Reader Responses

"Hey, there's no violin in this case!" — *Life with 7 Ms*

> … *"sweet and funny"*
> … *"very interesting"*
> … *"inspiring"*
> … *"thank you for sharing the joy"*
> … *"hilarious"*

… "Our sincere thank you for your most wonderful book. What a treasure it is. We have already shared some smiles reading through some sections."

… "I have enjoyed reading your family stories, often told from the "Ms'" point of view. Very entertaining style and content! Thank you for a heart-warming window into your life. Hilarious! Tender. Uplifting."

… "The many incidents that make this book are fascinating and I couldn't stop reading—laughing at times. First hand experience of joy, laughter, tears, all enjoyed tremendously!!"

… "Many emotions were stirred as I read from chapter to chapter. I heard myself laughing a lot. … Thank you so very much for affording us the joy (and sometimes sorrows) in sharing so candidly the growth and development of your incredible family in the treasury of stories in your book. I have truly enjoyed it!"

… "Many thanks for the book of your family. I read it in one day—I couldn't put it down."

Received after most recent annual letter (included in book):

"Thank you Louise for your beautiful 2018 family newsletter. You have accomplished so much over the years in keeping family unity so strong. So many families of today do not have this, and believe it or not your letters serve a greater purpose to society, to remind people to be families, to love each other, to be aware of what everyone is doing, and to be there for each other when the going gets rough.

Please continue, as in our modern world *'Hey, there's no violin in this case!'* may well serve as a model of what family should be, and will be a guide for those just starting out."

◆ FriesenPress

Suite 300 - 990 Fort St
Victoria, BC, V8V 3K2
Canada

www.friesenpress.com

ISBN
978-1-5255-5363-9 (Hardcover)
978-1-5255-5364-6 (Paperback)
978-1-5255-5365-3 (eBook)

1. Biography & Autobiography, Personal Memoirs

Distributed to the trade by The Ingram Book Company

Louise Holland

"Hey, there's no VIOLIN IN THIS CASE!"

Life with 7 Ms

1958–2018

Third Edition

To my family, with love

Acknowledgements

"Praise God from whom all blessings flow!"

Thank you …

… to my husband, Bruce, for his unfailing support day after day, year after year, and to our children, who provide the *raison d'être* for this book and whose permission to put them under the spotlight has been much appreciated. A special thank you to our youngest sons, Mark and Matthew, whose moral support and technical expertise brought this project to fruition: Mark for the colourful cover, Matt for the many hours of painstaking work on the computer, assembling text and photos into a readable format;

… to Margaret McKee, a dear friend who proofread this collection of letters, whose insights, gained over 45 years of observing the letter-writer and her family, have been most valuable;

… to family and friends who have encouraged me to share my writings; and

… to those photographers whose handiwork embellishes this family scrapbook.

Louise Holland
September 2006

CONTENTS

Foreword..11
Chapter 1: A Beginning..13
Chapter 2: 1961 to 1970..15
Chapter 3: 1971..21
Chapter 4: 1972..23
Chapter 5: 1973..26
Chapter 6: 1974..29
Chapter 7: Music, Music, Music...32
Chapter 8: 1975..34
Chapter 9: 1976..42
Chapter 10: Camp Letters..48
Chapter 11: 1977..51
Chapter 12: Letters to Daddy at Camp Qwanoes, 1977 57
Chapter 13: 1978..61
Chapter 14: Letters to My Parents at Quartzsite, 1977 and 1978...............67
Chapter 15: 1979..77
Chapter 16: Letters from England 85
Chapter 17: Letters to My Parents, 1979 95
Chapter 18: 1980..100
Chapter 19: Letters to My Parents, 1980 107
Chapter 20: 1981..111
Chapter 21: Letters to My Parents, 1981 118
Chapter 22: 1982..121
Chapter 23: Letters to My Parents, 1982 127
Chapter 24: A Christmas Digest, 1983..128
Chapter 25: A Christmas Digest, 1984..135
Chapter 26: Letters to My Parents, 1984 143
Chapter 27: A Christmas Digest, 1985..145
Chapter 28: Letter to My Parents, 1985 151
Chapter 29: A Christmas Digest, 1986..153

Chapter 30: Letters to My Parents, 1986 159

Chapter 31: A Christmas Digest, 1987 161

Chapter 32: Letter to My Parents, 1987 166

Chapter 33: A Christmas Digest, 1988 167

Chapter 34: A Christmas Digest, 1989 172

Chapter 35: A Christmas Digest, 1990 177

Chapter 36: A Christmas Digest, 1991 183

Chapter 37: A Christmas Digest, 1992 189

Chapter 38: A Christmas Digest, 1993 196

Chapter 39: A Christmas Digest, 1994 203

Chapter 40: A Christmas Digest, 1995 209

Chapter 41: A Christmas Digest, 1996 214

Chapter 42: A Christmas Digest, 1997 221

Chapter 43: A Christmas Digest, 1998 228

Chapter 44: A Christmas Digest, 1999 238

Chapter 45: A Christmas Digest, 2000 245

Chapter 46: A Christmas Digest, 2001 253

Chapter 47: A Christmas Digest, 2002 261

Chapter 48: My Mom 269

Chapter 49: A Christmas Digest, 2003 275

Chapter 50: A Christmas Digest, 2004 283

Chapter 51: A Christmas Digest, 2005 290

Afterword: First Edition 298

Chapter 52: A Christmas Digest, 2006 300

Chapter 53: A Christmas Digest, 2007 308

Chapter 54: A Christmas Digest, 2008 317

Chapter 55: A Christmas Digest, 2009 327

Chapter 56: A Christmas Digest, 2010 335

Chapter 57: A Christmas Digest, 2011 344

Chapter 58: A Christmas Digest, 2012 351

Chapter 59: A Christmas Digest, 2013 361

Chapter 60: A Christmas Digest, 2014 370

Chapter 61: A Christmas Digest, 2015 378

Chapter 62: A Christmas Digest, 2016 386

Chapter 63: A Christmas Digest, 2017 394

Chapter 64: A Christmas Digest, 2018 402

Afterword: Third Edition 410

Foreword

August 2006

This book has been 40 years in the writing. Year after year, friends and family graciously accepted our annual offering: a family letter that attempted to capture the year's activities. As long as thirty years ago, there were suggestions that the letters should be put together and shared more widely. Thirty more years of music, teaching, and children transforming into adults and producing children of their own, have come and gone. Parents have moved from Young Adulthood through Middle Age to The Best is Yet to Come. So the summer of 2005 was set aside as the Typing Summer. As I typed into the computer letter after letter, most of which I had not read for many years, several things became evident. Not only was I projected backwards into my own life as a young wife, mother, and teacher, but I noticed a consistency in the personalities and behaviour of my children—a consistency that stretched from childhood through adolescence and into adulthood.

It is not surprising that music, in various settings, turns up repeatedly, with seven children each taking lessons on both piano and violin, and the group performing in a variety of settings over the years—home, church services, schools, care homes, weddings, festivals, examinations—and with a mother who played the organ each Sunday and worked with dozens of piano students each year. Father's invaluable support, especially in the kitchen, surfaces year after year, as does our gratitude to a Heavenly Father whose faithfulness has been great.

A trivial item which is mentioned several times is the colour of a child's hair. Although my husband was very blond, and I was brunette, supposedly the colour of dominance, most of our children were blond as youngsters. My father insisted that the blondness came from his Swedish heritage. Now five of the children have dark hair, Father has lost most of his, and Mother is brunette no more!

Because my children are now in their mid-20s to late 30s, it is difficult to think of them as young children—until I reread the letters. And I both smile and shed a tear as vignettes flash through my mind.

A special gift came to me 16 years ago, after my parents moved into their condominium. Among the items given to Goodwill at the time of their move was a suitcase, purchased by a gentleman of good will. Finding my father's air force discharge papers in it, and assuming my parents would value their return, he arrived at their condominium with the papers, along with an envelope containing many letters that I had written to my parents from 1977 to 1987, during their winters in Quartzsite, Arizona. Along with two sets of family letters written from and to Camp Qwanoes in 1976 and 1977, tidbits of information found on old calendars, and two letters and a postcard from our trip to England in 1979, the Quartzsite letters have been a happy addition to my original writings, and perhaps give a behind-the-scenes, more personal, perspective. Comments in square brackets indicate my current, sometimes startled, reaction to what I have been typing or expand on what has just been written.

January 2019

Another twelve annual letters have been added to this book, thanks to the efforts of our son Matthew. So now there are sixty years recorded, our children have aged a decade, and we ourselves are even farther along the pathway of The Best is Yet to Come.

And we continue to thank God for an abundance of blessings.

Louise Holland
Victoria, BC, Canada

Chapter 1: A Beginning

It all started on a summer evening in August 1958. The lay pastor, Dave Vickers, who had just taken the church service at the Baptist church in Brentwood Bay, BC, learned that my family would be moving to Victoria in September. He asked if I would consider coming to the little non-denominational church, Lake Hill Mission, where he preached each Sunday morning. He wanted me to teach Sunday School and then play the piano for the church service. I agreed to this, and he faithfully travelled an extra ten miles each week to ensure that my sisters and I were in church. What he didn't tell me was that at the Mission's Wednesday night prayer meeting, the faithful parishioners had been praying that a suitable partner might be found for their dedicated young Sunday School Superintendent.

Bruce Holland was 22, tall, blond, handsome, and shy. I was 17 and equally shy. I was also interested in the young men from the downtown church, Central Baptist, who raced their cars up and down Pandora Avenue after the youth meetings. As a country girl, I was quite overwhelmed by the city scene. He later told me that he knew I was the one as soon as we were introduced. I, on the other hand, was wondering if the tiny gold pins would hold up my skirt hem until the end of the service.

BRUCE HOLLAND

A year and a half later, he asked me for a date, making his request from a phone booth so his family would not be curious. We went to the Ice Capades and then out for a snack at the Monterey Café. Fifty-nine years ago, eating at restaurants was a rare treat, and this country girl felt quite

Gibson's Photography

LOUISE FORSBERG

insecure in this setting. Following my date's example, I ordered a club sandwich held together with toothpicks, something I had never encountered before. It was a challenge to eat the sandwich without having it crumble into pieces in my lap.

DECEMBER 21, 1961

Nearly two years later, in December of 1961, we were married at Central Baptist Church. In the three and a half years since we met, I had completed Grade 12, two years of university (crammed into 14 months), and a year and a half of teaching. In order to marry on Thursday, December 21, the wedding anniversary of both his and my parents, I had to hire a substitute to cover my class of 42 lively Grade Twos and Threes.

We both thank God for bringing us together and for over 57 years of happy togetherness. It is the purpose of this book to share my perspective on raising a family of seven children. It has been a joyful journey!

Chapter 2: 1961 to 1970

Between 1961 and 1963, we lived in a beautiful little cottage on the Hollands' nearly-three acres of Christmas Hill property. After two years of teaching (me) and working in Holland Brothers furniture store on Fort Street (Bruce), we moved to Vancouver, where Bruce attended Vancouver City College. He took a course in social work, and I taught school at Sir James Douglas Elementary School on Victoria Drive. We attended Faith Baptist Church and still have contact with friends we made during those three years.

In August of 1966, we returned to Victoria and lived with my parents until we purchased our tiny house (750 square feet, no upstairs, and room only for a furnace and water heater below the house), which sat on the rocks in the middle of a pie-shaped half-acre near the northern end of Saanich Road. Bruce was attracted to the welcoming amber lights at the front door, lights he had seen as a teenager pedalling down Saanich Road from his home two blocks away on Quadra Street. I was enthralled by the sweet fragrance of a viburnum shrub's dainty pink and white blossoms beside the sidewalk. So an easy sale was made! We purchased the cottage for $13,500 at the end of 1966, with the understanding that we would put in a new furnace. This we did, with my seven years' superannuation savings. In an innocent foreshadowing of things to come, we had a very large furnace and hot water tank installed in the crawl space below the house. Although the hot water tank has been replaced several times over the years, the furnace served us for over 35 years before its demise in 2004.

In the spring, Bruce had taken courses in quantity cooking as he prepared to cook for four weeks at the brand-new and primitive Camp Qwanoes, situated on a large waterfront property between provincial and municipal parks in Crofton, 50 miles north of Victoria. Our Christmas letter from 1966 observed: "The campsite consists of 35

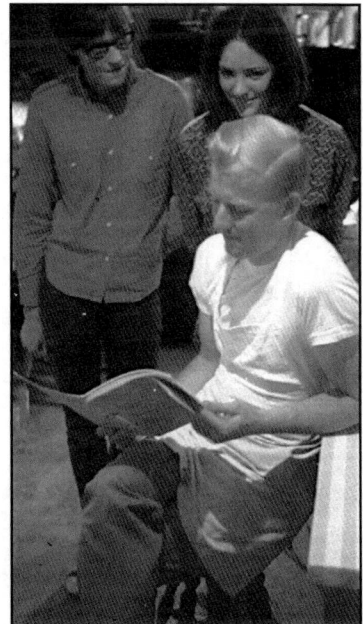

COOKING AT CAMP QWANOES

acres situated just north of Duncan on Vancouver Island, with over 2,000 feet of waterfront. When fully developed, it will be one of the finest anywhere."

The novice cook had many experiences, some interesting and some frustrating. Water from a well on the property was treated with bleach. The "dining hall" consisted of plastic sheets roped to trees. The young people recruited as helpers had to be reminded, after cleaning out the outhouses, to wash their hands before they handled food. One harrowing episode involved several pans of baked macaroni and cheese. The large old cook stove had been barged from Vancouver to Crofton, after being refurbished. The griddle top had been thoroughly scraped, scrubbed and polished, and the rusted oven walls and ceiling had been painted. Unfortunately, when the macaroni pans were removed from the oven, gray flecks of dried paint decorated the food destined for the stomachs of 100 hungry campers. Bruce does not have a clear memory of what happened next, but he suspects the casseroles were relieved of their ashy coating and served. And that oven was out of commission for the rest of the summer.

In spite of the month of 18- and 19-hour days, Bruce went back in succeeding summers for several more stints of camp-cooking, both at Qwanoes and on bike hikes sponsored by the camp.

In September of 1966, Bruce began work with what was originally named the Family and Children's Service and, after seeing at least three name changes over the next 30 years, retired in March of 1997. I taught Grade One for one more year, leaving elementary school teaching in June of 1967 and starting 52 years—and counting—of piano teaching that September.

In early December 1967, I wrote:

It's five o'clock in the morning, a second load of washing is spinning merrily through the machines and I can't get back to sleep, so I guess I must obey the one I promised to "love, honour, and obey" and write you a letter! No, I am not an early bird by nature, but lately I've been waking up during the night and often find it more efficient to get up and get some work done and then return to bed later on. Those of you who have not heard from us for a while perhaps would like to know what brings on this insomnia: Bruce

LOUISE AND NIECE CINDY-LOU WESTAWAY

and I are excitedly waiting for a third party to join our little household, due any time in the next three weeks.

We are thoroughly enjoying our cozy little home—"quaint" is the word often used to describe it—and find the addition of a crib, baby buggy, chest of drawers, etc., to the little "den" has indeed made it more snug. The mostly naturalized half-acre on which our home sits has provided much enjoyment as the seasons have passed. Not knowing what the previous owners have planted makes the garden interesting. Bruce has replanted a back lawn-border terrace in grass, which is much neater (this appeals to him) and requires much less maintenance (this appeals to me), and plans to do the next terrace down some time in the future. With an abundance of nooks and crannies, rockeries and lawns, oak trees and leaves, the gardening presents quite a challenge, but Bruce finds it a welcome relaxation after a week of varied but sometimes emotionally exhausting work at the Family and Children's Service. Bruce's family has spent much time and effort helping us get established here, with the painting, carpentry and renovating a 20-year-old house requires, so we are very comfortable. The most recent project is a little 5" x 6" swinging door, built into the laundry room door, through which our very spoiled black and white medium-sized cat, Gunther, can find his way to a warm bed.

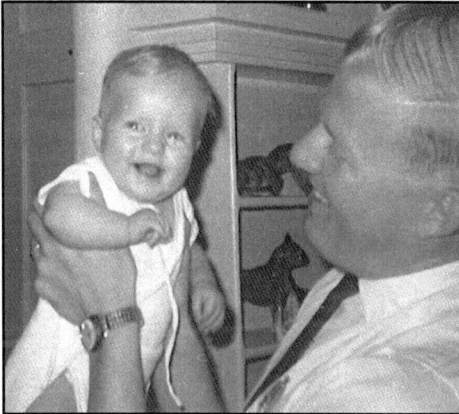

MARILYN LOUISE HOLLAND AND DADDY

At the end of 1968, Bruce wrote:

Perhaps the biggest event to affect our lives took place at 11:57 p.m. December 30, when **Marilyn Louise**, 5 pounds 15 ounces., entered this world. I shall now have to restrain myself from filling up the rest of this letter about the best, most beautiful, healthy, intelligent bundle of joy ever to bless the lives of two doting parents! ... We have had to ask ourselves several times whether we really have a baby, and Louise is already planning for six (?) more—sigh!! Just as good of course! *[I can't believe this. I had written "Five, Dear" in the margin. I can't believe that, either!]*

In 1969, the pen was handed over to a dainty, dimpled hand, as our first baby described her brother's arrival:

You probably have heard about our Thanksgiving present that arrived on September 30th, less than an hour after Mommy went to the Stork Shop—I think it's called the Jubilee Stork Shop—**Michael Bruce**, 6 1/2 pounds of little brother. This summer I thought Mommy looked a little different; she said something about the "shape of things to come" and I added "tum-my" to my vocabulary. Anyway, the three of us were very pleased to welcome "Mico" to our shrinking house. Mommy and Daddy seem to think he's quite special, even though he hasn't got nice blond hair like mine. *[Within six months, white-blond hair replaced the original brunette.]* I try to feed Teddy the way Mommy feeds Michael but just can't seem to manage too well; at least Teddy doesn't cry, and Mommy's baby does, sometimes. Sometimes he gets the "hinks," too.

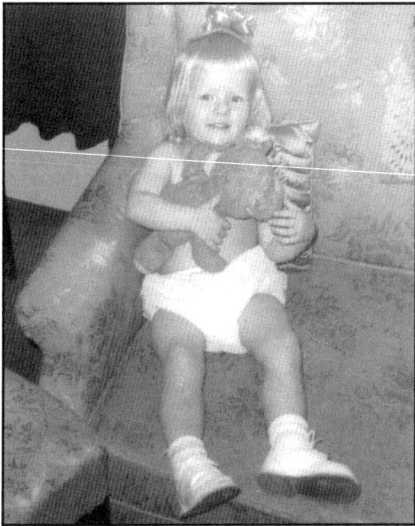

MARILYN "FEEDING" TEDDY

And in 1970, little brother took the pen:

I have been delegated the pleasant task of wishing you a happy, blessed Christmas time and God's best for you in 1971. At present, I am the littlest Holland (three pounds separate me from my big sister) and I answer to several names, including "Mike" and "Mikey." Mommy doesn't really like these; she prefers *Mich*ael, or Michael *Bruce*, depending on the severity of the situation, and often refers to me as "S.E." This stands for "Something Else," as in, "Marilyn was an extremely cooperative baby, but Michael is 'something else.'" Unlike my older sister, who is a gentle, sedate nearly-three, I feel it is every baby's right to be heard and seen, and if the latter situation is not possible, development of the former ability is most desirable. In line with Dr. Spock's information to Mommy, I complain when hungry, tired, prone (on bathroom counter or in bedroom crib), frustrated (when bobby pin/shoe/clothes peg/pebble/beetle is removed from mouth), or cutting teeth.

Our day is divided into four sections: morning, when Marilyn and I play together in our bedroom (Mommy puts up an extension gate to keep the toys from rolling out); early afternoon, when we have a nap (two to three hours; Mommy often crawls under the eiderdown with Marilyn for a little while); late afternoon, when Anne and Claire from next door come to play with us while Mommy teaches piano classes up in her classroom; and finally, evening, when we are ceremoniously coaxed into our respective beds after a story or two, or three, or four. My time with Marilyn in the morning is perhaps the most instructive, as she sings and "reads" to me and suggests which toys I should play with and which toys I really do not want. Our clothes closet and chest of drawers add to the possibilities of play.

On Wednesday afternoons Mommy teaches rhythm classes for little children at the Victoria Conservatory and we stay with Auntie Fran and Uncle Ken. Once I think I heard Uncle Ken whisper to Auntie Fran, "I thought it was Wednesday the day before yesterday."

As you may have gathered by now, I am not a Perfect Baby; however, I have learned a few techniques that help make up for this situation. For example, when Mommy's ardour begins to cool—this coincides with our third rendezvous in one night—I Turn on the Charm: soft little arms around Mommy's neck, little blond head drowsily placed on Mommy's shoulder, pathetic "It's my left molar, Mommy" whimper. When the heat is really on (for example, when I have opened the china cabinet), I go into the Winning Ways routine: a combination of Turn on the Charm and Sweet Innocence—"MOM-M!", interpreted by Mommy as, "Mom, how nice to see you here, too; would you like a tea cup?" Depending on the response, I find that if I temporarily relinquish my goal of emptying said cabinet and advance toward Mommy with bottom lip quivering, the odds are reduced as far as a seat-warming goes.

I have also tried to instruct Marilyn in my Exercise in Lunguistics. Apparently she wasn't aware that babies are supposed to lie on their backs, preferably in the middle of the floor, temporarily blocking traffic (Ed. note: in a 750-square-foot house, that's not hard), and express indignation against parental mistreatment (removal of sewing scissors or lamp cord from chubby hand). When Marilyn tries out this Exercise—she's not too good at it yet—Mommy just ignores it, but for some reason when I do it, she refers to it as a Temper Tantrum and I end up with a rosy glow down below.

Mommy and Daddy are just finishing their ninth year of sharing the same food and shelter, and report that they are still very pleased with each other. Daddy has been registered and re-classified—now he's a Social Worker 2, although he doesn't look any different to me—and still enjoys his work with the Family and Children's Service. Mommy passed her Piano Teacher exams in June and now is registered as a Music Teacher. (I wonder what all this registration does to our pedigrees.) She talked Auntie Peggy into bringing over Tara and Tanya for a "visit" each morning in July and August while she traipsed off to summer school. This is supposed to help her do a better job of teaching.

We have three additions to the family, one mahogany-brown, the other two an uncolourful beige ("easy-to-clean, doesn't show the dirt" is what the salesman said). The first is Daddy's present to Mommy—an old grand piano that he had refinished and which occupies a beautiful one-quarter of our living room. The other two have been referred to as "Bolts wagons" (as in "thunder bolts," I believe), abbreviated VW. In the old Austin, Mommy went through two stop signs with her foot on the brake, and Daddy's Rambler had flattened his wallet, so he got a VW bus for work and a VW squareback for Mommy; the carport Grandpa made is well-used. (Thinking of grandparents, Daddy has a story he likes to tell about my other grandparents. One Sunday he returned to Granny and Grandpa's house 6 1/2 minutes after we had left from our visit and they were already having a nap.)

I could tell you of all sorts of hair-raising experiences that I have had in my first year and a bit, but space and Mommy do not permit. In case you are afraid that I feel unloved and rejected, perhaps I should point out that each night when Marilyn says her prayers, she ends with "and thank You, God, for Daddy and Mommy who love me, and for my darling (!!) little brother Michael." Then she waits until Mommy says, "And thank You for Marilyn and Michael," before she pads off to bed with Teddy and Blanket. A variation of this occurs when we have company, but I won't tarnish her image.

Love, Michael

Chapter 3: 1971

Margaret Ellen took over as family scribe in 1971:

This is the fifth Christmas letter Daddy and Mommy have let escape from the confines of their untidy half-acre, and each one has come from a different member of the family. This year it's my turn.

My story begins just after last Christmas. It seems that my parents went shopping downtown to take advantage of the after-Christmas sales and spent a fair while choosing an appropriate set of cards for this Christmas. After much looking and discussion, Daddy

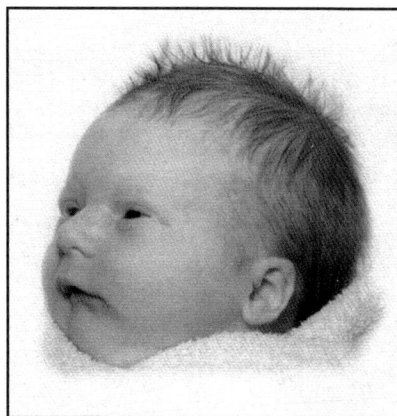

MARGARET ELLEN HOLLAND

decided he liked the one you have just received. Mommy agreed, and it wasn't until she got home that she realized there were three little towheads in the picture. When she pointed this out to Daddy, he just smiled.

I arrived October 6, 6 pounds and 15 ounces of squalling femininity, and received a happy reception from the two little blonds who already shared the tiny house with Daddy and Mommy. By this time, however, 3 1/2 months of hot, dusty and noisy construction had resulted in a somewhat enlarged house, so that now Marilyn, Michael, and I each have our own bedroom. (Mine, for some reason I can only guess at, is in the most remote corner of the upstairs.)

Mommy managed to get four weeks of teaching in before I arrived and—with a lot of help from grandparents, aunties, uncles, and Daddy—was able to return to her music room after a couple of weeks of taking it easy. The fact that I am a cooperative baby no doubt helps, too; however, this is not altogether by choice. Apparently a nurse from the hospital told Mommy I slept through the night in the nursery, so when I decided to try my luck the first night away from the hospital, my feminine intuition registered Mommy's disapproval. The next night I decided to wait until Mommy woke up before reminding her of her responsibilities. It was a long wait (until eight o'clock), but the improvement in her disposition was so remarkable I decided that the extra hunger pangs were worth it, and have made 6:30 or 7:00 a.m.

my usual rise-and-shine time ever since. *[I could have written the book on Tough Love!]* My big sister **Marilyn** will be four just after Christmas and is Mommy's special helper. She keeps her room tidy—closet doors are not only decorative, they are concealing—and helps protect me from the enthusiastic affection of my big brother, who refers to me as "Marker." On Wednesdays she goes with Mommy to the Conservatory where she is Mommy's youngest pupil. I understand she has all sorts of suggestions for Mommy as to which song to do next, or who should play which instrument.

Michael turned two a week before I made my entrance. He is Marilyn's shadow and mimic; Mommy calls him "Instant Replay." Marilyn's "Goodnight, Sweet" to me is echoed by his "'night, 'weet"; her (against-the-rules) bouncing on the chesterfield is immediately challenged by his catapulting from a chair. Maybe this is why our parents insist on an afternoon siesta. Daddy and Mommy feel certain Michael will someday be a mechanic or a doctor. Of four accessible clocks, three have had their personalities permanently altered; his cure for any "hurt" is a gentle kiss on that part of the anatomy that appears to be ailing.

It is now the end of November, and Daddy and Mommy have nearly got the house straightened around. Daddy has just finished his holidays. In January he became a night-duty social worker for the Family and Children's Service, which means he is on call for two weeks (5:00 p.m. to 9:00 a.m. during the week and all weekend), and then has two weeks off. This, and Mommy's teaching time-table, has allowed (allowed?? B.) him to develop his cooking skills, which are the envy of Mommy's friends (and Mommy. L.). His help also made it possible for Mommy to take two courses at summer school. Mommy and electric saws aren't too compatible, and the library was a little cooler than the 85 to 95 degrees our house baked in.

As you can probably read between the lines, life has been moving along happily and busily for us. Daddy and Mommy are thankful to God for the gifts they have been given. High on their list of blessings are friends and family who are so generous and helpful, and who kindly overlook the indiscretions of the under-4s in the family. Best wishes for 1972.

Love, **Margaret Ellen**

Chapter 4: 1972

The following year brought the family a wonderful surprise. This letter was written several weeks before Christmas; our surprise arrived two days before Christmas. I take up the narrative:

This is our family's sixth Christmas letter and now that each member of the family has had a turn, it is my pleasant task once again to wish you the joy that accompanies remembrances of our Saviour's birth and the blessings of a New Year.

Some of you may remember that two Christmases ago Bruce and I scurried downtown to take advantage of the Christmas sales and were taken aback, on returning home, to discover our choice of cards portrayed three little blonds; the third little blonde made her arrival the following October. Needless to say, we exercised great caution last Christmas in choosing cards! Apparently, however, the stork who patrols our area isn't too perceptive and has decided to add yet another bundle to our family, this one at some date between the end of November and the end of January—a happy surprise! Most of you know that we consider our children real gifts and find them a source of continuing pleasure. We must admit, though, that even we weren't counting on such an abundance of joy!

Our lives have been filled with blessings of every sort, and I hope you will bear with me as I sort out a few of the more tangible ones. At the rate the population is escalating at our home, it could be a long time before our letter represents Mommy's eye-view again.

Highest on the list is the man who calmly and efficiently presides over the variety of activities that take place under our assortment of roofs. In his capacity as emergency social worker, he on occasion brings some wee neglected mite home for a few minutes on its way to a foster home, sometimes for a cookie or a change of diapers; I am always impressed to see that other peoples' little people, at times grimy and poorly nourished, are cared for as lovingly as we try to care for our own little ones. When I am teaching, Bruce does nearly all of the cooking, a happy byproduct of his stint as camp cook several years ago and a large contribution which enables me to teach to capacity. He makes breakfast while I wash and supervise the dressing of three little people and pull together beds, and supper while I teach, and recently has baked tremendous quantities for my students' recitals. I bake when quantity, quality and efficiency are not required, i.e., when Marilyn and Michael "help" mix, cut out and decorate the shortbread with sterile (?) fingers and lick out cake and icing bowls, a questionable habit passed on from their mother.

LOUISE AND PARENTS

As the world's most fortunate wife, I can hardly believe my own studying days are at last behind me—it has taken me 25 years to complete a BEd instead of the normal 16—thanks mainly to a husband whose generosity towards my ideas and hopes goes far above the call of matrimony.

The little "Ms" who inhabit whichever four-foot square of the house Mommy and/or Daddy happen to be working in (and one of our purposes in enlarging our house was to allow each member of the family an area in which to work and play—dreamers we were!) provide us with all kinds of insights into life from a 24" to 42" eye-level, and more unsettling, into our own ideals and motivations. Marilyn's fifth birthday is December 30. She started Kindergarten in September and is enjoying her first exposure to the academic world. Each school morning she and I work for a few minutes at the piano, and while I feel quite sure Van Cliburn and Rubenstein need not feel threatened, progress is being made in relatively painless small steps. Michael, three in September, continues to be Michael. Unlike his sister, he rarely walks anywhere, but appears to be propelled by springs. With Marilyn, he takes part in my Wednesday "'servatory" classes and is quite adept, if enthusiastic, on the percussion instruments. A small-size replica of his daddy, he has become Daddy's

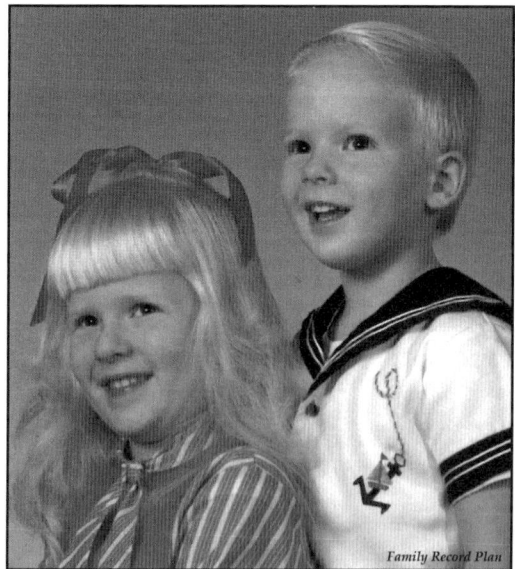

Family Record Plan

MARILYN AND MICHAEL

helper with Marilyn away at school, digging drainage ditches, raking leaves, piling wood, and chattering constantly. Margaret is a cheerful baby who "rolls with the punches," and greets any likely partner-in-mischief with a conspiratorial "da-da." The proud possessor of seven teeth, she crawls at an alarming rate (can manoeuvre the stairs as fast as I can), and is just taking her first steps. One of her favourite activities is lying across my feet when I practise the piano, untying my shoelaces if at all possible; the pedalling effects are not exactly musical. Other pursuits include emptying wastepaper baskets; chewing shoes, slippers and boots; and polishing off under-the-table crumbs.

While our home life and respective vocations occupy the largest share of our time and attention, we have enjoyed the many kindnesses of family and friends during the year. Grandparents who willingly babysit at a moment's notice, neighbours who provide playmates for the children while I teach, and others who share the delicious results of their hard work in the garden, friends who send along treats for us and the children, and who close their eyes (and ears) to said children's not-always-seemly behaviour— these add immeasurably to the joy of living. Grandpa Holland's masterful use of leftover lumber to construct a playhouse for the children is especially appreciated. And our participation in Sunday School and church activities provides a source of spiritual growth week by week.

DEGREE COMPLETED SUMMER 1972; GRADUATION SPRING 1973

Louise

Chapter 5: 1973

A year later, and almost a year old, our fourth child carries on the letter tradition:

May I tell you about myself? My name is **Melissa Ann**, and I was my parents' happiest surprise last year. I will be one year old two days after THE Anniversary (Mommy and Daddy's, Grandma and Grandpa's, Granny and Grandpa's, and Auntie Peggy and Uncle Wayne's *[December 21]*), two days before Christmas, and seven days before my

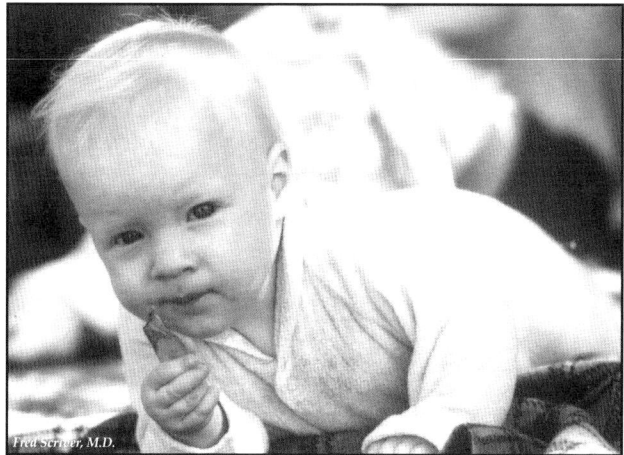

MELISSA ANN HOLLAND

biggest sister turns six. I am blonde (surprise!), giggly, cuddly, and my parents call me a ray of sunshine. Margaret calls me "Sissa" and is my very best friend, sharing my crib whenever possible and suggesting all sorts of suitable activities. A couple of months ago I, too, learned how to crawl up fourteen stairs to get back to the bedrooms and all the interesting drawers up there. The first time I did it, Mommy searched all over the house downstairs for me, only to discover that my rattle was making music upstairs. Our parents have only two eyes each, and that has its limitations when there are four pairs of legs carrying us to new adventures.

Now for the other members of my family. So far we have been unable to coax Mommy into adopting even a guppy, let alone a puppy or kitten. She says that with four children (she calls us "precious pets," which I think is a bit sticky), several students, and only twenty-four hours to a day, pets would not be looked after as they should be. (I think Daddy is a little more soft-hearted.) My gentle big sister **Marilyn** is in Grade One and has learned to print and read. She covers paper after paper with wiggly lines and straight lines. She had some trouble with equations (apparently a hereditary problem), and insisted that $3 + \underline{7} = 4$. Mommy said the new math was different, but not quite that different, so with both parents pooling their great knowledge on the subject and guiding her, she seems to have figured out how to add, even when the answer comes in the middle. She is progressing well on the piano. **Michael**, four in September, often sits just behind her while she practises and now he is able to play several songs, some with two hands. I think they're the same songs Marilyn used to play, except they take quite a while to finish. When Michael plays a wrong note, he goes right back to the beginning to start all over again; he says he *can* do it himself and Mommy says, "That's good, Michael," and tries to smile. An expert on anything that vibrates, turns, clicks, spins or in any other way moves (or is movable), Michael keeps Mommy, who is notably ignorant about mechanical gadgets, in a state of constant apprehension. At three and a half, he started vacuuming his room on Fridays, and the plaintive cry from Monday to Thursday is "Isn't it Friday today?"

I have an excellent instructress in my pal Maggie, although I doubt if I will ever acquire her finesse at problem-causing. By turns she is an actress (nearly 32 ounces of pickle juice on the kitchen floor: *"Me?"*); engineer (the contents of the toy shelves, toy cupboard and toy chest, evenly distributed throughout the house, will cover every square foot of floor area; the dispersal, i.e., scattering ability of vaseline, powdered milk, dishwashing detergent, Michael's marbles, and folded diapers have been rated 5, 3, 4, 1 and 2 by our two-year-old expert); problem-solving psychologist (Question: How quickly will Mommy become uncalm if I put porridge in my ears? Answer: Very.); and artist in a new medium: peanut butter. To my mind, this is **Margaret**'s *pièce de*

Fred Scriver, M.D.

MARGARET

résistance. I have seen her wait until Mommy pulls out the breadboard to butter the inevitable twelve slices of bread for lunch. The buttering time allows M3 to extricate the can of peanut butter from the cupboard below the breadboard, remove the lid, stir the contents with one hand and finger-paint a greasy pattern on the lid with the other, all the while sitting companionably at Mommy's feet, out of her range of vision. By the time Mommy gets to the peanut butter stage (this, too, is inevitable; Marilyn figures we had 392 peanut butter sandwich lunches last year), Maggie can hand up the can to Mommy, all very helpful and with the smile of an angel. And charmer; neither Mommy nor Daddy can resist little arms tight around their necks, and a little bottom wiggling with the pleasure of being hugged. And rumour has it that when we are all asleep, our parents come to look at us and Mommy kisses us and says, "Thank You, God," and "Aren't they beautiful?" and Daddy agrees, and covers us up very carefully.

The two people with whom we share our house are still working at social work and music teaching. They each say they wouldn't want a different job, so I guess they like what they are doing. The big girls from next door look after us for two or three hours a day the two weeks Daddy is on call and I get carried around and cuddled, especially by the big girl Maggie calls "Amm." Claire plays games with Marilyn and Michael and Margaret and we enjoy having two older sisters for a while.

MARILYN

Well, I see it's naptime again and everyone else is tucked in (including Mommy), so I'd better get my beauty sleep, too. We all wish you a Lively Christmas and an Abundant New Year, as we remember the One Whose coming we celebrate at this season: "I am come that they might have life and that they might have it more abundantly."

Love, Melissa

P.S. Daddy says to tell you that we went on a big adventure this summer: 1,500 miles pulling a little house on wheels behind us (Granny and Grandpa's trailer). We visited Auntie Harriet and Uncle Fred and Cousins Freddie, Eric and Patrick at Fort St. James for nearly a week. The other week on wheels was HOT (100 degrees in the Okanagan and the Fraser Canyon). Daddy called our trip a holiday, Mommy called it an "experience," and we called it fun. Marilyn said it was "funner" than staying at home.

Chapter 6: 1974

In 1974, a very new addition to the family carried on:

Hello from the newest Baby Holland! My name is **Melody Joy** and I arrived rather speedily on December 5. I am 7 1/8 pounds of cuddly brunette (repeat: brunette; Mommy finally has an ally!) and I have soft, fuzzy hair, velvety cheeks, a quivery chin, flickering eyelids, and a tiny mouth that puckers even when Mommy isn't kissing me. My parents think I am enchanting, whatever that means.

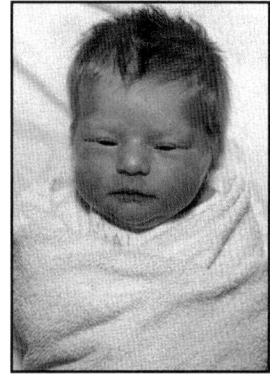

MELODY JOY HOLLAND

My biggest sister, **Marilyn**, will be seven on the second last day of December. Except for the contents of her bedroom (which are interesting but not always organized), she has managed to organize herself and her several activities into one interesting day after the other. In Grade One, under an excellent teacher, she learned to read very well. She haunts the school library and brings home several books a week. In February, she and Michael started violin lessons following the Suzuki method and now both can make some reasonably acceptable sounds on their one-quarter and one-eighth size "fiddles." In June Marilyn passed a test given to second-year piano students. She gets up at seven o'clock to practise both instruments, with Mommy watching, and Michael takes over just before eight for 15 or 20 minutes. Now that Margaret says she wants to hold the "fiolin," and now that I'm here to add a little variety to the scene, and there's always Melissa to stir up interest, Mommy gets wiggly lines across her forehead trying to figure out how everything will fit in. Granny showed Marilyn how to crochet a chain and she has produced ten feet of braided wool. (Daddy suggested she ask Granny how to start the second row.) Mommy tells me Marilyn is the kindest big sister a little sister or brother could have. She picks up all 28 pounds of

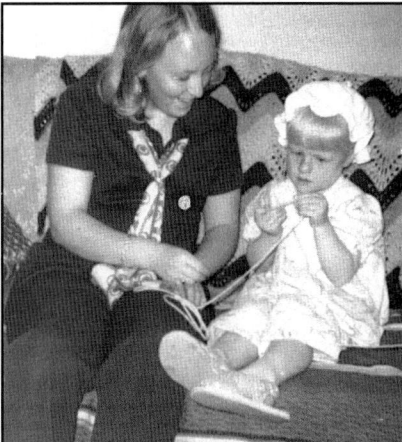

MARILYN WITH FRIEND CAROLE RASMUS

Melissa—she weighs 49 pounds herself—and pats her gently on the back when she falls down. And she's the one who insists that Margaret should be allowed to hear the bedtime story. "Come and sit quietly beside me, Margaret; you *will* be quiet, won't you?" is answered by Margaret's enthusiastic head noddings, which don't fool Mommy or Daddy for a moment, but usually result in three little heads following the book's pictures. Marilyn says that the sunrise looks like a "straight rainbow," and that the green light in her bedroom "rhymes" with the green sheets.

Michael turned five on the last day of September and credits his more satisfying experiences in life to the passing of that milestone. He insists that his cooperative helpfulness in the kitchen (baking cookies for Kindergarten, loading the breakfast dishes into the dishwasher, wiping small sisters' faces and hands), and his zeal for a tidy bedroom (at times, Mommy finds dirty clothes neatly folded away) have "something to do with being five." Mommy and Daddy get a play-by-play description of the Kindergarten activities, punctuated (when parental attention appears to be wandering) by "Guess what? D'you know what we did next?" He received a grown-up navy-blue suit for his birthday which makes him look just like Daddy, only smaller; Mommy calls them "Chip and Block." The other day he stayed upstairs while Mommy made the beds so Mommy "wouldn't get lonely," and exclaimed, while sitting in the big chair with Marilyn in front of the TV, "Look at the two good children—*us!*"

Margaret was "free" in October and is making great strides in most areas and slow steps in one; Mommy doesn't care to discuss the exception. May's three-word sentences ("No, I *won't*", "*Michael* did it", "I want *cookie*") have lengthened considerably: "Melissa eating toothpaste again—her *naughty* girl"; "I fold these cloffiss, 'Lissa fold these bibs and you fold the diapees, OK, Mom?"; and Mommy's favourite (during afternoon nap time when a spindly arm stretches across Owl, Elephant and Teddy to pat Mommy's neck): "I loving you to sleep, Mommy." Margaret joins Auntie Peggy

Family Record Plan
MARGARET

and Mommy in the beginning music classes and happily becomes a rocking-horse, turtle or dickey-bird, as the occasion demands. (Daddy says she marches to a different drumbeat, but Mommy says he isn't talking about music.) She likes music classes, just as she likes wearing several layers of shawls, scarves, Marilyn's, Daddy's or Mommy's shoes, and a colourful assortment of "wings, wibbons and blacelets."

Last year, Margaret encouraged Melissa in all sorts of adventures; this year Melissa enthusiastically offers her own suggestions. Like two little puppies, one tall and slender, the other Daddy's "lump of sunshine," Margaret and Melissa travel from one escapade to another. At present, the special activity is mural-making, using *le mur* as a surface for creative expression. **Melissa**, two on the 23rd, has her own artistic specialties, window-crayoning and felt pen facial decorating. Not only is she talented, but she is quick, producing works of art at a speed that defies Mommy's agility and Daddy's patience. Melissa's vocabulary, which for several months consisted of expressive grunts and pointings, now includes some real words: "up," "down," "p'ane (flies in the sky)," "beese (magic word)," "bish (tidies hair)," "yedsh (an affirmative)," and (most frequently used and therefore very clear), "MINE" and "NO."

My dad comes to see me here in the hospital and makes me feel as if I'm the most beautiful baby ever produced. Mommy tells me he's a 365-day-a-year, 24-hour-a-day social worker, although he receives cheques only for the hours the Department of Human Resources has him on call. He does a lot of work around the house so that Mommy can teach her music students, and is chief cook and baker. Mommy had six recitals in November, each with around twenty students and their parents, and Daddy baked mountains of loaves and cookies for refreshments. I was more or less (Mommy says "less") invisible at these concerts, but every so often a loud cymbal clang or a particularly discordant note on the piano made me very eager to see just what was going on.

Daddy superintends the Sunday School Junior Department at our church, which has eight teachers and 60 to 70 nine to eleven year olds. Mommy plays the organ and piano in church services and substitute teaches in Daddy's department. I am scheduled to join the Cradle Roll in a few days and will keep Melissa company in the nursery on Sundays.

Mommy has warned me that some perplexing situations await me at home. She suggests I might try to find the answers to these riddles for a start: Why is there a wooden spoon in the bathroom drawer upstairs? Why does Daddy find unopened mail in the wastepaper basket? Why does Mommy talk in a loud voice when Margaret uses Mommy's toothbrush to scrub out the toilet, or when Melissa brushes her hair with it? Why do Michael, Margaret and Melissa go with Daddy to take Marilyn to and from school? It looks as if I have an interesting year ahead of me. My family joins me in wishing *you* a most interesting 1975, too. As our Christmas card suggests, Christmas is a time of hope, and the Bible says our hope is in the One whose birth we remember at Christmas.

MARILYN HOLDING MELODY; MARGARET, MELISSA, MICHAEL

Love, Melody

Chapter 7: Music, Music, Music

A little sentence from 1974's letter—"In February she and Michael started violin lessons following the Suzuki method and now both can make some reasonably acceptable sounds on their one-quarter and one-eighth size 'fiddles'"—provides a matter-of-fact introduction to what eventually became an overwhelming component of our family life: the study of both piano and violin, and the sharing of our music in dozens of settings over the next nearly-20 years.

As the letters continue, many references will be made to this family project, but I would like, from the perspective of more than 45 years later, to outline what prompted such a huge investment of time, energy, and finances.

It was only natural that our children would receive piano lessons, as that was one gift I could give them. The violin lessons began after I heard a violin teacher, Frona Colquhoun, speak on the Suzuki method of teaching music. Frona, with a background in both traditional and Suzuki methodology, brought the Suzuki method to Victoria in the early 1970s. Michael had already demonstrated an aural acuity, often pointing out different bird sounds during the day, and waking up to sirens in the night, sounds to which his sleeping parents did not respond. The Suzuki method, or "mother-tongue" approach, in which children are taught to play an instrument much as they learn a language—by much listening and

FRONA COLQUHOUN

repetition, and only later on by reference to the printed score—seemed an ideal method for training a child with such a good ear. After two weeks of observing Little Brother's excitement with the tiny instrument, Big Sister decided she, too, wanted to learn to play the violin. And, in succeeding years, five more siblings joined in, and had the unique experience of performing with each other.

Frona worked with our eldest six over a period of eleven years, and gave the youngest, Matthew, some guidance just before her retirement in 1984. Other teachers, including Alice Tyrrell, Yasuko Eastman, Derry Deane and Dr. Elfreda

Gleam, took over as the years passed.

We believe that learning to play an instrument not only provides an opportunity to experience and share beauty, an avenue of self-expression, some self-discipline, and an academic achievement, but that it can provide a means of serving God and the community. We set modest academic goals for the children: achieving the Grade VIII level (Royal Conservatory of Music standard) on both piano and violin, and completing Grade 12 (high school graduation). Beyond that, they were free to pursue any further educational and vocational training of their own choice, aided somewhat by funds we had set aside for that purpose. The Grade VIII level in music provided a foundation for further study, if desired (five did go beyond this level on one or both instruments), and a lifelong appreciation of music.

Because there were so many children, we set up a structure of festival and examination involvements to ensure that each child would receive at least this basic training. As the years passed, festival entries included piano and violin solos, duets and ensembles; practical and theoretical examinations marked the calendar. For ten years, the family entered the festival's Family Class, performing a selection of classical and sacred pieces. Each year I arranged a hymn for inclusion in these performances, and these were also used in many other settings. A memory I treasure is when one of the children's teachers, invited with several colleagues to a tea and recital, was moved to tears as the family played an arrangement of "Jesu, Joy of Man's Desiring": four playing the beautiful flowing introduction and interludes (in harmony), the other three playing the chorale tune, as it appeared and reappeared throughout the piece. I remember the extraordinarily fulfilling experience of being surrounded by and helping to produce such beauty in the company of my children—a gift I will always cherish.

Bruce is often asked which instrument he plays. Although he played saxophone in the high school band and was band president, he was content to facilitate his family's musical endeavours from the sidelines. He provided meals to enable me both to teach my piano students and to work with our own children; transported children to violin and, later, advanced piano lessons; and enhanced practice sessions both by listening to repertoire and by giving a meaningful glance to any uncooperative performer. There is no way that the family could have performed in so many settings without their father's support.

Was it difficult? Was it worth it? Would we do it again? Yes, yes, and yes! Would we do anything differently? Probably—the time spent on music lessons, examinations, festival performances, and family concerts precluded much involvement in community sports. Most of our children did manage to fit in some sports activities, however, sometimes as a reward for diligent practising. All would agree that, as adults, they value their musical background and the family camaraderie that built up over the years of performing together.

Chapter 8: 1975

MELODY

Merry Christmas again from **Melody Joy** Holland! I have just turned one and am seriously considering how to manoeuvre without holding on to the edges of things. I have two big bottom teeth and two small top teeth, enough hair to put in a barrette (blonde; my beautiful brunette hair has deteriorated), a five-word vocabulary ("ma," "da," "ba," "ff," and "up"), three sisters, one brother, and the ability to clean a carpet of crumbs, pins, Lego, lint, moths and flies in sixty seconds flat.

As you may know, I live in a music school of sorts. My day starts with an hour of violin music, kindness of **Marilyn** [nearly eight] and **Michael** [six]. Sometimes Marilyn gets up before seven and goes to the music room to practise the piano. This is not, as you might think, due to great ambition or enthusiasm on her part; she has discovered that Mommy is not likely to suggest unacceptable changes in her wardrobe if a) she is dressed so early, and b) she has practised so conscientiously. I believe she was the only Grade Three girl to wear white sandals to school in November, and Mommy didn't say anything (well, hardly anything). Marilyn passed her Grade I Piano exam in June (with a mark of 84) and Mommy was the one who got butterflies. Michael plays both piano and violin with varying degrees of enthusiasm and proficiency. He and Grade One have hit it off very happily and he has discovered the thrill of reading by and

GIRLS IN PINK FLANNELETTE NIGHTIES—ONE OF MOTHER'S FEW SEWING PROJECTS (NOTE MARGARET'S GUM-RELATED SHORT HAIR)

for himself. (Marilyn's comment: "Well, if we can't watch TV, I guess we'll have to get out more library books.") Michael prints important messages like "Please do not come in while Michael is not in his room (by Michael)," and "Daddy I love you. You are very nice. I love you. I love you," and leaves them all over the house. He assures us that "Our Daddy is the best daddy in the whole tired world."

MICHAEL AND MARILYN

Margaret, four in October, calls me "the precious baby in the world." She is tall with long, slim fingers and short, straight hair, the length the result of an unfortunate misplacing of chewing gum. Margaret is learning how to hold the violin, plays little pieces on the xylophone and piano, prints the family's names, colours very carefully, and is sure she will soon be as old as Marilyn: "I'm four now, so there's just five and six, then I'll be as big as you, and then I can make Peter Butter sandwiches." Her favourite breakfast cereal is "Freddies," which has some serious implications, considering she has two Great-Uncle Freds, one Uncle Fred, and one cousin Freddie. Margaret enjoys dressing up. She recently received a scolding for wearing Mommy's diamond and pearl rings, watch, and French perfume. Last spring she brought Mommy a huge red tulip *[origin unknown, but dubious]*, with one dandelion placed carefully on each side.

Melissa is nearly three. She is sturdy and round, with short, pudgy fingers, long blonde hair, and a smile that occurs at the slightest provocation. She calls me "Sweet Melody," one of the few instances when she combines "s" and a consonant successfully. Usually words containing this combination suffer: "'Tay here, Dolly. I going to 'tore with Daddy." "MOM! Her say I 'tupid. I not, I 'mart." Last winter she exclaimed incredulously, "Daddy 'panked my hand!" I believe it had something to do with the half-empty porridge bowl she had placed on her head. Or it could have been the time she stuffed both ears with toothpaste. Her favourite lunch foods are "nucks and waisins" and she wears "lassgets" and "wibbons" in her hair (also "bwets").

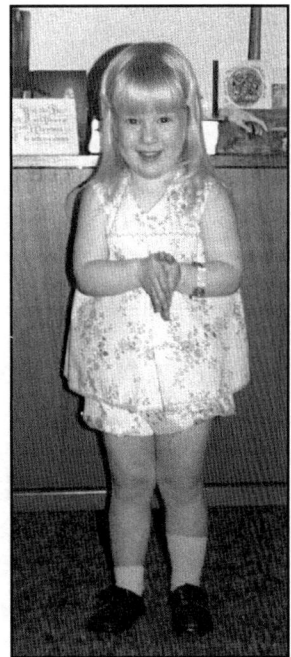

MELISSA

Melissa knows nothing of child labour laws; she often folds the face "cloffs" and bibs, clears the table ("See, I keeping the dishes 'traight, Mom"), and tidies up the family room. To Melissa, "Watch the puddle," means "See if your Sunday shoes are waterproof by wading through the deepest part." Although Daddy's patience nearly evaporated when he found her in a long-sleeved white shirt, playing in the fireplace soot, Melissa is convinced that "Allbody loves me." And she's right!

Mommy says if there's one thing she and Daddy don't suffer from, it's boredom. Daddy still works two weeks on/two weeks off and the rest of the family appreciates having him at home much of the time. He superintends the Junior Department at Sunday School and takes Junior Church with Mommy alternate months. He encourages Mommy in her music teaching and studying (now organ with Richard Proudman), and seems pleased that all of my sisters and my brother are involved in beginning music and/or piano and/or violin lessons. Mommy shares the organ responsibilities with two other organists at church and is on the Music Committee. Every so often she sneaks into her "office" and writes on a calendar covered with beautiful flowers and birds. If you like, I'll let you see some of her notes.

Friday, February 7, 10:00 a.m. Mother at table in study writing term reports. At last count, house contained five bedrooms and well-equipped family room. Children 3 and 4 snugly entrenched under desk, secure with several teddies, blankets, pillows, cutlery and dishes—a long siege? Mother appreciates devotion and desire to be near, but finds train of thought continually derailed. Child 4 climbs up behind Mother's back and hangs around neck at regular intervals. Mother remembers *Sesame Street* on at 11:00 a.m. :) Also that Kindergarten comes all too fast. :(

Tuesday, March 25, 4:00 p.m. School teachers for tea. Pleasant visit. Children quiet. Children *very* quiet. Mother goes to family room to investigate. Children 3 and 4 sitting at little table, paint brushes in hand, sharing a large glass of dirty water, in front of expanse of painted paper. New white shirts and pale blue pants now multicoloured. Mother upset. Kindergarten teacher *[Lenore Glew]* amused. (Melissa comments later that she *likes* Mrs. Glew.)

Monday, May 26, 7:00 a.m. Child 1 yells quietly in Mother's ear: "Time to practise, Mom." Mother says, "Again? Oh." Mother throws on scruffy old dressing gown, staggers down stairs and practises with eldest. **7:40 a.m.** Mother yells loudly through intercom: "Time to practise, Mike." Child 2 says, "Again? Oh *no*." Mother practises with second eldest. Father makes breakfast. **8:20 a.m.** Breakfast. **8:40 a.m.** Little girls dressing selves. Mother dresses Child 5. Father leaves for office visits; takes Children 1 and 2 to school. Mother still in dressing gown. Picks up dirty clothes from bathtub, takes to washer. Opens washer: washer filled with wet, clean clothes. Opens dryer: dryer filled with dry, clean clothes. Looks for large wicker basket—upstairs. Finds basket: filled with dry, clean, folded clothes. Mother distributes clean clothes, then makes way down to laundry room again. Empties dryer into basket, empties washer into dryer, fills washer. Ponders philosophy of housework. ... Phone rings: Other piano class supervisor needs mimeo before noon if possible. Mother says yes, grabs typewriter and stencil, types furiously; stencil covered with little red marks [*old Gestetner mimeograph stencil: waxed tissue, mistakes corrected with fluid similar to nail polish which filled in holes made by typo; letter/word retyped once fluid had dried*]. Child 3 (topless) pursues Child 4 (bottomless) through house. Child 5 in playpen; screams loudly when Children 3 and 4 out of range of vision. Mother types wildly on. **10:00 a.m.** Doorbell rings. Mother wishes she had dressed. Opens door 3/4", peers out, does not want to be seen. Student's parent wonders if child's book left in music room. "Sorry to surprise you, Mrs. Holland." Mother says, "Surprise, yes, ha ha." Mother finds key to music room, escorts parent to book. Children 3 and 4 escort Mother; Child 5 protests in background. Mother settles down again to typewriter. **11:00 a.m.** Finishes stencil. Father home, runs off 200 copies. Mother remembers laundry, goes to move wet clothes to dryer. Opens washer: full of dirty clothes. Washer not turned on.

Friday, July 19 Children 3 and 4 watching at front window as grandparents leave down path. Child 4: "I *like* those kids." Child 3, knowledgeably: "Those aren't *kids*. They're *people*."

MELISSA, MICHAEL, MARGARET, MARILYN

Sunday, September 21 Whole sunny weekend at trailer park in Sooke, except for Sunday morning services. **3:00 p.m.** Maternal grandparents arrive for visit and supper. Mother mixes pancakes while talking with grandmother. Mother going to quadruple recipe. Recipe says 1 cup milk. Mother talks to grandmother, pours in milk. After 8 cups, bowl very full, batter very thin. Grandmother says maybe add more flour; how many cups of milk in bowl already? (Mathematics vs. Mother; Mathematics wins again.) Mother adds cups of flour. No more baking powder. Grandfather goes to store to get some. Out of sugar, too. Mother adds honey. Grandmother and Mother take turns making pancakes. **5:00 p.m.** Still making pancakes. Pancakes all over trailer: in oven, on table, on shelves. **5:30 p.m.** Children and Father back from beach, pleased to see supper all prepared, and *so many* pancakes—yummy! Mother swears grandmother to secrecy.

Saturday, October 25 Father's birthday celebrated; grandparents, aunts, uncles, and cousins in attendance. Mother puts 39 candles on cake. Father blows out small bonfire in one try.

Monday, October 27   Father's real birthday. Opens presents: soft blue sweater from Mother, hair cream from Child 1, shaving cream from Child 2, razor blades from Child 3, Spanish soap from Child 4, peppermints from Child 5, all carefully wrapped and decorated (minimum wrapping paper, maximum Scotch tape). Shaving lotion from other grandparents. Mother says what with cuddly sweater and delicious shaving lotion, will not be responsible for possible consequences.

Monday, November 3, 9:45 a.m.   Father helping Auntie Dot move. Phones to say will not be able to take Child 5 for portrait: moving vans late, must stay to supervise. Mother was hoping to get some record-keeping done; wishes she had cancelled appointment. **10:20 a.m.** Mother drops Children 3 and 4 at Auntie Dot's old house and leaves for Studio 35, Nootka Court. Traffic unusually heavy, Eaton's car park packed: $1.49 Day! Mother wishes she had cancelled appointment. Street slippery, traffic at snail's pace; will Mother make it on time to appointment? **10:55 a.m.** Parked at last. Mother struggles down steep, wet street in high heels to Nootka Court; baby heavy. **11:00 a.m.** Photographer welcomes Child 5; Child 5 eyes him suspiciously, finally smiles. Baby placed on bench; baby screams. Mother

MOMMY ONLY HAS TWO SIDES

wishes she had cancelled appointment. Baby picked up by Mother; baby smiles. Baby placed on bench; baby screams. Photographer entertains with fluffy dog; baby narrows eyes menacingly. Mother empties purse in search of suitable plaything; no luck. Baby placed on bench; baby howls. Mother suggests photographer try to calm baby down while Mother goes outside. Mother paces Nootka Court, with protesting shrieks in background. Passersby wonder why coatless woman peeks furtively around corner into photographic studio. Shrieking crescendoes in spite of gentle persuasion by photographer. Photographer comes out and suggests perhaps another time? Mother wishes she had cancelled appointment. Mother dresses baby in bunting-bag; baby smiles. Mother says thank you, face red; baby says "ba-ba" happily to photographer, waves with both hands. Mother struggles up street again, baby waving to everyone, and smiling most winning smile. Mother forgets which floor car is parked on. Finds car, stuffs baby into car seat and makes way through traffic jam to Auntie Dot's new apartment. Moving men all over the place. Father upstairs talking to manager; Mother hasn't time to wait. Retrieves Children 3 and 4 and goes to pick up Children 1 and 2 from school. **12:10 p.m.** Starts making lunch: Children 1 to 4 at elbow; Child 5 howling. **12:20 p.m.** Father arrives home for lunch: "Why didn't you tell me you were going to pick the kids up from school?" Lunch not ready yet. Mother wishes she had cancelled appointment.

Thursday, November 6 Father away all day. Children home from school all day. Mother not terribly excited about day. **9:00 a.m.** Cookie-making starts: two bowls, four spoons, eight hands at work. (Child 2: "Like electric mixers, Mom, see?") Child 5 sleeps blissfully. **11:00 a.m.** 13 dozen cookies made, now cleanup. Children 1, 2, 3, and 4 watch *Sesame Street*. Mother cleans up pans and bowls. Children sample cookies. (Child 4: "But Mommy, I hungary. I *very* hungary.") **12:00 p.m.** Lunch. Mother reads *Mortimer the Friendly Dragon* to children. Children very attentive, except for Child 5 who wants more lunch. **1:00 p.m.** Children 3 and 4 put down for nap. **1:30 p.m.** Child 5 put down for nap. **2:00 p.m.** Children 1 and 2 working on leaf mosaic; glue and bits of paper everywhere. Storm hits: thunder, lightning. Child 2 cries. Mother wants to lie down, but doesn't want Child 2 to be upset, so waits out storm. Very dark outside: rain, hail. **2:30 p.m.** Mother tells Children 1 and 2 to be very quiet while she rests. **2:42 p.m.** Shriek from downstairs indicates disobedience. Mother has 4 1/2 hours of teaching ahead and is rather agitated. **3:00 p.m.** Mother gets dressed for teaching. **3:30 p.m.** Father not home yet; Mother apprehensive. **3:45 p.m.** Classes due to start. Mother leaves house for music room; hopes Department of Human Resources does not find out seven year old left in charge of four younger siblings. **4:15 p.m.** Father home; Mother breathes easier. Mother suddenly remembers that possibly she was supposed to be at violin workshop in morning. Mother asks Father please to phone violin teacher and apologize if workshop did in fact occur. **6:15 p.m.** Father tells Mother workshop did occur; teacher sure she told

MICHAEL AND A FAVOURITE ACTIVITY

SHARING RECITAL GOODIES

Mother. Mother must listen more carefully.

Wednesday, November 19, 8:40 a.m. Mother puts Oil of Olay on face. Child 4 watches intently. Mother goes down for breakfast. Father and Children 1, 2, and 3 at breakfast table; no Child 4. Aroma of cod liver oil drifts down hallway, followed by Child 4. Child 4 covered from nose down cheeks, chin and neck to shoulders with thick, white grease; long blonde hair stuck in Desitin diaper ointment. Child 4 has late breakfast. **8:40 p.m.** Recital over. Guests' coats piled high on bed. Student's mother sure she saw pile moving—perhaps cat? Mother says no cat. Pile of clothes explodes—small, hilarious boy. Mother's lecture drowned out by guests' laughter.

Monday, December 1, 11:45 p.m.   Final tuck-in for night.   Parents check assortment of beds and cribs. Child 1 snoring gently, woolly blanket in usual position over mouth. (Every birthday since fourth, Mother has suggested perhaps child now old enough to dispense with blanket? Response still negative.) Child 2 sprawled length of bed, feet on pillow, arm hanging over side; snorts grumpily when Father replaces in original position.   Child 3 on top of

MARILYN, DOLL WITH MATCHING BEDCAP, AND "SNUFFY" BLANKET

covers as usual, sleeping sideways, four barrettes above each ear; reaches up sleepily to hug Mother as Mother slides her back under covers. Child 4 surrounded by 14 "people" and collection of Lego, clocks and puzzle pieces; extension gates on top of crib form cage since Child 4, at 18 months, found standing on Saanich Road's yellow line. Child 5 scrunched up in south corner of crib, bottom high in air; blankets at

NEVER TOO YOUNG!

north end. Mother cannot resist impulse to pick up and cuddle baby. Baby smiles happily around soother. Father covers tiny body, knowing little bottom will soon be exposed again. Parents think of children's favourite hymn: "Father, we thank Thee, … Father in Heaven, we thank Thee."

Love, Melody

———————————————

From Mother: In 1975 we made our annual pilgrimage to Prince George. We have happy memories: five smiling little faces, snuggled into two bunk beds 48" from their doting parents; the off-key renditions of "Can a Little Child Like Me" (all four verses) while driving; a breathtaking variety of scenery; and the ferry ride, where Daddy swelled the comic book collection by buying four "comits" (bringing the total to five). However, for some reason or other, I found myself humming "Home, Sweet Home" rather often, especially on the return trip! These are some notes I made:

… Running around with cousins in Prince George, building forts, climbing (and falling out of) trees, it doesn't really matter what the children wear. With Vancouver and civilization just a few hours away, Mommy makes sure everyone is scrubbed up and in matching outfits. Daddy checks to see the trailer is secure, and we're off—almost. Melissa comes running around the trailer corner shrieking, "Mawgwet 'pit up! Mawgwet 'pit up!" Margaret has *thrown* up thoroughly, all over blouse, shorts, socks, shoes, car seat and car blanket.

… It is 6:45 p.m. and we should have stopped at that trailer park 80 miles back. Mommy has, with typical cheerfulness (?) and many interruptions, thrown supper together. The older two are fighting, the stew is sticking to the pan, the younger two are whining, the salad is wilting, the baby is crying, a fly walks across the butter, Daddy tries to say grace. … The baby suddenly and desperately needs a change of diapers.

… Cousin Ralph is an accountant, Cousin Marilyn a school teacher, both in their twenties with no children. They have bought a beautiful new house in Richmond, and Mommy and Daddy and children are invited to come for a visit. In 14 l-o-n-g minutes, Michael has splattered a blueberry tart on the kitchen floor two inches from the pale gold living room carpet, Margaret has lost her gum in that same carpet, Melissa has fingerprinted the glass coffee table, and Melody has spit up on the chesterfield. Marilyn pretends she doesn't know where her parents picked up the little barbarians.

"Be it ever so humble …"

Louise

Chapter 9: 1976

Here I am again, pen in hand, ink on face, shirt and pants, to wish you a joyful Christmas and a contented 1977. I am Melody Joy, and I am prepared to tell you all about my family.

The two big people who provide us with room and board will have shared credits and debits for fifteen years this December. The taller one still wanders in and out of the house at odd hours of the night; the telephone's ring and the pager's chirp seem to exercise great control over him. His travels take him through homes, offices, police stations, hospitals and courtrooms. Unlike the daytime jobs he shares with Mommy so that she can teach, his emergency work is endlessly varied. Our shorter, rounder parent spends large portions of her time up in the music room, at her desk, and on the organ bench. In May, she trembled through a Grade VIII organ exam, and hopes to tackle Grade IX in January. This summer she and Daddy took separate vacations: Daddy cooked for twelve days at camp at the beginning of July, and Mommy directed a junior girls' camp in the middle of August. Somehow our annual safari to Prince George got lost in the shuffle and our parents didn't seem to mind as much as we did.

Family Record Plan
MELODY

BRUCE DEALING WITH AN EMERGENCY

Our family is still composed of five "Mini-Ms": **Marilyn** (Big Sister), 9 in December; **Michael** (Brother), 7 in September; **Margaret** (Middle Sister), 5 in October; **Melissa** (Little Sister), 4 in December; and me, **Melody** (Baby Sister), 2 in December.

Marilyn is Mommy's second pair of arms and legs. If she had her way, she would spend life attached to a book, but unfortunately her parents' requests and the requirements of studying and music interfere all too regularly. She passed her Grade II piano exam in June and is coming along quite well on the violin. For the past two years at school, she has kept a diary. (Mommy says it's a more permanent version of

Show and Tell, or Tattletale.) Included in her writings are Psychological Treatises: "Gaby and Michael and I are going to stick around Mom and see if she asks us if Gaby can stay for lunch" (the erosion principle); a sprinkling of Words Originally Spelled: "For Christmas I would like the hole serries of Laura Ingalls Wilder books"; and Items of Intense Interest to All: "Yesterday it was my mom's birthday. Now my mom is <u>35</u>!" (Mommy didn't think the underlining and exclamation mark were all that necessary.)

Michael basks in his status as the only Holland grandson, surrounded by eight granddaughters. Like Marilyn, he prefers reading books to almost any other activity, except perhaps riding his bike. Like Marilyn, he is an unliberated child who has to meet his parents' demands, whether or not they coincide with his wishes; as a result, he plays both piano and violin with some proficiency.

MICHAEL

In May, he came home with a crumpled piece of foolscap that made Mommy forget the early-morning, "Oh *no*, not again." In large Grade One printing, it said: "MY Mother. My Mother is nice. I love her very very much. Sometimes she makes my dinner but not allwas. She even helps me with my music becus my Mother is a music techer. My Mother helps me with my violon too. Sometimes she helps me with things I do. My Mother is a speshal Mother thats what I tell her. She is a pretty Mother when I am asleep she kisses me. By Michael." He recently confided while peeling potatoes that "This is hard, but I'm doing it because I like you."

For a year, Mommy and Daddy have had two little girls (The Pair) and a baby (me) home in the daytime. Now the baby has nearly been replaced by another little girl, and a Crowd has formed (as in "Two's company, three's a ..."). This Crowd spends morning after busy morning upheaving the house, meets for lunch with the "Big Kids," and then disperses for the afternoon, Melissa to play by and talk with herself or to go for a ride with Daddy, me to my nap, and Margaret to Kindergarten.

Margaret scampers off with great anticipation and never seems disappointed with her afternoon's experiences; her lengthy report usually starts, "Today I did/didn't paint," which gives some idea of what she considers important. Margaret is tall and slender, with beautiful long fingers (a paternal endowment) that are gradually accommodating themselves to both piano and violin. She shares her bedroom with Marilyn and her bed with Holly Hobbie, alias Molly Holland, Raggedy Ann, three or four books, a handful of Lego, and as many pillows as she can filch from other rooms. She "reads" stories to Melissa and me with an authority that belies illiteracy; papers covered with letters, words and numerals printed by an increasingly-steady five-year-old hand can be found in nearly every room. The family individualist, Margaret has an excessive fondness for chives (which is fine until she uses Mommy's toothbrush) and chewing gum (used, as is found in wastebaskets and under church pews). At the beginning of this year, when asked by her violin teacher whether she thought Melissa (three years old a few days previous) should take violin lessons, too, she said, "I guess I'll let her come."

It will be Melissa's turn to start Kindergarten next September. Daddy is sure she will be able to manoeuvre through school on charm alone, blessed as she is with the most cheerful disposition imaginable (Daddy says she gets this from her father), white-blond hair to her waist (except on the sides, which are 5" and 7" shorter due to some do-it-herself barbering), blue, blue eyes and a smile that lights up the room. Daddy calls her "solidified sunshine," with an emphasis on "solid"; Mommy remembers that "Melissa" means "honeybee" and thinks of flowers and summer days and agrees the name is appropriate. Melissa and the English language are still not quite on speaking terms. Her version of a well-known nursery rhyme goes: "Little Miss Muffet sat on a puffet, eating her curtains away." "Bacuum upping" is a favourite job, as is "plugging out" the telephone when Mommy has a nap. When the two smallest rooms are in use, her cry is, "But Mom, I need to go *reely beely*." A typical reply, designed to confuse her easily-befuddled parents, is "I already did it, tomorrow."

Picking buckets of blackberries in a disreputable outfit that has seen several prickly Augusts is one of Mommy's favourite summer pastimes. More than once, she has hung suspended over a ravine, refusing to relinquish a handful of glossy berries, a testimony to the strength of blackberry vines. Margaret and Melissa happily follow suit, replenishing their playhouse larder with tin cans of berries and leaves. However, their domestic ardour suffered a setback in July when Mommy caught them picking "fuzzy little green balls" for their "supper." In August, the peach crop was rather scant, and The Pair received a further lecture on the unwisdom of getting within ten feet of the peach trellis.

Mommy and Daddy sometimes comment approvingly on the spare-time activities of my older siblings. However, although my resourcefulness is noted, too, it is not always, or even usually, with approval. Apparently filling my shoes with porridge while Daddy talks on the telephone, or rearranging the contents of dresser drawers (in the middle of the floor) are not considered Worthwhile Activities. Nor are transporting toothbrushes and toothpaste from room to room and redecorating the bedroom wall, and my T-shirt, with toothpaste and/or pencil. Standing on the organ pedals, hanging by fingertips on the lower manual, and "varooming" Michael's tiny trucks on the bench while Mommy practises are not acceptable, either. Even my efforts to speed up family routines receive no praise: as soon as Mommy takes out the big knife and a loaf of bread, I yell, "Wunch weady, 'body," two or three ear-splitting times, and everyone comes to watch Mommy make her sticky way through lunch preparations. She says it's hard to work with 2 1/2 children swinging from each elbow. My vocabulary has expanded greatly this past year, the most useful additions being "No," and "Don't want to." When Daddy's grace extends beyond two sentences—and I do know we have very much to thank God for—I accelerate things by interjecting a loud "Ah-min." As far as I can tell, the only reason I'm allowed to stay here is that I have dimples on my hands and elbows and I look very sweet when I am asleep. Also, I have learned to say, "I luff you," at the most advantageous times. (And Mommy still calls me Melody *Joy*.)

Our day begins with alarms ringing in Marilyn's and Mommy's rooms at six o'clock. After a few minutes, "Marili-in" is whispered several times and, from my room, I say, "Hi, Mom"; Mommy pretends she doesn't hear me. Pretty soon, "Yes, Mom," comes floating out of Marilyn's bedroom, followed by two pairs of slippers shuffling down the stairs. For the next three-quarters of an hour, Marilyn patiently endures Mommy's suggestions on the piano and violin and then heads up to the

music room for another session by herself. Our much-cuddled tabby, Tiger, sits under the piano keyboard next to Marilyn's feet. By this time, Michael is being cajoled into producing beautiful music. By eight o'clock, it's Margaret's, then Melissa's turn, and Mommy tries at least partially to match their enthusiasm. After porridge, it's off to school in a flurry for Marilyn and Michael.

Most days follow a regular schedule, with French, beginning music, piano and violin classes for the Big Four speckling the calendar at frequent intervals. Sometimes, Mommy scribbles on her calendar; you're welcome to read with me.

MARILYN, MARGARET, MICHAEL, MELISSA

January 1, 1976, 2:20 a.m. Mother finishes book, drifts off to sleep. **2:55 a.m.** Mother dreams wind is blowing drapes violently against wall. Wakes, finds Tiger batting a measuring tape around room. Mother hisses, "Psst!" but cat is too engrossed in play to respond. Father arrives home from call and evicts cat. Mother has difficulty getting back to sleep. **3:30 a.m.** Mother and illuminated dial exchange looks. **4:00, 4:30, 5:00 a.m.** Mother and clock stare balefully at each other. **5:30 a.m.** Mother falls asleep. **7:00 a.m.** Alarm startles Mother, who says, "Happy 1976" to self, unconvincingly.

January 22 Little Sister: "I amn't." Middle Sister: "You're wrong, 'Lissa. You should say, 'I *are*n't.'"

March 5 Little Sister: "Look, Mawg—three dogs!" Middle Sister: "No, 'Lissa—*two* dogs and one Dalmatian."

July 9, 8:30 a.m. Big Sister and Little Brother wash hands for breakfast. Little Brother dries hands on towel. Big Sister dries hands on Little Brother's T-shirt. Outraged cry issues from bathroom. **12:30 p.m.** Big Sister and Little Brother wash hands for lunch. Little Brother dries hands on towel. Big Sister dries hands in Little Brother's hair. Outraged shriek issues from bathroom. **5:30 p.m.** Little Brother washes hands for supper. Calls solicitously to Big Sister that bathroom is free, so she can wash her hands; vanishes. Big Sister enters bathroom, surveys self in mirror, pulls up metal handle for metal sink plug and fills basin with water. Starts washing hands. Suddenly water drains away. Perplexed, refills basin, only to have basin empty quickly again. Starts talking softly to self. After third emptying, starts talking loudly to sink, whereupon cabinet door under sink bursts open and Little Brother emerges with whoop of glee. Score is even.

August 18, 10:00 p.m., Camp Qwanoes, Crofton Mother makes way from cabent to cabent, flashlight in hand, checking to see campers comfortable (and quiet) for night. Youngest group is settled down on plastic sheet in open field; moon and stars illuminate row of sleeping bags covered with second sheet, secured at each end with small logs. Youngest camper says, "Kiss me, Mommy." Director hesitates, then kneels down to kiss eldest daughter good-night; decides that cabin-mates might feel left out, gives each one a peck on forehead. (Counsellor says, "Me, no thanks!") Mother returns to lodge to work on next day's programme. **12:30 a.m.** Mother descends into basement of lodge, knocks on door of work crew's room. Music drowns out knock; no response. Knocks again, louder; decibel level plummets. Mother says, "Have a good *sleep*, boys," plods over to own room, gets dressed in long flannelette gown, sweater, and heavy socks, and crawls into sleeping bag. Pulls up blankets over self and instantly loses consciousness. **3:30 a.m.** Unnerving drone tunnels into Mother's subconscious. Mother wakes uneasily to sound of wind bearing down on dense forest surrounding cabents and lodge. Tall firs, cedars and maples sigh in protest; lodge moans. (Mother enjoys rain, tolerates thunderstorms, but has unreasoning fear of high winds.) Lodge shudders. So does Mother. Suddenly remembers campers out on field. Rubs eyes vigorously, puts on glasses, heavy pink dressing gown and rubber boots, makes way across shadowy field with flashlight. Hesitates some distance from line of sleeping girls; does not want to originate Qwanoes "Legend of the Large Pink Ghost." All appears well. **4:00 a.m.** Mother crawls back into sleeping-bag. **5:30 a.m.** Mother aware of new sound. Wind is replaced with not-so-gentle splashing of rain. Mother remembers next day is Sports Day and thinks longingly of Saanich Road and home. Drags self out of bag, reaches out for glasses only to discover them already on face, puts on dressing gown, heavy winter jacket, rain scarf, rubber boots; picks up flashlight and umbrella and sloshes across field in search of campers. Sleepout site deserted except for plastic sheets. Mother decides that camp should have rainy morning sleep-in; goes to office upstairs, makes and tapes signs on both kitchen doors: "Breakfast at *8:30*, please." **6:00 a.m.** Returns to bed, resets alarm for 7:30 a.m., crawls onto mattress under sleeping bag, removing only rubber boots and scarf. **6:30 a.m.** Jangling of tin cans precedes alarm by 60 minutes. Mother stumbles to door, discovers nurse has been unable to sleep and is tidying up handcraft materials. Mother gets up to meet another exciting day at camp.

Monday, October 11, Thanksgiving Day Father and Mother decide to throw routine to the wind and take the family for a hike around Thetis Lake. Unwashed laundry, unfolded laundry, unironed laundry left behind; unpainted trim, unweeded borders, unwashed windows left behind. Parents and towheads tramp around lake. Brother and Middle Sister (true to form) up front, darting up and down side paths, covering three times as much territory as more lethargic members of family. Little Sister stomps along main path, examining fungi and leaves, humming to self. Sweater and pants, as usual, on backwards; shoes, surprisingly, on correct feet. Parents hold hands, separated every few moments by different pairs of little hands wanting to get in on the action. Big Sister brings up rear, holding Baby Sister's hand and trying to match pat-pat of tiny running shoes. Hikers making opposite circuit of lake note horde of blonds, comment on felt-pen X on Baby's cheek: "Guess that's so you'll find her when she gets lost!" Fragrance of fir needles underfoot, glint of sun on lake, green and gold pattern through trees, excited treble voices, and busy little feet on path: Mother thinks, "'The lines are fallen unto me in pleasant places'— Thanksgiving indeed!"

Saturday, October 23, 7:30 a.m. Violin lessons start at 9:15 a.m. on other side of town. Big Sister and Vivaldi Concerto in music room; Brother and Boccherini Minuet in living room; Middle Sister, Mother and tentative rendition of "Lightly Row" in bedroom upstairs. Little Sister tiptoes downstairs with Middle Sister's new doll; Baby Sister confined to kitchen-family room by extension gate. **8:00 a.m.** Desperate cry from Little Sister. Mother rushes downstairs to find Father's birthday cake (concocted previous evening by Big Sister, Brother and Mother) with two 3" craters on one side; Baby Sister nowhere in sight. Trail leads behind large chair: small, quivering child covered from elbows to eyebrows with chocolate crumbs. Brother says, "Guess the cake tastes OK, eh, Mom?" End of practice session.

I see we're running out of paper, and I'm not sure I want to share any more stories like that last one, anyway, so I'll close for now. My family joins me in wishing you God's best.

Love, Melody
P.S. The cake was good, and besides, I'm well-padded where it counts! xxoo

Chapter 10: Camp Letters

This chapter includes a set of letters mailed to and from Camp Qwanoes during the summer of 1976. In typing out and sending the letters to my now-adult children, I observed to them:

Dad was 40, I was 35, and you five were eight and down. There are two sets of letters: ours to Dad at camp, and his to us from camp (July); and letters from me at camp to you all at home, along with letters from you to me (August; I directed a junior girls camp). What you would find incredible today is that Dad and I communicated only by letter (I wrote him on Monday and Thursday); neither of us phoned each other, as that was expensive. No fax; no e-mail. And, as you know, Qwanoes is just over an hour's drive away from home!

I had not looked at the envelopes of camp letters for nearly 30 years, and was fascinated to find a happy assortment of letters and small items that could be sent to camp. There was money sent to Daddy from Michael (then six): two pennies, two nickels, and two dimes; felt pen pictures, still bright, drawn by Melissa (labelled by me: "clouds," "fire," "house," "grass") on one side of the paper, x's and o's covering the other side, and by Margaret (a tall house with chimney and smoke at a 45-degree angle, and a row of oxoxoxoxo across the back, with MArGArEt printed carefully underneath it. Mike's letter has nine hearts with "I love you!" in each one across the top, and dozens of x's and o's down the side and "Dear! Dad!" as the salutation (the exclamation marks with little hearts instead of periods).

His letter to Dear! Dad! on July 12:

"I am beter but Margret has a cold. Today I did the watering. I hope you do your cooking right. Today the Heals took Ginger. I hope you enjoy cooking. Today a man came and cut the grass near the rock in the carport. Love, Michael Holland."

MICHAEL AND A SIX-YEAR-OLD'S GAP

And on July 15:

"Thank-you for your letter. Yesterday we almost got out of catfood so we used the box. Then when I looked more closely I saw three more and I saw a big box of cat food and Marilyn thout it was the same as the one called purenia but the other one was liver diner so it wasn't the same." This letter also has loads of hearts and xo's and two boxes at the bottom with "specil" hearts and "specil" x's and o's.

Marilyn's July 12 letter:

"Dear Dad, this morning I woke up at 6:00. I did my two hours practising, then I played with the kittens. I feel much better. Margaret has a bad cold. After breakfast Mommy might let me go over to Gaby's to watch Mr. Dressup and Sesame Street. Love Marilyn xoxoxoxoxo" (all in beautiful Lake Hill School handwriting, just learned that year).

And on July 15:

"Dear Dad, I hope you're having a good time. I didn't really have a good time yesterday morning, Guess Why. Well, yesterday morning the kittens climbed high on that prickly [holly] tree. Michael and I and a few others were trying to get them down. I wasn't watching what I was doing and a bee stung me on the fourth finger on my left hand. Love from Marilyn" (also lots of tiny o's and x's).

With Marilyn and me at camp in August, there is only one letter, from Michael:

"To Mommy! (heart exclamation mark) Are you getting wet? It's rainning hard here. I hope you are having fun playing in the puddles. We are going to have supper at Granny's tonight. See you on Sunday. GrandMa came over last night to babysit. Tanya is playing with me. love from Michael". *[There's also an envelope for Mommy and Marilyn from Michael with half a stick of Trident gum, now petrified, in it. I presume one of us chewed the other half! And Dad sent a cute set of cards from camp, one for each of you.]*

In my July 12 (1976) letter to Dad I wrote:

Ms 2 to 4 are in the music room creating something for you. M1 and Gaby are bouncing a super ball around the patio; it just ricocheted between the rocks, and against the playhouse. ... M5 is wandering around my desk here—what an adorable tease. She just picked up an eraser off the desk, put it in her mouth, and when I turned to look at her, immediately pulled it out and replaced it on the desk. She disappeared a few moments ago, and has just come back with "sooie" (from her crib) … Melody calls Mom "Granky". Mom's not impressed … Byron and Viola came for the kitten this morning. Their kids were really excited. *[This is sad.]* Poor Tiger looked and called for the kitten for the longest time. She seems to have accepted it now.

And on July 15:

Dear Head Cook! I love you! So do 5 little angels (?), one of whom still insists in asking "Where Daddy gone?" several times a day … We get quite a lot done during the day in the way of music practice, and as *[my sister]* Peggy so aptly put it, "The house doesn't look any worse than usual!" Yesterday I cleaned off much of the graffiti in M4's and M5's room and vacuumed that room and my own—what a miserable job! *[Some things don't change.]* Michael (all too willingly) helped me sort out my drawers, so at least two rooms upstairs are reasonably presentable. I'll need an extra dose of adrenaline to be able to tackle M1 and M3's hideaway. … On Tuesday the kids *[Marilyn and Michael only at this time]* played their violins at the women's mission group and were very well received. Mrs. McKee (the president) gave them each a gift: Michael a horse figurine and Marilyn two figurines, a man and woman in old-fashioned costume. The kids were pleased and even more so when they discovered the "candy lady" (Mrs. Taylor) sitting behind them! She slipped them goodies a couple of times. At the tea afterwards, they had milk and many squares, etc.; as soon as the ladies saw their jaws were momentarily still, along came more treats.

MELODY AND CROCUSES

So there you have a "slice of life" from 42 years ago. I don't think I have looked through these letters since that time, and it brings a lot of memories flooding back. One memory is of picking blackberries at the end of August, sliding down a ditch at the side of Saanich Road, and extricating myself from the vines with great difficulty. Mark was born a few days later. I trust my daughters/daughters-in-law would not be so foolish!

Chapter 11 : 1977

By now, it will be apparent that the letter M figured largely in the naming of our children. Our first baby was named after a special aunt, Marilyn Holland (now Wilson). We liked the name Michael; my cousin, Michael Sparks, was a pilot, which gives some credence to the prophetic power of a name. Margaret was named after my sister, Margaret ("Auntie Peggy"). Melissa came along 14 months later, and we felt committed to an "M" name; as is noted earlier, "honeybee," the meaning of Melissa, suits our middle child. The name Melody seemed appropriate, given the importance of music in our home.

I am sure there are those who wonder at the numbering of our children: M1, M2, M3, etc., and assume that they must feel depersonalized by such labelling. However, they often use the same shorthand in relation to each other, and at least four have incorporated it into their e-mail addresses over the years.

The M tradition continued in 1977, and our sixth baby contemplates his name in 1977's letter:

Season's Greetings from the sixth arrow in Daddy's quiver. "As arrows are in the hand of a mighty man; so are children of the youth. Happy is the man that hath his quiver full of them..." (Psalm 127:4, 5b).

Mark Andrew is my name, and I'm glad it is, when I look at some of the possibilities. After Margaret announced to the Kindergarten class that "Mommy has a baby in her tummy," the Kindergarten teacher made the contribution, "Marvellous!" both as a suggested name and to express her sentiments. Daddy considered "Many" and "Much," but steadfastly turned down "More." Both he and Mommy rejected "Mistake." In fact, Mommy often quotes Bible verses that say we are "a gift," "a reward," and "an heritage," heady stuff for a group of towheads whose relationship to a wooden spoon is more than culinary. Uncle George had a suggestion, but Mommy said it was already in frequent use: "Melody, if you drink the cat's water again, your name will be 'Mud.'" And when Granny heard I was coming, she contributed "Mercy" ("Oh, Mercy!").

After a long, very hot summer, I decided to make my entrance nearly two weeks ahead of schedule. I figured the Labour Day weekend was an appropriate time, so I chose the evening of September 2, just in time for back-to-school festivities. Daddy was able to fit in my arrival between calls, and held and admired all 6 pounds 15 ounces of me when I was just a few moments old. To Mommy's surprise and everyone's delight, I was not Girl 5, but Boy 2, and I am apparently an image of the Michael of eight years ago. According to Mommy, I am a Beautiful Baby, and this assessment has been confirmed by a panel of experts (two grandmothers and a father —mine). Daddy assures me that my dark hair is only a temporary aberration, and will shortly be replaced by something more attractive, as Michael's was. Not only do I share Michael's birthday month, early arrival, hair colour, and looks, but I also shared his bilirubin problem. By September 10, my tan belied my English-Scandinavian ancestry and my doctor said that "Sir Mark" had to return to the hospital. (Mommy cried, so the doctor had two problems—a yellow baby and a crybaby.) There I lounged under an ultraviolet lamp with just a toque and eye pads on until I turned pink again; Daddy said I looked like a little elf all set to ski. When Mommy came back from the hospital without me, my littlest big sister was displeased with Mommy's irresponsibility; as she pushed my bassinet back and forth, she said, "Anyway, I 'tend my little baby boy is in here."

On my second homecoming, I was received even more appreciatively, and took advantage of my popularity to demand *tête-à-têtes* with Mommy every two or three hours, day and night. Mommy thought my theme song was going to be Rock—as in rocking chair—Around the Clock, but after a few weeks of testing her devotion, I finally relented. By the end of October, my parents could usually count on sleeping between midnight and six o'clock. My exemplary behaviour is rewarded by a violin and piano concert starting at 6:30 p.m., compliments of my three biggest sisters and my big brother.

May I give you a baby's-eye-view of the rest of my family?

As Emergency Social Worker, Daddy continues to field after-hours telephone calls. With shifts ranging from 16 hours (overnight) to 88 hours (long weekends), he covers many miles and accumulates reams of notes each two-week shift. He is superintendent of the Junior Department at Sunday School, and serves as a deacon and board member of our church. A year ago in May, he encouraged Mommy to take a Grade VIII organ exam. The surprising results were 87% and some scholarships; Mommy said thank you to God and to Daddy. Last January she took Grade IX (84% and some scholarships; thank you, again), and had every intention of attempting Grade X this past June. However, by the end of February, I had had enough of travelling across 2 1/2 octaves of pedals every day, so I pressed the panic button and Mommy viewed life horizontally for a couple of days. Organ lessons, choir accompanying, camp work, Junior Church and piano class supervision were quickly erased from the calendar as Mommy discovered she was indispensable in only one area—me.

Daddy spent the first three weeks of the summer holidays cooking at camp. His arrival home coincided with the beginning of a five-week heat wave, which enabled him to spend much time outside painting, gardening and consuming gallons of iced tea. Mommy spent the summer preparing meals, assembling teaching materials and assignments for her students, discussing (complaining about) the heat, and suggesting ways in which the children could happily while away the summertime: "Marilyn, you can vacuum the upstairs"; "Michael, the downstairs needs dusting"; "Margaret, I'd like you to fold this basket of clothes, and you can help her, Melissa"; "Melody, you put all the toys away in the sun porch." Rarely did the children make the mistake of saying "But there's nothing to do!"

Marilyn will be ten at the end of December. She is rapidly developing organizational skills (a euphemism for "bossiness") and helps our parents keep things on a relatively even keel. She shares hair styles, comic books, gum and philosophy with her room-mate, Margaret, who also displays developing leadership abilities. (Michael's comment on Marilyn's return from a week at camp: "Margaret was boss while you were gone.") Marilyn took her Grade IV Piano exam in June and puts in an hour on the violin and on the piano first thing in the morning, encouraged by a less-than-ferocious Tiger who sits at her feet or on top of the piano. Her favourite activity is sprawling out on the chesterfield, book in hand, with a Beethoven symphony providing 95 decibels of background. Marilyn's favourite food is cookie-dough.

Michael, eight in September, has acquired a positive attitude towards life in general (piano and violin practising in particular) that has our parents both delighted and baffled. His New Year's resolution, written at school, included, "I promise to be nice to my sisters," and "I promise to do my practising in the morning with my Mom without being grumpy." Instead of being dragged out of bed by Mommy, he has been known to tiptoe into Mommy's bedroom, tap her gently on the shoulder, and remind her that it's time to practise. The first time it happened, Mommy had met with me at 11:00 p.m., 1:00 a.m., 3:00 a.m., and 5:00 a.m., and would have given the piano and organ—and thrown in the violins—for eight hours of uninterrupted sleep. The novelty got through to her, though, and she stumbled out to enjoy Bach before breakfast with my brother. Michael enjoys writing stories and decorating them with parentheses, asterisks, dashes and exclamation marks; the first entry in his journal at school described *me!*

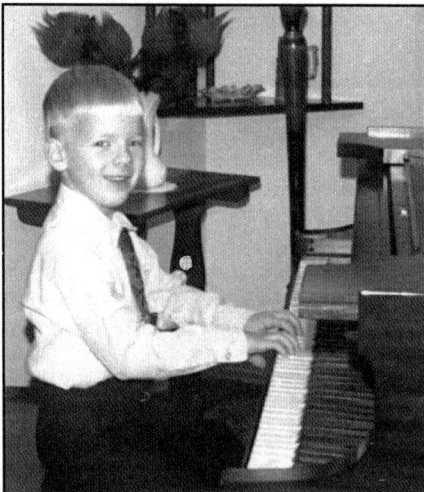

MICHAEL

Michael's favourite activity is licking out the cookie bowl, although I think he enjoys reading just as much; he has five flashlights to extend his undercover reading hours.

Margaret was six in October. As artist-in-residence, she delights in assembling 3-D pictures, using any scraps of paper and materials available; her belongings are readily identifiable by the flowers, hearts and "I love you's" drawn all over them. Although picture-making is her favourite pastime, Margaret, too, is required to spend time each day on violin and piano. She is also learning to read and is very willing to pass on her knowledge to younger family members: "Listen, Mel, this is what it says: -ing, -ring, bring." Margaret's artistry extends to her mode of dress; she appears at breakfast as an elegant "lady," a "gypsy," or a "ragamuffin," depending on the whim of the moment. Her favourite sleeping outfit is a long flannelette gown, gypsy scarf and sunglasses.

Melissa is my sturdy, cheerful, five-year-old sister. She and Melody entertain themselves (and our parents) by playing "house," "school," or "nurse" each school morning. After lunch, Melissa joins the Big Three and bounces off to Kindergarten, Show and Tell object in hand. Included among her activities are playing little songs on the (inevitable) violin and piano, and biting her nails (toenails). The latter activity is considered enviable by her less-supple parents, but is not encouraged. Melissa's ambition is to eat a whole banana *all by herself* (Large Family Syndrome). "Mark is small because he is babier than me," and "Please undo me up," are Melissa's contributions to the vernacular.

Melody was three at the beginning of December and has become quite independent over the past year, although a setback did threaten when I arrived on the scene. ("Yes, I know, Mommy; my dad say the same thing—I too big for diapees.") Pants and shirts are usually worn backwards and shoes end up on the wrong feet; the "elbow" of a sock lands on top of her foot and her clothes become "backwards out" when she undresses, but Mommy and Daddy are very happy to let her "do it by MYSELF." Melody's favourite toys are the 25 plastic "people" she carries around in a bucket and a little blue "bummy-rabbit" she tucks in beside me. As my unofficial herald, Melody announces to all who are interested, that I am "M*A*R*K A*N*D*R*E*W H*O*L*L*A*N*D," her "Little Baby Brother."

And that brings us back to the tiniest twig on the family tree. Although I am unable to make music, bake cookies, or chew on my toenails, I do have some accomplishments to my credit. I produce laundry at a rate designed to keep the Ivory Snow company afloat, I smile and coo for any reason and no reason, and I carry on animated conversations with the flowers on the upholstery and the cobweb decorating the lampshade. And, no doubt, 1978 will bring even greater exploits. A Happy 1978 to you!

Love, M*A*R*K

P.S. Here are some little stories I found on Mommy's calendar:

January 10 Brother reads joke to Big Sister, whose sense of the ridiculous is not as fully developed: "The other day in a restaurant I saw a man with such poor manners he was actually scratching his back with a fork. I got so upset at seeing this, I dropped my handful of mashed potatoes." ... Long silence ... Big Sister: "Where?"

January 11 Melissa [4]: "I like God, Mommy. I want to sit in His lap. You know, God isn't just in heaven; He's in my tummy and my heart, too."

March 5 Mother is driving Margaret [5] and Melissa [4] home from violin lesson. Mother scolds for misbehaviour: "And the next time you climb up on Miss Colquhoun's high chair, I'll take you out in the hall and spank you." ... Two-minute silence, ... then Mother hears: "OK, 'Lissa, we must remember—no more climbing that chair."

March 21 M4 asks for kiss. M1 says M4 does not deserve kiss, has been playing with Mother's perfume. M4 says, "No," just "watching" while M5, standing in second drawer, experimented with bottle of perfume.

March 24, 7:00 p.m. Father puts Ms 4 and 5 to bed: lights out, door shut, promise of "going right to sleep." **8:30 p.m.** Mother comes down from teaching; aware of upstairs hilarity. Greeted by "Hi, Mom, look at my hair." M4's waist-length hair plastered with bobby pins. "Me, too, Mommy," from crib. Mommy removes pins, turns off lights, delivers nocturnal ultimatum. On way downstairs, hears, "Love us, Mommy?"

May 31 (contributed by Daddy) Margaret: "Why are you putting my dress up there, Mommy?" Mother: "That's the ironing basket." Margaret: "That means I won't be able to wear it anymore."

July 25, 4:00 p.m. Mother at desk checking class lists. Older children outside, playing uproariously. Supper looms. Mother decides to check up on youngest child on way to kitchen. To consternation, discovers said child in garden digging around tomato plants with silver serving spoon, clad only in cherry-stained T-shirt, rapidly graying socks, and fine covering of dust. (Mother's hair matches socks.) Day is very hot, and Mother is very tired *[and nearly eight months pregnant]*; does not know whether to laugh or cry. During moment of indecision, small voice pipes, "I *like* you, Mommy—don't cry." Mother doesn't.

August 1 Margaret wants to tell Mother's fortune with folded paper. Mother chooses colour, number, number; at third number, Margaret reads "fortune": "You look like a fairy." Mother looks down at abdominal protrusion, thinks, "175-pound fairy?" and smiles; gives Margaret a hug. Father cannot contain his glee and receives withering glance from Mother. Margaret wonders at adult humour; thinks that it is a *good* fortune.

Melissa tells fortune next, first whispering to Mother that number 7 is the one to choose. Mother chooses colour ("Which one says 'red,' Mommy?"), two numbers, then 7. Melissa grins ecstatically while Mother reads "fortune": "I love you." Feeling is mutual.

Sunday, September 4, 3:30 p.m. Harassed father, aunt and quintet of blonds arrive at hospital to look over newest recruit. Nurse eyes small mob skeptically, suggests perhaps sunroom more comfortable visiting place than Mother's bedside? Visit to nursery window: children agree M6 most acceptable; M5 holds arms out, wants to take tiny boy from nurse through glass. Father has spent morning in Sunday School and church with children, followed by quick lunch and hour in court. Father's pager beeps at five-minute intervals. Auntie Shirley and Mother count noses while Father exhausts supply of dimes at phone; Father gradually becoming unstuck. Aunt suggests children tell Mother what they saw in church: "Two babies the same—that's what we want you to have next time, Mommy!" Mother smiles weakly. M3 regards Mother appraisingly, asks, "Why do you still have a big tummy, Mommy?" **4:00 p.m.** Father asks hopefully if it's time to leave. Mother says yes, dispenses kisses all around, shuffles back to bed to recuperate.

Sunday, October 16, 9:10 a.m. Family dressing for Sunday School. Mother working on smallest head, fixing fourth pair of pony tails; suddenly realizes footwear missing. Sends out FTS (Find Those Sandals) to four older siblings, who scurry from room to room, searching under beds, in drawers, through bookshelves, closets and wastebaskets. Youngest girl watches confusion with casual indifference. Finally Mother asks in exasperation if she knows where her shoes are. Immediate reply is, "Under my pillow." Search squad overturns pillow; finds five dolls, three hankies, assortment of blocks, and two small white sandals. Family only three minutes late for Sunday School … this time.

MELODY AND FRIEND EMILIE (BORN ON SAME DAY)

Chapter 12: Letters to Daddy at Camp Qwanoes, 1977

In the summer of 1977, our children were learning, among other things, to associate work with earning power (in this instance, carrying pails of rocks to the site where a rock wall was being constructed), as well as communicating with their father at camp. Here are some excerpts from that year's correspondence:

From Marilyn [9 1/2]:

July 2 "Dear Dad, I hope you are having fun and I hope you are having a good time. We are alright and tonight I am sleeping over at Gaby's house. I am working hard and so far I have $1.72 and I am getting more today. … I hope everyone enjoys your cooking. By for (just) now! Love from Marilyn Louise Holland" *[decorated with a heart with lots of x's and o's]*

July 8 "Dear Dad, I hope you are well and having fun. I am having more fun than I did at the beginning of the summer. On Wednesday (the one that just passed) Heather asked me if I wanted to go to Beaver Lake with her and Mom let me go. The water was cold so we didn't stay in very long. … I have counting today $5.57. When you come back I am hoping to get some new thongs for $1.98. My hand is getting tired so I'll have to stop. Love from Marilyn Louise Holland (P.S. Please write soon.)"

July 12 "Dear Dad, I hope you are having a good time and I hope you are well. We look forward to having you home. I hope you liked our letters. Thank-you for mailing us your letters, we have been waiting for them since you were gone. As you know I slept over at Christine's house on Sunday. It was great fun riding bicycles (Christine her new one me her old one) going to the store, playing cards and doing lots of other things. Catherine and Bruce went cherry picking and brought home 25 pounds of cherries. Guess What! They put on the asphalt and now its all black up there. So far (counting today) I have $6.84. Love, Marilyn Louise Holland"

From Michael [7 3/4] [All three letters are bordered with dozens of x's and o's, and "I love you" hearts are featured on them all—a lot of careful work for someone just out of Grade 2.]:

July 1 "Dear Dad, I hope you are well, and having a good time. We are having a good time at least, and everyone is well. So far I have a dollar and 63 cents, and am getting more today. I hope you're cooking is a great success, and everyone enjoys it. (Everybody is I bet.) Something else is coming at the end of the second week, but I won't tell you what it is, because that's a secret. Have a good time!!!! Love, your son Michael"

July 8 "Dear Dad, I hope you are having a good time. Mom and the girls are well, and I hope you are too. I hope everyone enjoys your cooking, and I really miss you. So far I have 5 dollars and 6 cents! Well, have a good time!!!! Love, your son Michael"

July 12 "Dear Dad, I am having a good time, so I hope you are too. I'm tired and it's 9:15 at night, so I have not looked at my chart, I don't know how much money I have. The weather's O.K. here, and I hope it is there too. I hope everybody likes your cooking !!!! Love your son, Michael"

Margaret [5 3/4] sent a drawing of herself and Daddy, both the same height (arrows pointing to each person in case there was any doubt as to who was who), with a note:

"Dear Daddy. Thank you for the cards. We love you. Margaret Holland." There is also a printing exercise, where the kindergarteners had to print over "I love you, Dad" five times. (My note: "This was for Father's Day, but Maggie had misplaced it.") There's a drawing of Daddy's bus; another of Daddy's camp with "Dear Daddy Happy Summer Love from Margaret (lots of kisses and hugs)"; one with "Dear Dad, I love you, Dad, we love you" (lots of hearts, x's, o's and underlining); and one with the family around the table (oval table with seven chairs radiating out from it, and seven placemats on it).

Margaret also obviously helped Melissa with her letter:

"Dear. Dabbythankyou.for.the cardswe.love.you" (S's backwards in her name). Melissa also feltpenned around her own and Melody's hand. And she "helped" Melody label her "free-designs" (whirls and squiggles) with "Welovyou" and "Happy summre" (the "re" at the beginning of the line because there was no more room at the end). *[Melissa was 4 1/2 and Melody 2 1/2.]*

Letters I wrote to Bruce give a slightly different perspective on the Days without Daddy:

June 29 The summer holidays have finally arrived with an explosion of kids in their play clothes and lots of sunshine. Today *[last day of school]* we woke up at 8 a.m., and Michael managed to get himself dressed, breakfasted and a note to Mrs.

Lampard written between 8:25 and 8:45. Needless to say, The Three were driven to school by Mother. *[I assume the other two came along for the ride.]* They walked home with their reports *[Ah, the good old safe days!]* and have busied away the afternoon in great spirits. ... I hope you have a fair amount of money set aside for your little capitalists. Last night Michael hauled 65 cents worth of stones, Marilyn 55 cents, Margaret 21 cents and Melissa 13 cents (also Gaby 52 cents). It was amusing to watch them from Michael's window, half-dragging their buckets across the yard. The stone-man was here setting in boards, some curved, for the cement, and voiced his approval of the chain-gang! ... M1 has tidied her bedroom, folded diapers and vacuumed the family room. M2 has folded dark clothes, vacuumed the upstairs hallway and stairs and supervised the watering (in between bike rides). The kids have been very good, with minimal fussing. M3 and M4 spent a fair time this afternoon putting camas seeds into bottles and Melissa has just come in with dried grape hyacinth heads to empty. Sticky *[cat]* has also just rubbed against my legs, much to Melody's amusement. ... After the Big Three had been scurried off to school this morning, Melissa, Melody and I were finishing our breakfast. Melody looked particularly sweet, so I smiled at her. Immediately Melissa said, "I'm a precious little girl, too, aren't I?" *[I didn't record my response, but I can guarantee that one little four year old got a great big hug!]* ... Melody tried to re-colour Sticky's white fur today with a red felt pen, but I caught her in time. ("But I *need* to, Mom.") ... *[After some suggestive comments to my husband, I made the statement, "I can't help but feel a little excited at the prospect of another baby!"]* ... Melissa told me she wanted to make her S's "like you guys," but I assured her Daddy liked them the way they are *[i.e., backwards]*. ...

July 1 It's after supper and M1 has gone over to Gaby's for the night, M2 is hauling stones, and Ms 3 to 5 are getting dirtier by the minute in the backyard. Michael did a super dusting job in the living room and family room (Windexed glass surfaces, too); I'm sitting at the table in the living room, so it's very nice. Marilyn vacuumed the whole downstairs thoroughly (actually moved things), so we could almost have company! I did a huge ironing in two stages. Fortunately, it's been pleasantly sunny but cool today and I sat down the whole time, so it wasn't too strenuous. *[I sometimes took the ironing board outside and ironed in the back yard; eccentric even then!]* ... Margaret just came in to go to the bathroom and I heard her muttering, "I don't really like it when Daddy has to go away!" She was by herself and didn't realize I was within earshot. She is so spindly and loving and helpful. ... Yesterday and the night before, I got a large amount of mending done, including putting eyes and nose back on a brown teddy. Needless to say, Teddy has been the centre of controversy since his return to circulation, with the three little ones squabbling over him. I also fixed Michael's teddy and found him fast asleep last night, hugging Theodore, in a spotless bedroom. I hope we can incorporate housekeeping into the fall routine; M1 and M2 are really very capable, and M3 most willing. I was happy to hear them singing away as they worked.

July 2 … I stopped at Sears for some Purdy's chocolates for Eric's birthday. Was somewhat conscious of stares as my troop and I tramped through—all four girls in matching ponytails, obviously closely related! *[Michael would have been there, too, and I was seven months pregnant.]* … You have such beautiful children, Dear! … Must go— Beautiful Child #5 has been in my gum again. … P.S. Cement *[for backyard ramp]* finished today; looks good (one small running shoe print on yesterday's cement— barely noticeable, but a good memento!)

July 6 … Melody is sitting in the wicker basket full of folded clothes, singing "Row, Row, Row Your Boat." …

July 8 … Your adorable children are writing to you, so who am I to do less! It's almost lunch time and I am waiting for some new potatoes (Bottens') to cook, Marilyn is vacuuming the hall ("How much, Mommy?"), Michael is practising the piano ("I'm trying to earn as much as I can before Auntie Peggy comes so I can send it to Daddy."). … I have a headache, partly due at least to the incessant noise on that parking lot *[adjacent to the back of our property]*. There have been graders and blasting and now a caterpillar filling in. The caterpillar travels very quickly back and forth, smoothing the surface; I sometimes wonder whether he'll go off the edge. … Yesterday morning Melissa had her eyes and ears checked, and a visit with the school nurse. Naturally the whole crew went, so it was another expedition! They've been behaving quite well. This morning I heard the water running and discovered Melissa and Melody drinking from the hose (Margaret manning the tap). Yesterday I caught Melody drinking from the cat's water dish. Margaret was mopping up the floor with that sponge mop. …

July 12 … There's the daintiest wee girl outside my office window squatting down, patting "my pussy"; needless to say, Sticky is lapping it up. It's been cool today, and the kids have had a great time playing hide-and-seek, and house ("house" being a cozy place under the house, or two chairs by my office door; two people, e.g., M4 and M5, share a "house" and make forays from it to other houses). I'm pleased and amused at their imaginativeness. There's been a minimum of fighting, too, which is good.

I recently wrote to my children: "I am so thankful that I was able to get these notes down for posterity, in spite of considerable discomfort and fatigue at the time. And there are descriptions of what I cooked for you all. It was a happy, sunshiny time, and I commented several times how fortunate Dad and I were, to have such wonderful children and a place for them to grow up in. I still feel that way!"

Chapter 13: 1978

It's **Mark Andrew** again, fifteen months and twenty-five pounds of mischief and energy, and I am here to extend my family's good wishes to you. It is our hope that you will have a blessed Christmas and a bountiful New Year. As family spokesbaby, I have all sorts of things to tell you about the people who live at my house.

Ralph Steele

MICHAEL HOLDING MARK

First, me. Mommy wrote a letter to Auntie Harriet on September 1, the day before my first birthday. I will shamelessly quote part of it: "Mark is just adorable, so soft and blond and blue-eyed and cuddly." Mommy assures me that she still feels the same way about me even though there have been three additional months of cupboard upheavals, fireplace explorations, dishwasher reorganizations, and laundry, always laundry. Some time ago I learned to nod my head back and forth quickly in a horizontal direction. This feat amuses my brother and sisters, especially when they ask me such questions as, "Do you like porridge?" or "Are you going to take music lessons when you grow up?" Apparently the above-mentioned attributes (softness, cuddliness, etc.) counterbalance such antics, and the fact that "ma-ma-ma" has recently been added, after much prompting from one parent, to the staccato "da-da-da" of several months, is in my favour, too. Since early November, I have been reminding my parents (yet again) what "toddle" means, as I stagger from exploit to exploit. Daddy says I walk like a penguin, but I understand it's over two-fifths of a century since he became ambulatory, so I guess he forgets how difficult it is to maintain that 90-degree angle with the floor, when 180 degrees exert such a pull.

Melody's philosophy seems to be: Why walk when I can 1) run, 2) skip, or 3) gallop, and why talk when I can 4) hum, 5) sing, or 6) whistle? She turned four at the beginning of December and has been in Mommy's beginning music classes for nearly two years now, which gives her opportunity for options 1–6 at least once a week. In September, with much nervous giggling, she started her violin lessons, on a 1/16 size

RHYTHM CLASS

violin, and enthusiastically practises several times a day, whether or not Mommy feels like it. ("If I play Twinkle *two* more times, do I get *two* more Cheerios?") One day Melody was rocking her doll, and explained carefully to Mommy that she was "not a *really* mother, just a *pretend* one." In April, Marilyn, Michael, Margaret and Melissa presented two at-home recitals for family and friends who have, by choice or of necessity, been especially helpful (French teacher, pastor, etc.), and Melody distinguished herself by sprawling full-length on the carpet and snoring gently through the last half of each programme. This was quite disconcerting to our parents (especially to our mother, who looks for the day when Exemplary Behaviour is the rule rather than the exception), but far less unnerving than a concert on Mayne Island in July, when hymns, concerti, minuets, gavottes, etc., were accompanied by a clear, perfectly pitched, and very audible, whistle. Unfortunately, Mommy was at the piano facing the violins. Daddy was at the back of the hall walking a small, squirming baby (who shall be nameless), so Melody was completely uninhibited. That morning my whole family, plus violins, had travelled by speedboat to Pender Island to give the same programme, without the whistling obbligato.

    Melissa continues to approach each day with enthusiasm and good cheer. Her sixth birthday is just two days before Christmas. Until November, she displayed a typical Grade One gap at the front of her mouth. (Since "Scissors Saturday" a few weeks ago, she has also had a matching gap four inches higher.) Although she appears to have no trouble with reading, and has a willing audience in

MARK, MARILYN, MICHAEL, MARGARET, MELISSA, MELODY

Melody and me, she has maintained her ability to spice up the English language: "Mommy, Margaret hit Melody hardly"; "See, the water's frozening"; "I think school is very fun." And Melissa is the one who sits in church patiently through a 30-minute sermon, after participating in 20 minutes of violin music, and whispers to Mommy at 3 1/2-minute intervals, "Are we being good?" (Daddy has tied in "being good" with a stop at the Dairy Queen on the way home.)

Margaret has been the family jack-o'-lantern for the past few months. In September, her smile resembled a small checkerboard, and by the middle of October, corn-on-the-cob was scratched from the menu. Margaret is affectionate (especially toward me; she even took me to her Grade Two class for Show and Tell), generous ("You can have this quarter if you guess right: heads or ears?" Margaret didn't know about antlers), and loves small creatures, especially a ladybug named Mary Ellen, who lived in a jar on her dresser. One day Mommy took the stairs four at a time after a blood-curdling shriek registered downstairs, to find Margaret weeping uncontrollably. Marilyn, torn between tragedy and comedy, and holding her sides,

MARGARET

gasped, "She thinks she's stepped on Mary Ellen and squashed her." Mommy managed to quell the rising wail and somewhat hesitantly examined the sole of Margaret's foot. Fortunately, the culprit was a piece of grass from Mary Ellen's home; Mary Ellen herself soon came strolling across the bedspread, to everyone's great relief.

Mommy often tells me how fortunate I am in having **Michael** as "such a good example." (She says this when Michael is within earshot; I think she is counting a little on the power of suggestion.) Last June Michael completed Grade Three with a "mixed-bag": a gold award for physical fitness, piano and violin contributions to the primary assembly, four Excellents, Grade Two Piano, and three detentions. After the second detention (received for kicking a soccer ball after the bell had rung), our parents established Still Another Rule:

MARGARET AND MOMMY

$1 forfeited from allowance (equals the folding of ten baskets of clothes), one week no biking, and one week (equals one or two hours) no TV. The next unwarranted detainment will cost $2 and two weeks.

Michael started Grade Four with a heavy hand, too, his right one, the result of a disagreement between his bicycle and himself. The bicycle suddenly turned west;

Michael continued on his way south, where his chin and wrist had a close, crunching encounter with the pavement. Michael's only concern was the "XO from your ever-loving MOTHER" which someone had inscribed on the plaster; piano and violin assignments were viewed with a barely-concealed satisfaction. Because our parents employ child labour on a regular basis, Michael has the privilege of paying for some of what he considers the necessities of life. Last spring he purchased a tape recorder to enable him to listen to his violin pieces more consistently. However, at times, unmusical and less-than-inspiring sounds fill his bedroom: "This is MA-RI-LYN

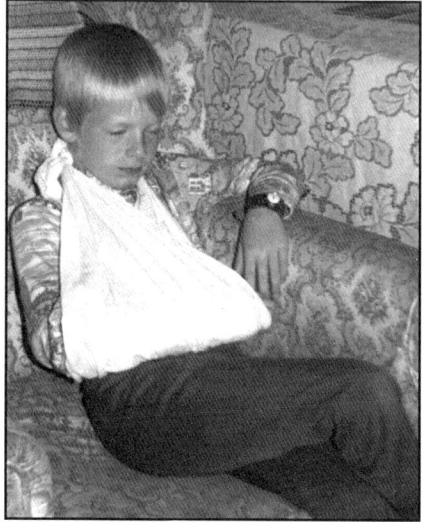

MICHAEL UNABLE TO PRACTICE

LOU-ISE HOL-LAND and I'm talking into my bratty little brother's tape recorder and he doesn't even know—HA HA HA!" The recorder came closest to confiscation the day Mommy, downstairs, heard part of Vivaldi's A minor Concerto repeated,

MICHAEL IN CONCERT

upstairs, with exactly the same inaccuracies, and discovered the tape was providing the "practising" and my hero was stretched out on the bed reading a book. (Mommy doesn't give detentions; only lectures.)

If you have managed to make your way through the above paragraphs, you will have received some glimpses of my biggest sister. On the positive side, **Marilyn** continues to practise both piano and violin faithfully, with encouraging results. She passed Grade Five both in school and on the piano in June. She will be eleven five days after Christmas, has almost reached the five-foot mark and enjoys wearing her hair down to her waist when out of Mommy's range of vision. (Mommy wears pony-tail elastics permanently attached to each wrist. Michael carries elastics, too, but I don't think they're for pony tails.) Marilyn helps Mommy with office records, tidies *her* side of the bedroom, folds innumerable baskets of clothes, keeps a narrowed eye on the activities of her siblings, and usually has her schoolwork up to date. For some reason or another, she doesn't get into *too* much mischief.

Mommy and Daddy will have made seventeen revolutions around the sun together just before Christmas. Aside from church activities, social work, music teaching, and ensuring that small bodies are in the right place at approximately the right time, covered with an adequate amount of clothing and filled with the required amount of food, they lead quite uneventful lives.

Our family's involvement with music has some advantages, one of which is travelling to points north in a heavily-laden VW bus. Since May, the children have presented programmes on Pender and Mayne Islands, and in Parksville, Brentwood, Sidney and Duncan, in addition to testing the patience of different groups in Victoria. Mommy's prayer is that they will 1) be competent enough 2) to be a blessing, and 3) make enough mistakes 4) to keep them humble. She says 3) is answered with regularity. She also says that her week, and Daddy's, officially begins at eleven o'clock on Sunday morning when our church reverberates with "Praise God from Whom All Blessings Flow."

In the course of a week, Mommy hears many things. From the scribblings on her calendar, I have been able to compile a list of Things Mother Would Rather *Not* Have Heard.

January 7 Margaret (Grade One): "Mrs. Scoates helps me with those hard buttons." Melissa (Kindergarten): "And Mrs. Baxter does up *my* buttons, only now there's only one left."

February 12 Melissa: "Mommy, Melody put stickers all over the window, and they all say 14 cents on them." *[These "stickers" of course were postage stamps with glue on the back that happily merged with the condensation on the cool windows, resulting in an attractive art display—attractive at least in the mind of the three year old who assembled it. The parents let the stamps dry and affixed them to their letters with glue.]*

March 8 Lab receptionist to waiting room full of patients, in a voice guaranteed to be heard at the Family Planning Clinic three blocks away: "Mrs. Holland, is Melody 06 or 07 on your medical card?"

March 22 Just before Margaret and Melissa play a piano duet. Margaret: "We would like to play 'Skip to the Lou.'"

March 25 Easter Sunday, five minutes before the service is due to begin. Marilyn: "Hey, there's no violin in this case!"

April 4 Marilyn: "I thought you wore that shirt yesterday." Michael: "I did, only yesterday I had it on backwards. See, there's still jam on the back."

May 14 Melissa: "... And when I play in the playhouse, I tell Mrs. Baxter that I'm the mother, Christine's the baby, and I say, 'You've got to do what I say because I'm bigger than you and I'll hit you if you don't.'"

June 6 Ten minutes before a concert at the Juan de Fuca Centre, a 20-minute drive from home. Marilyn: "Margaret, didn't you put your violin in its case when I told you to?"

October 3 Marilyn: "Look at that long silver line on the carpet. Oo—oo—oo—

GROSS! It's a *slug* from the apple box."

November 10 Margaret: "Mommy, what is a lice? My book says 'A LICE IN WONDERLAND,' and there's just a girl on the front."

November 12 Auntie Peggy: "I see he's walking, Louise. You've never got past that stage before, have you?"

November 22 Halfway through a recital. Student: "Mrs. Holland, someone's thrown up on the carpet."

November 26, 9:20 a.m. Marilyn: "Is it OK if I wear this jacket for my solo? You can hardly see the safety pin." **12:50 p.m.** Margaret: "No, I didn't use any soap. I didn't want to waste it." **4:40 p.m.** Melissa: "Mommy, when you were born, did they have any schools? Did they have any churches?"

Love from Mark

This is from another 1978 calendar (Marilyn is 10, Michael is 8, Margaret, 6, Melissa, 5, Melody, 3, and Mark is 5 months):

February 2, 6:10 a.m. Baby greets day with volume on high. Mother takes him into bed for breakfast. **6:30, 6:32, 6:33 a.m.** Alarms ring; bedrooms come alive. Child 1 shivers her way into clothes, makes bed, puts sign on bed for benefit of bouncing siblings: STAY OFF THIS BED! Gathers up piano and violin music and violin, strides toward music room. Children 2 and 3 reminded by Mother that early rising will ensure reduction of after-school practising; statement greeted coolly. Children 4 and 5 patter up and down hallway, in and out of bedrooms, under feet. Mother puts baby face-down [*this was 40 years ago!*] in middle of bed, pats encouragingly; baby soon drifts into less chaotic dream world. Mother tells Children 2 to 5 that Child 6 must not be disturbed, goes downstairs with Child 2 to take swipe at a Seitz Concerto. Flips on intercom to music room, obtains dutiful rendition of Handel Sonata. Sets Child 2 on course, returns upstairs with two small violins, expecting to find Children 3 to 5 fully clothed. As is frequent, expectation is great; realization is not. Three bedrooms are empty. Cheerful twittering seeps out through closed door of Mother's bedroom. Upon entry of Mother Quail, covey of flannelette-clad chicks alight off bed. Tiniest bobwhite lies on back, chortling at sisters' antics.

And the same calendar recorded an incident at the other end of the year:

Parents are going out for supper with violin teacher, Frona Colquhoun. Mother paints nails a bright fuchsia for the first time in fifteen years. Father mumbles something about Jezebel. Children watch, fascinated; niece/babysitter [*Cindy Westaway*] gives advice. Son comments, "I wish I was 42 so *I* could take you out."

Chapter 14: Letters to My Parents at Quartzsite, 1977 and 1978

For several years I wrote to my parents wintering in Quartzsite, Arizona. They both were supportive of our efforts with our expanding family, especially my mother, who had taught school at the elementary level for many years. She was an excellent listener, and appreciated sharing the details of our family life.

December 28, 1977 ... Dear little Melissa's birthday (23rd) nearly got lost in the shuffle, but fortunately she had the persistence to keep reminding her harried parents it was her birthday. The tea set *[gift from grandparents]* was an instant hit. I think Bruce got a picture of the middle four hovering around the box the set came in, sipping tea. (Melissa amazes me at times with her ingenuity; she immediately emptied the box, turned it over, set it, and proceeded to serve the other three, all the while chattering away as if we weren't there. Tonight she came into my bedroom with a rectangle of white paper taped across her forehead and announced she was a nurse. She'd be a cute one.) *[And 14 years later she would be working with exquisite china at Sydney Reynolds, 15 years later entering nurse's training.]* ... Marilyn and I went shopping on the 27th. She's so self-reliant and yet she often insisted on holding my hand. (And, in two or three years I understand she—if a "typical teenager"—won't even want to acknowledge her parents in public—oh dear!) ... The children loved their Christmas presents. Michael sneaks his book under the blankets (has five flashlights) and keeps me informed as to what he reads.

December 31 Midnight! 1978! I hear the cannons booming and horns tooting. I guess I'll go up to the music room and kiss Bruce *[working on reports]*. (Footsteps upstairs—wonder who's up.) ... It was Michael. He came down to be the first to wish me Happy New Year, dressed in his smallest pajamas. He looked so dear shivering on the bare kitchen floor.

January 6, 1978 ... This morning I was feeding Mark. I had told M4 and M5 to get dressed, but they were zooming up and down the upstairs hallway instead. I heard a sudden shriek from M5, and M4 proudly announced that she had scared her because she was "Drackeela." Melissa Dracula?! ... After school, while I was teaching, Bruce took all six to the library to pick up a new set of books and then went shopping at Woolco. When I came down at supper, I was greeted by four girls wearing new slippers (30% off apparently). They looked so cute and were so excited! … Melody sings her day away, Mark sleeps his away, and Ms 1 to 4 slave theirs away (according to them).

January 12 … Yesterday I reminded (i.e., nagged) Michael for the severalth time that he still had his piano practising to do. "I hate piano—haven't got any pieces—can't do this—don't want to do that," etc., etc. Nevertheless he found himself at the keyboard forthwith and it wasn't five minutes before I heard him yelling upstairs, "How's that, Mom? Doesn't it sound good?" It did. (And Mother adds another white hair to the collection.) … Marilyn's biggest tragedy at present is a cherry Chap-Stick that keeps breaking (or being used by Ms 3 to 5). She dearly would like a "lip smacker," but they cost around $3, so her chintzy mother bought her the other for 59 cents. … I was on the phone last night blithely talking to a student's parent when Marilyn slid a note to me, "Mom, could you please put the little girls to bed because they are pretending to use your raser!" End of conversation.

January 24 … Michael and I took a walk around the neighbourhood on Saturday. (He had squabbled his way through a basket of clothes and we both felt the need for fresh air and isolation.) We noticed you have four yellow chrysanthemums in bloom in your front yard. We walked down through the subdivision-to-be and discovered the house facing Saanich is empty. The lake was so pretty. The sky was gray and every so often a seagull would wheel up against it and shine in the sun. The dazzling white against the gray was breathtaking. Michael was impressed, too. … As you know, our kids haven't moved that fast *[musically]* because I want them to be competent on both instruments and cannot afford the time to make any one of them spectacular on either piano or violin. I feel in the long run this will be more valuable even if in the short run it might not be as impressive. … I write this as I say good-bye to Bruce and Melody who are off for a couple hours of shopping. She has promised to "look after Daddy." She's so sweet in the navy-white jumpsuit that Marilyn used to wear seven years ago. She had your white ribbons on her pony tails and went bouncing up the ramp in front of Bruce. Michael took his walkie-talkie to school for show-and-tell and his teacher sent him outside and talked to him, much to the entertainment of his class (and surrounding classes, including Big Sister's.) … Margaret announced one day that she had been reading with the "Bunnies" that morning. She had been a "Beaver" until then, so I wondered if she was having problems. *[I am sure that these discriminating labels are not used now.]* Her teacher said she wasn't trying to sound out *fl, bl, cl*, etc., words and would rather not pay attention, so she had kept her back to read with the other group as well. I said I didn't mind where she read (I don't) as long as she is doing her best, but I didn't want to miss an opportunity to help her if she needed it. The teacher was pleased at my interest and sent home the supplementary reader (*Laughing Letters*—quite difficult phonetically) and M3 and I have been reading through it. I made a set of flashcards using the reader's vocabulary (132 "strange" words) and she manages to get through them in 8 minutes now. It was originally 15 minutes; we're aiming for five and then she gets a "surprise" (don't know what, yet). The next day she was back with the Beavers and reported Mrs. Scoates was very pleased with her work. Apparently the flashcards were the problem, and the extra drill (which she enjoys) is helping her. Her printed exercises are beautiful. … I hear M6 demanding lunch. He is just beautiful and the cuddliest little fuzzyhead around. …

February 8 … Margaret and I have been working at the flashcards and she finally hit her 5-minute goal yesterday. When I told her, her little face went pink with excitement, and she was very pleased. She got to choose from my box of prizes and chose a large chocolate bar (which she shared) and a package of six pencils and sharpener. She tells me that reading is going much better now. Two of her words were "velvet" and "satin," so I sent along a velvet dress and satin ribbon for her to show the children. (She asked me to. When I asked how many other children had also brought exhibits, she said no one else had. "I told Mrs. Scoates you would for sure, Mommy!")

[By 1978, the music situation had really heated up, with the four eldest working on both piano and violin.] The last two days have been the best practice-wise for a long time. Mark has slept until 6:00 a.m. and is fed by 6:30 a.m. Marilyn's alarm goes off at 6:15 a.m. and she's up and dressed by 6:30 a.m. She and I work 6:30 to 7:00 a.m., 15 minutes on each instrument (get M2 on the move by 6:45 a.m.), and then she goes the next 1 1/2 hours on her own. (That's the day's requirement for her.) Mike and I work from 7:00 to 7:30 a.m., 15 minutes on each (get M3 on the move by 7:30 a.m.); he finishes another half-hour on each instrument on his own. Margaret gets the next half hour and then works another half hour, and Melissa gets the last half hour and some more after the other three are gone. It works quite well. All are coming along really nicely. They complain, but I notice they're quite pleased to be able to play if someone comes. With the big two, I've been giving them a cup of hot chocolate (and marshmallows—shame!) at 6:45 a.m. and this goes down well! … Frona *[violin teacher]* wants our children to do a mini-recital some time in April or May here at home. *[Here's where it started!]* Probably they will do it twice, once for family and once for friends (pastor, doctor, etc.). There should be violin solos (two or three each), duets, quartets; piano solos and duets, and even M1 accompanying M2, M2 accompanying M3, and M3 accompanying M4. … Marilyn and three friends baked cookies all Saturday afternoon, with #2 to 5 overseeing the project. Bruce wound up his shift with 22 calls and got in at 4:00 a.m. Sunday. We struggled out to Sunday School and church—Marilyn played a beautiful offertory—and Bruce left again at 3:00 p.m. I took the six to Gosworth Road church for their evening service (6:00 p.m.). We had promised to provide music. …

[On Monday, March 6, 1978, during the only extended session we ever had with vomiting (two weeks of violent sickness that was plaguing the school), I wrote:] … I'm sitting on Melissa's bed upstairs with a wary eye on the bathroom. On Friday, Michael distinguished himself by throwing up at school just before three o'clock. (Mother distinguished herself by not hearing the phone when the school rang home. Mother was sleeping, phone unplugged.) Friday night Melissa got in on the act, all over her bed. Saturday afternoon Margaret did it, all over the hall carpet and bathroom. This morning my alarm went off, and immediately M5 started vomiting. I managed to get a diaper spread out in front of her and then she stopped. She didn't do much, so I'm sure she's on the verge of more. I ponytailed her hair back and tied a diaper around her neck and she's sitting on a small, overturned tub in the bathroom right next to the toilet. Margaret has decided she feels sick again, too, so is sitting on the over-turned diaper pail beside her. I've put a diaper on the floor for their bare feet and over the heating vent beside the toilet. I'm halfway through folding a wicker basket of clothes on Melissa's bed. I'm grounded, and Ms 1 and 2 know it; they're dragging their feet about practising on their own. … I've just taken another look at the tableau here: Margaret and her smaller version sit on their respective "thrones"; Melissa is in the hallway against the wall with a whole row of dolls set to watch any action if it's forthcoming. (And yet when Melody started throwing up in her bed, Melissa was lying on her stomach, head under her pillow.) Michael has just started his violin, and Marilyn has snailed her way to the music room. …

March 11 … Melody waited until night time and then deluged her bedding. (Also hit the bathroom floor again Tuesday.) What a week! By Tuesday night Marilyn had emptied the contents of her tummy and Bruce spent the night doing likewise. I had a doctor's appointment for Ms 5 and 6 and had to be at the lab by 9:30 a.m. on Wednesday. Bruce was incapacitated; both bathrooms had to be available at a moment's notice. I started at 6:30 a.m. and by 9:15 a.m. I had cleaned up two messes, got two ready for, and delivered to, school (Michael, Margaret), got two bathed and ready and myself ready for the doctor, fed five breakfast (plus M6, of course) and had been upstairs and downstairs innumerable times. … Wednesday's trip to the doctor had its funny spots. As you can imagine, the three of us left in a flap, but once we were on our way, I decided we weren't going to waste such a gorgeous day, so I pointed out the beautiful blossoming trees. When I got to the parking lot, I realized I had zero cents in my purse and the parking lot now has a 25-cent meter. We parked up a block and walked, me with Mark on one arm, and Melody holding my other hand. Suddenly there was a wail from her. I had visions of her throwing up again, but finally, through all the blubbering, she choked out that her gum (1/10th stick of Orbit) had fallen out of her mouth. I assured her that she could have some on our way home. Once we got into the lab—the lab technician had raised her eyebrows alarmingly when she saw the medical card went right down to 07—Melody refused to cooperate as far as the specimen was concerned. "You go first, Mommy." Mommy did, but to no avail. We went up to the doctor's office, and later returned to the lab, where the conversation (mostly mother to three-year-old child) ranged from pleasantries ("What a big girl!") through thinly-veiled bribes ("There's a nice piece of gum in Mommy's coat pocket.") and complaints ("Please hurry, Mel; this hurts Mommy's back.") to threats ("If you don't go before I count to ten, I'll chew the gum myself.") That last one precipitated the waterworks and I soon had my sample. ... **Later** I've just taken the three musketeers out of the tub where they've been languishing in a bed of foam, generously put there by a brother whose willingness to fill the tub was tied to the promise that he could use some of Mommy's pink bubblebath. Additions were made as required, so that by the time Mother got upstairs, there was one glorious mess. Seven facecloths were in use, with two ice cream pails and an assortment of plastic toys. I carried a shivery M5 into her bedroom and she was so sweet. Really, the pleasure is worth the bedlam! ...

March 25 ... Marilyn had in her mind that she wanted some of her friends for a sleepover Friday night, and when Marilyn has something "in mind," parents had better give up! Anyway, she invited five friends to sleep over (music room) and, of course, Not-So-Little-Brother wanted to know why *he* couldn't—the usual reaction. So he invited Emlyn Ngai, who is in his room at school. Marilyn and Gaby vacuumed out the music room and set the tables and piano benches in a row to make "houses." (I bet Granny never foresaw her tables being put to such a use.) The girls put their sleeping bags, pillows, teddies, books and comics underneath and seemed very satisfied. Marilyn had put up six signs: "Gaby sleeps here," etc., and had arranged a circle of chairs up in the corner so they could have a "meeting." Needless to say, Tiger and Sticky were part of the group; Ms 2 to 6 weren't. Aside from the cinnamon toast which Bruce made for all 11, and the Easter egg hunt which I rigged up, they were no extra trouble at all. The girls are very self-reliant, and the boys play very nicely together; they are working on some experiments and this keeps them out of the girls' hair. ...

Tomorrow Ms 1–4 play for the offertory. We were asked last Sunday, as there had been very little Easter music available, and we've worked up an arrangement of two hymns, both entitled "Praise Him!" ... I told M1 and M2 which ones we were doing. They, of course, knew the melodies, but had never played them. To both Bruce's and my surprise, they played them virtually note-perfect the first time, by ear. They don't realize how fortunate they are; however, they are becoming reconciled to the fact that music lessons are on the agenda until they are 16! Even M3 and M4 had little difficulty in learning their song. They do one, "Praise Him, Praise Him, All Ye Little Children" with the older two; then the older two do two verses of the second song; and then all four do the first one again.

March 26 (Sunday evening) … Marilyn's guests gradually filtered away yesterday until all were gone by four o'clock in the afternoon. They seemed to be in good spirits, in spite of sleeplessness and the overindulging of chocolate eggs. (*I did not buy the eggs.*) … This morning we were awake by 7:30 a.m. and it suddenly struck me that perhaps we were expected to play for the 8:45 service, too. I couldn't get in touch with the man who had asked me (at least, I wasn't about to phone him so early), so I assumed the worst and got everyone ready. By twenty to nine we were turning into the parking lot and were in the usual panic as violins had to be tuned before 8:45, and it takes longer than five minutes. I told Marilyn to give everyone a violin and to move quickly. To her horror, she picked up Melissa's violin case and discovered it was empty. (Michael had carried the violins to the car.) After a predictable explosion from Mother, the four musicians and I scurried down to the front where I tuned Marilyn's violin quietly with the piano while the organ was playing. I then took it and tuned the other two out in the lounge—not the ideal tuning method. Bruce went to get the fourth violin for the eleven o'clock service. At nine o'clock, Pastor Holmes announced the offertory and said how pleased he was to see the Holland children ready to play the offertory. I told Melissa to stay in the pew. As I got up, Bruce came rather quickly down the aisle and handed me the offending instrument, which I tuned with the piano and handed to Melissa. Melissa stood with the others, looking as pleased as only Melissa can look (Michael looked relieved), and everything went well for both services. The man who had asked me was delighted to learn that we had come out to the early service; he had been afraid to ask us as he suspected it would be quite a job to get everyone ready (understatement!). The girls wore their yellow dresses [*sewn by my mother: long dresses with full skirts, flounces, and yellow and green tops—one of several sets their grandmother made over the years for their performances. The girls looked like daffodils in them.*]. A wedding had left its arrangements of yellow chrysanthemums at the front so the effect, though certainly not planned, was most cheerful. …

MELISSA IN CONCERT DRESS

[*That summer we took the family to Mayne Island, where we had been asked to give a concert. I wrote from the motel:*] It's 4:00 p.m. and we're on holiday! The biggest (Bruce) and littlest (Mark) are snoring happily in one bedroom, Marilyn and Michael are flying Michael's airplane outside, and the three little girls are colouring in colouring books, one each (29 cents). Since I started writing, M3 went outside and was tackled by M2, with much noise ensuing. Both are confined to the other end of this room in chairs, supposedly still and quiet.

This morning we hiked through beautiful forest to Edith Point where we had lunch. It is very secluded and somewhat treacherous in spots, but we were very careful. After lunch we went "shopping" (two stores, quite well-supplied) and bought a few supplies, including the colouring books, plane, and a comics digest for Marilyn. When we came back, Michael assembled the plane. On its maiden flight, it landed 20 feet up in a maple tree, so he and I took turns trying to dislodge it with a knitted ball. The ball also became enamoured of the tree! It and the plane finally were detached by a flying running shoe, and the plane (95 cents, made of balsa wood, powered by an elastic band) has given much pleasure. Yesterday we went to Pender Island by launch (speedboat) and had a good time. (Two hours by ferry, ten minutes by launch.) The church is an adorable little community church with a pump organ for accompanying—quite an experience. The children were very well-received both there and back here on Mayne in the afternoon. Mayne's service was held in a school gym and was well attended. On Pender, a pleasant and somewhat familiar-looking man came to say how nicely the children played. I thanked him and searched my mind frantically for the name to go with the face. When he recognized my bafflement, he said, "Frank Churchley," and I nearly had a stroke on the spot. Dr. Churchley was my Music Ed 305 prof eight years ago, the first summer I went back to summer school. He teaches, among other things, piano classes at UVic, and wrote a series of textbooks for use in B.C. schools. Several people had been introduced at the beginning of the service, but he hadn't been, which was just as well. Apparently he and his family are holidaying on Pender. Back on Mayne, one of my students and a family from Central were in the audience. Small world.

November 9 … It's a chilly, clear evening, and the end of a beautiful day. The children were off school today due to interviews, so we went shopping, had lunch out, and went to Beacon Hill Park. We shopped at Woolco and Woodward's (and you'd think some people had never seen six apparently-related children all in one place before), then had lunch at the new Viteway cafeteria for lunch. Can you imagine six tired children and two harassed parents trying to figure out what to have for lunch? The servings were very big, but we managed to get around them anyway. The Park was just beautiful, so colourful and crisp, with many ducks and seagulls around. … We knew our time there had come to an end when Melody slipped and fell in. Fortunately, I was able to grab her by the scruff of the neck, so she got only her feet wet (and coat dirty; we dropped it off at the cleaners on the way back). … Taking the children on an outing like today is really a hassle, but it's worth it (I think). As we went down Saanich Road in the morning, the train crossed the road, to everyone's delight. I think we could have gone home again and they would have thought it was a successful outing! Michael reminded me of the time he and I went blackberry-picking when he was in Kindergarten and the train whistled so loudly that I dropped my bucket. I had forgotten that myself. I didn't remind him that he was a perfect pest that time, whining and complaining and wanting to go home. (Last summer when I took him with me to get him away from the girls, he sat patiently and read a book while I picked; that was when his arm was broken.)

We went for our interview yesterday afternoon; Marilyn stayed home and babysat. We took Michael with us, and he played with his soccer ball in the schoolyard and read a book in the car. We left the baby sleeping and the four girls drawing and printing stories on the kitchen table, and when we came back an hour and a half later, they were still at it. Needless to say, it would likely not have been that peaceful if No. 1 Son had not been with us. The teachers were embarrassingly kind about your grandchildren. I think one of the nicest things was what Mrs. Scoates said about Melissa. She said she had tended to lean on her to help others and run messages because "the Holland children know how to take requests and can be depended on to do it right." Melissa is one of the better readers, apparently. Marilyn's teacher said they (two teachers) had graded low and were still forced to give her two Excellents; two Very Goods were one or two marks short of the same. ... Michael's teacher, Mr. Eng, said Michael is a very bright boy and raved on about his performance in all areas. He ended by saying maybe he could play the violin some day; did he have any other interests? When I said that he also played the piano, he was pleased. Mr. Gillion (Margaret's) said Margaret was well above average, and that her work habits and quickness were very similar to Michael's. ... Melody is lying at my feet, head on her precious pillow, chomping away on a piece of cheese toast from supper, and singing something about bells at Christmas. Disneyland is over and I can hear explosions in all areas, so I guess I'd better go. P.S. Mark walks all over the place now—so proud of himself. What a darling! ... I just found a note in the upstairs bathroom: Oct 8/1978 I want to have a Dolley For ChRistMAS. I love ChRiStMAS. Oct 9/1978 it was fun today because we didn't have to prandids I like today. (Melissa's efforts. I assume "prandids" = "practise.")

November 28 ... This week I had six recitals. Shirley *[Bruce's sister]* made 500 bran muffins for refreshments. These were served with cheddar cheese alongside, and were well received.

December 16 ... Last Saturday, the Neufelds took Melissa over to Saltspring Island with them to choose Christmas trees for themselves and for us, from a tree plantation. Ours is a beautiful, thick tree, and should be fun to decorate. Needless to say, Melissa really enjoyed the experience. She continues to do well at school and amazes us with her super marks. Michael played the chime bars (mine) as an accompaniment for the Junior Choir at Wednesday night's school concert. (I accompanied the choir.) Marilyn is one of a group of girls who wash up the staff dishes at school (Grade Six privilege, I guess). Margaret played in the ice and mud at school while waiting for me the other day, in her Sunday School coat. Melissa and she had the dirtiest shoes I have ever seen, after testing the same patch of ice and mud. Peggy was here while we were getting ready for the concert; she ended up

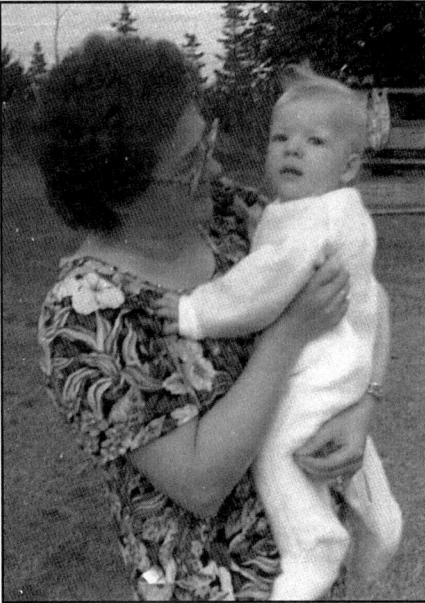

MOMMY AND MARK

washing Melissa's good shoes to make them presentable. ... Melissa reads by moonlight to Melody. Mark is walk-running now and is into everything. He's just a pet, and a tease. That smile would just melt you. ...

December 30 (Marilyn's 11th birthday)
... On Christmas Day, I tried to lift up that big laundry basket by leaning over it and holding on to the handles. It was very full and very heavy, and my back protested, with the result that Bruce had to haul me up off the floor with what I assume was an "acute back sprain" (according to our medical book). The kids had played their violins in church on the 24th, so were freed from playing on the 25th, but we went to the service, anyway. Shirley asked if we could bring over the violins on the 25th, so I had been "encouraging" (!) them to play through a solo each and a couple of group pieces just before you phoned. I could hardly move, and had just finished telling Bruce that I thought he had better go without me (tears; the whole bit) when the phone rang. ... We all went to Shirley's and had a pleasant time, but every move I made had to take the back into consideration. Hildegard [*head physiotherapist at Jubilee Hospital, Bruce's aunt*] sat beside me and massaged it; she said she could feel which muscles were in spasm. Uncle Gordon offered to take over, but I said I thought she was doing just fine! ... Things have been really heavy for the last six weeks. In that time, there was the week of recitals, followed by a couple of weeks of writing 120 reports [*most of my teaching was class work, hence the large number of students*], and working on that [*Christmas*] letter. Then there were 120 cards for my students, around 150 of our own, and nearly 200 letters inflicted on people at church (no cards; the church people all sign a common card in the foyer and the money saved goes toward a missionary project, this year Saanich Church). There were, would you believe, several requests for that letter, and several very kind comments. Up to today, in December there have been three birthdays here, tea over at Westaways (16th), practising with and accompanying the Junior Choir at school (13th; also four practice sessions—fun,

though, and Michael always seems pleased; he's in the choir), a cantata (16th and 17th), supper at Bruce's folks (21st), a really happy visit with Wynne and Eric [*my brother*] on the 24th after the Sunday school concert, supper with Frona on the 28th, and maybe some other things I can't remember… On Monday (New Year's Day), we will have 26 for supper here. The turkey weighs 28 pounds! … I had to smile at Tory Craig's Christmas card note: "Thank you for my 'Christmas Delight and Chuckle'—I think Mary Ellen came to visit us the other evening. 'Someone' was walking across our dinner table while we were dining. Oh well—as long as it wasn't A lice in Wonderland ha! ha! ha!—just <u>priceless</u>. Keep up the good work, you two. Sounds like fun over there." Can't you just hear Tory saying that?! … I have a multi-choice in front of me once I get off this typewriter: I can mark workbooks (start teaching tomorrow), fold clothes, work on Festival entries (due by the 21st), have lunch (Bruce has a lunch meeting, so made the kids' lunches and even left mine and Melody's in the fridge), and/or crawl into bed. Want to bet the last two get it?

Chapter 15: 1979

Mark took up the pen again:

Before you take the plunge into the sea of words below, my family would like to wish you a joyous Christmas and a blessed New Year. We have much to thank God for, and we trust this has been your experience through 1979, too. "Great is the Lord, and greatly to be praised!"

December 31, 1978 By the end of 1978, after three December birthdays, the six of us were 11, 9, 7, 6, 4 and 1. On the 24th, **Melody** made her official debut with the Big Four, playing a two-note harmony part for "O Come, Little Children" during the offertory. As soon as she had finished playing her part, she was supposed to stand in rest position while the others played "Joy to the World." However, her violin remained aloft while Mommy played the next introduction. Upon realizing that "Joy to the World" was likely to be given an unrehearsed fifth part, Mommy tried to signal Daddy to whisk away the superfluous violinist. Daddy remained transfixed in his seat, and a cooler head took over as **Melissa** delivered one swift, well-aimed kick sideways. Although the smallest violin remained at the ready for two verses of "Joy," no offending harmony was forthcoming. (Appropriately enough, a few days earlier, Melody had despairingly proclaimed, "Melissa is wrecking my whole life.") Minutes later, Melody sat on Mommy's lap, listening intently to the choir's buoyant rendition of "Angels We Have Heard on High," and whispered to Mommy, "Who is Glo-o-o-ria?"

MARK

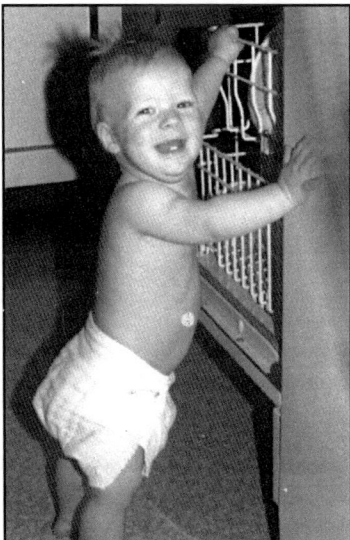

MARK THE HELPER

Melissa also had her problems with the vocabulary of Christmas. Practising a reading for Sunday School, she came up with, "In the days of Horrid the king," and, a couple of verses later, "They presented unto Him gifts of gold, frankenstein, and myrrh." The second bit of originality brought forth a peal of laughter from Big Brother, which reduced the little reader, whose only knowledge of monsters comes from *Sesame Street*, to tears.

Daddy's Christmas was more cheerful. **Margaret** gave him an original cookbook, compiled by her Grade Two class. A well-deserved tribute to his culinary abilities, it was inscribed, "To my best father Love from Margaret." (Mommy was a little unsettled to learn that all of Margaret's classmates had given the book to their *mothers*.)

January 29, 1979   January brought a welcome return to schedules and organization. (Mommy wrote that. *I* was sorry to see our lovely tree go; it smelled so good and the shiny things were so touchable.) Mid-January produced snow*drops* (as distinguished from snow*flakes*—this for the benefit of our friends and relatives back East), and late January gave us 'flu. Our parents try to instill in us a capacity for sharing; apparently this means in sickness as well as in wealth. Daddy considered mimeoing a form letter: "Dear Mr./Mrs./Ms. _____, Please excuse M _____'s absence on _____. She/He is recovering from [ ] a fever, [ ] a sore throat, [ ] a cold, [ ] a cough, [ ] aches, and/or [ ] _____, and is returning to school in the interests of preserving parental sanity."

With Melissa's increasing skill in the Language Arts, little notes and lists began appearing on doors and dressers. A list of "overdo book" was, unfortunately, quite extensive. A sign was posted on the southwestern bedroom door: "No one under the age of twelve (12) is allowed in here. KNOCK FRIST." No doubt Melissa was influenced by a sign on the northeastern door: "DO NOT ENTER! BEDROOM OWNERS ONLY! IF YOU WANT IN KNOCK FIRST, THEN IF YOU ARE INVITED IN COME IN. IF NO ONE ANSWERS <u>SCRAM</u>!" The authoress of the preceding piece of literature also attached a less-elaborate label to the end of my crib: "Cutie."

February 27   I guess I shouldn't have mentioned January's snowdrops, because February gave us some snowflakes, much rain, little sunshine, and a deluge of "Merry Valentine's Day" cards manufactured by Margaret. Two large valentines are still decorating a bulletin board, and probably will for some time to come. They proclaim, in flattering overstatement, "To the greatest, the best and the only Dad," and "To the greatest, etc., Mom." **Marilyn** was responsible for these. Melissa had Mommy rummaging through the bathroom drawers when she announced she needed Q-Tips on her valentines. Melody and I helped by applying glue; at times paper and glue actually connected, but not often. Melody also provided a romantic touch by singing "On top of pizzghetti all covered with cheese" to the tune of "Old Smoky."

March 31 Among my varied activities in March was an effort—unappreciated; fortunately my derriere is well-padded—to straighten out the buffet. By the time I had lined up seventeen of the best glasses on the wooden chairs nearby, word had filtered down to the other end of the house that "**Mark** is breaking glasses." (This was not quite accurate, as only one met an untimely end.) I have decided to leave buffet-organizing to the bigger people. Also, hearth-hopping. In spite of the balloon the nurse made for me out of a surgical glove, I can't say I enjoyed the hospital sewing session after head and hearth collided.

For the rest of the world, 1979 is the "Year of the Child." Our parents decided that for our family, this would be "Year of the Trip," so Daddy bought a handful of plane tickets and notified his English relatives of the planned invasion.

April 27 April brought family recitals, an operetta, a cantata, and the Music Festival (piano classes). At one recital, Margaret started a piano duet with an audible, "One-two-buckle-my-shoe" (and the duet was in 3/4 time). After another recital, our teetotalling mother was somewhat startled to read a thank you note Margaret had written: "Thank you for the chocolates. … Since my mom didn't really want one, she had rum."

Melody figured out how to play "Hot Scotch Buns" on the piano, using one finger, and commented that there were two kinds of "tooth": the kind in your mouth, and the kind where "you practise and then you do it again—that's the 'tooth' time." Thinking of teeth, Melissa has taken Margaret's place as the family jack-o'-lantern. The Tooth Fairy mused on the inroads of capitalism when she slid a quarter under Melissa's pillow only to find these instructions on a scrap of paper with a strategically placed arrow: Put money here.

August 21 May and the first half of June sped by in a flurry of more Music Festival violin and piano classes, examination preparation (in company with many of Mommy's students, Marilyn and **Michael** took piano exams: Marilyn Grade VI, Michael Grade IV), and packing and repacking. (I was especially good at *un*packing.) From June 8 to 11, Melody's temperature refused to stay below 102 degrees and kept rising to 106 and a little above. A urinary tract infection was the culprit, and on June 18 she had minor surgery which made her quite uncomfortable for a couple of days. With regular classes, extra exam lessons, Daddy on duty, three recitals on the 19th, and a plane reservation for the 21st from Vancouver, our parents were wondering if The Trip would even get off the ground.

But England was not to be spared. At noon, on June 21, we kissed our grandparents and our closest neighbours goodbye, piled into our heavily-laden VW van, and chugged out to the ferry for Vancouver. Mommy's parents came along for the ferry ride and shared a delicious lunch that Granny had prepared for us. After leaving the van at our cousin's place in Richmond, we checked in our baggage (eight tote-bags, five violins, one stroller and five large suitcases) at the airport and tried to look like the sophisticated travellers we weren't. Mommy says I mustn't bore you with too many details of our trip, but I'd like to tell about the excitement when we landed in London. Back on the ferry (many hours before), our ex-teacher grandmother had given the five eldest each a package of Chiclets, an unusual gift from her and very much appreciated by them. Although instructions had been to save most of them for England, one pair of ears had failed to transmit the message, and our parents were chagrined to find their eldest son, dressed in his best pants, immobilized in his plane seat by fifteen Chiclets' worth of adhesive. Twenty-three

hours of wakefulness had done nothing for their *joie de vivre*, and at least one of them would gladly have turned the plane around and headed straight back for Vancouver if she could have.

London's otherwise sunny welcome was the forerunner of forty virtually rainless days. For ten days we lived in a large apartment on the outskirts of London, and went into London each day by clattering train (ten

FAMILY IN LONDON, ENGLAND

minutes) or tippy double-decker bus (thirty minutes), passing mile upon mile of brick residences, most displaying at least a tiny rose garden. Although the places we visited (St. Paul's Cathedral, Westminster Abbey, Buckingham Palace, the London Zoo, etc.) were quite interesting, I think my sisters and brother would agree that the trains, buses and subway were the most fun. Trains whooshing in unexpectedly from either side ("All of you—*stand against the wall!*"), and buses pulling off before Mommy could get to the magic number (six) or Daddy could check to see that diaper-lunch bag, stroller, camera and wallet were also aboard, were pure excitement. A highlight for Michael was sighting the Concorde overhead several times; for Margaret, finding innumerable half-pennies and wrapped candies on the sidewalk. Shopping English-style was quite an adventure, too. Aside from the problem of converting English prices to Canadian by multiplying by two and a half, there was the necessity for bringing along one's own carrying bags. More than once in London, my parents found themselves back on the sidewalk with armloads of unwrapped groceries. When Mommy discovered that Pampers cost more than $4 a dozen, she bought two flannelette crib sheets, cut them in two and made me four Canadian-style diapers. (The English disposables, while cheaper than Pampers, precipitated several damp incidents that Daddy would rather forget.)

We soon adapted to the different English terms: flat (apartment), lorry (truck), motorway (highway), sweets (candies), lift (elevator), etc., but the English equivalent of our "How are you?" threw Mommy the first time she heard it. When asked, "Are you all right?" Mommy had mentally to check herself to see if, in fact, she was "all right," before she dared answer, "Yes, I'm fine, thank you."

FAMILY READY FOR A CONCERT IN ENGLAND

From July 2nd to 16th we imposed on Daddy's most generous aunt, uncle and cousins, out in the countryside near Uttoxeter, Staffordshire. Their house is surrounded by miles of rolling, green fields, and was a peaceful contrast to London's noise and dirt. (At least it was peaceful until we arrived.) Auntie Vi ordered 21 pints of milk twice a week, and loaf after loaf of bread, and she and Cousin Sandra busied themselves feeding and entertaining us. Uncle George and Cousin Henry took over where they left off. Uncle George has a toad living in his cold frame; Cousin Henry has a three-wheeled car and supplied us liberally with chocolate biscuits made by the factory where he works. The children had played their violins in a Baptist church in London, and they shared their music in two Pentecostal churches in the Midlands. I think they found this quite exciting, although the habitual "grumble-before-we-practise" was alive and well, even 6,000 miles from home. We explored the countryside and did some more shopping. Daddy and Mommy went shopping in Grandpa Holland's birthplace, Burton, and received a six-pound fine for overparking 15 minutes. (Margaret worked that out to $1 a minute.) Our parents had managed to find some bargains—a rarity in England—and were a little downcast to see their hard-won savings demolished by an overenthusiastic ticket dispenser.

Our last two weeks were spent on the outskirts of the East Anglian town of Norwich. We were given the free use of the Rockland St. Mary rectory, which included a large fruit and vegetable garden, and the vicar and his family even loaned us their station wagon while they were away. Within 20 minutes of our arrival, both Margaret and Melissa had learned to ride junior-sized two-wheelers, and wobbled around and around the yard in great jubilation. The large rectory was only three years old, and was situated across the driveway from the parish church, which was many hundreds of years old. Each Sunday the children played their violins at a different country church, accompanied by Mommy on small pipe organs. At the second church, the organ was at the back in the balcony, so Mommy had to keep an eye on her violinists by using a mirror, a new experience for both them and her. The

flat, lush farmland (barley and sugar beets), the narrow country roads edged with corn poppies, common mallow, tall grass and prickly hedges, the many buildings and shops we explored, the afternoon spent sailing on the Broads, and the kindness of the people, all strangers to us when we arrived, gave us a memorable ending to our stay in England.

In order to rest up for our flight home (for some reason or other, our parents do not

REHEARSING FOR A CONCERT IN UTTOXETER

consider ten hours of flying with their offspring the most restful experience), we stayed overnight in London on the 30th. On our arrival in London from Norwich, as if to tax our guardian angels' abilities to the limit, we used a London taxi. The taxi's capacity was set at four persons. However, because the youngest four of us were considered "non-persons" due to our ages, all eight of us plus luggage (which had been joined by another large suitcase) were allowed to ride together. Margaret, Melissa and Melody carried on a running commentary as we veered in and out of rush-hour traffic, identifying the landmarks of four weeks previous: the Tower Bridge, Pall Mall, Piccadilly Circus, etc. Mommy kept her hands over her eyes for most of the 30-minute ordeal, venturing to peek out occasionally through her fingers in horror. No doubt her nervousness was heightened by driving on the left side, but for this trip the driver also insisted on turning completely around in an attempt to carry on a conversation with Daddy. Daddy was unusually uncommunicative.

After a comfortable night's stay in London, we flew home on the 31st, leaving London at four o'clock in the morning and arriving in Vancouver at 6:30 p.m. (2:30 a.m. London time), and home around 11:00 p.m. We couldn't get into our beds fast enough, and even I cooperated by going straight to sleep. Daddy said that was no great accomplishment, as I had slept for just the last hour of the flight home, providing my family with entertainment and good company for the first nine hours.

September 26 For the first time in my life, I have my parents, my home, and my sisters' and brother's playthings all to myself for a most gratifying length of time. At 8:45 a.m. (give or take a few minutes depending on who has lost a shoe or misplaced homework or forgotten to brush his teeth), my five siblings explode out of the house for school: Marilyn to Grade 7, Michael to Grade 5, Margaret to Grade 3, Melissa to Grade 2, and Melody to half a day of Kindergarten, all at the same school. (I leave you to contemplate on what must be the principal's evaluation of the situation.) All is tranquil from 9:00 to 11:30 a.m., while I explore, rearrange, and generally create havoc amongst the treasures I find lying around. My mother spends many unprofitable minutes encouraging me to make more consistent use of the porcelain apparatus in the bathroom. (I figure that if she has spent twelve continuous years changing diapers, she won't mind a few more months.) You may recall that immediately after my birth, my sisters put in an order for twin boys. At times,

Mommy actually gets quite enthusiastic at that prospect, and then she catches me emptying the cutlery drawer into the dishwasher, or floating my tugboat in the toilet, or removing my shoes and socks for the fourteenth time in one morning, or clomping around in her best high heels, or emptying the jar of gummed shiny stars into my damp little hands (the effect was spectacular), or

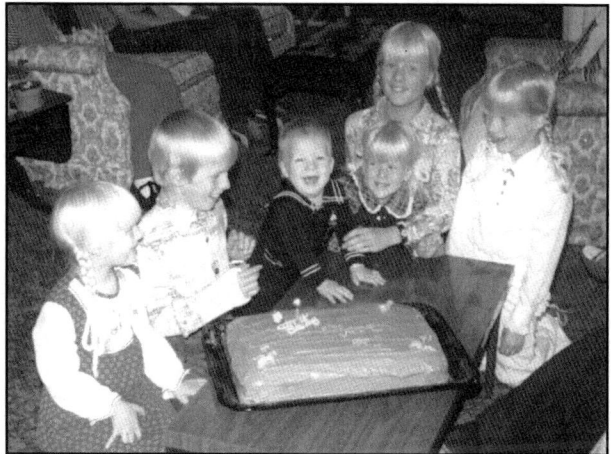

MARK IS 2!

leaving teeth marks on the soap (or worse, Desitin on her toothbrush), and she reconsiders: "Two of *him*?" However, when I suggest that maybe I am a "ba' boy," she is always quick to say that no, I am a "good boy," "such a sweetheart," and a "little pet," so I guess mother-love has its blind spots.

October 19 October saw Daddy out in a Saanich orchard, collecting 300 pounds of sweet, juicy MacIntosh apples (windfalls, but unblemished), most of which Mommy made into buckets of applesauce for freezing. I received my first barbershop haircut, and Mommy said her baby was gone. Margaret made a set of place cards for the family; even Sticky and Tiger, our controversial cats, rated carefully-decorated designations beside their dishes on the porch.

One rainy Tuesday morning, Mommy and I went on an excursion: a walk to and from school to see if we could find the necklace Margaret had lost the day before. Going to school was fine. I carried Melissa's recess treat all the way, sloshing through the puddles in my little white boots; Mommy carried the umbrella and held my free hand. The return trip, however, was something else. Halfway across the school yard, I decided I had had enough exercise and doubled myself into an immovable crouch. Mommy foolishly thought I was bluffing, and walked nearly a full block without me, but she hadn't reckoned on the little turquoise lump crouched defiantly in the middle of the playing field. Whoever coined "mad as a wet hen" has never contended with a wet, frustrated mother. A "Come *on*, Mark" (ignored), a "Get *up*, Mark" (ignored), and a "Right *now*, Mark" (ignored), were followed by a firm swat on an area normally covered by trousers. This was *not* ignored, and soon we were on our not-so-happy way again. Two blocks, twenty minutes, and several mother-child confrontations later ("Mark, must you behave like a two year old?"), and Mommy was ready to deposit me on the nearest doorstep. Suddenly she suggested we might find some juice when we got home—instant *détente*! For the next four blocks, I trotted along amiably, and Mommy chalked up another lesson in the Art (Strategy?) of Dealing with Small People.

November 29 I am writing this to the accompaniment of Melody's violin. She is practising "Silently Night" ("A 1 A 2, A 1 A 2, down, down, up"), so I guess we're coming close to that special time of the year again. Our unruly half-acre relaxes under a carpet of orange-brown leaves. The weather is sunny and clear, which allows the children to walk home at lunch and after school. When they complain, our parents tell them how rosy their cheeks are, and point out that their appetites certainly don't suffer. Sometimes Margaret whiles away the mile by playing her recorder.

Daddy made a long list of jobs that just were not getting done, and two of our friends have spent several days building new cupboards, renovating the downstairs bathroom, erecting a greenhouse (*Daddy's* playhouse, although I know Mommy will enjoy the flowers), and completing many other projects. We children are especially pleased with a 12' x 32' concrete slab near the playhouse (*our* playhouse), with a tetherball in the middle and a basketball hoop at the end, mounted on an oak tree. Daddy, paintbrush in hand, gives the finishing touches, often in the wee hours of the morning.

My older sisters and brother have at last been given permission to share the news that both Mommy and our family are expanding. I can't see what all the excitement is about, especially as I am destined, God willing, to become the Old Baby as of late April or early May. (That line of diapers stretches still farther into the distance.) On second thought, perhaps a Miriam or a Matthew will be able to take over as family scribe next Christmas. (Although Mommy's attitude towards twin boys seems to have deteriorated, Margaret has chosen two names, anyway: Major and Minor.)

Love, Mark

Chapter 16: Letters from England

42, Alleyn Road, London
June 23, 1979
Dear Mom & Dad,

Hello from the land of brick houses, roses, birds, fast drivers and expensive food! Our house here in Dulwich is immense. Each room is larger than ours at home (12' ceilings, 8' doors), but it is laid out in what Bruce refers to as "typically English" fashion, i.e., inconvenient. It has four flights of stairs and has recently been carpeted throughout and redecorated, most of it quite tastefully. Everything is *clean*, which I appreciate.

We slept for hours last night, after a less-than-restful nine hours on the plane. After going to bed at eight o'clock, we woke up around three in the morning and went back to sleep until 9:30 a.m. The time change (eight hours ahead of home) hasn't bothered us at all. Perhaps the plane's three meals (8:00 p.m. our time: sandwiches; 10:30 p.m.: turkey crepes with all sorts of goodies; and 3:30 a.m.: omelette with fresh pineapple and strawberries) conned our systems into thinking we had had breakfast and lunch when we arrived here at 1:30 p.m. (London time; 5:30 a.m. our time). We just had a small meal around six and went to bed. The birds woke up here at 4:30 a.m., as well, and what a racket. They're much noisier during the day, too.

Bruce has taken the children to a nearby park and I'm supposed to be cleaning up after supper (roast, potatoes, carrots, cucumber, tomato, ice cream). We went shopping this afternoon and it was quite an experience. Each little shop specializes in something different. Bags are not provided, and everything comes in such small quantities. We bought a bag of flour in the largest size available: 3 1/3 pounds (1.5 kilograms) for 46 pence (just over $1). They had strawberries that worked out to about $2/lb. (We didn't get any.) Tomatoes are 40 pence ($1)/lb. Strangely, our Earl Grey tea was about the same as we would pay at home.

Milk is delivered every day (including Sunday), and the milk bottles look like fat pop bottles (one-pint containers). The milkman also sells bread, potatoes, eggs, and other odds and ends. The dustbin (garbage can) is cleared twice a week. Every plug-in here has a switch which must be turned on before you can use the appliance.

We go through two doors before we get to our first flight of stairs. The first door has two locks, two bolts, and a burglar alarm; the inner door has two locks. The neighbour who lives permanently in the lower floor of the house says this is a high-risk area for theft. It would take an ingenious thief to get in, but it's sure a nuisance getting in and out ourselves.

The back yard is lawn surrounded by many varieties of roses. The owner (a friend of Mrs. Ireton's, who looks after the house in his absence) lives in Singapore. He has left the family silver and crystal here, so I picked a huge bouquet of roses (from the front, too) and filled a silver pot with them. The table is about 12' long, so the arrangement looks really elegant!

Sunday Today we walked to church (about 10 blocks) and really enjoyed the service. Next Sunday the children are to play their violins. The church is Chatsworth Baptist, rebuilt 20 years ago after being bombed in 1944. Aside from the accents, the format and content of the service were very comparable to ours. The pastor has a Scottish background (McKie) and knows Pastor Moore, who was at Central for three years while Pastor Holmes went back to Ontario. The people are very friendly and kind.

There are quite a few black people in this area. Yesterday when we were out shopping, we saw a black baby dressed in snow white: frilly bonnet, long dress and booties. She smiled at Michael, who was appropriately pleased. The black people are always immaculately groomed.

Monday Bruce is making supper as I write. Marilyn has a postcard she wants to mail, so I'll try to send this, too. Before I forget, I meant to tell you at the beginning that we really enjoyed having you come over on the boat with us, and the lunch set us up for the rest of the day. The kids were really pleased, too.

This morning we woke up to rain but decided to make our first foray into downtown London anyway. We bundled up in sweaters and raincoats (I brought the winter lining for my jacket), took an extra sweater (not needed) and some sandwiches and cookies, and splashed our way down to the local train station (ten blocks away). Fortunately, it wasn't a heavy rain, but we were still quite a soggy lot waiting on the edge of the loading platform. The train (I believe the first I have ever ridden) took us right into the heart of London in about ten minutes, and then we got on a "London Tour" bus to see two hours' worth of famous brick and concrete. The size of the place and the crowds of people are mind-boggling. We complain about Victoria being laid out illogically—you should try to make sense of the streets here. Modern (ugly) concrete buildings fill in the spaces between ancient (dingy) brick buildings. The traffic is continuous and noisy. Amongst all the clatter and bang you often come across blocks and blocks of lawns and flowers. In the outlying area, there are rows and rows of brick houses, each attached to the next, with a tiny front yard and quite large back yard. Most are carefully kept. I asked a saleslady what an average wage here was, and she said around \$500/month for a woman. With food two to three times what we pay, there's still no shortage of liquor and tobacconists' shops, and cosmetics.

Wednesday I didn't get this mailed on Monday, so you're going to get even more rambling. Yesterday we went downtown by bus (double-decker)—hair-raising the way those things sway around corners. It was hard at first to realize they are not "toys" over here, but the main means of everyday transportation. We shopped around in a small town on the way and then took another bus to inner London. (The City of London is only one mile square.) We thought the children would like a boat ride down the Thames so we spent an hour and a half on that. It was really very interesting.

Today we took the bus again (Bruce bought a "go-as-you-please" ticket in Victoria and he feels we've already had our money's worth) and transferred to the subway (underground London is as complicated as aboveground London) to see the Tower of London. Unfortunately, the T of L tickets we bought in Victoria were sitting on the kitchen table at 42 Alleyn Road! So we went somewhere else on the subway, had lunch in the courtyard of St. Paul's Cathedral, and explored the Cathedral after lunch. We climbed right to the top of the Cathedral (hundreds of steps spiralling upward, quite safe but still scary for Fraidy Cat here). The view of the city was spectacular (366' up). The kids also fed the pigeons in Trafalgar Square. Melody said a pool had "green bubblebath" in it (actually algae), and I was concerned about the pigeon droppings; depends on one's perspective, I guess.

We went to buy (Pampers) disposable diapers for Mark: \$4 per dozen! I decided we'd invest in half a dozen flannelette diapers. No such thing; terry towel ones were \$8 for six. So I bought two flannelette crib sheets (\$4), and cut each of them into two super-size diapers [which I hemmed by hand]. The small English disposable diapers (about \$1.20/dozen—what we pay for Pampers at home) can be used as liners (they're lined with plastic but are more like a large Kotex pad), and we're always going to be near washing facilities. Anyway, I don't mind rinsing out one or two diapers a day by hand if I have to.

We plan to go to the Tower tomorrow (tickets are already packed) and probably the Zoo.

Tonight we watched a Victor Borge special on TV. He performed with a London orchestra and was a panic. At one point he played "Humoresque" and always played the wrong notes when he went up high. Our kids were in fits over it. They really appreciated the whole thing; you can imagine Michael laughing, can't you!

Must close. We're going to try to leave early tomorrow. Today the weather was just right. Actually, so far it has been nice; I'd rather it wasn't too hot, anyway.

Do say hello to Bruce's mom and dad. I plan to write them more thoroughly from Uttoxeter (Auntie Vi's). It was fun to have both sets of grandparents (and

"Auntie Bottens") to see us off.

Love, Louise

July 7, 1979 *[postcard]*
Hi again!

We're at Bruce's relatives and having a very good time. The house is on 3/4 acre, surrounded by miles of rolling farmland—just beautiful. The kids (Ms 1 to 5) sleep in two tents, covered over by a larger third tent, and have plenty of space to play. So far the weather has been good. The smell of hay and sounds of birds (thrush and magpies included) are such a pleasure after London. Auntie Vi and Uncle George and cousins Sandra [35] and Henry [34] are most hospitable. I'm sure their food bill is soaring out of sight. (They're favourably impressed with everyone's unfussy appetites!) Margaret and Melissa are planning to write postcards to Mr. Gillion and Mrs. Scoates, but the addresses are home in Victoria. I've addressed them to you, so could you please check the phone book and re-address them: Gillion - Buckingham Close; (E.) Scoates - Barkley Terrace. I don't know the numbers. They probably should be sent in envelopes from you to them. Thanks.

We all are well. The violins have already been well used. We're here until the 17th.

Much love, Louise

The Crest
Marchington Woodlands, Uttoxeter, Staffs., England
July 13, 1979 *(Thank you for your letters!)*
Dear Mom and Dad,

Hello again, still from this beautiful spot. I'm sitting on the edge of the bed, as there's no other free space. This house is about the size of Granny's, and each room is just crammed with stuff (I've often heard Bruce's mother comment on it; nothing is thrown away!), and at times it's almost claustrophobic. However, the outside is all lawn with garden, surrounded by the inevitable hedge, and off in every direction are miles of green, rolling fields. The house is on top of a hill (hence The Crest—I'd always thought the name referred to a symbol), and the views are spectacular.

July 16 Today is our last day here, and Auntie Vi and I have just done a huge wash. *[When we first arrived at The Crest, Auntie Vi asked what time I did the washing. I,*

THE LAUNDRESS

used to daily laundry chores, said, "Usually in the morning." She had meant what day of the week did I do the laundry, so we decided on which two days of the week we would do it. The (wringer) washer was kept in a storage room, under a lot of other things, so it was quite an effort to keep on top of the wash.] It's threatening rain, but until now the weather has been most cooperative, not too hot, just warm and comfortable, and the children have been able to play *outside!* They're quite tanned and I think a fair degree "bonnier" ("bonnie" meaning "plump"), if the quantities of milk and bread consumed are any indication. Melody has had a few "accidents," but I think it is because she sleeps in until 10:00 a.m. and can't make it into the house in time, or both toilets are in use. She is very well otherwise and has been good about sleeping in the tent after her initial hesitancy. Michael was playing soccer with a (second) cousin the other night and got stung by something; there was quite a welt and a tiny hole. However, he didn't swell much until yesterday (36 hours later) when I was surprised to see that his right jaw was very swollen. I gave him some Chlor-Tripolon (anti-histamine) and by this morning it was right down. The children played at another Pentecostal church yesterday, both afternoon and evening, about 40 minutes each time, so it was good his left side was not affected. As well, Margaret developed a fever and earache a couple of nights ago (had had a head cold for a day first), but seems to be on the mend now.

We rented a car here in Uttoxeter for 83 pounds for 10 days. (London: 152 pounds for seven days). It is a Morris Marine estate car, a small station wagon. We've travelled all over the area looking at castles (some incredibly large and beautiful), zoos, potteries (a pottery museum where the different stages of china-making are open to the public was fascinating), picnic grounds, etc.

I'm almost used to the left-hand driving, but I don't think I'll ever get used to the narrow town streets and country lanes. In the towns, one is not safe even on the sidewalks. If two trucks meet, they both mount the sidewalks and the pedestrian learns to move quickly, sometimes a little difficult when the sidewalk is only a yard wide and is against a brick building. The lanes are so pretty. The road itself is about 1 1/2 car widths wide. Each side has another 1/4 car width in grass which, due to labour problems, remains unmowed, six feet high, filled with flowers and weeds. On both sides are hedges of hawthorn, holly, honeysuckle, etc., absolutely impervious. The cars travel at 35–40 mph on these lanes (I'm sure we would have 20 mph signs posted at home), which is fine as long as one is alone on the road. The yard is very safe here, fortunately. A three-year-old boy a couple of houses down the road was hit by a delivery van and critically injured a week ago. Auntie Vi says there are no fences on the other property and she has narrowly missed the little boy and his two-year-old sister more than once herself. The lanes curve and you don't know what to expect around the next bend, especially with the tall grass at the edge.

The children have been sleeping in two tents under a larger one and this has worked well. After the first night, it was decided by common consent that the four girls would sleep in the slightly larger of the inside tents, so Michael sleeps in solitary splendour in the other one. (It was supposed to be a 3 + 2 arrangement, not a 4 + 1 one, but M2 is not the most docile bed-mate!) The first night there were "fairies" on the lawn just before midnight, but that kind of nonsense didn't last long.

Tomorrow we take the train (two changes) to Norwich. The people there volunteered us their car, and a guidebook here shows all sorts of interesting things to see in Norwich, including 900-year-old buildings.

Lunch is almost ready so I'd better clear the table here. I'll try to add more either later on today or after we get to Norwich.

Norwich, July 18 We arrived here just after two o'clock, after leaving Uttoxeter at 9:15. The two changes went relatively smoothly, considering the amount of luggage involved. (If eight adults were involved, it wouldn't be quite so bad, but it seems the smaller the child, the greater the amount of luggage!) The Bawtrees are just super—we were all greeted with a kiss from both of them and transported six miles out of downtown Norwich to their home in "Jumbo," their van (minibus). (Norwich is pronounced Norrich, but you probably already know that.) They had thought their holiday was to start on Monday, but instead it was Wednesday, hence the overlap of families. You remember her [Mrs. Bawtree's] description of this place; it's that and more. Rev. Bawtree is vicar (with two other clergymen) for 11 small churches in this parish; the church next door (dates from 900 AD) is his and the old rectory is right beside it. This new rectory was built three years ago on the lawn of the old one. The old horse and coach stables are on the other side of this house. The children have all sorts of toys in these buildings and our kids are having a ball. Within ten minutes of landing, their four and our six were playing together uproariously—riding bicycles (M3 and M4 both learned how within 30 minutes on two little bikes), tricycles, feeding the rabbits (Flip and Flop), cuddling the cats (Tigger and Snowball), observing the terrapin (turtle; don't know his name), and exploring the premises. The children are 13, 11, 9 and 6, two girls and two boys; the eldest and youngest are boys. The Bawtrees are in their mid-30s and so friendly and exuberant. Can you imagine preparing your own family for a three-week holiday, welcoming a family of eight, feeding them supper and breakfast, and then leaving by 8:30 a.m., all with a lot of talking and visiting? Rev. Bawtree is much like Doug Harris and has a wry sense of humour. His wife is lively and so generous. As I write this, I am seated in the study where I can look out sliding windows (a foot off the ground—the family uses them as doorways; they're also in the living and TV rooms) at a garden full of raspberries (lots), strawberries (just about over), carrots, potatoes, black currants (just ripening; I am to freeze some if I have time—also to freeze beans), cabbages, onions, broad and string beans, and a couple of other vegetables I can't identify. Upstairs are two double bedrooms, three single bedrooms, a toilet (with a tiny sink, about 15" across) and bathroom. Downstairs are this study (where the Bawtree children were to have slept last night; as you can imagine, they all filtered upstairs to sleep with our kids), an office (duplicator, sewing machine, etc.), an entry hall and cloak room, a large living room, an average-sized dining room/TV room, a large kitchen (seated 14 quite comfortably last night), another toilet ("loo"—the accepted term, not vulgar as I had thought) and laundry room. The washing machine is a small one, and I think longingly of my Maytags (not the first time, either). So you can see we are quite comfortable. We have the use of their other car, a small station wagon, which we understand is held together with washing machine parts. Apparently Bob collects scrap metal to help finance the second car and has been able to keep it running this way, too. Lois was telling us that they just got "Jumbo" back from the garage after extensive repairs and were a little concerned about the cost, which they feared would be around 300 pounds ($750). On Tuesday they asked the garage owner what the bill would be and he said they weren't finished and hadn't totalled it up yet. On Wednesday they received an anonymous cheque for 182 pounds from a lawyer in London and on Thursday, they were given their bill: 182 pounds. You probably remember her comment in her letter about possessions being not very important (therefore we were welcome to use them freely); I hope I can be that trusting.

Bruce has gone shopping for groceries and I've prepared potatoes, carrots/ beans, and raspberries for supper. I've also fixed up some ham scraps that Bruce is going to incorporate into an omelette, and iced a chocolate cake that the 11-year-old girl baked for us the other day. I just heard the car return, so I'll be interested in how Bruce made out. (He made out fine except for the one-way streets and putting the tomatoes on the bottom of the bag.)

On the train we passed immense fields of potatoes, sugar beets (provide half of Britain's sugar requirements, and judging by the terrific amount of sugar consumed, that must be a lot), cabbages, etc. Apparently this area (East Anglia), near the coast and opposite France, is the warmest section of England and provides many of the vegetable and grain crops. There were also miles of larch trees, planted in rows. They are used as pit-props in mines. Unlike the Midlands, which are hilly and grassy and dotted with sheep and cattle, this area is quite flat. I prefer both areas to London! We certainly are fortunate to be able to visit three such different areas. Even Melody is taking some things in. We were climbing a spiral stairway in a tall tower on Saturday, and suddenly she said, "This is like St. Paul's, isn't it, Mommy?" In London we had climbed (1000+ stairs around and around and up) to the top of St. Paul's Cathedral (366' high) and had a fantastic view of London. (For the previous six days I had been having what I assume was a miscarriage and my gynecologist-in-residence said such a climb would be good for me! I certainly suffered no ill effects and by the next day there was no trace of the problem. There was a lady doctor three houses down from us in London and I had written out my medical history for her in case we had to get her, but thankfully, that was not necessary.)

While I was working in the kitchen, Melody came flouncing in with a frilly pink nylon dress (from the stables) over her trousers and T-shirt. Her hair was stringy with perspiration and her face was smudged with dirt, but she insisted on doing some "ballet" dancing for me. She hummed the music and pirouetted and bowed her way around the kitchen until her cheeks got even pinker. She's sure a sweetheart. I hear Sweetheart 6 is just getting up so I'd better deal with him.

BALLERINA IN TROUSERS

July 19   We've just walked around the houses here. The church is not too big, but quite pretty. The inside has been modernized, but I understand the outside (stone in cement) is nearly 1,000 years old.

I'd better get this finished so you'll get it before we get back. If you think of it, could you save back copies of the *Colonist* for us, please, if you have any? We cancelled our subscription when we left.

Our plane leaves London at 4:00 p.m. July 31, arriving in Vancouver at 6:30 p.m. Those will be the longest 2 1/2 hours, I'm sure! (Nine and a half hours, really.)

Much love, Louise

July 25, 1979
Dear Mom,

I thought it would be fun to mail this *[birthday card]* from England, so it may arrive early (then again, it may be late if the mail gets disrupted). Everywhere we've shopped I've looked for one that would have "Mum" on it—the English way!—and also would not be too expensive or too large to mail! So Happy Birthday!

We are having a grand time here in Norwich. On Sunday the children played at a pretty little Anglican church and we went to that rectory for a cup of coffee on the lawn. Three vicars share eleven churches because they are small, so there aren't regular services in any one church. The vicar responsible for Sunday's services had four services to do that day in different churches. On Monday that vicar and the other one not on holiday invited us to a third, very large, 110-year-old rectory for a picnic lunch and then a sail on the "Broads" (beautiful canals that meander through the farmland; the Norfolk area is noted for them). Bruce and Marilyn and Michael went sailing and I stayed back at the rectory and visited with the wife and another friend. We sat in lawn chairs and then took the children for a several-mile walk down the lanes. (The sailing was from 1:30 to 6:30 p.m.) This rectory is on three acres of beautifully wooded land, but is not kept up, understandably, because of the family's busyness. The wife also nurses half days and there are four children from 15 down to 9. She was wearing bluejeans and sandals and yet managed to look graceful and elegant.

From what we have seen, housekeeping, at least to Canadian *[textbook!]* standards, is not a priority; being friendly and helpful is. This is good, but seeing a large fluffy cat on the counter beside a slab of cheese made me revert back to Canadian ways!

Last week we went to Norwich Cathedral. It was a special day and the church had at least 15 flower arrangements in it, each one eight to ten feet across: all sorts of flowers and branches—just beautiful. The old stone and the stained glass windows made such a contrast with the greenery, and the ceilings are very high. We happened on a rehearsal of Mozart's "Sparrow" Mass with choir and orchestra—what a setting! We hope to attend an organ concert there tonight. *[Did, and received comments on how well-behaved the six were.]*

Several days we have taken our lunch and gone shopping (i.e., sightseeing; we don't buy that much). Unlike London and Uttoxeter, Norwich is clean and well-kept. The cobblestone streets are picturesque, and the downtown core is modern and busy. The outlying area—we are 6 1/2 miles from downtown Norwich—is like our prairies: flat, with fields of sugar beets, vegetables and grains, and some cattle, the fields all defined by hedges. The trees (elm, beech, ash, etc.) are very tall and leafy, so restful.

Mark has just been wheeled past the study window by Margaret, both very happy. He is one adorable child, and the potential for spoiling is enormous! This morning, service wasn't quite quick enough to suit him, so he got a pint of milk and his empty bottle and crawled upstairs with them. He's added several things to his vocabulary; when he's in trouble, he yells "Ma-Da." (Melody told me this.) I hear the rabbit is out for the second time. I caught him (in the gooseberry bushes—*ouch!*) last time.

I caught him—*ouch!*—in the gooseberries again and have scratches to prove it. Lois Bawtree says usually when he escapes he heads for the hedge and works on a tunnel. Apparently he hasn't got it finished because he hasn't left the yard yet. It was a panic trying to catch him—eight people vs. one bunny—or should I say, seven people vs. one bunny and his ally, Mark! Mark is now stripping the raspberry bushes to his height. I've frozen about 20 pounds of black currants and several bags of scarlet runner beans as well; we've been having broad beans one day, and string beans the next.

Marilyn and Michael are going to mail this on their bikes and are champing at the bit, so I'd better finish. Someone has just come to borrow a lawnmower. I wonder how Bruce is making out; knowing the Bawtrees, it's probably fine, but we don't know who's who.

Love, Louise

Chapter 17: Letters to My Parents, 1979

January 18 … A week ago I cut up old Christmas cards, using the paper cutter, into gift tags for next year. The day I was doing it, Melody *[just turned 4]* wanted to hang on my elbow and I didn't like her so near the blade, so I got the idea of cutting up the leftover paper into jigsaw puzzles for her. She spent the rest of the time making these six- to eight-piece puzzles at the other desk and was as good as gold. She took an envelope for each one and carefully put one set in each and then printed her name on each envelope. Some came out MEODY or MELDOY, but I was really pleased at her ability to concentrate for such a long time. She would put the envelopes on her left side, then choose one puzzle at a time to assemble, undo it back into its envelope, put the envelope on her right side in a neat pile, and announce to me each time that she had another one done. She really is good company. When I tell her that Mommy loves her, she often says, "And Mommy loves Mark, too, doesn't she?" I'm not sure if that pleases her, but I hope so. Mark is just a panic. If he thinks you're displeased with him, he covers his left eye with his hand and peeks through his fingers. Or he looks sideways instead of straight at you. He's a lovely little chunk of boy and so cuddly. … I saw something cute yesterday when I was on the phone in Bruce's room. The door was open, and as I sat on the bed, I suddenly saw Melody streak into the bathroom, pull down her pants, desperately jump up on the toilet, urinate, slide off again, pull up her pants, all without the benefit of toilet paper. To my amusement, she then put the lid down, climbed on top of it to turn the tap on, and very carefully washed her hands with much soap and an equal quantity of water. All this was done without her realizing that I was watching; after all, when one goes to the bathroom, one always washes one's hands, right?

… Bernie *[Neufeld]* has a terrific sense of humour. Last night she commented on Sunday's choir piece. It was difficult, and both piano and organ (me) were accompanying it. She said as soon as she noticed the pianist had a page-turner and the organist didn't, she watched to see what would happen. Apparently, at the first page-turning, the organist gave the page a hefty swat (which was clearly audible in their balcony seats), and the page stayed where it was supposed to. She said it wouldn't have dared to flip back! The things I do that I'm not even aware of!

… I told you a couple of days ago that I was feeling depressed. I'm sure part of the problem was that I'd got up early and had had absolutely no cooperation in practising with my little sweethearts, so much of the time had miserably gone down the drain. It has been their habit lately to prolong getting up, and getting dressed, to three-quarters of an hour, and then there's just not enough time for really valuable practising. Anyway, yesterday I had a brain-wave. I was setting my hair and thought that I would be ready to start working with them in about five minutes, so I took the timer upstairs and announced that anyone up and dressed in five minutes would get a treat. In two and a half minutes, four bright, alert, greedy little children were standing in the hallway outside the bathroom, dressed and raring to go. (The treat was a stick of Orbit gum.) We had super practices, and the gum was greatly appreciated. When I told Peggy, she said a) she could strangle them, and b) now that I know that they are capable of doing it, they should be penalized for disobeying. [*Auntie Peggy was actually our children's ally, enjoying their antics, lending a sympathetic ear on occasion, and eventually teaching each in turn at Pacific Christian School.*] I'll go along with that to a point, but I'm afraid I fully sympathize with their unwillingness to get up, so I thought I would try a compromise. This morning I set the timer for 15 minutes and said that they had to be dressed and have their beds made. I said nothing about being punished if they didn't, although I had mentioned within their hearing that "someone" had suggested they deserved punishment if they didn't shape up (they immediately said, "Auntie Peggy," but I didn't give them the satisfaction of telling them who), and I said nothing about a reward, either. However, they all were prompt, and at breakfast they found a Scotch mint at their places, and seemed pleased with that. (Did I tell you about the time they had a scoop of ice cream on their granola for breakfast?) It's to their advantage to get a good swat at their music before school, partly because they're fresher then and partly because they're freer after school. I consider it an investment in their future, and it would take a lot to give it up, especially when every single one is coming along so nicely. It's not easy, though.

November 2 … This morning I finally got together with Michael to work on his large piece. He had been picking away at it all week, neglecting the new, very difficult part, and playing over the old, easier part to keep his father convinced he was practising. Anyway, we tackled it, and I suggested he play it ten times before breakfast. It had taken him seven minutes to struggle through it once, under my nattering supervision, so naturally he wasn't too enthusiastic about my suggestion. However, the second time through took four minutes, and times 3 to 10 took one minute each, virtually perfect. Naturally, I had hoped to be able to leave him for times 2 to 10, but as would be expected, I sat through times 2 to 10, and both of us were very pleased with the results. It's like working with a porcupine! He catches on so quickly, though, once he sets his mind to it. Margaret has been just a pet with her work. She carefully goes down a list that I prepare for her, and does what she is told. Today I checked through all her exercises, and she had obviously worked on them all week; she had also memorized a concerto, which is quite advanced—only her second week on it. … I don't think there's anything harder that I do, but when things go well, it's more than worth it. They really are dears.

The weather has been quite good lately, and there has been the usual grumbling about having to walk home at noon and after school. They don't realize how pretty they look, with the blond, and blue, and rosy cheeks. Their appetites don't suffer, either!

Saturday night … Michael is having a bath downstairs, and the three little girls are being bathed lovingly (?) by their big sister upstairs. The motivation is pretty high, because I promised them they could watch a Charlie Brown special tonight from 8:00 to 9:30. It was my suggestion, and followed some very good violin lessons today, and a productive practice time just before supper. When we get a head start on their week's work on Saturday night, it goes much easier the next week; unlike the early morning practices, there isn't quite the time pressure, and I can see the problems through properly. They all are doing so nicely; Margaret sight-read a whole concerto movement through, with very few errors. It was filled with bowing problems and weird notes, and yet she managed to figure them out mostly on her own. Having heard the other two play this piece over the last two or three years no doubt made it easier for her, but I was most impressed with her determination. Normally, a piece that size would be spread over two or three weeks, divided into five or six smaller sections. She probably will have it by memory for next Saturday, the way she is going.

… I mentioned that the kids still walk home from school whenever their indolent parents can finagle it. Just after I left the typewriter, Melissa straggled in and presented me with three pink clovers and two pretty leaves; no comment was made about walking. Margaret followed, music in one hand, recorder in the other. Apparently she had been playing the recorder all the way home. In the long skirt she was wearing, she looked like a little hippie. Biggest Sister dragged herself in, and, predictably, grumbled about having to walk. All three (and Michael, who had run) were lovely and pink and managed to put away a good lunch. They are so much fun.

November 16 … We're just home from the teacher visits. What a hoot! And how very fortunate we are. Marilyn's teacher, Mr. Taaffe, started off by saying it would be a short interview as he had nothing to say about Marilyn except she is one of the top students in the class. She is helpful, polite, etc., etc., and did we have any problems? We didn't, so we sat and talked about the other four, whom he also befriends on occasion. Michael's teacher, Mr. St. Clair, said that these interviews regarding good students were always … I supplied "painful" and he laughed. He is the super musician and computer nut, who has Michael eating out of the palm of his hand. Margaret has Mrs. Mosher, who was Marilyn's Grade 4 teacher. She has

Margaret pegged to a T, and is very good for her. She says Margaret can be a chatterbox (not when she herself is talking, though), but that just a look from her brings immediate cooperation. (I asked her if her face goes pink, and she laughed and said that was so, and that Margaret is very sensitive to criticism or reprimand.) She also said that Margaret wants desperately to be among the best, if not the best, at everything, and that, fortunately, she is able to achieve this. Mr. Gillion said he had requested that Melissa be put in his class, and he has no problems with her. He said she is very bright and it is all he can do to keep up with her. She zaps through her work and then suggests to Mr. G. what would be a suitable project for her; he usually agrees, and both are happy! Melody's teacher, Mrs. Baxter, says M5 is now coming out of her shell and is joining in with the others more. (She won't know what has hit her when she finally comes all the way out!) Did I tell you about the Halloween "concert" the Kindergarten children put on for the parents? Melody stood at the front, half a head smaller than her classmates (she is the youngest), and refused to sing the first song or two. I had suggested she change her turquoise tights to pink ones, which she had, only I hadn't checked the pink ones before she went. There she stood, rolling up her jumper, exposing two large holes, one in each knee! Mrs. Baxter told us she had problems at first getting her to keep her clothes on; when she got hot, she would just take off her sweater and jumper! Needless to say, there was a certain amount of merriment in the interview (actually in all of them), and Melody, too, appears to be in good hands.

We came home to find Ellen [*our friend who helped with housework for many years*] working away upstairs, and five good (according to their teachers) students sitting downstairs watching Mr. Dressup; the breakfast dishes, milk, cereals, and sugar container (which Mark had obviously been into) were on the table, and the family room itself looked like the aftermath of a tornado. Oh well; I guess one should count one's blessings. Marilyn had peeled some potatoes and carrots, but not "that other thing"—a turnip. She didn't know what it was! …

ELDEST FIVE AT LAKE HILL SCHOOL

December 20 It's 10:30 p.m. and things have finally settled down enough for me to get pen and paper together. The children and I have just finished their school concerts (Tuesday's long dress rehearsal, concerts Wednesday afternoon and evening) and we're all bushed. In addition to choir accompanying (me) and Kindergarten accompanying (Marilyn, and she did very well), our Favourite Five played about 15 minutes' worth of violin music to cover up the operetta's scenery changes. Melody was Mary, holding a large doll, in her class's contribution. Melissa's class sang and quoted the Bible account of the Christmas story; Melissa gave the title, reference and first verse in a voice that would match a hog caller's! Michael and Marilyn were both in the senior choir which accompanied the operetta, and Margaret was in a speaking choir which did "This is the House that Jack Built." (I provided skipping music for the people acting it out on stage.) Marilyn and Michael are both involved in their respective class parties tomorrow and Bruce has to pick up and deliver the ordered food—one lot from McDonald's and one from Brownies. I've just wrapped presents for each of them to give classmates (names from a hat). Central's cantata (Ms 1 - 4 are in the children's choir which took part) has been televised as CHEK-TV's Christmas Day special, and that, too, has been on the go. And Auntie Vi and Uncle George [from Uttoxeter, England] have been hiding here for several days, until tomorrow night's anniversary celebration [Holland's 50th; family brought them to Canada as a surprise]. ... There's a loaf of sandwiches to be made for Melissa's party and I told Bruce I would make them, but I see he's started and he has to get up at 5:30 a.m. Must go. [Some things never change!]

December 28 It's 11:20 p.m. and Bruce is out on a call (had to take the police with him on the previous call), and I thought I'd say hi to you. ... Today I feel normal for the first time in several days. December has been extremely busy, and the last two weeks were incredible. In addition to the regular family and school activities, there were three school concerts (18th, 19th and 20th) at which the children played; a Golden Anniversary (21st, 22nd); S. S. rehearsal and concert (23rd); playing at the Gorge Hospital (24th a.m.—Margaret's tail-gut broke and her violin fell apart about one-third of the way through the programme—TEARS!); a lovely family visit in the evening—including Scrivers (Uncle Fred [doctor] diagnosed Margaret as having mumps); playing at church Christmas morning (M3 played anyway, then Bruce took her home immediately) and Christmas supper for 20. And Bruce was on call from the 24th on. For the last three Sundays, I ended up playing for the early service and the evening service as well as Sunday School and 11:00 a.m. church; also Jr. Church for 9th, 16th, 23rd (Bruce's off-call weekends). We have no commitments from now on, and I've been able to get a good rest, after two sleepless nights with Margaret (temp. to 105—no fun). I would not choose to follow such a tight schedule, but I am most grateful to be given the strength to manage it. This unscheduled time is doubly appreciated. [I would have been five months pregnant with Matthew.]

... I've had several strong suggestions that I incorporate these Christmas letters into a book. Maybe one day. It seems such a bother now, and my main purpose in writing them is to share our happiness (do the letters sound happy?!) and provide a record for the children.

Chapter 18: 1980

As was mentioned in an earlier chapter, the children were encouraged to help out, and sometimes even received payment for their efforts. They started purchasing some items with their own money: shampoo, toothpaste, some school supplies, some clothing—of their own choosing. It was interesting and sometimes amusing to note their reactions to the prices of what they wanted, in relation to their earnings. An even more important reason for ensuring they had their own money was that they had something to share with others. And they were given the option of tithing their treasure into the Sunday School offering.

This chapter (September diary entry) records some of the wheeling and dealing involved with the children's money matters.

M*A*R*K's Diary

December 31, 1979 Yesterday was **Marilyn**'s twelfth birthday. Our garden celebrated by presenting her with mauve primroses and yellow pansies. (The day after Christmas, Marilyn had presented our parents with a carefully-prepared list entitled "Things I Want for My Birthday." She had crossed out the "I Want" part and rewritten "I Wouldn't Mind"; I think it's called diplomacy.) This morning, **Margaret** commented that she hoped it would snow soon, "or else what's December for?" I guess she forgot that December is for three sisters' and three cousins' birthdays, five family anniversaries, and the most significant Birthday of all.

This year, in addition to school concerts (three), a cantata, a Sunday School concert, and playing the violins for several groups, my family marked Grandma and Grandpa Holland's Golden Wedding Anniversary on the 21st with a family dinner, and on the 22nd with afternoon and evening receptions at Auntie Shirley's. We had kept Auntie Vi and Uncle George from England hidden at our house from the 16th to the 21st as a surprise for our grandparents. These gentle English people adapted remarkably well to the ungentle Canadian activities that swirled around them here.

Margaret may be forgiven for her slightly sour view of December. On the 24th, the violins were partway through a programme at the Gorge Hospital when the tail-gut on her violin snapped, flinging the bridge to the floor; the tailpiece and strings hung forlornly under a shower of hot tears. That evening complaints of soreness behind her ears finally registered. (It is only when grumbling reaches a certain level of frequency and volume that our parents pay any attention.) Christmas Day brought a quite impressive case of the mumps. Even so, Margaret was bundled up and taken with the family to church. Near the beginning of the service she, on her newly-repaired violin, its chin rest well-cushioned, joined her brothers and sisters in playing several Christmas carols. Daddy immediately took her home and tucked her into bed, where she spent the next several days.

Christmas Day started with the mumps and ended with a turkey dinner for twenty. In between, presents were opened and savoured. Everything I unwrapped was greeted with, "Oh *wow!*" After all the wrappings had been demolished, I regarded my sisters' new dolls sadly and queried, "*My* baby?" I guess I'll have to be satisfied with all the "taddies" I "cubber" up so carefully each night, and Mommy assures me I soon should have a real, live baby to fuss over.

Yesterday, after a few days of relaxing and enjoying each other's new toys, games and books, my brother and sisters were recruited into Operation Tidy-Up. From the depths of her closet, **Melissa** produced six petrified peanut butter and honey sandwiches left over from her class party on the 21st. We enjoyed them, even if Mommy looked a little green afterwards when we told her.

January 31, 1980 January brought us seventeen inches of beautiful, beautiful snow. The end of each day saw at least fifteen pairs of mittens drying out on the clothes rack, accompanied by innumerable hats. Margaret, typically, always kept a dry pair of mittens stored in her toque. On January 10, I created a little excitement by raiding the refrigerator and downing the miniature strawberry milkshake our doctor had recommended for my sore ear. My parents had been doling it out to me for three days, and had plans to continue for the next seven days. Neither was impressed by my thoroughness in placing the empty container and lid carefully in the dishwasher. Mommy put her fingers in my mouth and gave me a drink of soapy water and soon my Amoxicillin and I parted company. Daddy muttered something about $6 and made another trip to the drugstore.

February 29 My sisters and brother don't appear to have too much trouble at school. (One was heard to state that "School is easy, compared to home." The remark was brought on by a parental reference to practising.) The eldest four usually receive an Excellent in Spelling, but I suspect that at least one teacher is being overly generous. Melissa has a sign over her bedroom library: "Book Scedchwell," and our parents received an enthusiastic Valentine card with the message, "I love you Mom and Dad! SPEACAILY you!" The other day Mommy found a scribbler Melissa used in Grade One for "Vicktashin."

My parents have been trying to wean **Melody** from her afternoon nap, in preparation for Grade One. Despite her desperate attempts to stay awake, however, she is often found sitting in the large family room chair, quietly snoring. During the last week, Mommy found her asleep on pillows in the hallway upstairs, in her bed under a Richard Scarry book (still open to a special page "to show Mommy"), at the

SWEET SLEEPYHEAD

foot of the stairs (using the bottom step as a pillow), and with her head on Mommy's desk, where drowsiness had overcome her as she checked off her list of Valentine names.

Melody practises the violin and piano after lunch most days. Recently she made a discovery: "The right hand plays the treble notes, and the left hand plays the ones in the basement." Her ambition is to have long hair like her sisters; she keeps track of its growth by the number of "wobblies" used for each braid.

"*My* bed, *my* toys, *my* Daddy"; "I don't wantta"; and "No, Mom," reflect my current attitude towards life.

March 31 Today was not one of my Better Days. In the course of a few hours, I received three scoldings, a slap on the hands, and a swat on the bottom for various misdemeanors: at 10:00 a.m. for making moves towards the front yard (and Saanich Road), at 11:30 a.m. for plugging in an extension cord (I still don't know if those bobbypins will fit in the other end), and at 1:00 p.m. for standing on Marilyn's pillow to hang out of the upstairs window.

Later on this afternoon, I cut my mouth on Daddy's razor, and removed a large piece of fingernail with **Michael**'s scissors. This evening I emptied half a bottle of Mommy's best perfume onto her dressing gown. When she tells me these are things I must not do, I usually answer, "O̲K, Mom," which is safer than "OK̲, Mom," which she says is "chicky." At the end of the day, Mommy and I sat on her bed in the moonlight. She sang something about the moon and the old oak tree, and even told me I was one she loved, so I guess she doesn't hold a grudge.

April 30 From the 17th to the 19th, the whole family (excluding me; my grandparents had the pleasure of my company) took part in a violin workshop in Vancouver, under Dr. Shinichi Suzuki's leadership. The final activity was a concert at the Orpheum Theatre, where over 300 violinists covered the stage by the end of the programme. Mommy travelled everywhere with a fully-packed suitcase, and tried not to dwell on its significance.

Two nights later (eleven days ahead of the calendar), our newest baby indicated quite

DR. SHINICHI SUZUKI, FOUNDER
OF THE SUZUKI METHOD

dramatically that he was on the verge of disembarking. Mommy completed her class, spent a quiet night confined to a hospital bed, and in fifteen hectic minutes presented the intern with my tiny brother—Matthew Norman, seven cuddly pounds of blue-eyed blondness hung on 22 1/2 spidery inches.

Matthew's Diary

May 31 Hello from Grandpa Holland's namesake! My brother next up has turned his pencil over to me, hoping that I can contribute a slightly different perspective on life in our home. Mark Andrew's point of view is constantly changing, as he patters from one misadventure to the next. I am immobilized, and must depend on both my wits and my lungs to bring about a change of scenery.

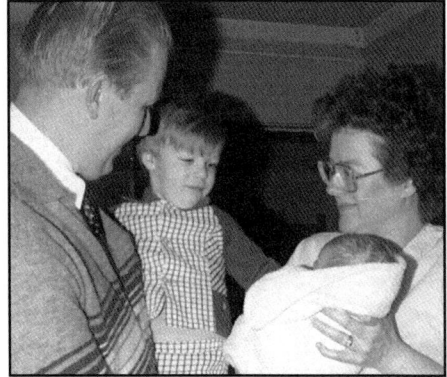
MARK MEETS MATTHEW

Mark is a most solicitous big brother. He calls me "Mashew," his "tiny baby brudder," and adds, "I *like* it." He pats me and kisses me very gently (and usually receives a kiss from Mommy; I wonder if there's a connection).

Last evening the children played their violins and the piano in a 50-minute recital at Linwood Court. As we left the house, Daddy mentioned, to Mommy's consternation, that he would drop us off and leave, as he had an emergency call to attend to. In order to maintain my reputation as the Best Baby Ever, I chose to sleep through the whole programme. As it was, there were tense moments as Mommy tried to send inaudible messages to Mark without removing her hands from the keyboard. She told him later that wandering from chair to chair, crawling under tables, and skipping amongst the violinists (ducking to avoid collision with the smaller violins) were not positive additions to the concert.

Today I experienced some uncoordinated jostling as Mark, holding me by the armpits, struggled to lift me out of my bassinet, which rested on the living room carpet. Airborne, I travelled towards the kitchen, Mark's "Mommy—baby cwying" ringing in my ears. I understand at times like this it is customary for one's life to flash before one's eyes. Perhaps it is due to the brevity of my life, but the only flash I saw was my mother breaking all sprinting records as she came to my rescue.

June 30 From March to June, the children presented several recitals, both at home and for senior citizens' groups. Auntie Shirley made the four girls matching navy-blue jumpers and white tops, and white tops for Daddy, Michael, and Mark, too. To go with the outfits, Daddy bought ten or twelve pairs of white socks at $1.49 Day, so it was with a little dismay that Margaret's report of a birthday party was received: "We all took our shoes off, but Mrs. Wiebe said *I* didn't have to because of the holes in my socks."

Mark's vocabulary continues to expand. That interpersonal relationships do not always operate at a high level is reflected in his newest acquisitions: "That isn't fair"; "Don't bother me"; "Get lost!"; "Marilyn," (or "Michael," or "Margaret," or "Melissa," or "Melody")—you *bad boy*"; "You did it on pripuss"; and *"Go away*—he's *my* brudder!"

July 31 Keeping the laundry under control appears to be one of Mommy's favourite pastimes. At least she passes a lot of time doing it. Three weekends ago, Daddy, Michael and Margaret returned from camp and added the contents of their suitcases to the collection already in the laundry room. Daddy had been cooking for 148 campers in a hot kitchen and came home with nine days' worth of laundry. Margaret contributed a respectable six days' worth, but Michael's pile was surprisingly small. Upon closer examination, it was discovered that not only had his pajamas and several outfits escaped use (he had slept in his clothes), but his soap was in excellent (and its original) condition, and his toothbrush rested neatly in its case, uncontaminated by either toothpaste, water, or teeth.

While Daddy was at camp, my adventurous grandparents (Forsbergs, who happily for us, live just two short blocks away) invited us down for supper. Afterwards, the children went to a nearby playground, where Mark missed his footing on the slide and tumbled earthward, catching the back of his head on the steps. He and Mommy spent two and a half hours in Emergency, a first for her and a third for him. (In addition to the forehead stitching of last year, Mark landed in that busy place after a rough-housing session with my biggest brother. Just before the doctor took a look at it, his arm clicked back into place, and the doctor diagnosed the problem as "supermarket sprain," sometimes received by children whose parents drag them impatiently through the store.)

Four years ago our Christmas letter contained Melissa's rendering of "Little Miss Muffet", which included "eating her curtains away." Melody's 1980 version might well be copyrighted by Weight Watchers: "Little Miss Muffet … eating her curves away."

August 31 Two more days until school—and Mark's third birthday! Today is the end of a "structured" summer. (Mommy's Thesaurus has two synonyms for "sanity": "structure" and "afternoon nap.") Each of my instrument-playing siblings accumulated fifteen hours of practice on both instruments during July and August; they also played for several groups. In a burst of enthusiasm, Margaret created a collage with the message "Music is so fun," which Mommy thinks should be a permanent addition to the music waiting room.

Nearly four weeks ago, Mark suddenly took a great (overdue) leap forward and I found myself the recipient of all the family heirlooms, flannelette division, a motley collection accumulated over twelve and a half years. Occasionally people suggest

Mommy write a book on large-family living. (Daddy says she already does—each Christmas.) She says she might, when the 36-Hour Day comes into effect, and she has a title chosen: "For Two Pins" *[written when diapers were held together by safety pins]*.

September 30 *[Michael's eleventh birthday]* One of our parents' mottoes is, "If a child can do it, a *child* does it." Little extras are associated with an allowance, which is, in turn, associated with chores. Not only are my brother and sisters becoming canny shoppers, but they are gaining a firsthand knowledge of capitalism:

Profit "I got them three for a dime. You can have one for a nickel."

Loss "I paid 50 cents for it. I just ate the edge of it; I'm not hungry anymore. It's yours for 25 cents. 15 cents?"

Subcontracting "I'm getting 25 cents for this line of laundry. I'll give you five cents if you'll distribute it."

Negotiations "If you'll do the watering for me, I'll do your basket of clothes."

Management-Labour Confrontation "No, you can't put 'watering' on your list. The rain did it for free." "This room is not considered tidy until all the shoes are upstairs and you've checked under the chesterfield for toys. Until then, no TV." "Forty-five minutes and your bed still isn't made? Give me that book."

October 31, 7:30 p.m. There are peculiar goings-on here tonight! Although it is cold and rainy, my six older brothers and sisters insisted on going for a walk in the dark, clad in some extraordinary outfits. Marilyn's version of a housewife elicited a comment from Daddy which Mommy has forbidden me to record; Margaret, Melissa and Melody were "beautiful ladies"; Mark was a clown; and Michael put on a curly brown wig, sparkly earrings, a dress, sandals, much artificial colouring, and Mommy's old furry coat to make the Beautiful Lady Trio a Quartet. In between glimpses at the newspaper and entertaining me, Mommy answers the doorbell and hands out bags of caramel popcorn to other strange creatures. **8:30 p.m.** Daddy's bedraggled sextet has just arrived home, shivering, but pleased with the results of their neighbourhood scrounging. (Only two of the neighbours recognized the glamorous brunette.)

MICHAEL AS A "BEAUTIFUL LADY"

November 30 A few weeks ago, our parents' most recent investment arrived, in twenty-one pieces: three bunk beds. The two older girls share one, in a room labelled: "Notice to anyone thinking about entering this room—DON'T." Melissa and Melody share another, and my two big brothers share the third, which is placed on the wall opposite my crib. Michael refers to the upper bunk as his "eyrie," and spends hours (some illicit) in it, devouring books, catalogues (specifically Radio

Shack publications), and the contents of a 480-candy jar he won at a Fall Fair.

Marilyn has enjoyed her first three months in Grade Eight at Pacific Christian School. One day she went off dressed for Clash Day in mismatched shoes, socks, hair ribbons, hair (one braid, one ponytail) and an outrageous combination of colours. She was quite pleased with her artistry until Daddy casually remarked on the way to school that he hoped she had her dates straight. A few uneasy moments passed, and then she caught sight of a similarly-attired schoolmate.

A few weeks ago, Mark started learning to hold the "bliolin" and sometimes joins in a bow at the end of a programme. A favourite activity is sitting on the carpet beside the couch, "playing Lego wiff Maffew." (He plays; I watch.)

For the past few days, there's been an undercurrent of excitement running through our household. There is talk of presents and concerts and parties and large meals. Mommy goes shopping and stores her purchases in a large box. Melissa and Melody have festooned their bed with green chains held together and weighted down with a controversial number of staples. They join the other three in a five-part rendition of "Gesu Bambino" on the violins. My dad likes this piece and tells me it was written in honour of the most important Baby who was ever born. Daddy also told me it is his hope that I, and my brothers and sisters, will grow up to love and serve the One whose birthday celebration occupies so much of our thinking and activity.

We hope that you, too, will have a joy-filled Christ's-Birthday celebration, and a blessed New Year.

Love, **Matthew**

SEEN AND HEARD …

January 12 Mark bathed, in clean pajamas, playing in tub with sisters—soaking wet …

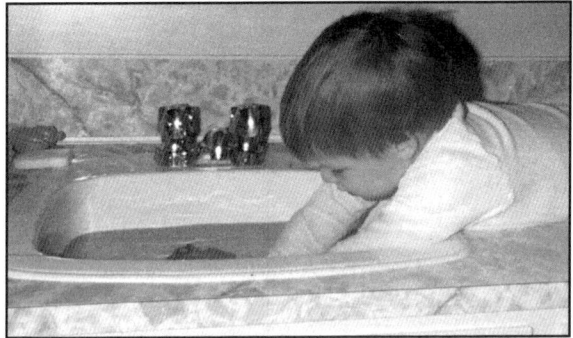

MARK LOVES WATER

January 13 Mark, who refers to himself as "Markie," in response to behaviour suggestions: "No thank you, Mom." …

January 22 Melissa, self-described as a "maiden," folding *both* baskets of laundry …

April 12 Melissa, shoeless, with "bare feet on" …

April 19 Melody wearing "arm necklace" (bracelet) …

December 16 Margaret and Melissa wearing long dresses for school choir performance at Rec Centre: "Everyone's wearing one. This girl in Grade 3 has a pink frilly one." Total in long dresses: three …

Chapter 19: Letters to My Parents, 1980

January 20, 1980

Dear Mom and Dad,

... It's ten o'clock on a Sunday evening, and Bruce isn't back yet from church. I've just put Mark down; he slept several hours this afternoon and has been keeping me company all evening. He's so much fun. He had an ear infection before Christmas which flared up again a couple of weeks ago, so the doctor put him on a ten-day series of antibiotics instead of five days. About a week ago, he drank seven days' worth of the medicine, so we had to get the prescription renewed. I made him throw it up, first by putting my fingers down his throat, and then by giving him a solution of dishwashing detergent in water (hospital's instructions). I don't think the medicine is that lethal (penicillin), but didn't like to take chances. The little character was carefully placing the empty bottle upside-down in the dishwasher when Bruce caught him. The medicine tastes like strawberry, so it's little wonder he likes it. I suspect he may also have had a mild case of the mumps during this past week, too. Marilyn and Michael came down with them Saturday and Sunday a week ago, and are still a little chipmunkish. Marilyn was quite sick with them, but Michael had only one day of temperature and has been quite active (often negatively so; what an inventive pest!) throughout; Marilyn has been lethargic all week, but was much better today. ... I am very well, as long as I get my rest in the afternoon, and a reasonable night's sleep. The baby is kicking and squirming; it seems I still haven't got over the fascination of a new baby's movements. ... I made alphabet books for Melody's kindergarten class. The first day Melody asked the teacher if she liked "Mommy's printing," and the teacher said it was beautiful (she wouldn't have dared not to), and this was duly reported, with great excitement. ... Mark talks a lot now. Everything is "Markie's" and whenever I do anything for him, he says, "Thank you, Mom." He has tremendous bladder control except when it counts. ...

February 5 ... Melody came down with the mumps on Thursday, so we've had the pleasure of her company since then. Marilyn stayed home with her on Sunday (the babysitting problem is getting closer to a solution all the time, as Marilyn ages!); Melody insisted she would rather have had Melissa. She slept with me for the first three nights (the temp really soars with mumps, but fortunately is controllable with aspirin), and appears on the mend now. I guess we didn't tell you she had a cast on her arm in December. She had been carrying a huge Lego model airplane down from Michael's bedroom and somehow tripped, scattering the pieces all over and gaining a green-stick fracture in her right arm. The bone is bent, not broken, but requires a cast; often happens to children, whose bones are more pliable and less brittle than adults. She even had Dr. Morrison cut off the cast carefully so she could bring it home and show it to her class at school (Show and Tell—ugh). She had to play at a concert with it on (Sons of Norway), and was quite enthusiastically received. She's "crackerjack" [her Grandpa Hjalmar's expression] on both piano and violin, so well coordinated and enthusiastic. She and Mark have been having a great time together the last few days; she's very good with him. And he is a walking entertainment committee. This morning I went up to the music room to see how Marilyn was faring, and there he was, sitting on the bench beside her, dressed in his dressing gown and boots (never his own), banging away on a triangle while she played. He was right in time, too, and the piece moved quickly. He still hasn't caught on to being trained, but has increased my exasperation by saying, when I'm changing him, "It's fonny, eh, Mom?" Mom assures him it isn't "fonny" and gives him Lecture 42-a on How BIG Boys Use the Toilet … Last night he crawled in with me at 4:00 a.m. and was so cute and cuddly. He just got up and under the covers as if it was his perfect right. … I had turned off my light at 11:30 p.m. and was just about asleep when a peculiar rolling noise in the bathroom brought me to life. I suspected, correctly, that it was one of the cats playing with a toy, as no lights were on. When I took after the culprit, she bee-lined for Marilyn and Margaret's bedroom and disappeared into the closet. I found her curled up in a very cozy house, her own, assembled by Margaret (with disrespect for parental decree): a large box, complete with blanket and Cat Chow. I was so mad I turned on the light (had to, to find the beast), but the two guilty room-mates slept innocently on. By the time I threw Tiger out, I was wide awake. At 2:00 a.m. I woke to make my nightly trek to the biff, and then Mark arrived a couple of hours later. After a night like that, 6:30 a.m. is rotten. … The kids do practically all the folding. I just organize the loads and see they get through the machines while the little slaves are at school, and the baskets are all ready by the time they get home. I also make a list of what they have to do after school: finish practising, if any; tidy bedroom; sort out drawers; fold clothes; homework, etc., etc., with little boxes beside each item. They all seem to enjoy checking off the boxes, so this works quite well.

February 7 … [dd typed at end of previous line] You can see Mark just had to experiment with the typewriter. I've just finished reading the paper, with constant interruptions from him. He's so sturdy and busy and interested in everything. He has (another) black eye from hitting the bottom of the upstairs handrail; he runs from one thing to the next. The scab is starting to peel, which distresses him, so after much whining and getting little response from me ("Leave it alone, Mark"), he finally solved the problem himself by applying a strip of masking tape just below the "hurt." No more complaining. … Bruce is making lasagna for lunch, under Mark's supervision. Michael will be ecstatic. You know what a complainer Michael can be. The other day I picked them up for lunch just at noon, to be sure they got back half an hour later for a staff-students basketball game. When M2 asked why I was right on time, I told him, and he said, "Great! I'm not going to complain any more. But you know, it's awfully hard not to complain!" At least he recognizes his problem. Fortunately, he has two things in his favour: he is enthusiastically happy when things do go well (according to him), and he is immensely pleased when he finishes a project satisfactorily. One principle I use with him is, "I refuse to deprive you of the satisfaction of doing that job well." The "job" may be practising, or tidying his bedroom, or rewriting a paragraph, etc., and the above statement is usually followed by, "Now get on with it." Poor Michael. *[For years I have tried to remember exactly what that sentence was; I didn't realize I had recorded it.]*

February 27 … Yesterday Melody came home with a long-coveted prize: a medallion (laminated manilla tag, actually) which stated, "I can tie my shoes!" She has developed a thing about words (wonder why?). *[Instead of the requisite five pictures for each alphabet letter page, she and I had collected up to 25, which Mrs. Baxter gamely labelled, a tremendous contribution to a Kindergarten student's vocabulary. I still have her alphabet book here, and Mark's as well.]* She has asked me several times why we use the words we do: "How do we know which words to use?" Yesterday she asked, "Are we God's puppets?" At least she's thinking. Her wetting problem seems to be a thing of the past. Since Christmas there's been only one wet bed, and up to then we could count on at least one soaking a night, even if we took her to the toilet at 11:00 p.m. or midnight. Just after Christmas, she announced that she wasn't going to put on her usual three panties plus plastic pants, but would wear just ordinary "big-girl" panties. I didn't say anything, as I had long since assumed she might even have a permanent urinary problem, and it would be cruel to make an issue over it. Since then, no problem. I suspect it was just a question of maturation, because her attitude has always been good. She had a croupy throat last night, so I took her into bed with me; she's so dear—dainty and delicate, and so cooperative.

I'm looking at a monstrous (as in very large) Valentine Melissa made for me. It says, "God loves you! Speacaily you!" And the child is at or near the top of her class; don't you think the standard must be suspect?!

Yesterday I was at Coffee Hour (for mothers of pre-school children; I guess I'm a charter member). A request was made for prayer for the parents of a ten-year-old girl who is not recovering from a serious brain operation. That kind of thing just puts bands of ice around my middle (heart?). Anyway, at lunch time, our ten-year-old casually mentioned that he'd had two reading tests at school and had scored at the

99th percentile. When asked to define that lofty description, he said it meant everyone else was below him. Mr. St. Clair had said, "I'm not going to read out many marks, but you won't be surprised to know that Michael scored very well on his tests, and it's not easy to score so high on both of them." Of course, said son got a mini-lecture on what his response (at least mentally) should be to such success, and so far I think he's pretty well got the right perspective. *[Thank You, Lord.]* What a responsibility we have. The strange thing is that I don't think we demand such a high standard, and we certainly don't put in extra time doing remedial work or pulling strings at school. I'm convinced that some of Michael's early-morning grumpiness is due to his reading well past the time we think his light is out. I have to hide all new Reader's Digests; he has read almost every book around here. He took one out of the church library, and was told by the librarian that it was an adult book—it is, I've read it—and replied, "I know, I've already read it." (He bought a science encyclopedia for over $100, quite a sacrifice at $6/month allowance, and spends many hours engrossed in it.) … Marilyn won a prize for her Science project *[a row of bottles filled with water to make a major scale]*. One of the sweetest things about Marilyn's project was the pride the next four took in Big Sister's display. Bruce took them and all her trappings back to school on Monday, and said it was cute how they all wanted to carry things into the school for her. I took Michael to the Fair last night, and he was so pleased when she got her award. I think I'll write a book on the advantages of a large family! …

March 17 … Wednesday the teachers came for tea and an uproarious time was had by all! Our children are so fortunate to have such long-suffering teachers. Michael's teacher from last year (Mr. Eng) and this year (Mr. St. Clair) discussed all sorts of things with him (camera, music, trip to England album, etc., etc.) and he was elated for the next 24 hours. He hadn't been sure they would want to come. They all left between 5:15 and 5:30 p.m. after arriving at 3:30 p.m. … On Friday I went to Uncle Jim's memorial service at Hayward's. *[Jim was my mother's brother; it must have been hard for her to be down south at that time.]* It was short but very lovely. I sat with Auntie Kaye and Uncle Fred and tried to look inconspicuous (eight months pregnant, 180 lbs., in my furry winter coat?). In the crowd afterwards, an elderly man peered at me from several angles and finally said, "Are you Anne *[my mother]*?" When I identified myself, he said, "God bless you," and told me he was Auntie Grace's twin brother. Everyone was very nice to me and, later on, when I was teaching, Auntie Kaye phoned to thank me for going. …

Chapter 20: 1981

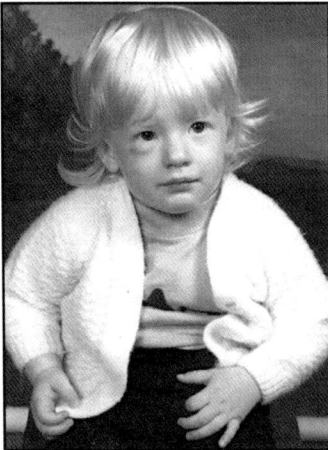

MATTHEW

Matthew continues:

May I re-introduce you to the people who share my house with me?

My dad has just completed fourteen years in social work with the Ministry of Human Resources. Whether or not he is on call (two weeks out of four, from 5:00 p.m. to 8:00 a.m. each night and all weekend), or off call, he is able to spend much of the day at home. This gives Mommy opportunity to prepare for and teach her classes, and it allows us to enjoy our dad and him to (I think) enjoy us. He says he finds our happy, if rowdy, home a source of encouragement when he spends so much of his working time with people in distress. He continues to ensure we are well-nourished by cooking up stews, soups, and casseroles, and vast quantities of muffins and biscuits. In October, he gathered over 300 pounds of windfall apples, a large portion of which he and Mommy made into applesauce to freeze.

In June, Mommy finished 21 years of teaching, 19 1/2 years of marriage, 13 1/2 years of nonstop diapers (and silky heads, and dimpled hands) and, most traumatic of all, her fourth decade. This summer she emptied our many borders and rockeries, refilling them with wheelbarrow after wheelbarrow of soil and compost, replanting hundreds of bulbs, and covering it all with bedding plants she and Daddy found on August 1. The plants came along very quickly, as did the chickweed. A patch of greens under our lilac tree illustrates the dangers of putting seedy swiss chard in the compost box. Mommy also faithfully watered the weeds at our back door, and was rewarded with six ice cream pails full of blackberries for our freezers. She scrounged another eighteen buckets of berries from a friend's yard, along the roadsides, and up-Island. (Some of the scars still haven't faded.)

Mommy usually plays the organ for the 11:00 a.m. service at our church. Daddy is on call two Sundays out of four. This means that my six older siblings who sit five rows back, behind four rows of elderly men and women from the Central Care Home next door, are, at times, comfortably removed from parental nudge or warning look. Rules have been set forth (no gum, no comic books, no dolls, no paper airplanes, no arguing, no elbowing), but there are times when our mother feels quite helpless, with hands and feet restricted. Even her one means of supervision (glance, frown, stare, and/or glare) was scuttled when she realized some of the elderly people were intercepting her signals and looking at her in perplexity.

Clothing and the washing/drying/ironing/mending thereof demand a fair amount of our parents' attention. Not only are there enough clothes to cover us decently now, but all the in-between ages are represented in our closets and drawers. My mother refers to this immense wardrobe as the In-House Thrift Shoppe and our style as Hand-Me-Down Eclectic.

In July we spent nine days at the Rathtrevor campsite, Parksville, our grandparents' trailer providing a haven on a spacious plot cleared from the salal and ocean spray shrubbery, nestled against cedars and firs. A very short walk through the woods brought us to the beach, where we spent hours swimming, building sand cities, flying kites, and toasting in the sun and sea breeze. With running water half a block distant, toilet facilities a block away, and electricity non-existent, we soon adapted to rising and setting with the sun. Mommy, as chief cook and laundress, said the first large raindrop was a signal for our immediate return to Victoria; happily, the sky smiled down on us for our entire stay.

Our very courageous friends, Doug and Mary Harris, decided that our parents needed, as well, some time away on their own. They volunteered to look after us for nearly three days in August, while Daddy and Mommy camped near Nanaimo. We had a hilarious time with our foster parents. Our mom and dad seem to have been able to manage somehow without us, although I understand they found their first meal a little eerie—no interruptions, no spilled milk, no disagreements; just the clicking of forks and spoons on plates, and great stretches of silence.

MARILYN IS 14

Marilyn will be fourteen at the end of the year, is in Grade 9 at Pacific Christian, and participates enthusiastically in the youth activities of our church. Although she probably will not appreciate my telling you, she has discovered, contrary to what her research at home might suggest, that not all boys are pests. She passed her Grade VIII piano exam in June, and is well into Grade IX work. Her pieces on the violin are also at that level, and our parents wonder how she manages her music, homework, chores and shampooing (she is usually warmed shoulders to waist by a yellow, wavy cloud) without apparent strain.

Marilyn continues to share a bedroom with Margaret, whose creative activities make tidying their mutual lodgings a challenge. Although Mommy tells Marilyn that it is good for her to learn to live with someone less tidy than she is (using Daddy's adaptability as an example), Marilyn is not convinced that *any*one needs all the paraphernalia Margaret accumulates on her bed and desk and in their cupboard. On the bedroom door hangs a cheerful WELCOME, enhanced by a photograph of a kitten, carnations and bows. When the room's occupants are not feeling so hospitable, however, the sign is turned over, and one is greeted by a hawk, a hapless mouse in his talons, and the fearsome message: GO AWAY! DO NOT ENTER OR WE WILL E-A-T YOU. This threat has not been carried out yet, partly because Michael keeps turning the kitten side out.

Although practising ranks somewhere between "Arising When First Called" and "Enduring a Haircut" on **Michael**'s Favourite Things list, and must be squeezed in around patrol duty, basketball practice, swimming lessons and Battalion, he plays both piano and violin with a flair that leaves Mommy wondering whether there really *is*—as she tells her students—a connection between effort and achievement.

A few months ago, a neighbour gave Michael an old record player and amplifier. He fixed it up, placing the record player on his dresser top and attaching the speaker to the book shelf beside his bunk. On Halloween, he hung the speaker out of his (upstairs) bedroom window, weatherproofing it with a black plastic bag, and played *Chilling and Thrilling Sounds from the Haunted House* for the benefit of the trick-or-treaters who were already contending with a driving rain. I'm sure no one thought the house was really haunted, with a light on in every room, and an assortment of blonds doubled over with laughter at the front door; and Mommy told the visitors not to be worried if they heard some strange sounds on their way down the path.

The child of reactionary parents who not only severely limit the contributions TV could make to their children's happiness, but also refuse to purchase such necessities as Barbie houses, **Margaret**, ten in October, is learning to make do. She has made her own doll house from a cardboard box, a shower (waxpaper box with waxpaper shower window), a toilet (small box with an appropriate hole; lid attached), and a cupboard (containing one-inch hangers made from bare "twistem" wires). Margaret's non-conformity won her a prize on St. Patrick's Day when she dressed all in green—from green running shoes to green ribbons and barrettes, in addition to green freckles on her face. She never complains of boredom. (Rarely do her sisters and brothers, either; they know that our parents always have several suggestions for using time wisely.) Once—only once—she provided her own percussion section by practising the piano with a peanut shell encasing each finger. Margaret is a most affectionate "little mother" to Mark and me. The first time she bathed Mark, all appeared fine until the next morning. As Daddy wet Mark's hair for Sunday School, bubbles started to rise, and he was subjected to a second rinsing.

Melissa, the middle member of The Trio, will be nine in a few days. In September, she fell from a rock to our cement patio, breaking her left leg. With the exception of swimming lessons and cross-country runs, she has maintained her regular activities these past two months, with characteristic cheerfulness and a hippity-hop. She, Margaret and Melody spend hours turning the upstairs into Fisher-Price Village, a suburb of Lego City downstairs. The Three play restaurant, arranging "meals" of bits and pieces of toys and scraps of cloth or paper, if something more palatable cannot be wheedled from the kitchen. Melissa's handprinted menus for Dad's Place ("Food—Yum!") detail such delicacies as "toast (any topping)," "ginger-ail" and "cold slough."

As I write this (December 3), **Melody**'s seventh birthday is just two days away. In company with her brother and sisters, she prefers reading to sleeping and has shared many books with Mark and me. Melody's loss of teeth threatens the Tooth Fairy with destitution; her rapid growth leaves behind a wardrobe of little-girl clothing that, Mommy reminisces nostalgically, has served (at least) four little girls well. Melody and Melissa are co-hostesses in the bedroom for the holiday camp-ins, when sheets, held down by many books, are strung from bed to dresser to floor to make tents. The addition of sleeping bags, pillows, blankets, flashlights, snacks, reading materials and two or three participants from neighbouring rooms, and the subtraction of too much parental interference, make festive occasions of discretionary days and some Saturdays.

Mark is enthusiasm incarnate. Shopping with Daddy is *"great"*; his new ("previously-owned") overalls are *"super"* ("See, there's pockets in the back and I can do the buttons myself"); his fleet of tiny cars is *"fantastic"*; his chocolate pudding is *"excellent"*; *Sesame Street*'s Pinocchio is *"far out."* I understand he is supposed to harbour negative feelings about me, but so far he has kept them well-concealed. In fact, he often tells Mommy and Daddy to "Come and look at Matthew in his crib. Isn't he bee-*yoo*-ti-ful?" (Needless to say, our parents always agree.) Each school morning, Daddy delivers Marilyn to her school and

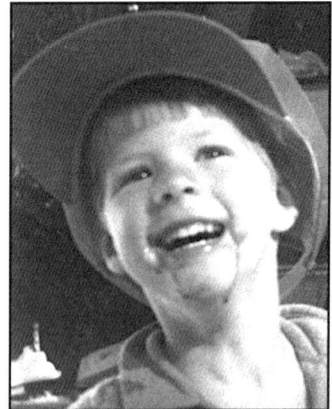

EVIDENCE OF CHOCOLATE ICE CREAM

then returns for the remaining four. Usually, however, five straggle into the car, the fifth and smallest carrying an ice cream pail full of treasures and his cheese-and-crackers "recess treat," bursting with excitement at the prospect of a trip to school.

Each Saturday morning at 8:45 a.m., Mark bounds up to the music room, violin case in hand, hair parted and slicked back in honour of the occasion, to greet his violin teacher, Frona Colquhoun, who faces four hours of dedicated, painstaking work with our family. Last spring, he and Mommy worked on a two-note harmony part for "May Song." The older five, as a group, played six pieces in the Festival, including "May Song," in addition to numerous piano and violin solos and duets. Mark's pudgy three-and-a-half-year-old fingers captured his two notes at approximately the right times; I suspect the fact he was overpowered by two full-size, one 3/4-size, one 1/2-size, and one 1/4-size, violins—his is 1/16-size—was fortuitous. The adjudicator designated him "family mascot" and wrote "Bravo!" on the children's adjudication. (Mommy hauls out the paper and rereads it whenever she gets discouraged by the early-morning foot dragging.)

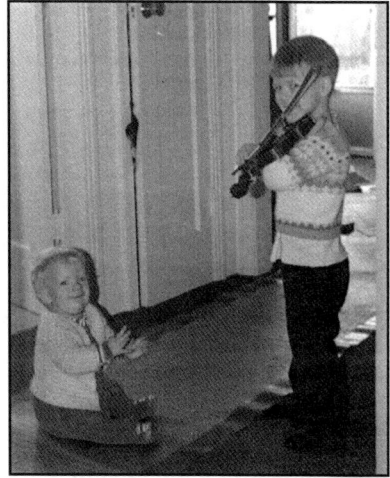

AN APPRECIATIVE AUDIENCE

Mark knows that parents often have a dampening effect on a child's wishes, so he has learned to preface most requests with "Say 'yes,' Mom." More than once our mother has been brought up short by something she has, absentmindedly, agreed to. Mark's evaluation of a summer salad was, I fear, shared by other junior members in the family: "I like it all, except for the awfulcado." He sometimes watches *Little Prairie on the House.* Recently Mommy observed him line up two rows of "people" and then march a bride doll down the aisle between, accompanying the whole procedure with a boisterous "Here comes the prize." (Daddy was out, and Mommy wasn't about to disillusion him!)

As the family baby, I have no responsibilities beyond assembling an interminable Christmas letter. In spite of the attention lavished on me, I must confess I am not too adept at anything besides charming my family. My musical career didn't get off the carpet when Marilyn found me lying under the piano, strumming a full-size violin with a vibraharp mallet. I have a two-word vocabulary ("Mommmmm" and "Daaadd"). My stagger has evolved into an efficient walk-run that propels me from one scene of devastation to the next. (My parents cannot figure out where the "pitter patter of little feet" originated;

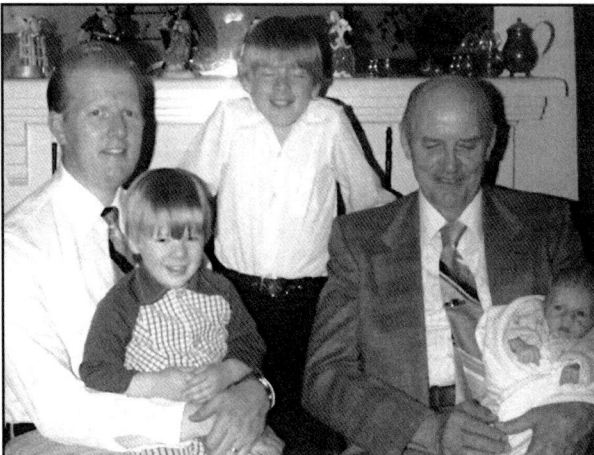

THE HOLLAND MEN: BRUCE, MARK, MICHAEL, NORMAN, MATTHEW (1980)

certainly not at our house, where thumps, bumps and crashes are more typical, especially when the parents are downstairs and the children upstairs.)

Life here does not always move along smoothly (according to Daddy, the understatement of understatements), but I think my family is quite happy most of the time. Our graces always include thanks to God for the many good things He has given us. However, we were all greatly saddened when our beloved Grandpa Norman Holland was taken from us suddenly on October 25. Although we believe such a separation is temporary, it is very hard to realize that we will not have his lap to perch on, nor hear his encouraging voice again during our lifetimes. We are surrounded by many reminders of his love for us: a bathroom vanity he made Mommy and Daddy for Christmas several years ago, secretly, in his workshop, after taking measurements to be sure it would fit in its awkward space in the downstairs bathroom; our much-used playhouse, made out of scrap lumber left over when we tripled the size of our tiny house ten years ago (he oversaw much of that construction, too); carvings and handmade furniture; many small and large repair jobs around the house; and most recent, the beautiful electric train set for which he constructed a plywood base, and meticulously painted in roads, a lake, etc. Grandpa pretended he didn't notice our less-than-perfect behaviour; Grandma says he thought we were a "fine bunch" and was very pleased that one of us has his name. We were fortunate to have had Grandpa while we did, and we will miss him very much.

Love, **Matthew Norman**

P. S. Here are some stories you might enjoy:

GRANDPA NORMAN HOLLAND

April 18 Marilyn and Margaret return from London Drugs; wrap and present parents with Easter gifts from family: gum for Mom, gum for Dad, chocolate cookies for both. Parents try to ignore voices in background. (Marilyn: "You still owe me 97 cents." Margaret: "The card was 60 cents. I couldn't find a 30-cent one.") Melody tiptoes away. Rustling of paper and rip of scotch tape are followed by presentation to Mommy: small book (*Noah's Ark*) and her own tiny notebook, received as a prize at Christmas, inscribed, "Mother can keep this for all April and 2 days in May. By Melody."

June 2 Four piano exams are scheduled: 10:45 a.m. (Melissa, Grade II); 11:17 a.m. (Margaret, Grade IV); 11:41 a.m. (Michael, Grade VI); 12:12 p.m. (Marilyn, Grade VIII). Marilyn is writing a special math exam until mid-morning; Father takes other three downtown to examination centre. ... Grade II and IV exams are completed. Father is to return girls to school, then pick up Marilyn; suddenly realizes that 11:41 a.m. candidate has evaporated. Frantic trip to nearby Radio Shack produces wayward student, who is accompanied wordlessly to examination room. … Eldest child enters hall at 12:10 p.m. Fortunately, examiner is running a little behind. Also fortunately, Mother is unaware of near-disaster (at school accompanying choir); blanches when informed of incident. … **Mid-July** Marks are received in mail—quite acceptable. Second child *[Michael]* tops family scores. Mother bites tongue.

June 26 Father is at camp. Mother, set to drive self and offspring to church in 12-passenger van, hoists herself into seat, buckles up, checks to see that seven other buckles confine her passengers; glances in mirror and is unnerved by septet of tense little faces peering back at her. Uneasy tension is broken by Melissa's reassuring message to her companions: "Just pretend everything's normal." (Eldest child's loyalty also suspect, after safe arrival home: "I just pretended Daddy was driving.")

November 7 Father and son are washing cars on the driveway. Strange figure appears from Lakeview Avenue across Saanich Road: long, heavy navy-blue coat, preceded by huge toy dog, and accompanied by other parcels. Margaret is returning from a bazaar up the street. Still clutching the remains of her $1.50, she proudly displays her purchases: the dog (25 cents); a plastic silver trophy cup for Daddy (one cent); three pairs of earrings for Mommy (five cents each); a plastic car for Mark (one cent); a stuffed rabbit for me (10 cents); a vest for herself (10 cents); a swimsuit for Melody (10 cents); comics (four at five cents each) and books (two at 10 cents each) for Marilyn, Michael and Melissa; and three cloth butterflies (25 cents), and two African violets (free) for the house.

Thursday, December 17, 6:15 p.m. Father takes children to (Lake Hill) School 45 minutes ahead of Christmas concert; mother is to come in second car just before concert starts (teaching until 6:15 p.m.). All is going well until it is time to leave. At 6:40 p.m., Mother is dressed in silky, red rose-patterned black dress, shiny red patent sling pumps, glittering earrings and black velvet jacket; it will take her less than 10 minutes to get to the school. Problem: Car keys have disappeared. She searches frantically through purse, checks music case, and other totally impossible areas of the house, but no key. Realizes she will have to make the 20-minute walk (10- to 15-minute run). Throws on a pair of old running shoes, slings shoes over fingers, rearranges case and purse in the other hand and starts marathon, with a light drizzle guaranteed to turn hairdo into a frizzy mess. Runs down Saanich towards Quadra. To immense relief sees neighbours (Padgetts) just about to turn on to Saanich from Eagle Rock on their way to the school; they take her in. Changes into dress shoes in car, runs into auditorium and slides on to piano bench, flushed, steam rising over head, just in time to hear principal say, "And now let us rise for 'O Canada.'" … Later, after arriving home, while looking for something else in purse, she discovers, resting in a side pocket of the purse, the elusive keys.

Chapter 21: Letters to My Parents, 1981

February 4, 1981

Dear Mom and Dad,

... I feel better (more energetic) than I have for a long time, and am so thankful that bronchitis is not in the picture. When I look back a year ago, I can't see how I managed. (Mind you, the discomfort was worth it. M7's a delight!) Mark is coming along very well on his "bliolin," and should be able to play a very simple harmony part with the others in the Festival. *[Mark was 3 in September 1980.]* It's a challenge to maximize his concentration span; you wouldn't believe some of the gymnastics (mental and otherwise) that I go through! Matthew is thinking about crawling (but not much) and continues to be placid and cooperative, except when we start up the stairs for bed, or when I lean over to put him into his playpen. Then he arches his back and starts complaining. And he's strong, so he becomes quite an armful.

February 7 ... (10 minutes before three hours of recitals, and 20 minutes after five hours of violin lessons) Matthew is learning to crawl; it's really sweet how he lurches forward and sideways and he's so pleased with himself. He sure doesn't lack for attention. Must go. Students arriving.

February 23 ... It's a sunny spring day up here—a bit cool, but lovely and bright. The snowdrops are nearly over, but are rapidly being replaced by daffodils and crocuses. And it's a draggy Monday morning (i.e., I'm dragging), but everything is going well. ... Marilyn [13] is becoming more away-from-home-ish (?) than ever, visiting one friend for a birthday supper, babysitting (7:30 p.m. to midnight Friday), and sleeping overnight at another friend's. She is allowed these privileges as long as homework and practising are up to date. It's amusing at times to see what efforts she is willing to go to, to ensure that all her commitments are met. No complaints from her parents, though. She was baptized on the 8th, entirely of her own volition.

Michael is coming along well at everything (except for the odd interpersonal relationship which I won't elaborate on.) *[Being surrounded by four relatively compliant sisters must have been a trial for Michael at times!]* His teacher gives him A for his notebooks (he periodically checks through to see how neatly the students have their notes arranged), so Michael has become a real fusspot as far as his homework is concerned. Can't complain there, either. He's also become very helpful in loading the dishwasher and peeling vegetables, caring for Matthew (he just loves his little brothers), vacuuming, etc. And the nice thing is that much of the grumbling is disappearing, although the odd mumble indicates that sometimes there are other things he would rather spend his time on. Margaret has just completed a massive "research" project on Horses. She went to a birthday party on Saturday (there's a party for one of them almost every week; I'm getting to be an expert on assembling birthday presents), and won everything worth winning. She had gone off in a long yellow dress (Marilyn's, originally) and announced that she'd had fun playing Cops and Robbers; she'd worn an apron over the dress to keep it clean. Melissa and Melody have spent a lot of time with me practising, as almost everything they do needs supervision. All five are working up things for the Festival. Melody reads different readers to me in spare moments. She's doing well at school, the fifth to Mrs. Scoates's credit.

We had the teachers for tea on the 12th, and it was a lot of fun. (I just saw Tiger leap up after a moth in the sun above the wide-open crocuses—beautiful.) I don't know what the newer teachers think of such an activity, but the older ones accept the invitation each year very graciously. You probably know that there are several factors at work here. If you've read *Future Shock* (Toffler), you'll be aware of the rapid depersonalization of our society, and our tendency to take people and services for granted, and to regard people as expendable and interchangeable. The main reason for our "tea" is to express our gratitude to the teachers and to let them know that we value them as people, not just as a commodity. I only wish all children had the same opportunity; although our children are instructed not to talk about it at school, it is possible that others in the community are aware of it and may ascribe the wrong motives to it. (Melissa's teacher told me that the reason Margaret is in Mrs. Cochran's class is because when they were sorting out the classes last June, she said she wanted a Holland child because she had never been to a Holland tea! Needless to say, this was not repeated in the children's hearing. Margaret is very happy with Mrs. Cochran, too.)

… Bruce has just asked me if I will make lunch. He has business to attend to. (Imagine that!) He is, of course, as dear as ever. He's just going off [call], after a hectic two weeks.

… My little boys are such good company. Mark chatters and plays away and tries to keep Matthew entertained. Matthew crawls (lurches) all over the place, and clicks and clucks in imitation of anyone foolish enough to do it, too. They're real sweethearts.

March 17 … Things are very busy here. Exams and Festival cast a shadow (and quite a bit of motivation) over everything. Last Thursday we pulled the children out of school and took them to Vancouver to see an outstanding display of old instruments gathered from museums all over the world (a once-in-a-lifetime opportunity). We rented a tape to hear a narration of several exhibits, along with a sample of the sound produced by 25 instruments. (There were hundreds in the display.) The Bottens [older neighbours; Mr. Botten played cello in the symphony] came with us, leaving at 6:30 a.m. and returning at 9:30 p.m.; they're amazingly resilient! Saturday night Bruce and I went to an Alumni (Royal Conservatory of Music of Toronto) party and left Ms 1 and 2 as babysitters. I phoned home at 9:30 p.m. to find M1 asleep (also Ms 3 to 6), M2 awake, and M7 crying. Michael made him some milk, and we got home at 11:30 p.m. to find Michael playing with, and enjoying, Matthew. Matthew is just a darling. He stayed two nights (Wednesday and Thursday) at Bruce's parents' place, and apparently more than met their expectations.

... Margaret responded to her teacher's challenge to dress up for St. Patrick's Day. She went off with curly hair tied with 8 green ribbons and decorated with two green barrettes. Green shoes, socks, pants, and T-shirt completed the outfit. She had me put green (eyeshadow) rouge on her cheeks as well as green freckles. The idea was to see who could wear the most green.

March 18 ... Melissa's teacher (choir leader) said she enjoyed Melissa's summary of our excursion to Vancouver: "Lunch at McDonald's and supper at Denny's"! I assured her we had done more than that.

Margaret brought home an enormous cardboard ribbon with "1st", "Dynamite!", "Terrific!", "Amazing!", "Wonderful!" printed on it. Apparently she was the "greenest" student yesterday. (Melody was, the day before: she threw up all over her desk, books, and self after lunch and had to be brought home. Mark threw up while he was sleeping with me yesterday afternoon; fortunately just the bedspread and I got it. Both of them came back to normal very quickly. Mark downed a small chocolate bar and a piece of apple after supper!)

... We've been watching a sparrow empty the birdhouse outside the kitchen window of feathers, string, hair, etc. She's made innumerable trips to a nearby branch, where she drops her garbage into the breeze. I guess she wants the nest to be her own. I wonder if she'll pick up some of what she has discarded!

Chapter 22: 1982

"'Tis the season" … to rake oak leaves and clean out eaves troughs; to put in an order for Grandma Holland's delicious mincemeat; to polish up last year's carols and add a new arrangement to the repertoire; to try to coordinate gift lists with finances and time for making and shopping; but mostly, to pause in gratitude to God for His Gift of our Saviour: "Thanks be to God for His incomparable Gift."

My family and I (Matthew) send to you our warmest greetings for a blessed Christmas and an optimistic New Year. In case you are confused as to who's who at our house (even our parents occasionally lose track), I'll remind you: Marilyn [nearly 15] and Michael [13] are our teenagers; Margaret [11], Melissa [nearly 10] and Melody [8] form The Trio, and Mark [5] and I (Matthew [2 1/2]) are the inseparable playmates who round out (finish off?) the family.

Michael (Grade 8) joined **Marilyn** (Grade 10) at Pacific Christian this year and appears to be thriving on the challenges of high school. The highlight of his year was a seven-day bike hike through the San Juan Islands in July with twenty other thirteen

TWO BUDDIES

to fifteen year olds. Although our parents (one in particular) were a little apprehensive to see him go, they were delighted to have him return hale, hearty and several shades darker. Michael is an avid AIA and Vikings (basketball) and Canucks (hockey) fan. The prospect of an outing to the university to a basketball game, or of watching a Canucks game on TV, often provides the motivation for conscientious (if disgruntled) efforts on piano and violin. (I suspect, however, that he enjoys playing his Bach Concerto along with the taped orchestration as much as we enjoy listening to it.) The highlight of Marilyn's year may have been the Youth Camp at the end of the summer, or it may have been the Young Peoples' graduation banquet in June, when she was the blushing recipient of a fragrant yellow rose corsage. (I could elaborate on this topic, but Mommy says I probably have said too much already.)

Margaret's interests extend from basketball and swimming through music to art. Her affectionate, non-conforming style continues to embellish family life; she has a fund of original ideas from which her younger sisters all too willingly draw. **Melissa** quietly accumulates her thoughts on paper. Her special birthday gift to Mommy was a "novel" (à la Nancy Drew), "The Wedding Bell Mystery." **Melody** is the chief clothes-folder-and-distributor at present, but even she can't account for the strange pair of socks that ended up in Mommy's drawer (one mine, the other Mommy's). She is not very tall, so she stands on the chesterfield arm when she folds the sheets.

Mark and I have inherited the Fisher-Price and Lego villages (although at times there are as many as six of us working together on projects), while The Trio's interests have turned to setting up house, with elaborate (cardboard box) ovens in two bedrooms, beside which are located rows of empty spice containers, cereal and shortening boxes, small bottles, etc. The dolls and teddies who reside here have been recruited to form an instant family for each junior mother. The attic was raided for small clothes. Daddy was shaken a couple of months ago to see Mommy folding tiny baby outfits; his colour returned when Mommy assured him the girls were dressing *their* children. One day, our parents discovered The Trio returning from a friend's house across the road, half-carrying and half-dragging a playpen, a doll's crib, several bags of doll's clothing and associated paraphernalia, and dolls of all sizes, shapes and states of dress. As well as these maternal activities, the girls set up store in the music room, with labels and price tags on stock garnered from every corner of the house, and even ask their teachers for extra worksheets to "play school." I will not bore you with a description of the effect these activities have on the orderliness of our home. (No doubt our faithful, loving friend, Ellen, who contributes to our parents' sanity by helping clean house twice a week, could add a few choice thoughts on this subject.)

Since September, Mark has propelled himself into the Kindergarten room each school afternoon, carrying at least one Show and Tell object and flowers (if our mother has been persuaded to arrange some), and perhaps even some fruit or vegetables for a class snack. He offers a running commentary on life around him: "The tea bottle is burning"; "It's a good thing we have lots of butterflies or else we wouldn't have any butter." He again joined the family in a couple of violin pieces at the Music Festival in May, and bounces through Mommy's rhythm class and a beginning piano class; his current favourite is "Oats, Peas, Beans and Barbecue." Dr. Suzuki would probably cock an eyebrow at his announcing of a recital solo last spring: "I am going to play 'Wrinkly Stars.'" He may not have grasped the implication when he requested we sing, "Praise Him, praise Him, all ye naughty children." Our eldest sister supervises his piano practice (as well as helping Mommy with two classes of young piano students), and is hard put to match his enthusiasm. (Mother thinks back ten years: three small children, a fourth imminent, the four year old learning CDE and CBA on the piano.) Our mother, who is second-in-command in the kitchen during the school year, decided a small talk was in order after hearing Mark's comment as he rolled out cookie dough: "Daddies do it; ladies don't."

The child development books say that I am at the age where routine and proximity to Mother are major considerations. In perusing Mommy's calendar-diary recently, I came across an entry that suggests she doesn't always appreciate my desire for closeness: "M7 <u>underfoot</u>" (underlining hers). For months, Mommy and Mark practised the violin in the bathroom while I sat, listening, on the counter. Even now, I am given a perch on top of the big piano when the others practise as a group. The interesting goings-on at such times—the apparent harmony in performance is, alas, not always indicative of what has occurred during practice sessions—and acrophobia keep me obediently positioned out of harm's way. The kitchen high stool allows me to get very close to the suds when someone is washing dishes, and, after dragging it into the laundry room, I can reach into the washer and hand Mommy the wet clothes. I have been known to fill the dishwasher with toy cars and to join my siblings in the bathtub, freshly bathed and dressed for bed. I am doing my best to make the transition away from flannelette rectangles as gradual as possible, as I understand it may be traumatic for Mommy to give up a fifteen-year habit.

Several times in the past year, it has been our family's privilege to share programmes of violin and piano music, both in our home and in a variety of other settings. My sisters and brothers were asked to play in the Festival Highlights concert at the McPherson Playhouse on May 11. Aside from the threat of being swallowed up in the billowing curtains, this was an exciting event. Daddy held me in the wings, and we waited for Mark to return to us after his contribution to the ensemble. [*Reference to family by MC of concert, before giving out awards to more conventional performances: "... those beautiful blonds with their violins, and they were superb."*]

During the summer, we had several extra-special guests to family recitals: Daddy's Grade One teacher, Blanche Hagerman, who still has lists of most of her classes from the 1930s on (Daddy's name was listed among more than forty in her 1942 class at Cloverdale); a teacher who went to high school with both of my grandmothers and taught with Mommy sixteen years ago at Quadra School, Kay Horner; and Mommy's junior high school music and art teacher of twenty-seven and twenty-eight years ago, Larry Miller. [*Larry passed away in April of 2006, in his 90s. I am indebted to him for his encouragement; I still have the accompanist's copy of the music textbook the high school choir used in the Music Festival the year I was in Grade 8, as well as a tiny set of salt and pepper shakers in the shape of a treasure chest and map. He, as our English teacher as well, had taken us through Treasure Island and this was a gift to me for*] *accompanying the choir. Twenty years ago, he gave us his old violin which has been used by several of our children. And he used to enjoy reading our Christmas letters.]*

Miss Hagerman, who taught with Mommy at Cloverdale School twenty years ago, now in her 80s, resides in the Gorge Hospital. In spite of the arthritic discomfort involved, she insisted, to our delight, in accepting our invitation. She, in turn, invited us to present the same programme at the Hospital. This was one of our more interesting recitals. Daddy dropped us off at 7:00 p.m.: seven children, one mother, one high chair and an assortment of noiseless toys (for babysitting purposes), nine violins (including three extras; this was the scene of a snapped tail gut two-and-a-half years earlier), one bulging music case, and one heavy metal music stand. Daddy's call kept him away until 9:45 p.m. In the interim, the children and Mommy were occupied with their music for well over an hour. Miss Hagerman supervised me, and I entertained both of us by dropping peppermints down her front. Following refreshments and visiting, Margaret pushed Miss Hagerman in her wheelchair into the elevator. The eight of us, plus the trappings listed above, accompanied our hostess back to her room. Hospital personnel tried to ignore the jumble of equipment spread across the glassy floor, as well as the multitude of small and larger blonds who kept appearing in doorways and from behind pillars. And we have been invited back to present a Christmas programme on December 17.

There are, however, some low points in our music endeavours, the most consistent being the 6:30 a.m. "Time to get up, gang," and parents who don't seem to understand that practising is not high on their offsprings' lists of priorities. Even so, the Music Festival and examinations are tackled each year and give evidence that at least some progress is being made. Michael, Margaret and Melissa passed Grades VII, V and III piano exams with respectable standings. (Michael's 85, near the top for Victoria, was more respectable than even he had dared hope, when viewed in the light of preparation efforts.)

A kaleidoscope? A circus (multi-ring)? A merry-go-round? Our parents have not decided which best describes their circumstances, as elements of each colour the day's events. Our father's actions are dictated largely by the telephone and pager during his "on-call" hours, and by our family's needs and wants during his time "off-call." His quiet, authoritative presence helps "keep the lid" on potential boil-overs. Our mother continues to be blessed with our dad's practical and moral support, an almost-overwhelming number of requests for teaching, and a great joy (and sporadic frustrations) in sharing our lives. A poorly-coordinated involvement with a refractory geranium and a very sharp butcher knife resulted at the end of June in the near-severing of .75 cm of thumb, a throbbing trip to the Jubilee's Emergency Ward, and a more permanent appreciation of the value of healthy fingers and the necessity for care and safety.

When the kaleidoscope begins to blur, or the circus threatens to escalate into pandemonium, or the merry-go-round moves from the usual Allegro to Presto or even Prestissimo—I referred to Margaret's theory papers; Mommy says I chose appropriately—our parents remind themselves of the great privilege they have in being entrusted with such "dear, sweet" children (a cheerful elderly friend's description). Daddy ponders on the scriptural reference to the "olive plants round about thy table" (Psalm 128; Psalm 127 also puts in a very good word for us), and is mollified. Mommy re-appraises her "fruitful vine" status and reminds Daddy that she isn't looking forward to the interlude between children and grandchildren. (Daddy flinches.)

My mother's parents have spent several winters trailering in Arizona. Mommy and Daddy have decided to give us the experience of a desert Christmas, so we are planning to leave on December 20 in our van and drive through Washington, Oregon, and California to Arizona. Our grandparents have suggested a visit to Disneyland, and, characteristically, have offered us the use of their trailer for our stay. We children are tingling with anticipation. Our parents' demeanour is somewhat more subdued; perhaps the prospect of 3,000 miles of togetherness is a factor!

Love from **Matthew**

P.S. Here are some little stories for you:

OFF ON A TRIP!

Sunday, June 6, 6:30 p.m. Eldest child asks permission to attend youth fireside at Willows Beach after service. Faces Grade VIII violin examination Monday morning. Mother, as accompanist and worrier-in-residence, makes strong recommendation that daughter observe a 10:30 p.m. curfew. **11:45 p.m.** Lateness of arrival home leads to negative comments from maternal parent. Daughter sheepish and non-communicative. (Mother later learns that moonlit hike around Swan Lake with three friends was added to agenda.) **Monday, June 7, 11:00 a.m., examination waiting room** Eldest child, Mother and teacher await summons to exam. Mother leaves room three times in next twenty minutes; daughter and teacher remain calm and collected. **Tuesday, October 19, 3:15 p.m.** Eldest child opens letter from Royal Conservatory of Music of Toronto: " ... the mark you received ... for Grade VIII Violin ... highest in the province. ... qualified for the Silver Medal Award." ... Grin illuminates entire house.

Sunday, September 5, 12:30 p.m. Family straggles in from carport, parents trying to decide on lunch menu. Mother opens back door, is confronted by eldest daughter just returned from fifteen days at camp. Discovery greeted by siblings' whoops of joy; sisters hug and kiss, small brothers attach themselves firmly to each leg; second eldest gives friendly thump on shoulder and admits he's glad she's back. **10:00 p.m.** Mother makes nightly patrol through upstairs bedrooms. Takes fifth child on drowsy trip to bathroom, trying to ensure Happy Face on calendar (child's idea; Mother tries to forget that kidney surgery may be slated for October). Pats and re-covers children of varying sizes and positions; thanks God for the immeasurable wealth snugly enclosed between seven pairs of sheets.

Tuesday, October 12, 9:00 a.m. Children (finally) all off to school, except for two little boys who are building a village in the family room. Mother remembers Mark has not done violin practising. Reminds second son, whose response is negative. Third son shouts, "Me! Me!" Extricates 1/16th-size violin from under piano, places it on living room table. Jumps up and down excitedly while Mother opens case. Grabs bow, chanting, "Up-down-up-down, roun' 'n' roun' 'n' roun'." Older brother halfheartedly shuffles in to watch proceedings. Mother tempers tiny boy's enthusiasm by gently uncurling long, spidery fingers from bow and replacing them in more orthodox position. Child's left arm placed across chest, violin tucked under chin; arm and bow guided across strings: "Matthew plays the A string, Matthew plays the E string." Violin tucked under right arm, bow dangling from right hand; feet placed together, and bow is made. Older brother delighted with feat; hugs and twirls novice around coffee table. Undertakes own practice session cheerfully. Follows instructions carefully, while little brother sprawls on carpet, directing cars and trucks around Mother's ankles.

Friday, October 29, 8:00 p.m. Fourth, fifth and sixth children put to bed. (Seventh has had three-hour sleep in afternoon, and, as is his habit, plans to spend the evening with his doting parents.) First child at youth group meeting. Second and third children reading in bed. Father out on call. Mother typing downstairs. **10:30 p.m.** Explosion upstairs. Mother takes stairs at speed that could have placed her in Intensive Care. Sixth child balanced on toy chest at end of first and third child's bunk, glass shards glinting on upper bunk, floor, and through scalp of small delinquent. Blood streaming from two superficial wounds. Overhead light fixture minus glass shade. Forlorn victim sobbing, "I'm in big trouble. I'm in BI-IG trouble." Chalks up sixth visit to Emergency.

Chapter 23: Letters to My Parents, 1982

January 31, 1982
Dear Mom and Dad,

... For the first time in several months, I'm home on a Sunday evening. I've got the kids to sleep by 9:00 p.m. (meant staying up on my bed reading and uttering fearsome pronouncements at regular intervals), and now have just my darling little boys to keep me company. They've both had a good afternoon nap and are raring to go. They play together so well; they're drawing pictures with felt pens. Matthew has managed to decorate both face and hands. Mark is very proud of his family portraits. He's such a sweetheart. Matthew comes and presses a typewriter key at one-minute intervals.

February 5 ... Michael chose the big Valentine's card. He came back from London Drugs with several other purchases and the card, and when I asked for the envelope, he said he hadn't got one, and that the sales clerk had suggested he needed one, too. He said he could get one at home!

My students had three recitals on Saturday (students-only), going from 3:30 to 7:00 p.m. They went very well, but after violin lessons from 8:45 a.m. to 3:00 p.m., I felt the day had come and gone very quickly. Everyone is well here.

Melody's [Kindergarten] assembly (all 17 minutes of it) was really sweet. Bruce's mom came and Melody made a big fuss over her five guests (Mark and Matthew, too).

Chapter 24: A Christmas Digest, 1983

EDITORIAL *by Louise*

It is no doubt part of the "Middle-Aged-and-How-Did-We-Get-Here-So-Fast" Syndrome, but it seems a very short time ago that we were assembling 1982's annual imposition. It is not until we scan the three calendars we allow to intimidate us, or pore over the exercise books, or glance at the pile of recital programmes that we realize how full and happy the past 365 days have been.

Although each person in the family has his or her own activities and projects, it is the family outings which we as parents particularly value. We not only thank God each day for each other and the seven others, but we are grateful to Him for the opportunities for serving through social work and music and for the good times we have together. (And we probably learn even more from the not-so-good times!) As well as presenting programmes at several places on Vancouver Island and in Vancouver, and spending nearly three weeks on the road to and from, and in, California and Arizona last Christmas, we had the privilege of living in a friend's condominium at Mount Washington's ski resort for a week in August. Surrounded by snowcapped mountains, alpine meadows and flowers, we were forced by the isolation (no radio, no TV, no telephone—wonderful!) to rely on each other and a certain amount of ingenuity for entertainment. We left the mountain one day to replenish supplies in Courtenay. While there, we played our instruments for an old friend (100 in July, and still very spry), Mrs. Elizabeth Pickard.

We and our family especially appreciate the encouragement of acquaintances, friends, and family over the past year, and extend our very best wishes to you for a Happy Christmas and a peaceful New Year.

LIFE'S SOMETIMES LIKE THIS

Sunday, January 9, 11:20 a.m. After referring to church bulletin, Mother opens hymnal on organ to hymn 317. Pastor announces number. Mother gives resounding introduction to hymn on right page. Baffling silence replaces usual 500-voice response. Pastor turns and asks quietly, "317?" 317 on *left* page. Glowing blush evident to back row of balcony.

Tuesday, May 31, 2:00 a.m. Mother's dream crumbles into chaos, forces her to a drowsy consciousness; aware of quiet sobbing in room next door. Upon inquiring, learns that fourth child has headache. As Father is on call and sleeping downstairs, Mother suggests child join her for rest of night. Child ready to crawl into bed when Mother asks where head hurts. Child says at back, and adds casually that she fell out of upper bunk, catching wooden toy box on way down. Mother turns on light, is distressed to find waist-length platinum rapidly turning strawberry blonde. Does not dare explore source of colouring, but races downstairs to waken Father, who helps rinse off wound. Trip to new Helmcken Emergency ward nets several stitches.

Wednesday, July 13, early morning News filters through household: carnival in afternoon! Parents are occupied with own pursuits, not overly interested in outside activities. **2:00 p.m.** Slight drizzle has dampened "booths" but not excitement of organizers (Ms 4 to 7). Parents are coaxed outside, given four pennies each, one for each booth. Cannot help but be infected by children's enthusiasm. Melissa is at lemonade stand, ladling out dubious concoction. Melody dispenses kisses at second stand. Mark is at pebble throw: "Here's four pebbles, Mom. ... You can stand closer. It almost went in. Here, I'll put it in and you can get a prize." Matthew wanders between booths as Apron Man. In exchange for penny, lets parents choose prizes out of pockets; Mother is lucky recipient of Hot Wheels car, Father is overjoyed to win ping pong ball. Sudden deluge sends participants for cover. Parents excuse themselves and return to more mundane activities.

Friday, July 15 Mother squats beside youngest, who snuggles against her in apparent affection, breathing softly in right ear. Mother soon realizes tiny boy is engrossed, not in expressing devotion, but in trying to see through her eyeglasses: "Hey, guys, come wook in Mommy's gwasses!"

Monday, November 7 Father checking phone bill. Perplexed to see Washington, DC, call listed. Operator cheerfully responds to inquiry: "Someone at your house have a beef with the President of the U.S.? That number's the White House." Mother confronts eldest son with evidence, elicits shamefaced admission that he had experimented with the number given in a magazine. Mother comments that she hopes his bank account is in good shape and informs him that the cost is sixty-six .... cents.

PERSONAL GLIMPSES

Marilyn Almost 16 and very sweet (adjective contributed by maternal parent; may be deleted when proofread by daughter). Has not, however, evidenced much enthusiasm for car license. Prefers playing piano to washing dishes, playing violin to vacuuming. (Required to do all four.) Considers siblings 6 and 7 special gifts from parents: takes each in turn on bus and to the "big M." Finds sharing accommodation with creative whirlwind trying at times. Suggested to parents that claustrophobia could be reduced if additional bedrooms were added onto already-sprawling residence.

Michael   Shares small bedroom with little brothers; seconds older sister's suggestion re. barracks. In Grade 9 at school; into volleyball, basketball, computers, violin, piano. Achievements include Grade VIII Piano, evading the barber (see related article, "A Haircut", near end of letter), mending broken calculators and stereo components (desk probably the only one in town with a soldering iron as a permanent fixture). Regards two-year wait for car keys as interminable.

Margaret   In Grade 7; therefore, one of school "wheels" and developing appropriate assertiveness. Source of handcrafts and other artistic projects which continue to spill out of her half-bedroom. Enthusiastic volleyball and basketball player; working on life-saving badge in swimming. Practising towards Grade VI Violin exam in January, Grade VII Piano exam in June. Joins two younger sisters in dressing dolls in cast-off baby clothes. (Mother reminds eldest sister, who cannot refrain from disparaging comments, that, at the same age, *she* had *real* babies to play with.)

Melissa   Lives up to her "honeybee" name: industrious, bringing attitude of sunshine and flowers to family routines. Within two hours of school closing in June had "school" in session in music room; organized summer Drama Club (see "advertisement" at end of letter). Appears to have book growing at end of right arm; uses gaps in activities at social gatherings to pursue her reading. Writes primers for Mark's reading practice (sample title: "Jim the Cow"). Often up at 6:30 a.m. to practise, in order to free up after-school time; tried 6:00 a.m. once, was surprised parents did not show more approval.

Melody   Almost 9, in Grade 4. Has rigged up Jolly Jumper and baby mobile in bedroom, along with wardrobe of baby clothes for larger dolls; bassinet full of dolls impedes flow of traffic around end of bunk. Hopes fervently that Granny will make her a full-sized doll like the one Granny made for her church's pre-school. Along with senior members of The Trio (Margaret, Melissa), collects stickers, soaps and serviettes, with predictable effect on housekeeping. Offbeat sense of humour occasionally brings her to edge of reprimand; redeems herself with inspired prose: "Mothers are magnificint and marvalas. They are so nice and kind that you will not want to leave them."

Mark   Free spirit identifiable by unbuttoned coat/jacket/sweater, undershirt hanging out, knotted shoelaces and 110% interest in current activity. Grins with typical Grade One gap; amassing small fortune at Tooth Fairy's expense. (Top front teeth ended up parallel to roof of mouth a summer ago after confrontation with wooden horse at Beacon Hill Park; resulted in eight stitches on lip, four-tooth gap, and difficulties with apples and corn-on-the-cob.) Mother's change-purse also gradually emptying as "15 minutes on violin = one star; ten stars = one dime" formula conscientiously followed by junior opportunist. One 15-minute session often occurs during 45-minute lunch break; goal is eventually to buy lunch kit with earnings so he can stay at school for lunch.

Matthew At three and a half, everyone's pet. Soft, cuddly and demonstrative: "I wuv you *so* much." Mark's inseparable companion when Mark is at home; Daddy's shadow when Mark is at school. Earns sticker for each good violin practice session. Wants to do everything *himself*, including resining bow and putting on shoulder pad. Mother feigns tranquillity as fragile instrument receives well-meant but sometimes uncoordinated attention. Incarnation of summer *insouciance* last July: lolling in the sunshine in the buff, glistening from the sprinkler, calmly licking a popsicle. (Ed. note: but not for long.)

Bruce Guides and supports family endeavours. Drove 4,000 miles last Christmas in exhilarating company of eight closest relatives. Makes five to eight trips to schools most days (typical Wednesday morning: M1's piano lesson at 7:15 a.m.; M4 to Lake Hill's computer class at 8:00 a.m.; M1 and M2 to Pacific Christian for 8:30 a.m.; Ms 3, 5 and 6 to Lake Hill for 9:00 a.m.). Cooked meals and drove van for 10-day Banff-to-Jasper bike hike for 21 campers in July. Continues to enjoy challenge and variety of emergency calls; often tempted to bring home neglected children. Working on house addition plans with designer; wonders if major repairs on both halves of "Cadillac-in-two-parts" (i.e., two 1970 VW's) will allow second storey to materialize. Is putting Grandma Holland's gift (Bosch bread-maker) to good use, as loaves, buns, muffins and cookies spread out across the counter-tops.

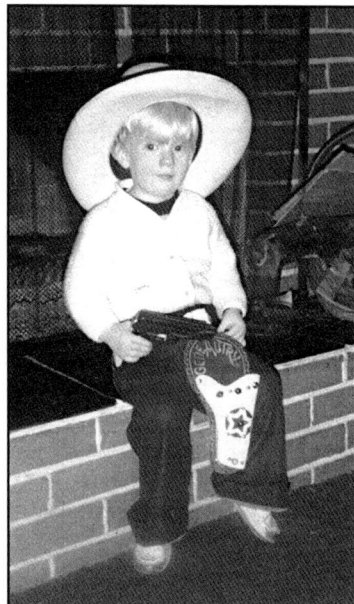

COWBOY MATTHEW

Louise Cannot quite figure out where day has flown. Organizing and teaching piano classes; supervising the progress of homegrown seven on violins (six of whom also chip away at the piano repertoire); arranging pieces and programmes for different groups; dealing with several loads of laundry each day; attempting to keep a step ahead of offspring (often satisfied if not farther than half-a-step behind) and trying to find time to "stand and stare," and count blessings, seem to fill each twenty-four hours to overflowing. Attends both "Mothers' Coffee Hour" (for mothers of young children) and "Second Cup" (for mothers of teenagers) at church; reassured to learn that family idiosyncrasies are "normal." Cannot believe that fifteen years of diapers and seven babyhoods are behind her. Finally disposed of most baby things, many only as far as southwestern and northeastern bedrooms.

FAMILY STORIES

"A Different Christmas" *by Melissa*, Grade 6:

Last Christmas we went to Arizona and California to have Christmas with Grandpa and Granny Forsberg, who usually leave Victoria for part of the winter. After three and a half days of driving through rain and snow, we arrived in Anaheim to find two pots of Granny's home-made soup bubbling on the trailer stove, as well as Grandpa's home baking and all kinds of fruit. We had turkey dinner in the sunshine at the trailer court and spent most of Christmas Day in Disneyland. We didn't want to leave, but we still wanted to go to Arizona. On our way to Arizona, we went to the San Diego Zoo and had an unsettling ride in the sky tram.

In Arizona, we stayed in a trailer park in our grandparents' trailer. We also stayed with our friends, the Howarths, at Sun Lakes, for two days, and played our instruments for the residents of this retirement centre. *[Family later learned that a gentleman from Sun Lakes commented it was worth his move to the centre just to hear "those children"—a highly motivating bouquet.]*

The huge farms of the Sacramento, San Joaquin and Imperial Valleys, which spread for miles in all directions, were very impressive, as were the orange, grapefruit and lemon groves, and the palm trees.

We went to an open market in Quartzsite, Arizona, where people (called tailgaters) sold odds and ends on the tailgates of their trucks. We went to the old prison in Yuma.

One of our favourite times was when we lay on the four large Motel 6 beds (two units side-by-side, with an open door between) and watched funny old movies on the two TVs, stuffing ourselves with taco chips and popcorn, while the rain poured outside. By the time we got back to Seattle, Matthew was an expert on recognizing the signs for McDonald's, Denny's, Shell Oil, and Motel 6.

It was a lot of fun going down south for Christmas, but we were very glad once again to see our 4031 sign hanging from the oak tree.

From Melody's tattletale diary written at school:

In the Easter holiday, my family and I went to Vancouver. We were supposed to catch the seven o'clock ferry, but my big brother got up about six o'clock so we missed it. At the ferry terminal you should have seen my mom's face when she found that we missed it. My mom said, "We have to be at a concert at ten o'clock." All of a sudden a voice came in the booth saying, "Don't let them on. They have a vent." So we got on the 8:00 ferry. We played our violins and went to the Harrises' house. It was fun. We got to bed at 11:00! In the morning we went to Stanley Park. We fed the squirrels. It was fun. Then we went to the ferry. My mom had to be home because she had piano lessons to teach. But another miss and another awful face. Well, *I* had a good trip!

"A Haircut" *by Michael*, Grade 8 [*taken from a journal written at school*]:

Aaagh! I got a haircut! What a traumatic experience! It was really scary. First you're led from the car. If you falter, you're a dead man. Then you walk along a long hallway, your footsteps echoing with every step. Every nerve screams, "RUN!" But you're frozen. You can't move. You keep walking, mechanically. Then you see the executioner, grinning evilly. The light glints off a pair of razor-sharp scissors. You're forced into a chair at gunpoint. The executioner goes to work. All guns are trained on you in case you make a break for freedom. But you are proud. You do not say a word, or even wince when he cuts your hair off in masses. Then you see yourself in the mirror. You're bald! You scream in horror and slump to the ground, unconscious. When you come around, you're in a dark alley, listening to the screams of another tortured person. You gather up your strength and limp home.

Letter from Melody [received at home four days into camp session; designed to allay parental fears]:

"I've been having a great time at camp. … Today a girl in my cabin almost drowned when she was doing her swimming test. Meals are going great, too. Well, that's all I can say, so goodbye. Love, Melody"

SEEN …

… A picture made by Matthew in Sunday School: "God made my family," with nine Cheerios for the respective family members; a large poster of the family's feet, pasted together by Mark at school; another one with enough paper dolls to represent everyone; and yet another with catalogue figures peering out of the windows of a bus (our apologies to the teachers involved for the extra work)

… Mother's birthday card: "If kids could choose their mothers, a mother as nice as you … Would have so many children she wouldn't know what to do." (Mother smiles at appropriateness of latter half.)

… A blue ribbon for Father on which is printed: "Father is **F**antastic, **A**ctive, **T**errific, **H**andy, **E**xcellent, **R**ich."

… A "note" (2 1/2' x 12') given to Mother by school's Junior Choir: 102 unique self-portraits or pictures with a musical motif, thanking her for accompanying the choir.

... AND HEARD

... Matthew, whose Rs and Ls end up as Ws, after an electrical failure: "That weally fweaked me out." (Often waves to next-door neighbour, "Wiz.")

... Second child to touch dishwasher in (against-the-rules) lunchtime or after-school dash: "First—worst; second—best."

... Mark, playing with Matthew: "I'm Garfield, and he's Odor."

... Matthew's comments when asked to draw "the Baby Jesus in a manger": "This is God in a Baby"; "Does God ever wear a hat? Sometimes?"

Advertisement

Chapter 25: A Christmas Digest, 1984

EDITORIAL *by Louise*

It is a wet, windy November evening. Father is on a call, Children 1 to 4 are, respectively, at church (Young Peoples' coordinator), at UVic (volleyball: linesman), in Abbotsford (midget girls volleyball tournament: player), and at UVic (spectator); a request for babysitting has had to be turned away. Children 5 to 7 are at my elbow. Child 5 officiously dictates 40-word November spelling list to Child 6, who earnestly blackens scrap of paper with letters. Child 7 watches procedure, trying to keep track of position of words on master list. The fire sputters amiably and I decide to take stock of the countless blessings which have been strewn across my family's path this year. A favourite hymn runs through my mind: "Great is Thy faithfulness! Great is Thy faithfulness! Morning by morning new mercies I see. All I have needed Thy hand hath provided—Great is Thy faithfulness, Lord, unto me!"

A year ago, we capitulated to the musty attic-ogre who subsisted on the leaks from the attic ceiling; a new roof became a necessity. This, combined with crescendoing complaints from at least two family members, one who shared a bedroom with a creative cyclone, the other who stepped over his little brothers' sleeping forms to crawl up into his bunk, initiated a 1,200-square foot, four-month building project that has given us, in total, seven bedrooms, two bathrooms, a kitchen/living room, and two small storage rooms across the second storey. Echoing the principle that "Work expands to fill the time available for its completion," the paraphernalia associated with each inhabitant has also expanded to fill each room to a cozy clutter.

The addition is perhaps our largest tangible blessing. However, we do not take for granted the privileges of good health, rewarding occupations, opportunities for service, and a warm, if chaotic, family life. We hope the following pages allow you to share in our joy. We extend to you our love and greetings of the season.

SCENE IN PASSING ...

... Matthew, helping to wash the cars, collapsing backwards into a full bucket of soapy water (very embarrassed) ... three night-gowned sprites playing tetherball in the moonlight at 4:30 a.m. on a warm summer morning, after helping Father load up for his ten days of camp cooking … a permanently-extended dining table, able to accommodate eleven or more … Mark, tears on both cheeks, riding high in the cab of a garbage truck after the garbage men took pity on the six year old waiting in vain to be taken home for lunch. (Three sisters had taken violin exams in the morning and returned home for lunch. The family suddenly realized at 12:30 p.m. that a member was missing.) From Mark's journal the next day: "I got left at school and my dady forgot me at school and the garbman saed would you luik too com with me in the garb troc war do you live 4031 sanich rod." … a worker from the church toddler department rushing across the parking lot, small towhead in arms, trying to catch large blue van turning on to Pandora Avenue … Mother, landing on what should have been a resounding opening chord for "O Canada" at school assembly, baffled at mild sound emitted by piano (Matthew, sitting on the bench beside her, had figured that if Yamaha piano at home and Yamaha piano at school had same label, perhaps they also had same mute pedal; they did.) … an entry in Michael's Grade 2 diary (uncovered when the attic was emptied) which attests to the power of peer pressure: "Kevin changed my mind that the best thing on my birthday was a water pistol instead of a game of chess." …

PERSONAL GLIMPSES

Our family has grown to include Tim, the fine young man who has found shelter in the new suite upstairs; beautiful Lisa [5] and her equally beautiful and bouncier brother, Jonathan [2 1/2], who spend three days a week with us (satisfying Mother's craving for the pitter-patter of *little* feet and providing play-mates for Matthew), and Greg [7] and David [5] whom Melissa oversees once or twice a week (and who form a happy quartet with Mark and Matthew). We will, however, subject only those who share a common surname to closer scrutiny. (The writer of Personal Glimpses has considered putting the spotlight on still another young man who has developed an affinity for a blonde accompanist—a mutual affinity, it would appear—but has decided that at least some discretion is in order.)

Marilyn [nearly 17] in Grade 12, is working at the Grade X level in piano, trying to assimilate enough music history to pass an upcoming exam, taking occasional lessons from the Symphony's first violinist, and helping coordinate the Young Peoples' activities. She greatly enjoys the company of her tall, dark and handsome friend (whose outer attributes are more than matched by a fine sense of purpose and dedication to the Lord's work and a generous disposition that accommodates both his accompanist and her entourage). Marilyn spent August in Antigua (West Indies), helping construct a Youth for Christ building, distributing Bibles—it was Antigua's Year of the Bible—and playing piano and violin on radio and TV programmes, pedalling her bicycle all over the island, acquiring an impressive tan and developing a ravenous appetite. Her first breakfast at home consisted of six slices of toast; lunch was requested two hours later. Fortunately, this was a temporary aberration. Although she has not made the time to acquire a driver's license, she has expressed a wish for owning a Subaru "hunchback" some day (the terminology eliciting a hoot from her now-taller brother).

Michael [15] has brought a blessing (well-disguised at times) into the family in the form of a paper route. Dad refers to it as a course in the school of hard knocks; Mom, as a short course in psychology. Two alarms conspire to rouse the would-be businessman from an abbreviated night's sleep at 5:00 a.m., except for Friday, when mother and sister have the privilege of sharing each other's company and the night's offering of frost and/or rain and/or wind (and solitude; occasionally moonlight and stars; early-morning fragrances, including a tantalizing aroma drifting down from Bunsmaster; and breath-taking sunrises over Swan Lake). Michael, too, takes sporadic lessons with the patient concertmaster who coached him through his Grade IX Violin exam in June. Volleyball and soccer fill up any spare time; a keyboard synthesizer and access to four wheels (topped by vehicle) are, he hopes, part of his not-too-distant future.

Margaret [13] in Grade 8, has joined Marilyn and Michael at Pacific Christian. Her work on piano (Grade VIII) and violin (Grade VII) has been threatened by the increased demands of homework and volleyball, and a new school, but so far she seems to be coping. (A few days ago she received her report: an A+, six A's, and two B+'s. She must be coping.) Margaret continues to embellish family life with her artistic projects.

Melissa [almost 12] is fast becoming the family entrepreneur. After substituting for Michael with Mom on Fridays, she was given her own 60-paper route right in our neighbourhood. She often runs to school for 8:00 a.m. sports practices, and serves on traffic patrols, as kindergarten monitor, lunch monitor, and assembler of choir music. She usually fits in the required amount of practising on her instruments. Melissa doesn't get into too much trouble.

Melody [just turned 10] lives in the upper southeast corner with a large collection of teddies and dolls, including Martha, Granny's metre-tall gift to her. Over her bed, a 3-D needlework picture of a small blonde girl on a swing, braids flying, also from Granny, shares the sunlight that streams into her room. A

MARTHA, GRANNY'S GIFT TO MELODY

voiding cystogram during the summer indicated that her kidney problem (reflux in the ureters) seems to be abating, and surgery has been, barring infections, indefinitely postponed. Melody continues to be the chief-folder-and-distributor-of-clothes. She earns a small stipend each day for keeping the music room in order for Mother's teaching.

Mark, in Grade 2, follows in his sisters' path of communicating via notes, although his phonetic spelling can be a little jarring to the reader. A set of "Plans" surfaced a few days ago, the result of some boisterous activity involving Melody, Mark, Matthew and the two boys Melissa babysits: "1. Write a note, then attack. 2. Attack! 3. I will crall under the bed. You attack!" (Discretion is the better part of valour?) This is stapled to a second, perhaps alternate plan: "1. Spi on Melody when shes out. 2. Be carful! 3. Attack when Melody is out and when david is in," which bears the terse comment, "We better do it cwik." The more contemplative side of Mark's nature shines through the caption on a recent Christmas picture: "I love you god! I love everyone god But I love you the most." Mark is a sports fan (atic?) who can quote names of hockey players and scores as easily as his own name and address; the knees of several pairs of pants bear ragged testimony to his athletic endeavours. His Auntie Marilyn gave him a cherished set of key-ring plastic hockey cards. These he has attached to an interlocked set of garters pilfered from the old sewing machine drawer. (Mother doubts he, in the age of pantyhose, knows what a garter is!)

From Mark's Grade One Journal: "Our Adishin"
[Written at school and unedited; Grade One teacher was phonics enthusiast.]

MARK IS SIX

Early February: "We are getting a nwh adishin on er huws and I cant wate untel the nwh adishin is on."

February 17 (in a burst of unwarranted optimism): "Are huos is almost finisht."

February 29: "I wus clenen the adick … I am glad we are getting a new addison but we haf too pay a lot ov mune."

March 5 (more optimism): "The men are wrcing on the roof now and They are nerle thrwh now."

March 26: "I was clening the addishon but one of them sed now We can mes it up a gen."

April 12: "The men hav been nocing into my sisters room and the linen closet And they are

HOUSE AFTER ADDITION

almost finisht."

May 8: "They've don the painting already. Now all they really have to do is put in the care pet."

May 11: "They have put the lits in the new part and they work now except the Bathrom but the fan works and the headrs work."

May 27: "They've put the under laer carpet and the top laer of carpet."

May 30: "The ploumer put the singk and a toolet and it works to and things that he cut for the singk he gave to me."

June 8: "My bed is all redy made so is my brothers and after the painting it should be finished and we are going to be putting in the specers for the stereow."

MATTHEW

Matthew races toward Kindergarten at an alarming rate (September 1985). Long and spindly of frame, yet soft and cuddly, he continues to bring great happiness to his big sisters and brothers and to his parents. He is easygoing and cooperative and plays by the hour with Mark, when available, and with the other children who come to be cared for. He is, in spite of his special position in the family, required to empty wastebaskets, hang small cloths on the rack to dry, fold clothes, and run errands for the older members of the family. Mother recently told him that, contrary to his observation, kale leaves are not "weeds." Watching the builder planing a door during renovations, he described the process as "taking skin off" the wood.

Bruce fields a variety of calls each two-week shift. He is responsible for the whole Capital Region (Malahat, Gulf Islands, Port Renfrew, as well as Greater Victoria) when he is on duty, and must have the resources available to troubled people at his fingertips. To complement the sometimes-sad, sometimes-annoying aspects of his job, he spends much of his off-duty time keeping the household running smoothly. Chauffeuring offspring to school, lessons, and games is largely his responsibility, as is most meal preparation during Louise's teaching months. He, with the rest of the family, is enjoying the prospect of having Grandma Holland and Auntie Marilyn living only four blocks away.

Louise's activities range from the sublime (playing a five-part arrangement of "Jesu, Joy of Man's Desiring" with the five biggest violins) to the ridiculous (waiting recently for 95 minutes at the shack for the day's newspapers; at least the company—her first son—was good). The summer found her spading over garden plots and digging through several years' accumulation of compost, in an effort to make the backyard more productive. (A friend's comment, at the compost heap: "My, such *delicate* work, Louise!") One pile of beautifully fragmented leaves yielded several treasures: Melody's watch (still working), a serving spoon, two tennis balls, a small rubber ball, several pencils, an eraser, and a tuberous begonia and date pit, both sprouting. Louise still works with dozens of piano class students, as well as overseeing her own children's progress in school and music, and planning violin/piano programmes for churches, hospitals, care homes, etc.; Festival and examination involvements keep her on her toes. One of the challenges in her life is keeping ahead of the demand for shampoo, white sports socks, clean gym strip and/or team uniforms, and notices to be signed for school and church.

From a Paper-Person's* Diary

(*coined at 6:30 one morning as Mother handed a customer, who had suddenly appeared at his front door, his paper: "Oh, it's the … uh … paper-person.")

4:50 a.m. on a summer morning   Obedient to the poster suggestion at the newspaper station, Michael is training his "back-up" staff: walking down the centre of Lodge Avenue, draped in a carrier bag, he is flanked by Margaret and Melissa, one delivering to the south side; the other to the north. Mother sits in the car a block back, keeping an eye on proceedings. A police car materializes out of the blackness and stops beside Michael. The policeman wonders if Michael is the spotter for a gang of thieves, asks to see the newspaper's front page to check the date. After hearing Michael's explanation of the early-morning activity, comments, "I see—a family operation." Glides up past Mother, who smiles brightly, unaware that family's reputation had been endangered.

6:25 a.m., August 29 Michael is out on 113-paper route; parents are fast asleep. Phone rings: "Is Mike there? I tried to catch him to ask him to stop delivery tomorrow." Father responds to request as civilly as drowsiness will allow.

6:55 a.m. on a drizzly fall morning Mother and son have been out delivering in the rain, Mother scarfless in short-sleeved blouse, soaking but warm (10 minutes of delivering = removal of jacket; 20 minutes = removal of sweater); plans to have a warm bath and shampoo sodden hair on return home. Son has delivered upper end of Falmouth, relaxes in car as Mother delivers final paper at lower end. As Mother appears, son decides to enliven the gloom by switching all car lights on and off *à la* disco, illuminating his partner in delivery, who makes a couple of curtain-calls in front of car. Mother is suddenly aware of two figures emerging from behind partition of light towards her—our two pastors' wives out for a walk. Mother wishes, unsuccessfully, for immediate absorption into nearest puddle.

7:10 a.m., November 23 Whole family has been out delivering papers, boys on Michael's route, girls on Melissa's. (Mark: "I delivered three *by myself*, and Matthew did one.") Group spills into Smitty's for breakfast, tries to ignore comments: "There's one way to fill a restaurant!" "Eating away all the profits, are you?"

6:15 a.m., November 25 Father and daughter are distributing newspapers through apartment building, Melissa on fourth floor, Father on third. Inebriated young man staggers down hallway, asks, "Ish there a fourth floor in thish building?" Father answers in affirmative, hurries up stairs to beat elevator and check on papergirl. Stranger shuffles down hallway, across one newspaper, picks up 405's paper, falls into apartment 404. Father knocks on 404, requests return of paper, replaces it at 405's door. Finishes other deliveries and returns to check that 405's paper is still at door. It is.

Roses / Thorns ...

... our spacious new accommodation and grandparents who stood behind us financially / the heating bill ...

... the 93 the family received from the Music Festival's adjudicator / the less-than-70 (although a pass) Marilyn—along with three-quarters of those taking the exam—received for her Grade X Piano, necessitating a redoing of that formidable test if she wants to go on to an Associateship ...

... the TV taping in early April, just days before Matthew's fourth birthday, when the "baby" played the first variation of "Twinkle" with his proud siblings (Mother had no time for pride. She was terrified when she realized that she, confined to the piano by a lapel mike, could not follow the usual procedure of setting up his violin for him. For the first time in his life, and in front of cameramen who said they did not want to do any retakes, he manoeuvred his 1/10th-size instrument on to his shoulder and performed quite adequately. Just before the taping, Melody had dropped her bow on the concrete floor, snapping it; the teacher gave Melissa's bow to her, Melissa took Margaret's, and Margaret took an extra one from a violin case. Everyone agreed, wisely, that it was best that Mother not be enlightened until after the taping.) / Bruce's first accident in thirty-two years, a rear-ender just days after his brakes had, supposedly, been fixed; thank God, he and Matthew escaped injury …

ALL SET TO PERFORM

… Melody's silver medal for violin (the highest mark in BC for Grade II, 90%, a companion to one Marilyn was given in 1982 for Grade VIII) / 5:00 a.m. on dark, rainy, windy mornings and the realization that if your *Times Colonist* customers are to receive their newspaper, you and your flannelette sheets must part company; and then you must come back home to practise …

… the steady income earned on the paper route / collecting that income …

… the generous gifts of clothing from slightly-larger cousins, aunts and friends / the laundry…

… the gift from a lady at church of a very good student violin; when it is refurbished, Melissa, too, will have a full-size fiddle / practising that fiddle …

Chapter 26: Letters to My Parents, 1984

November 5, 1984

Dear Mom and Dad,

... It's 6:15 a.m. and I'm hoping to mail this before school. Michael has been out since (I assume) 5:15 or 5:30 a.m.; it's a relatively mild day. I was able to get him some zipper-and-lace boots to keep him warm and dry. There's been no talk for several weeks now of giving up the route. ...

... The boys Melissa babysits are good company for Mark and Matthew. (They're 7 and 5.) Their mom works 12-hour shifts (head nurse at VGH Emergency) and Melissa looks after them one to three days a week. The younger one comes home with Bruce at 11:30 a.m. and has lunch with us, the older one comes at 3:00 p.m. with the others, and they stay until 8:30 p.m. (Our two little guys go to bed at seven.) Melissa earns $1.50 per hour per child: 14 x $1.50 per day. From that she pays Bruce 75 cents per child per meal and 10% of her earnings into the "Family Fund" (our "entertainment fund"), and $1/hour to her parents for babysitting the Kindergarten child from 11:30 a.m. to 3:00 p.m. (also goes to the Family Fund). For an eleven year old, it's quite satisfying! Our other Tuesday-Wednesday-Thursday two are a delight, as well. Their parents are very appreciative of the help and the F.F. swells by $75 each week. We hope to get a good amount paid off our building debt next June. When I think of last November (government strike, and a house plan bill for $1,200 when we had expected $300-400), I am very thankful.

... We hope to have a family recital here on the 25th. The children have to play on the 12th of December for Mrs. Holland's bowling group, the 20th for Emmanuel's "Keenagers" (turkey dinner at noon first; we've done it two other years and it's very nice), the 24th for Cobble Hill church's Sunday School concert, and probably our church on the 25th. We may play on the 2nd at Parkdale. Last night I got out some Christmas music and did some planning!

Bruce had his first real accident in 32 years last week. He rear-ended a car in front of him, although he had at least two car lengths to stop. The brakes had been fixed the week before, so he's not sure what happened. The front of the van (VW) is smashed, but neither he nor Matthew was hurt. (The man he hit was drunk.)

... Geordon took Ms 3 to 7 out on Halloween. He put on a sombrero and heavy poncho, and looked very Latin-American! He's sure a neat person; I couldn't wish for anyone better for Marilyn. His parents are really missing him. He says he often used to talk with his mother for an hour in the morning. He phoned me for an hour last week and chatted about all sorts of things. He had sensed I was concerned about Marilyn's music and schoolwork. She understandably wants to be with him whenever she can manage it. He is very supportive; he's really proud of her. He writes poems and they're good. Peggy even read one to her English class, much to Marilyn's embarrassment!

MARK KNOWS WHAT MOMMY ENJOYS

… Margaret went to Vancouver (Abbotsford) overnight on Friday for a volleyball tournament. They won all four games. Margaret took her (new) heavy quilt with her sleeping bag, plus several other unnecessary items. Bruce had taken away a large pillow and several stuffed animals, or it would have been *many* unnecessary items! She's a real sweetie, and seems to be doing well at school. Last Sunday (28th) we played at the Duncan church for the eleven o'clock service. When we got home, I helped Margaret collect leaves from our yard for a science collection. She needed 50, but we found 86 which I could identify [*I don't believe this*]; there were three or four more which I didn't know [*that I believe*]. We pressed them between newspapers and table leaves, so they are nice and flat.

… **Later** Mark is home with a cold and complains of a slight earache. He and Matthew are drawing pictures at my elbow. They're real dears!

… Wynne sent over a load of neat clothes for the girls. I wonder if she knows how much they enjoy choosing from the box, especially now that they are required to buy their own clothes with their earnings!

Letter sent by Mark, Spring 1984
Dear Granny and Grandpa!

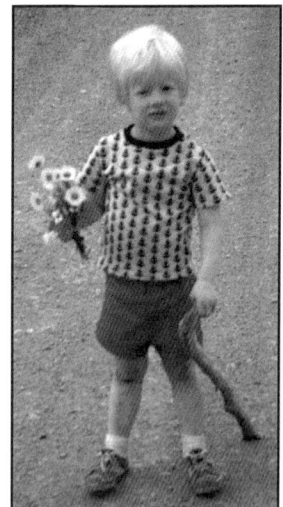

MATTHEW ALSO KNOWS
WHAT MOMMY ENJOYS

I hope you are feeling good. Grandpa's part: the Vancouver Canucks beat the Oilers and Islanders in overtime and Canadians in overtime and Whalers 4-3 in overtime. Granny's part: Melody's plant is growing in her bedroom it's name is snowdrop.

Love from Mark

Chapter 27: A Christmas Digest, 1985

EDITORIAL *by Louise*

1985 brought us our first high school graduation and our last Kindergarten entry, nostalgic milestones each. For thirteen happy and beneficial years, our children attended Lake Hill Elementary. With the prospect of another thirteen, and the proximity of a Christian school, we made the difficult decision to transfer the youngest three (Melody, Grade 6; Mark, Grade 3; Matthew, Kindergarten) to Pacific Christian, where they have joined the next three up (Melissa, Grade 8; Margaret, Grade 9; Michael, Grade 11). The serious little four year old, long hair waved and barretted, whom we entrusted to Mrs. Glew's care thirteen short years ago, has become a young lady. She, her parents, and her next five siblings are very grateful for the training and kindness they received at Lake Hill.

We also appreciate Pacific's positive input into our children's lives, and find it satisfying—and efficient—to have them all attending the same school. It is our prayer that they will learn to serve the Lord by serving others, both with their music and in other areas. We were gratified one sunny Wednesday in June, when Melissa shared the Citizenship trophy with another Grade 7 student at Lake Hill's morning assembly, and Marilyn was given the School Spirit award at her graduation at Pacific in the evening.

Grandpa Hjalmar (Forsberg) is one of fourteen children. This summer, the Forsberg family had their first reunion, in the drought area of southern Saskatchewan. I got to meet my six living aunts and uncles and a multitude of cousins. Except for the heat (100 degrees Fahrenheit and above, most of the weeks we were away), our visit to the Prairies was interesting and enjoyable. As one of four granddaughters carrying my grandmother's name, I was a little unnerved to stand in a windswept hilltop cemetery beside a tombstone marked "Louise Forsberg," the name to which I answered for twenty years. Actually, on closer inspection, the name was the Swedish *Lovisa*. How I would love to have known the grandmother who had her first child in Sweden at 16, and her last in Canada at 43. As a West Coaster, I found the flat lands and gently undulating hills, even in desolate conditions, quite fascinating, and could not help but admire the tenacity of the prairie farmer.

For several months we have had the inestimable privilege of sharing our roof with our church's interim pastor, Dr. Bill Sloan, and his wife, Maxine. The Sloans, with their loving and lovable cocker spaniel, Laddie, have endeared themselves to us as they offer encouragement and the wisdom of lifetimes in pastoral work. They claim, diplomatically, to be unaware of the decibels which reverberate through the other three-quarters of the house. We are not looking forward to their departure.

Church responsibilities, school assignments, sports activities, music lessons, family concerts and paper routes propel one week into the next. We thank God for the opportunities He has given, and for the strength and enthusiasm to meet each day's challenges.

We send to you our love and best wishes for 1986.

PERSONAL GLIMPSES

Ralph Steele

BRUCE AND LOUISE

Marilyn [almost 18] Fulltime student at Camosun College, taking a two-year course towards an Associateship in Arts and in piano teaching and performing given by the Victoria Conservatory. Enjoys her more unstructured schedule. Time is filled with study, practising, performing, accompanying.

Michael [16] In company with older sister, sports a learner's driving license. Hopes to take flying lessons, perhaps next summer. Provides a masculine strength to family musical ensembles; assists Mother with one piano class each week. Enthusiastic volleyball player; competent referee.

Margaret [14] Recently modelled one of Mother's dresses from twenty years ago, which *fit* her. Continues to tackle life with great energy and originality, following her own drummer. Received first-class standing in Grade VIII Violin in June.

Melissa [almost 13] "Honeybee" undertakes most tasks cheerfully and efficiently. Sidelined this fall with tonsillitis and pneumonia; shared a $40 bottle of penicillin with Margaret, Melody and Matthew and then downed sulfa drugs as well. As a "paper routist" (her response to a questionnaire's "Occupation?"), maintains a "Miscallenious Folder for Paper-route."

Melody [almost 11] Stomps purposefully through the early-morning gloom on Marilyn's paper route. Managed first-class marks last June in both piano and violin exams at Grade IV level. Gave enthusiastic report of life at camp in August, including episode where cabin-mate threw up on her sleeping bag, and was subsequently sent home when the nurse found white spots at the back of her throat.

(Mother had tuned out this distasteful item, and several weeks of Melody's coughing, but heard echoes of it in mid-September when the doctor, referring to Melody's and Matthew's throats, said, "Mrs. Holland, have you ever seen tonsillitis before? See the white spots?")

Mark [8] The Canucks' most loyal fan. Spends hours hitting around a tennis ball or puck on cement pad at back, aided by over-size Canucks shirt (kindness of Grandma and Auntie Marilyn), bicycle helmet, baseball glove and hockey stick (won by Grandpa Forsberg at a Cougars game many years ago). All pants are double-patched at the knees.

Matthew [5 1/2] In spite of spare frame, provides satisfying competition for Mark on backyard concrete. Still at demonstrative stage, bestowing frequent hugs and kisses on parents: "I don't know why I love you so much when you're always asking me to fold the laundry."

Bruce Continues to field a variety of calls each shift. Chauffeurs offspring hither and yon. Buys groceries in great quantities, cooks meals of comparable size. Helps out on paper-routes as schedule allows.

IT STARTED HERE

Would like to read morning paper before 10:00 p.m., but rarely does.

Louise Teaches. Organizes and gives concerts with family. Keeps an eye—and two feet—on family's four paper-routes (and an ear on whether or not the appropriate rooms evidence stirrings of life at 5:15 a.m.) Referred to as the "Abominable Snow-woman" by family carriers, as November snows adhered to her paper-route scarves (three), sweaters (three), and slacks (two pairs). Invested in a heavily-quilted winter coat, which gives her the same dimensions as last year's Christmas tree (harvested from our front yard): width almost equalling height.

LIFE'S LIKE THIS

Thursday, June 27, morning *Times Colonist* Living Editor telephones, requests talk with Mother on subject of teaching children music; interview to be next morning at nine o'clock if possible, with children to give a short recital. Mother has strained back severely, moves through rooms by hanging onto furniture and walls, finishes teaching year that evening at 9:00 p.m. House is in late-June shambles. Family leaves for Saskatchewan on Tuesday; house, especially upstairs suite, must be cleaned up. Family to give concert Sunday afternoon. Four eldest children involved in Youth for Christ skate-a-thon this evening from 7:30 p.m. to 12:30 a.m., then paper routes at 5:15 a.m. Melody has piano exam 11:00 a.m. Friday. Mother says no, then reconsiders. Violin teacher's comment from years before rings across consciousness: "Someday you may be able to help other parents with your experiences as a parent and a teacher."

Friday, June 28, 9:00 a.m. Mother welcomes beautiful young woman into one area of house where guest should not trip over foreign objects, introduces Rebecca Wigod to children, who have managed to remain upright for previous four hours. Editor responds appreciatively to children's mini-concert, talks with Mother over a cup of coffee for nearly an hour. Mother impressed and delighted with guest's refined yet warm and friendly manner. Photographer takes children's picture; leaves with journalist. Skater-carriers immediately doff concert outfits and collapse into beds.

Thursday, July 18, afternoon Family arrives at Tillebrook National Park, Alberta: treed; paved roads; manicured lawns; gravelled trailer-sites; cooler temperatures (mid-80s). Mother is pleased that campsite appears so clean and safe; relaxes in trailer, reads rules and regulations of campsite, notes warning against feeding and harassment of animals. Serenity is broken by daughter's excited report that eldest son has captured a gopher. A la Farley Mowat, Michael has enticed rodent from its hole with bread, lassoing it as head appeared. Mother brings scissors to cut string, along with lecture on consideration for wildlife.

Wednesday, September 18, 5:15 a.m. Mother drives son to paper shack; plans to do Marilyn's route, as well as half-dozen papers on Michael's. Drowsy duo enters shack wordlessly, starts counting stacks of papers. Mother takes six of Michael's papers, suggests addresses she could do; son grunts assent. Mother returns to car, shifts into neutral, then suddenly wonders if addresses really did register. Returns to shack to check, halted in mid-sentence by thunderous crash: car has rolled three car-lengths down incline into telephone pole (Mother's first accident in 22 years of driving). Son's comment: "You were lucky; the car could have rolled out on to Quadra and across into the gas station." Mother does not feel particularly lucky.

Tuesday, October 22, 5:15 a.m. Mother returns from Thrifty's (where Margaret's and Melissa's papers are picked up) with unsettling news that benches are empty—no newspapers. Two carriers find warm spots on carpet near heating vents and lie down, fully-clad, for second sleep. Another removes winter clothing and crawls back into bed. The fourth gets out violin. Mother makes four more trips to Thrifty's, three to corner of Lodge (1 1/2 miles) for Marilyn's and Michael's papers, and finally an excursion right down to the newspaper plant where, at 6:50 a.m., bundles are spilling from conveyor belts into trucks—several hours late, due to a press breakdown. Few tentative raindrops escalate into downpour. **7:15 a.m.** Margaret's and Melissa's papers available. Horizontal carriers become vertical, make short work, with parents, of two routes. **8:30–10:15 a.m.** Marilyn's and Michael's papers delivered in drenching rain by bedraggled middle-aged assistants.

Wednesday, November 27, 5:30 a.m. Temperature minus 10 degrees Celsius. Wind blowing. Two feet of snow, car immobilized. Marilyn has mononucleosis; Margaret and Melissa, 'flu. Father, Mother and eldest son trudge mile and a half to get Marilyn's and Michael's papers; papers large and heavy. (Father has already carried Melissa's to Mac's [*convenience store*] for safekeeping, Margaret's home until later.) Mother hums "Winter Wonderland" alternately with Father's "I'm Dreaming of a White Christmas." Mother uses Father as windbreak, steps in footprints behind him, adds "Good King Wenceslas" to repertoire ("In her master's steps she trod ..."). Son does not join in; suggests parents save energy for walking. **6:00–9:30 a.m.** Well-insulated trio ploughs up and down driveways, across lots, gradually works its way through four routes, with some help from Melody on fourth route. Customers' appreciation is satisfying. **9:00 p.m.** Forecast: more snow. Mother ponders, as has become her habit, on what children get their parents into.

SCENE IN PASSING ...

... Large blue van, pulling trailer, bearing what appears to be nine Arabs, trekking hundreds of miles across prairies to family reunion. Temperature in low 100s: family stops at gas stations to soak towels; wet cloths draped over head and shoulders provide a primitive sort of air-conditioning ... Marilyn receiving $10 (American) for a poem (below) to be published in a magazine ... Notice on Melody's door: "Please be patient. God isn't finished with me yet." (Small notice attached to it: "Maybe, but we sure like what He's doing.") ... A fortyish assistant carrier sloshing through three-inch puddles in twenty-year-old brevitts, soaked to the skin ... Another assistant carrier at least half dry, thanks to a voluminous rubber cape over his shoulders (our version of the Caped Marvel) ... A motley group of sweet-seekers: a small clown (suited in his brother's hand-me-down of ten Halloweens ago), a Canucks hockey player (what else?), a cowgirl and a Scottish lassie escorted by two "Colombians," ponchoed and sombreroed, one very dark, the other very fair ... Mother and daughters searching in thrift store outside Langley for white slip a couple of hours before a concert, after Mother realizes she packed only a black slip (Melissa found a quite acceptable one for 40 cents.) ... Family providing an hour of classical and Christmas music in the drawing room at Craigdarroch Castle (Castle largely restored to splendour of 1890s, decorated throughout with a wide variety of period Christmas decorations and handcrafts) ... Father, a nongambler, sheepishly accepting $250 cheque from circulation manager ("bingo" cards distributed for free with newspaper as promotion; numbers printed in newspaper each day) ... Mother's birthday card from Melody: 44 cents attached, with the cheery comment, "Almost 50!" … Note on bedroom door: "TOOTH FAIRY—Please stop by. $1.00 is your fee (molar)" …

On the Paper Route (or What You Might Not Experience if Your Alarm is Set for 7:00 a.m.) … absolute peace-and-quiet, broken only by the squawk of a blue heron overhead, or the whirr of two hundred ducks leaving Swan Lake, or the barking of the neighbourhood's watchdog(s) zealously guarding their territories, or the buzzing of a street light … writing a note for a customer by starlight … reaching the bottom step quickly and unceremoniously after touching down on unseen frost … a flock of pigeons, bronzed by the sunrise, wheeling overhead in formation … a snowy wonderland at 5:00 a.m., tinted a shell pink by city lights … leaning into a bitterly-cold wind blasting snow into the face … a black asphalt driveway transformed into a gold leaf mosaic, thanks to a line of stalwart poplars beside it … a baby rabbit scrinching over the frozen grass in the moonlight … a variety of early-morning fragrances: juniper shrubs; smoke from a freshly-lit wood stove; innumerable flowers; wet autumn leaves crushed underfoot; sweet fir … the Creator's jewels: a sapphire sky, spangled with diamonds …

"The Sunrise" *by Marilyn Holland*

One morning I went down to the water's edge to watch the sun rise.
Closing my eyes for awhile, I just sat and listened.
I heard the waves crashing down, playing upon the rocks,
Then rolling softly over the smooth sand.

As I opened my eyes
I felt a slight breeze blowing ocean spray across my face.
Sensing a warm glow on my face,
I opened my eyes fully to receive the radiance of the bright yellow rising sun.

The rays of the great star were a contrast
to the dark ripples of the ever-flowing fluid.
The mood created by the scene also brought about
a mixture of emotions within my being.

While the insistent pounding of the surf demanded attention,
There was a peacefulness,
a calming effect,
provided by the gradually ascending fireball.

It was as if the natural beauty
put forth by this gleaming light
Reflected and represented its Creator,
Displaying His infinite power and might.

Chapter 28: Letter to My Parents, 1985

January 6, 1985

Dear Mom and Dad,

... Happy New Year! I couldn't find writing paper more appropriate *[snowman]*; our snow is still hanging around in two- and three-foot drifts, dirty and slushy. At least the sidewalks and roads are clearing. The side roads are still quite treacherous. It was beautiful, though, but sure put a strain on the paper-people who live here.

... I'm glad you are tolerant of our Digest. A lot of people have been nice about it. You know how ambivalent I feel about exposing so much trivia, and yet there are so many who ask how it's coming, or could they have one, etc. One of the more hard-boiled teachers at school commented that he hates Christmas letters but he enjoys ours because it's so honest!

... I've just hunted up an acceptable pair of runners for Mark *[Grade 2]* to take back to school tomorrow. They're an old pair, so I've put laces with stars in them. Just before Christmas I had to go to school to accompany him on his violin; he was playing a rousing piece as a solo within the class play, and then "O Christmas Tree," while everyone sang. The music was no problem. But I was appalled to see what he was wearing at the rehearsal: an old pair of Melody's runners, flapping from instep and around. How he walked in them without tripping I'll never know, let alone do P.E. in them. (He's been put in with the Grade 3s for sports because he's so good. They say he's a natural athlete. He still drags himself out of bed as soon as he hears the paper carriers are home, tears open the paper to the sports page, and checks to see how the Canucks are doing. It's surprising how well he can read now he's in with a more traditional teacher.) I vaguely remember Mark taking those old running shoes, in quite

MARK IN COSTUME

poor condition, as a temporary measure, but we planned to get him another pair as soon as we could. We, of course, had forgotten all about them. And Mark is not one for the niceties of dressing. I've never seen a kid so unclothes-conscious. He wears raggy pants to school; he'll wear the same scruffy things day after day if we don't stop him; he wears sweaters inside out and backwards. But he is the neatest little guy; he's so transparently honest and non-manipulative, and wouldn't hurt a fly.

MARK IN PERFORMANCE

… Things have been happily busy around here. We were scheduled to play at Parkdale on the 30th, but that was cancelled by the snow. We are re-scheduled for January 27; it is a potluck supper first, and should be fun. Before Christmas, we gave several full concerts (mostly Christmas music) and took part in school and Sunday School concerts. We played at Cobble Hill on Christmas Eve and our church on Christmas Day. Next weekend we're slated to play at Fraserview Mennonite Brethren Church in Richmond, and poor cousin Marilyn (with her four) is bedding us down. We were asked to do this last summer, and I just learned today that it's a big church, but I've got to remember that our own church is big, and we do our best whether it's big or little. *[I used to say we played for Jesus, and anybody else could listen in if they wanted.]* On the 27th we played at Mt. Edwards Court Care Home, and an elderly man (member of Central) said he had more money than he knew what to do with, and we could use it better than he could, so he would send us $100. He did! I double checked with the authorities at the Home, and they said he often does that sort of thing, to accept it and enjoy it.

THE FAMILY

Chapter 29: A Christmas Digest, 1986

25TH WEDDING ANNIVERSARY

EDITORIAL *by Louise*

Twenty-six years ago this month, a young man asked a young woman to marry him. Twenty-five years ago this month, on the anniversary of both sets of parents, the seven sparkling diamonds were joined by a wider gold band inscribed inside with "Louise-Bruce 21-12-61." Nineteen years ago, the second of twenty Christmas letters was composed early one morning as a mother-imminently-to-be battled insomnia. For better and/or worse, each year has brought its quota of joys and vexations, and many have been chronicled both for the satisfaction of capturing life as it rushes past and for sharing the fun and foibles of an expanding family. (A few years into the above union, one partner asked the other why he had not chosen a more glamorous, sophisticated acquaintance of theirs. His answer, "I thought life with you would be more interesting," has continued to haunt him; he has yet to complain of boredom!)

Together we thank God for His many gifts to us. Each day is greeted with "This is the day that the Lord has made. We will *rejoice* and be *glad* in it." (Sometimes, particularly after a very short night, or at the prospect of the daily loads of laundry, the emphasis becomes "We *will* rejoice … .")

We, on behalf of our children and ourselves, would like to thank families and friends for their support, guidance, and love over the years. We are truly blessed.

PERSONAL GLIMPSES

Bruce Continues to field emergency social work calls at all hours of the night and across the weekend for two out of four weeks. Frustrated at times by "wild-goose chases" where hours of organizing and counselling are voided by uncooperative client. Has acquired wide knowledge of social resources available in BC, also of geography of Capital Region, as he deals with people in all areas and circumstances. Child protection is priority; occasionally takes police along on house calls. Puts years of camp cooking to use each day as he prepares meals for up to ten with efficiency and flair. Is grateful for normal chaos of own family.

Louise Gives thanks every day for the dear, patient husband who supports her varied schemes. Enjoys her expanding family which includes, in addition to seven of the home-grown variety, a young man who refers to her as "Mom"; a pair of bright-eyed brunettes, Lisa [7], and Jonathan [4], who join the tribe three or four days a week; and Laura, a gorgeous blonde curly-headed New Year's baby whom Marilyn babysits each week. Is almost halfway through twenty-seventh year of teaching. Starts most days with an invigorating walk through the neighbourhood, distributing papers so that her children can have at least one sleep-in morning each week.

Marilyn [Almost 19] In her second (and concluding) year of an Associateship programme for piano teaching and performing at the Victoria Conservatory of Music. Looks forward to a month's excursion to Colombia at Christmas to visit with the Rendles, who have a prison ministry in Bogotá. Worked with Youth for Christ as junior leader and choir director in Antigua, West Indies. With her roommate, Carolin Pinno (a voice major whom she accompanies), rents the upstairs suite, (hopefully) acquiring domestic and financial skills in the process. Teaches several piano students, helps Mother with her classes, accompanies, leads Junior Youth for Christ choir. Acquiesced to a *Times Colonist* request to take on another neighbourhood route. Faithfully pries herself out of bed most mornings to provide her customers with their breakfast reading, although paper delivery probably ranks as eleven on a list of her Ten Favourite Things.

Michael [17] In his final year of high school. Continues to participate in family concerts, although formal music lessons have given way to sports and acquiring as much information about flying as he can assimilate. (Completed theory requirements for Grade IX in May; has Grade VIII Piano and Grade IX Violin behind him.) Has spent many hours perfecting volleyball skills, as well as refereeing games. Drives 12-passenger van to school each morning, entrusted with the safety of his five younger siblings.

Margaret [15] Accompanied Marilyn to Antigua in August, violin in hand. Managed first class standing at Grade VIII level, Royal Conservatory of Music, for piano and violin; continues work on both instruments and theory. Paper route is closest to home; has made friends with many of the neighbours, some of whom had previously viewed the paper carrier (a new one every few weeks) with distrust. Produces hand-made stationery (place cards, note paper) with dried flowers, grasses, cones. Won Toyota volleyball jump and scholarship to UVic's summer volleyball camp. Receives very good school marks, as well as teachers' comments regarding socializing in class; older brother's nickname, "Mag" (for Magpie), is perhaps appropriate.

Melissa [Almost 14] (Jonathan's "Missela") Belies her "blonde" appearance by bringing home school reports liberally sprinkled with A's. Continues with both instruments at Grade VIII level. Joined Margaret in 2 1/2 months of volleyball, several times a week (Mother not totally approving). Occasionally takes over kitchen; organizes and prepares meals efficiently, to parents' delight. Churns out cookies by the hundreds, to children's delight.

Melody [Almost 12] Continues to study both piano and violin. Has maintained Marilyn's first paper route for nearly a year now, and distributes her Regal catalogues across all the routes. Joined forces to set up a large "Next-to-the-GARAGE-SALE" (in the music room), where her Regal items, Melissa's cookies, and Margaret's stationery were sold. Meeting and visiting with friends and neighbours made the effort worthwhile. Although probably the youngest (and smallest) Grade 7 student at PCS, has added experiments with the curling iron and makeup, and collecting tapes of questionable musical value, to her activities.

Mark [9] Zealously follows progress of Canucks hockey team. Was able to quote scorers of recent game—Canucks won 11 to 5—by memory and without taking a breath. Aided in piano study by eldest sister and Mother. Channels some of his considerable energies into violin studies, under the dynamic instruction of Yasuko Eastman.

Matthew [6 1/2] Continues to learn both good and bad from his older brothers and sisters. Joins Mark in devouring Section B of the newspaper (the sports pages). Helped provide wedding music for neighbour's daughter (Maria Wille); especially enjoyed Clarke's rousing "Trumpet Tune in D" played by seven violins, to which Maria walked down the aisle. (Violinists at front had superb view of procession.)

LIFE'S LIKE THIS

Christmas Eve, 1985 Mother and Father have been out on paper routes for several weeks without a break, due to snow and carrier sickness; have not had a chance to take the two little boys Christmas shopping. (Older "tycoons" have already wrapped their gifts.) Mother is snug in upstairs bedroom, surrounded by presents and wrapping paper. Little boys want to help; unhappy they have no gifts to give. Mother suggests smallest child give sesame snaps and peppermint drops to each family member; cuts out wrapping paper for him. Little towhead labouriously prints "To" and "Love from" on each gift tag. Second youngest disappears, reappears with bag of "gifts," which he, too, proceeds to wrap: a pen and some gum for Dad, a lavender sachet and gum for Mom, a brass cannon for Marilyn, a Canucks sticker (this a sacrifice!) for Michael, a small basket containing a china dog for Margaret, a lamb picture with "The Lord is My Shepherd" printed on it for Melissa, a book on Vancouver Island for Melody, and a picture of mountains for Matthew. All gifts wrapped with love and enthusiasm.

December 27, 1985 For several days preceding Christmas, Mother has been complaining about the many hours spent tramping the sidewalks each morning, in addition to her own teaching and the family's performing responsibilities, and the usual Christmas preparations. Apparently grumbling has registered, and, unknown to her, youngest five have decided to give her a morning off. Rising at 3:30 a.m., they scurry out to the boxes in front of the house, count and assemble papers and set out to deliver them before 7:00 a.m. **5:45 a.m.** Mother is pleased that children have put themselves out for her, a little concerned when she pictures her five and eight year old children out on the sidewalk and inside an apartment building at 4:00 a.m.

March 11, 1986, 8:30 p.m. Most of family is away for the evening. Melody and Matthew are playing upstairs, Father is on telephone at far end of house, and Mother is teaching in the music room. Matthew becomes aware of peculiar burning smell. He and Melody go down to kitchen to investigate. Melody catches sight of flames on sink; screams for Father, who drops receiver, runs to kitchen, grabs and drops burning bowl into sink. Dishwasher cord has short-circuited, setting Braun mixing bowl on fire. Fine black soot has infiltrated all nooks and crannies. Professional cleaner (sent out by insurance company) will scour out kitchen next day. Family does not like to think about what could have happened.

May 1, 6:30 p.m. Family arrives early at recital hall in preparation for Family Group performance in strings section of Music Festival at seven o'clock: violins to be tuned, music to be organized.   Discovers that harpist (printed on programme at a later time) is performing. Mother, startled, checks watch, learns that harp class was re-scheduled for 6:30 p.m. so that performers from Vancouver could catch ferry. **7:15 p.m.** Family's turn to perform; piano

SEVEN VIOLINS

is nowhere in sight. Grand piano used for previous Festival classes has been taken back to store. (Organizer knew harps would not need it; did not see family entry.) Old, out-of-tune piano found behind curtains, dragged out. Violins are tuned after a fashion. Performance begins with eldest six playing "Gavotte" by Martini, in two parts. Mother catches sight of youngest son exhibiting extreme discomfort in wings at other side of the stage; rushes across back of stage to check out problem. Fortunately, second item is Vivaldi trio for eldest three. Next two girls take little brother to nearest restroom; are back in time for third and fourth pieces. Performance ends with a resounding rendition of "I Sing the Mighty Power of God," after which Mother quietly wilts and resolves never again to get involved in such an event. (Family receives substantial mark; Mother's resolve begins to weaken.)

June 3, 4:30 p.m. Melissa is assisting Mother with beginning music class for four and five year olds, as Margaret is unwell. In introducing her to class, Mother asks students if they know how many children live with her and Mr. Holland. Children aren't sure, so Mother lists names, and children count on fingers. Fingers twist and brows furrow. Mother asks how many children? Colin says, "Ten"; Jonathan answers, "Fifteen," and Brice proclaims, with an unnerving authority, "One hundred and twenty-five!"

November 9, 5:00 a.m. Mother awakes to sound of wind. Remembers last November's two weeks of ice, snow and blizzard; afraid to look out in case ground is blanketed in white. Extracts herself from warm, comfortable bed, gets dressed in layers of scruffy paper-route clothes. Knocks on three carriers' doors as she makes her way downstairs and out to roadside to haul in bundles. Leaves rustle around her; telephone wires whine; rain spatters. Delivers part of Margaret's route, aided by drowsy trio; enjoys escort of dancing leaves on her rounds of Eagle Rock. Pauses to take in view of city glittering below. **7:15 a.m.** Michael, Melody and Mother drive along Lodge Avenue towards home and are confronted with loose newspaper pages floating up lane. Michael retrieves one, discovers it is dated November 9. Three carriers check several houses along Lodge; papers still intact. However, lawn at 991 Leeds Place provides dance floor for whirling and twirling pages. Offspring cheer Mother on while she tries to gather up elusive sheets.

November 21, 11:40 p.m. Alarm pierces sleep of several family members, who grope around on night tables trying to extinguish annoying sound. Wail continues even though alarm buttons are pressed in. Eldest son and youngest daughter suddenly realize smoke alarm is source of sound. Catapult themselves out of bed and down stairs two at a time. Steam billows along hall and up stairs past alarm. Dishwasher hose has split and is spewing water and steam all over kitchen. Water on floor extends to hallway. Drawers are filled with water, all linens soaked, three pumpkin loaves a soggy mush. Ceiling drips. Parents join children and contemplate scene with dismay; thankful alarm didn't signal fire. **December 1** Parents give up on fifteen-year-old dishwasher and turn it in on new model. Father says, "Happy Anniversary to us!"

November 27, 3:30 p.m. Children bring home school reports for parents' scrutiny. Youngest hovers around edge of group, finally allows family to see report. Older brother teases him about "poor" marks. Child is not sure if brother is serious; teacher had seemed pleased with his work. Mother points to teacher's printing (four marks of 100%), asks if he knows how many wrong that means. Answer is "Five? Ten?" Child smiles in relief when Mother enlightens him.

THE "LITTLE BOYS"

SEEN AND HEARD ...

... note found in Mother's jacket: "Mom, doesn't the flowers in front of the pulput (?spelt write?) look pretty in the sunlight?" ... nine-year-old violinist leaving the concert platform with his white shirt somewhat askew; buttons have been put in wrong buttonholes all the way down front—close relative of six year old who wore play running shoes to a wedding because 1) he could not find his good leather shoes, and 2) the gray matched his gray pants. Mother has long ago handed in her Motherhood and Good Housekeeping badges. ... an older teenager, three seconds out of sleep, trying to receive a telephone message through the first object his hand found: a bottle of hand cream (item contributed by sisters) ... Father confronting an unkempt young man at 6:00 a.m. in a paper customer's carport, stealing from the customer's freezer ... a question from Melody (rhetorical, as Melody assumed her parents would not give her an answer; one wouldn't, and the other wouldn't dare!): "How did Grandpa, who is quite skinny, and Granny, who is only a moderate size, have such a large child?" ... a sign of true love: SFU student who spends most weekends on the Island, usually in the company of a young lady who is as fair as he is dark; sacrifices early-morning sleep to escort her on her paper delivering ... a case of *déjà vu*: a seven-year-old music student whose mother was in Mother's class at Cloverdale School 25 years ago ... Michael, head momentarily turned sidewards, running full tilt into a parked car on PCS parking lot, denting car and left knee in the process; Mark, complaining about "splinter" in foot picked up from living room carpet—both in Vic General's Emergency Room, Michael sporting a tensor bandage and limp, Mark an incision where doctor removed pointed 1/2" of a sewing needle ... Matthew, upstairs, calling out triads through the heat register to Mark, downstairs at the grand piano ...

Chapter 30: Letters to My Parents, 1986

November 23, 1986

Dear Mom and Dad,

Thank you so much for phoning yesterday. *[This would have been a big deal for my parents, as a long-distance call was expensive and would have seemed even more so to them.]* It was fun "visiting" with you. I didn't know the sound would still be all right even with four phones (at least) off the hook. Hope your phone bill isn't too high. ...

Bruce spent all day yesterday cleaning up, after our kitchen got "steam-cleaned." When the hose on the dishwasher burst, it spewed hot water and steam throughout the kitchen, filling drawers, dripping from the ceiling, running behind the stove and fridge, etc., etc.—a real mess. (The smoke alarm was triggered at 11:40 p.m., or we might have been under three feet of water, instead of three inches!) I had papers at 5:00 a.m., violin lessons (Mark and Matthew) at 9:00 a.m., teaching at 10:30 a.m., concert at 2:30 p.m. (Melody played; I accompanied), teaching at 4:30 p.m. and helping Melody collect at 6:30 p.m. No time for boredom! During the night it rained very heavily. Often that happens and it stops by 5:30 a.m. Not so today; it poured and poured and I was out in it for over two hours, on Margaret's route. Once you give yourself over to the idea that there is no way you can stay dry, it's not so bad; I was warm as long as I kept moving. Actually, I quite enjoyed it. Must be a reversion to childhood! Michael, Melissa, Melody and Marilyn were out in it, too, but not for as long. It's a real hassle keeping the papers dry, because your hands and jacket get soaked and so easily touch the paper as you pull it out to put it in the holder. Several places don't have holders, and the porches were drenched, so I had to come up with different places to put the papers. I'm glad I have the stamina to tramp around for miles! It's such fun doing things with your children!!

December 17 ... Hello at long last! I'm at Lake Hill's second Christmas concert (dress rehearsal Monday afternoon, first concert last night) and have time to put in (i.e., use wisely) before I play for the Junior Choir. I also play for the Senior Choir at the end of the programme, so will have nearly another hour's wait. I'm in the staff room right next to the auditorium, so I can keep an ear on things. Tomorrow night I play for the cantata at PCS's concert at the UVic Centre. ... The boys' violin teacher has a concert (informal) on Saturday afternoon and I'm to accompany Mark and

Matthew and some other students as well. I have just tomorrow afternoon's classes to teach, so things are gradually winding down.

… Today Mark's class had to sing on the ferry going to and from Tsawwassen. Everything was fine until 7:40 a.m. (He had to be at school by 7:45 a.m.) He had slicked his hair back (he's quite handsome, you know), had on his Sunday pants and shirt, and suddenly realized he couldn't find his good shoes. The entire family did a complete search, but the shoes weren't found. (They were at school, not accessible to the kids on the ferry bus.) Mark went off in his old gray running shoes. I forgot to ask him if he was put in the back row. I sure hope so!

December 19 … Must get this off! Lake Hill's concerts went very well. I ended up with a beautiful Royal Albert serving plate, a musical note pad and a large bouquet of flowers (that I'd like to share with you!). I don't like receiving gifts. I know the choir directors appreciate my kind of playing; it is satisfying to be able to do it.

… Today I rehearse solos with Mrs. Eastman's students for a concert tomorrow. Tomorrow night Marilyn (Auntie) is taking us out for supper for our 25th anniversary, to the Olde England Inn *[where our wedding reception was held]*. When I think of the trying circumstances of 25 years ago (Thursday night, mother of the bride making dresses, etc.), I am very grateful! Marilyn and her sisters had better be more considerate! *[They were.]*

Chapter 31: A Christmas Digest, 1987

EDITORIAL *by Louise*

Yesterday (November 26) I picked a vine-ripened tomato in our back yard. This morning I made up an arrangement of chrysanthemums, nasturtiums, and primroses gathered from under a blanket of oak leaves. We have had an unusually dry summer and fall in Victoria, and it is hard to realize Christmas is so near.

Over the years, many Christmas letters contained news of yet another welcome addition to our family. This year, we also received an addition, equally welcome, but at the other end of the family! In August, Marilyn became Mrs. Geordon Rendle, and we are delighted with our new son.

A few weeks before Marilyn's wedding, in anticipation of her possible move to Vancouver, the family gave a benefit concert for two world relief organizations. We were humbled and encouraged by the warm support given to our concert and by the overwhelming enthusiasm of family and friends in launching Geordon and Marilyn on their new venture.

PERSONAL GLIMPSES

Marilyn Has acquired a new surname (Rendle), a wonderful husband (**Geordon**, son of Georgia and Don), a new address (1504 Oak Crest Drive) and a new appreciation for home-cooking, 4031 Saanich Road-style. Teaches piano. Directs Youth for Christ choir. Studies Spanish at UVic, with intention of eventually working in Colombian or Spanish prisons.

Michael Graduated from Pacific Christian School in June. Maintains two paper-routes and part-time job at Laurel Point Inn. Was given the use of a generous friend's BMW to pick up his date for graduation; appeared quite elegant in tuxedo and tails. Haunts used car lot in search of just the right set of wheels. Aims to take up flying in near future.

Margaret In Grade 11 at PCS. Is working towards

Gibson's

MARGARET

Grade IX Piano (passed Grade IX Violin with First Class Honours in June). Juggles music lessons, volleyball (Senior Girls), babysitting, paper route. Is developing artistic and business skills by making and selling stationery, sachets, and dried flower arrangements.

Melissa A year behind Margaret; on volleyball, soccer and basketball teams (Junior Girls). Working towards Grade VIII Violin (passed Grade VIII Piano in June, with Honours). Upkeep of bedroom sometimes suffers in the attempt to balance schoolwork, sports, music, babysitting, paper route and small business (making and selling cookies).

Melody Became a teenager December 5 (which means there are, for 25 days, five teenagers in the family; Marilyn's birthday is December 30). Joins two older sisters on Honour Roll at school. Flits through three apartment buildings almost every morning, delivering 70 papers. Is preparing for Grade VI Piano

Gibson's

MELISSA

exam in January (received Silver Medal for Grade VI Violin results in June). Continues to sharpen business skills selling Regal products. Plays hard at volleyball (Midget Girls).

Mark [10] and **Matthew** [7 1/2] Inseparable duo who take piano lessons with big sister and mother, violin lessons with Yasuko Eastman. Hit hockey puck around by the hour on cement pad in back yard. Attend "Boys' Brigade" and "Tree Climbers" at church. Provide "go-fer" service for rest of family.

Bruce and **Louise** Still social working and music teaching and trying to keep loose ends of family life from unravelling. Thank God for privilege and responsibility of overseeing large family, and greatly appreciate help and support from family and friends in both church and community. Managed to spend two days on own at Qualicum during summer—a real treat. Muse on pastor's assurance that trials and tribulations bring patience; figure in another few years they may be eligible to join Job's elite!

SEEN AND HEARD ...

... (March 31) Michael driving his family plus seven violins from Victoria to Nanaimo for a concert, through pelting rain, then 1", 2", and 3" inches of snow (winter's only snowfall); family alternates between fear of very slippery road and fascination with surrounding fairyland ... Melody, describing three stages of life: "There's young, old and mediocre" (comment not too well received by parents) ... Matthew, looking at parents' photos of 25 years ago in Mother's locket: "These pictures were when you and Daddy didn't wear glasses. It must have been the *olden* days." ... Margaret's photo in the *Times Colonist*, as the "cool carrier" who won 96 litres of ice cream in a subscription drive draw (The good news was her prize; the bad news was that she had to give her weight to *Times Colonist* personnel: she had won her weight in ice cream!) ... Margaret as the Queen of Hearts at school ... Margaret winning $100 for an essay ... Michael working as a busboy at Laurel Point Inn until 1:00 a.m., sleeping in one of the paper boxes at the edge of our property until the papers were delivered at 3:00 a.m., then delivering his 140 papers by 6:00 a.m. ... a 20-foot lilac tree in the back yard decorated with a basketball, tennis racquet and hockey stick, defying family's attempts to dislodge them ... five-year-old Jonathan (who, with his sister, Lisa, were almost-members of our family for three years), having just eaten a lunch of salmon sandwiches, raisins, nuts, carrots and milk, asking, "What's for dessert?" "The raisins and nuts are dessert." "Yes, but they're *healthy*. What's *really* for dessert?" ... Michael and two friends canoeing out to an island in the middle of Beaver Lake and setting up a tent ... at 2:00 a.m ... in the pouring rain ... in November ... Melody, opening a bundle of newspapers on the last day of November, only to have half-a-dozen snatched by a gust of wind and distributed up and down Saanich Road; she recovered three, replaced the others at Mac's ... the family giving a concert at Fairfield United's 75th anniversary celebration; Grandma Holland, at 80, has attended the church for 67 years ... Granny Forsberg, also 80 (a classmate of Grandma Holland's 65 years ago at Vic High), replacing several feet of lace around the veil attached to Marilyn's (and Mother's) tiara (Mother had cut off the original lace 16 years previously to make a bride-doll dress for Marilyn.) ... Mother steaming around the Saanich-Quadra-McKenzie triangle at 5:30 most mornings in a 3/4-ton, 12-passenger van, dropping the girls' newspapers in strategic spots (at four-thirty one morning came across a gorgeous Honda motorcycle parked outside an apartment; marvelled at its beauty and empathized with son's interest in such vehicles) ... Melissa adding three inches to her height over the summer; now taller than her three sisters, and very slim (our chubbiest chunk of cheer 12, 13 and 14 years ago) ... Mark bringing the Tooth Fairy to near-destitution as his last baby tooth hangs by a thread ... Father and Matthew setting off for "Tree Climbers" each Tuesday night in identical T-shirts (Chip and Block; Block tries to match Chip's enthusiasm!)

A MODERN FAIRY-TALE

Once upon a time (actually, the summer of 1984), a Tall, Dark and Handsome (TDH) young man was asked to join a youth group travelling to the West Indies. Several months earlier, a Petite, Blonde and Pretty (PBP) young lady had signed up for the same project. According to an interested observer (TDH's aunt, choir leader for the group), the plane was barely airborne before TDH had manoeuvred into a seat beside PBP (a.k.a. Angelic Bit of Fluff, the aunt's description). Before the four-week stint on the hot and dry island of Antigua was completed, the parents of PBP/ABF received a message from the two young people to the effect that "We know we're meant for each other; the Lord has great things for us to do together." The generation gap yawned wide as the parents tried to assimilate this startling news, especially as PBP/ABF was all of sixteen and a half, and TDH less than two years older.

Two summers and two youth projects (one separated: he in Colombia assisting his parents in their prison work, she in California working with juvenile delinquents; one together, again in the West Indies) only validated 1984's declaration. PBP/ABF and TDH flew down to Bogotá for Christmas of 1986 (thanks largely to the paper route PBP/ABF valiantly struggled with each morning for several months as a preface to her studies at the Conservatory). TDH's parents were as delighted with their son's choice as PBP/ABF's were with hers. A dainty ring, set with a diamond and two emeralds (the jewel for which Colombia is noted), became a prized item of jewellery, and plans were underway for an August wedding.

TDH finished his third year in criminology at Simon Fraser University, PBP/ABF her A.A. from Camosun College, and A.V.C.M. in both piano pedagogy and performing from the Victoria Conservatory. TDH applied for a position on the Saanich police force and was one of four selected from over 900 applicants. August 10, the third anniversary of the first date in Antigua, a Monday, was chosen as THE DAY.

Ralph Steele

AUGUST 10, 1987

On August 10, 1987, in a ceremony officiated by Pastor John Wilson and Reverend Ernest Kennedy, in the company of a church full of family and friends, Marilyn Holland became Mrs. Geordon Rendle.   After a beautiful organ-violin prelude by Reverend Doug Harris and his wife Mary, Marilyn's three sisters (bridesmaids, wearing gowns sewn by their 80-year-old grandmother) and her three brothers (two ring bearers and an usher) picked up their violins and ushered in their big sister with Clarke's "Trumpet Tune in D."   Kristen and Jennifer Steele were flower girls. (Marilyn had been the flower girl 16 years earlier for their parents, Ralph and Marilyn.)   Geordon's brother, Andy, was his best man; friends Terry Stauffer and Hugo Ciro were groomsmen.   The groom's uncle, Ian Rendle, and the bride's aunt, Marilyn Wilson, signed the register as witnesses.   The groom's mother sang "Wedding Prayer," accompanied by the bride's mother on the piano. Clara Knight, a high school friend of the bride's mother, not only arranged the flowers, but also catered the reception tea for several hundred guests, allowing the bride's parents to enjoy the festivities.

Both families are deeply grateful to God for bringing together Geordon and Marilyn. Little did the parents know twenty-six years ago, when they were all still single themselves, attending the same church, that their children would someday meet and marry.

Chapter 32: Letter to My Parents, 1987

January 27, 1987

Dear Mom and Dad,

… Michael, Margaret and Melissa are in the throes of exams, and are frantically studying; at least they are when I ask them to do the dishes, vacuum, etc. Our Music Festival is a month early. … What a hassle to choose pieces, let alone get them to an acceptable standard. And (would you believe) these children are not always cooperative. Oh well, at least Daughter 1 seems to see the value of her training now. Her pieces sound just beautiful. She has a graduation recital on May 14 at the Young auditorium at Camosun, an hour's length. She and Geordon have been the centre of attention of late: Geordon sang (she accompanied) last Sunday night, and then the pastor interviewed them as to what they had seen in Colombia, what their plans were, and other more personal things (Where did he propose to you? What do you think of your inlaws-to-be?), which had the congregation in gales. They both handled themselves well, although Marilyn had to fight down some giggles to get the answers out. She does speak well in public (enviable), and of course Geordon has never had a problem in that area! He had his suit on, looked great, and she was wearing a bright Colombian skirt with a frilly white blouse and Colombian earrings and necklace (beads and pottery) and had her hair loose and wavy. I know it's wrong to be proud, but I must admit I was so thankful that she is doing what she is doing and is such a good example to the rest of the gang (as is Geordon). I would have liked her to wait until she is 30 before she leaves home [!] and would just as soon she didn't have her mind set on working in Colombian prisons, but that's not for me to control. Because it was Youth Night, Michael, Margaret and Melissa joined a flautist in an unaccompanied piece for the offertory. The rest of the family was watching all this quite happily; I love observing the little boys taking everything in, so happy with big people around who think they're quite special. (They are!)

Chapter 33: A Christmas Digest, 1988

EDITORIAL *by Louise*

The wild geese fly overhead in formation to and from Swan Lake. For the twenty-second time, we are watching, helplessly, as our triangle of earth buries itself under a crunchy layer of oak leaves. We go out to deliver our newspapers in the dark (sometimes in the moonlight), and return before sunrise. The whitened rooftops and glittering grass suggest it is time to dig up the geraniums and store them in the greenhouse. Several continue to bloom on the front steps, oblivious to the potential for disaster should the temperature dive. Grape hyacinths have already sent up sturdy leaves, and snowdrops are making a tentative appearance. Christmas cannot be too far away!

At this season of our Saviour's birth, we take great joy in extending Christmas greetings to our friends and family. We have the confidence that the God who has been faithful again in 1988 will continue His faithfulness in 1989; we wish this for each of you, too. " ... God shall supply all your need according to his riches in glory by Christ Jesus." (Philippians 4:19)

SEEN AND HEARD ...

... Mark and Matthew trudging the long half-block to Pay-Less Gas with a supper for Mike ...

... Baskets of dirty laundry ...

... Mom (as five PCS students scramble out to car at 8:17 a.m.): "Matt, get one of the girls to brush your hair on the way." Matthew: "It's OK. It looks like this after recess anyway." ...

... Baskets of wet laundry ...

... Melissa's photograph decorating the *Times Colonist* in honour of International Carriers Week (Her cousin, Sonya Westaway, was given the same honour, as well as a trophy and watch.) ... Melissa, surrounded by cookies, pre-empting the front of the *Saanich News*, to illustrate family's Operation Eyesight benefit sale; Matthew, knee-deep in plants and dried grasses, taking over the *Gordon Head News*, with the same inside story: "Over $1,100 is being sent from a most fortunate and grateful family to help those with eyesight problems." …

… Lines full of drying clothes …

… Question on theory page, Grade I level: "How would you play Bars 4 to 6?" Expected answer: "Crescendo to the third E." Student's answer: "I wouldn't." Teacher pencils in, "Oh yes, you would!" …

… Baskets of dry laundry, ready to be folded …

… Colour Day at school: Mark and Matthew decked out, respectively, in 28 and 19 green items …

… Note from student to "Mrs. Haland": "to the best peainow teacher I ever had" (Mother admires spelling, reminds herself that she is this sweetheart's *only* piano teacher to date.) …

… Baskets of dirty laundry …

… Mark and Matthew searching out beverage cans in neighbourhood ditches for school project; haul 105 cans to school in early September, giving boost to house score …

… Baskets of wet laundry …

… Five ducklings swimming with their mother on our front pond for two idyllic days last spring; their disappearance had us wondering whether they had made their way to Swan Lake or had been dispatched by crows or raccoons …

… Dryer whirling through load after load …

… Our boarder, Doug, 6' 3" and lanky, scrambling over neighbouring fences to retrieve his cockatiel, returning with Spud perched on his shoulder …

… Baskets of dry laundry, ready to be folded …

… Geordon, one of Saanich's "finest," patrolling the municipality in a blue and white squad car, keeping an eye on—amongst other things—his paper-distributing inlaws … Geordon, speaking to several hundred young people at YFC's Full Circle in September …

… Baskets of folded laundry, ready to be distributed …

PERSONAL GLIMPSES

Michael obtained voting privileges on September 30. In February, a schoolmate of his, Doug Van Dyke, moved in with Spud, his cheerful cockatiel. In September, two UVic engineering students, Glen Halvorson and Mark Doerksen, came to live here. Two other motorcycles have joined Michael's; Mark's car occupies a spot near the end of our driveway, keeping a wary eye on the family cars (and their drivers).

Margaret, 17 in October, now has her driver's license and **Melissa**, 16 in December, peruses the driver's manual with more than passing interest. Both play on PCS's volleyball team, as well as taking piano and violin lessons at the Grade X and IX levels. (When her parents are not looking, Melissa joins as many sports activities as she can; she won the Junior Girls sports trophy in June.) **Melody** just turned 14, and at five feet of determination also studies violin and piano. The Trio's honour standing at school is jeopardized by the demands of sports and music, and their early-morning paper routes. They all have to turn away requests for babysitting. Melissa keeps an eye on neighbours' houses and pets while they are away on holiday (Melissa's Minding). She also tutors a Grade 2 child in reading and arithmetic for an hour twice a week. Although she enjoys the challenge, and her student appears to be progressing well, she commented, "It's hard work!" (Her mother and grandmother could have told her that.) In her final year at high school, Margaret works with a couple of students on the violin, as well as making dried flower arrangements and decorating stationery (Bits of Beauty).

Big sister **Marilyn**, 21 at the end of the year, supervises her three youngest siblings on the piano, in addition to teaching several other students. She conducts the YFC choir (nearly 50 strong, including her three sisters; Mike works the sound system), and accompanies the Police Chorus. In the summer, she and **Geordon** moved into the top floor of the Rendle home. Grandpa Rendle, in his mid-80s, occupies the main floor, and Andy, Geordon's younger brother and a UVic student, makes the lower floor his headquarters. Marilyn has just started an intensive secretarial course at Sprott-Shaw.

Mark and **Matthew** continue their relatively carefree existence, meeting the requirements of violin, piano, newspaper and notice deliveries (Mark's Messages) with good-humoured resignation. Mark has added a low and mellow sound to the family repertoire: Auntie Marilyn gave him her beautiful euphonium to play in the school band. Matthew is developing an interest in plants, as he stocks his Matt's Plants shelves with all kinds of green plants and dried grasses and flowers.

Bruce's job as emergency social worker is very demanding. As more and more ugly incidents of child abuse surface, additional pressure is put on him and his co-workers to find solutions to family breakdowns. As well as maintaining calm and order in our household, Bruce oversees the shopping and cooking for our exuberant, hungry group. I, as the spoiled half of this partnership, am free to teach, work with our children both in music and in their mini-businesses (licensed under Holland Family Enterprises), play the organ or piano on Sundays, attempt keeping on top of family schedules, and try to keep ahead of the laundry. My goal is to have at least one empty laundry basket on the premises at all times, but success is elusive!

LIFE'S LIKE THIS

December 16, 1987, 2:00 p.m. Family is providing 45-minute concert for the Women's Canadian Club in the Empress Hotel ballroom. Arriving a few minutes ahead of programme to tune violins, is instructed to wait in the conservatory until time for their contribution to the afternoon's activities. To her consternation, Mother learns she and children are to be presented to the lieutenant-governor's wife, Mrs. Rogers. Fortunately, guest of honour's graciousness smooths over family's ignorance of protocol. Family invited to stay for tea, a pleasant ending to the afternoon. (Michael adds black vest to outfit and leaves for ten-hour stint at Laurel Point Inn.)

June 15, 1988, 10:30 p.m. Mother finds youngest child in Margaret's bedroom, scolds him for not being in bed. Child meekly makes way to bunk. **June 16** Mother's birthday supper. Array of gifts presented to beaming recipient. Matthew carries his card, using both hands, over to her: a clown holding 47 balloons, each one numbered and covered with a penny. "Happy Birthday, Mom" stands up in wobbly letters. Inscription at bottom reads, "I love you Love Matthew xoxo." All is meticulously coloured. Second inscription reads, "Designed by Margaret, brought to life by Matthew." *[2019: Mother still has card with pennies intact, barely hanging on to card with yellowing scotch tape.]*

June 23, 9:45 a.m. Melissa, Melody and Mother wend their way through traffic towards examination room for violin exams at 10:13 a.m. and 11:49 a.m. Mother, as unstrung accompanist, comments on inconvenience of examination spacing, wishes Melody's exam were scheduled an hour later. Youngest daughter assures her time is correct, rummages around in music case, holds up form and shrieks in dismay: examination is scheduled for *11*:13 a.m., Dr. Gleam (their long-suffering teacher) will be on her way, and what will we do? Mother wishes she had gone berry-picking.

July morning Box of unpaired socks has been overflowing for weeks. Youngest three have decided to see who can find the most pairs. After laying a line of socks snaking from family room through kitchen and around living room, each child takes a sock and "walks the line," trying to find its mate. Father muses that were parents to do it all over again, a) white socks would be outlawed; and b) every child would wear one-size-fits-all navy-blue socks.

July 31, 2:00 p.m. Geordon and Marilyn and Margaret, in the company of 23 other Youth for Christ team members, leave for Bogotá, Colombia. They will work a month in the prisons with Geordon's parents, who have spent nearly twenty years ministering to the medical, spiritual, social and economic needs of Colombian prisoners.

August 30, 7:00 a.m. Mother returns from Melody's paper route, dressed in light summer dress and old running shoes; left arm and side are smudged with ink from newspapers. Decides to dig in garden before getting washed and dressed for day. **10:00 a.m.** Wheelbarrow-loads of compost have been incorporated into newest bed. Mother is hot, tired and even dirtier. Enters back door on way to bath just in time to hear front doorbell ring. Reluctantly peeks out through crack in door to discover two nicely-dressed young men on doorstep. One asks, "Did your son tell you? We phoned from Clearbrook late last night to say we would like to look at your suite." Mother had not been told ... **September 6** Glen and Mark arrive to take up residence in the suite and add another happy dimension to family life, as they join nine others around the supper table (11 or 13 others for Sunday meal). Glen commented after taking the tour of suite and house by dishevelled landlady, and learning of family's activities, "I wouldn't mind staying here just to see how it works." He might now say, *"If it works"*! [*And he stayed for six years!*]

November 22, early morning Mother battles 85 km/h winds and pelting rain for an hour and a quarter on Margaret's day off. Rain pricks arms. Clothing is drenched. Unenthusiastic carrier keeps pulling up rain-weighted slacks and wiping eyeglasses, tries to remember benevolent spring and summer mornings, when birds and sunshine, not wind and rain, are the paper carrier's companions.

Chapter 34: A Christmas Digest, 1989

EDITORIAL *by Louise*

We extend to you our Christmas greetings and a wish for God's blessing in the New Year.

It is unsettling to realize how many changes a year can bring and yet reassuring to be reminded of God's goodness and oversight during both the good and bad experiences. During 1989, another graduate was thrust out into the real world, three boarders have left (Geoff has moved in, and Glen is returning in January), a foster girl has come and gone, and innumerable young people have entertained and been entertained by the young people who live here.

With the church, school, work, YFC, music, and sports activities that fill our days, we have to fight for family "together" times. Capitalizing on newspaperless statutory holidays, we have twice spent overnight in a motel up-Island, "vegging out," as the next generation says. Our 12-passenger van trundles over the Malahat, loaded with ten family members, an assortment of pillows, teddies, books, junk food, and much merriment. It is surprising how much relaxation can be found in thirty-six hours away from the regular schedule. And Geordon's breakfast cornbread is a treat!

In February, we were invited to participate in the Saanich municipality's "Zomba" concert at UVic Centre, in aid of a developing African city. We spent the first of July weekend at churches in Ucluelet and Tofino. The generous and friendly response to our music made our sixteen years of music lessons and performances worthwhile. We have just been asked to join the Police Chorus in a benefit concert at UVic next March 24, a real privilege for us.

Mark's euphonium (courtesy of Auntie Marilyn) and Michael's bass guitar (courtesy of the church, with lessons from our outstanding music pastor, Ken Dosso) add new sounds to our environment. Unlike the violin melodies which, according to a neighbour, "pour out of every window," the bass guitar throbs downwards through the floorboards from Mike's west end room; the euphonium reverberates upwards from the living room, and makes one wonder if perhaps the *Queen Mary* is docking at the front steps.

SCENE IN PASSING ...

... Granny and Mother collaborating on Granny's book, with Mother learning many things about family that she had never known (Granny has contributed towards family's new computer; Mother can put final draft on a disk, once she learns how to use machine.) ... Easter Sunday baptismal service, at which three sisters (The Trio) give evidence of their faith in Christ (Parents are grateful for influence and encouragement of pastoral staff, youth and Sunday school leaders, and many others in the Christian community.) ... Jennifer and Helene, our two French-Canadian billets who stayed with us for a week, plus their 22 class-mates, plus PCS's 24 host students, in our living room, acting out skits in "franglais" (fractured English); house rocks with laughter ... youth group from church wall-to-wall in same room for after-church firesides ... three volleyball teams buying and consuming $90 worth of pizza while visiting with PCS friends, within the same four walls ... two teams spending two nights in sleeping bags on music room floor ... Margaret, radiant at graduation in a coral satin dress designed by self and Granny, and made by Granny, receiving a bursary towards her music studies ... Mother, frustrated by inability to gather dozens of beverage cans strewn around Ucluelet and Tofino for PCS fundraising; Father refusing to stop van every hundred feet (Son-in-law suggests we hang member of family out window to scoop them up as we go by. Although suggestion is not taken, Mark and Matthew return to school in September with collection of over 300 cans.) ... discovery that while family and violins are in Ucluelet, Mark's good shoes are in Victoria; sixth violinist performs in stockinged feet ... eight members of family, including Auntie Marilyn, fanned out over the Carey Road-Glanford Avenue area on a hot August morning, distributing flyers. ... Melissa starting her sixth year of *Times Colonist* delivery on November 12; Margaret to do likewise next March; Melody well into fifth year ... "Uncle Ed" Robinson visiting here from Saskatchewan for three days in October, discussing flying, sports facts and figures with Mike, Mark and Matthew well past younger two's bedtime (family's first opportunity to meet cousin on Grandma Holland's side, a lawyer-sportscaster-pilot) ... Melody's bedroom the morning after she had shared it for the first time with Tubby, her ten-week-old Siamese kitten: plant stand and three potted plants strewn all over the carpet (Auntie Marilyn's comment: "But he's only a *baby!*" Melody knows she has an ally in her aunt. Family has since learned that a Siamese kitten: climbs, cries like a baby, and enjoys digging in any available dirt.) ... Margaret helping Matthew's teacher coach girls' and boys' volleyball ... Mark's team winning Richmond Christian Schools tournament ... Family listening to glorious 2 1/2 hours of Handel's *Messiah* with baroque instruments at UVic Centre ... Mark and Matthew recognizing "He Shall Feed His Flock," which Marilyn and Michael have played as a violin duet for many years ... whole family mentally singing through intricacies of "For Unto Us A Child

Is Born" … Matthew roused from slumber to stand for "Hallelujah Chorus" …

LIFE'S LIKE THIS

Sunday, June 18, 1:00 p.m. Father sits at table opening Father's Day cards and gifts. Family watches with interest. Mother is pleased with special card she had found him. Father opens her offering, hesitates, bites lip and thanks her; cannot suppress amusement. Closes card, but is challenged by family as to reason for twinkle in eye. Second daughter opens card, reads, "To Bruce, Love from Bruce"; Mother is not pleased with self.

Friday, November 10, 10:30 a.m. Parents have been trying to get away for mini-holiday (day and a half) since 8:30 a.m. when children were dropped off at school. Phone rings incessantly; laundry, dishes, and tidying up beckon; papers have still not arrived, will need to be delivered in rain and heavy traffic after school. (Mother concerned, as she was prepared at 5:45 a.m. to take bundles around Quadra-Saanich-McKenzie triangle as usual; now Margaret will have to.) Mother had been unable to get reservation at Point-No-Point, hit upon idea of staying at Geordon and Marilyn's peaceful, quiet house, as they would be at 4031, keeping the lid on. Request was granted with enthusiasm. (Geordon's happy comment: "And the price is right!") **10:30 p.m.** Parents arrive at 2785 Murray Drive after day exploring downtown, topped off by dinner date at the Chantecler with Granny and Grandpa, who had helped fold and collate most recent flyers. Note from son-in-law informs parents of chilled goblets in freezer, white grape juice in fridge; fireplace set for lighting; appropriate ("mellow") tapes near tape deck; home-canned peaches and pumpkin loaf available for breakfast. Parents smile at such thoughtfulness.

Sunday, December 10, 6:00 p.m. Church orchestra begins 20-minute prelude of Christmas music before Sunday School Christmas service: Margaret, Melissa, Melody and Matthew on violin; Mark on euphonium; Mother on vibraharp, then organ. Mother wishes two eldest had been able to join in. **6:25 p.m.** Organ solo tries to set jubilant tone for service with "Gloria in Excelsis Deo." **6:30 p.m.** Service underway with series of Christmas Scriptures alternating with choirs. After third reading (Isaiah 9:6—"For unto us a child is born …"), eight violins (five youngest plus three friends) are set to come onto platform from both sides to play "For Unto Us A Child Is Born," following polyphonic vocal arrangement of soprano, alto, tenor and bass entering in turn, from Handel's *Messiah*. Packed church is in darkness; floodlights illumine platform. Mother has been alternating between organ and piano, assumes violinists are in place. Most are; four appear at one side, three at other. Father and Melissa notice one-eighth of group is missing, rush through lounge and lower floor trying to find him. Melissa returns to line; violinists file up on platform. Mother hesitates, makes mad dash through side door in case errant musician, who has spent hours practising piece, has turned up. Returns to piano, plays introduction. Each set of two violins enters in turn; half-size violin manfully brings in bass part, somewhat overpowered by one 3/4-size and five full-size instruments. Meanwhile, missing violinist, who had been upstairs under misapprehension there was more time before performance, enters Fellowship Hall where closed-circuit TV displays "Group of 7." Violinist "freaks out"—his term—as he realizes he should be playing with them. ... **Later** *Eight* violins, plus three flutes, enter auditorium for "Silent Night" offertory.

PERSONAL GLIMPSES

Marilyn completed a 10-month secretarial course at Sprott-Shaw (in 6 1/2 months; her parents say it is those piano fingers!) and is working full time at an insurance office and teaching several piano students. She directs the Youth for Christ choir and accompanies the Police Chorus and does her best to join the family for concerts and other activities. **Geordon** spent several weeks in a series of ankle-to-thigh casts after shredding knee ligaments playing basketball last January. After an enforced "holiday" of six months, he was loaned to the Victoria Police Department Crimestoppers team for a few months, and is only recently back in a Saanich patrol car. He narrated a segment of Crimestoppers for TV; we now refer to him as our son-in-law, the celebrity! He and Marilyn have invested in a house overlooking Portage Inlet and are experiencing the trials and tribulations, and benefits, of home ownership for themselves. Their month (June) in Mexico, working in the prisons, will probably be their last trip for a while, although their goal still is missionary service in a Spanish-speaking country.

Michael celebrated his birthday at the very end of September, a sunny reminder of the morning 20 years previous when he, in typically impetuous fashion, arrived two weeks ahead of the calendar, to be greeted by the doctor's quiet, but urgent, "O2." (It was, fortunately, only later that his mother realized the full implication of the order; by then he was crying lustily.) As this is written (December 13), Michael is back in Downsview, Ontario, for further testing for the air force. He has been so busy with his job at Pay-Less Gas, YFC (lights and sound), the bass guitar, and sports, that he is quite happy still to be at home and we enjoy his contributions to family life.

In September, **Margaret** entered the two-year diploma programme at Camosun College for violin. With the exception of English, all her courses are taken at the Victoria Conservatory of Music. Private lessons, pedagogy and Kodaly classes, chamber music and orchestra fill her calendar to overflowing (and mean Mother has to check Margaret's schedule to see if she has the use of her car).

Melissa, nearly 17, has just taken a music history exam and is now preparing for a violin exam (Grade IX) in January. She works on the youth executive at church and eagerly anticipates high school graduation in June. We appreciate the happy, cooperative middle of our family; her cheerful "OK, Mom" at 6:00 a.m. every morning makes that part of the day tolerable.

Melody, just turned 15, presides over her world from a well-organized, colourful bedroom. The receiver on her telephone is rarely cool, nor are her bedclothes, with a small kitten generating warmth between the sheets. By the end of June, Melody, too, should have reached our suggested goal for musical studies: at least Grade VIII on both piano and violin.

Mark tries to balance our parents' musical expectations with a passion for sports, usually with good success in both areas. He generally receives cooperation from the rest of the family in our flyer distribution which has grown from small notices regarding a lost cat put out across paper routes, to flyers distributed by 2,500s.

Matthew is also in the intermediate section of school, three grades (Grade 4) behind Mark. For the first time, he receives academic evaluation in letter grades; older siblings regard his string of A's through narrowed eyes, especially as his first report also contained a positive comment regarding his setting ability in volleyball. Mother is not too excited at the prospect of a sixth volleyball fanatic in the family.

Bruce faces new scheduling in 1990, as his duty worker job takes on a four-day-on/four-day-off pattern, and he will have to take his calls in an office, not at home. His two-weeks-on/two-weeks-off routine of fifteen years, which required 196 on-call hours over the first two weeks, and none for the second two, has worked well for the family. Bruce continues to help coordinate family activities, providing excellent meals for family and boarders and projecting an air of serenity over family busyness. **Louise** is almost halfway through her thirtieth year of teaching (twenty-third in music) and finds satisfaction in following the progress of students from past years, as they move through the musical ranks. She oversees the family's little businesses, which gives her opportunities for nonmusical activities (gardening for Matt's Plants; dealing with local businesses and walking, and walking, for Mark's Messages; and substituting on the girls' paper routes).

Love from the Hollands

THE PARENTS

Chapter 35: A Christmas Digest, 1990

EDITORIAL *by Louise*

1990 has nearly passed. We thank God for His goodness towards us again this year, and we wish you His best for 1991. In these days of uncertainty and turmoil, how reassuring it is to remember that "God is our refuge and strength, a very present help in trouble." (Psalm 46:1)

Our days are punctuated by activities relating to church, school, music, social work, teaching, and business. Parents seem constantly to be commenting on doors left open (at two degrees Celsius in November), empty gas tanks, lights left on in unoccupied rooms, extraordinary phone bills, overflowing laundry baskets, and depleted refrigerators—all byproducts of ten people sharing the same house, vehicles and telephones.

With our young adults now involved in many other pursuits, it is more difficult to meet requests for family concerts. However, this fall we performed in several settings. One Sunday in September we took part in services at White Rock Baptist Church in the morning, and at South Delta Baptist in the evening. In October, we played in Vancouver for the wedding of a former boarder, and provided nearly an hour's music at the reception. A special friend from over 30 years ago, Kathleen Agnew, had asked if we ever were on the mainland to be sure to play at her church. Arrangements were made for the weekend of the wedding, and we were somewhat unsettled to learn that Seven Oaks Alliance in Abbotsford is not the little rural church we had envisioned, but has nearly three times the seating capacity of the McPherson Playhouse in Victoria. The congregation was very kind to us and helped us realize what a privilege and responsibility our music brings with it. All seven play in the church orchestra when it accompanies congregational singing every few weeks—five on violins, Michael on bass guitar, and Mark on euphonium. Mom leaves the organ and hammers on a vibraharp. Another highlight was playing some of our own pieces on the Police Chorus programme at UVic, as well as providing a violin descant for one of the choir's pieces.

Our household consists of Glen Halvorson, our amiable, tolerant UVic boarder who is into the third year of his association with us; cousin Patrick Scriver, who is Margaret's age; the home-grown eight; and three cats: our aging tabby, Tiger;

Patrick's elegant Katie, fluffy white and tortoise; and Tubby, Melody's entertaining (and not-too-bright) Siamese. Geordon and Marilyn sometimes turn up with their sheltie, Zoe, and their temperamental yet lovable cat, Evita; and Geordon's brother, Andy, drops by with his miniature toy pom, Punkin. As those who do not totally approve of animals in the house, the Holland parents have come a long way!

Louise's sisters, Harriet (head ICU nurse from Montana) and Jeannie (Jeannie's House of Fashions, Medicine Hat) have both moved back to the Island this fall, after an absence of over 20 years. Louise, Eric and Peggy are enjoying renewed contacts with them and with each other. The Forsbergs look forward to celebrating their golden anniversary at Christmas with almost all of the seventeen grandchildren present.

PERSONAL GLIMPSES

Bruce continues fielding off-hours social work calls, with a new and not completely welcome change: he now must take all his calls at the office during "core" hours. He then comes home in the middle of the night (providing he is not on a call) and remains on duty, but from home. This enables him to put messages for the day staff directly on the computer, but it keeps him away from the family for much longer stretches at a time. As a result, other family members must, of necessity, do more of the cooking while Louise teaches, and this is a positive development.

Louise is again privileged to work with several piano classes and finds much satisfaction in watching her students gain the benefits of disciplined practice. Now that the eldest five have been seen through to at least Grade VIII level on violin and piano, her attention tends to focus on the two youngest, who are currently studying piano with their big sister. They spent several profitable years with Yasuko Eastman on the violin, and are now under Dr. Elfreda Gleam's tutelage. In addition to teach-

ing responsibilities, Louise oversees the family's little businesses. Mark's Messages has just finished another large flyer distribution, putting out 11,000 flyers (with the help of several other families) over nearby neighbourhoods. Computer and photocopier are humming for the weeks leading up to the quarterly distribution.

Marilyn has just taken on a position as half-time (25 hours)

MARILYN IN FRONT OF THE YOUTH FOR CHRIST LOGO

Youth for Christ worker, conducting the choir (which will again present its musical, three Sundays out of four, from January to June at various churches), working in girls' ministries, and studying through the comprehensive YFC internship course. The other half of her working time is spent teaching piano. She also accompanies the Police Chorus, and travelled to Wales and Holland with the Chorus in May. She and **Geordon** continue to open their home to church groups, friends, colleagues and family. A couple of weeks ago, nearly 40 YFC members spent Friday night and Saturday at their home. Geordon will be working within the school system as liaison officer starting in January, and looks forward to this new challenge.

Michael turned 21 in September. A few weeks ago he received his private pilot's license. Although he was offered managerships in both Pay-Less Gas and 7-11, he decided to work for North Douglas Distributors, filling orders in the warehouse for a few months, and more recently driving the delivery trucks, saving as much as he can for his anticipated entry into Trinity Western's flying programme next September. Much of his considerable energy is directed into YFC commitments, badminton, volleyball and bass guitar.

Margaret is working through her second year of the violin diploma programme at the Victoria Conservatory of Music, and at the Grade X level on piano with Wendy Maggiora. Music from the Baroque period to the Twentieth Century wafts through the house, giving much pleasure to the rest of us. Margaret helps Mother with a class of younger students and uses the computer to assemble some ads for our family flyer, as well as providing illustrations for the flyer. She occasionally umpires league volleyball games.

Melissa, after fourteen years of music lessons (and reaching Grade IX on both piano and violin), is taking a break from formal assignments. On the waiting list for nursing at Camosun College, she is working at the Sydney Reynolds china shop downtown, her first experience with a 9 to 5 job. She and Margaret both spent a couple of months at Camp Qwanoes during the summer, in several different capacities.

Melody, after completing Grade VIII on piano in June, is also taking a respite from weekly lessons. She spends considerable time in the company, or at least within hearing distance (via the telephone), of her friends, and just completed another strenuous season of volleyball which included a five-day trip to Smithers. In Grade 11, she claims to enjoy physics, chemistry and math. She hopes her learner's license will be available immediately after her sixteenth birthday (December 5); there are at least five other family members who do not share her enthusiasm at that prospect. Melody has been promised a free weekend at camp in March if she doesn't remove the wide elastic band around her neck (given to her by her fellow campers at a retreat in November) until then. Fortunately, turtlenecks suit her.

Mark has crossed the parking lot at PCS to the high school campus and Grade 8.

He works at the piano and violin and plays the euphonium in the band, and participates in as many sports as he can manage. He could be seen at the end of November with other family members delivering their portion of Shopping Opportunities; he was the one in the fluorescent pink cap and psychedelic striped shorts (his home economics project).

Matthew, the only family member still in the elementary school (Grade 5), continues to progress well at school, sports and music. He joins Mark in collating and delivering flyers, and in substituting on paper routes in the area. He has developed into a fine art the skill of reading books surreptitiously at mealtimes.

SCENE IN PASSING ...

... five youngest (18 down to 10) inhabiting grandparents' redecorated trailer on the driveway in May and June; pillows, teddies, books and snacks filling in empty spaces (Parents have difficulty finding workers for household chores.) ... Mother out delivering flyers and newspapers with offspring, dressed in comfortable cast-off T-shirts decorated with young peoples' projects; Father suggesting that wearing shirts labelled "Milk Run" (an event sponsored by BC Dairies) and "30-Hour Famine" (a World Vision project) borders on hypocrisy ... Melissa, glowing in a royal purple satin gown decorated with 18 satin roses, designed by herself and Granny Forsberg and made by Granny, graduating from PCS last June ... Grandma Holland patiently collating hundreds of flyers for us ... letter of resignation to *Times Colonist* at end of 1989, resulting from many mornings when carriers were up at 5:30 a.m., only to find drop-boxes empty (Family has managed to adapt to 7:00 a.m. alarms, after years of early risings.) ... Melissa taking Grade IX Violin exam in middle of Grade 12 final exams (re-scheduled from January due to examiner's accident), managing to pass all comfortably, graduating with a string of As and Bs. ... Melody, dressed in friend Hugo's business suit, white shirt and tie, for "Formal Day" at school ... Brian [6] and Tommy [4] arriving several sunny summer mornings, knapsacks and lunchkits in hand, ready to spend the day with Mark, Matthew and parents—a delight to babysit (Tommy even reminded us after lunch that it was naptime!) ... Lydia Tuttle and her three daughters sharing the upstairs suite during July and August, while she took a course at UVic ... Marilyn conducting a Police Chorus practice, with her mother at the piano (Burly policemen treat petite substitute conductor graciously, chuckle when little blonde diplomatically sets her accompanist straight.) ... Bruce cooking for a ten-day backpacking hike in the Rockies, spending three days by himself at a hot spring while hikers climb Mt. Robson ... Geordon (who also does much of the cooking) risking the excellent relationship he has with his mother-in-law by bringing his father-in-law a Herman cartoon: Herman's wife looms over Herman, who is dressed in his kitchen apron, and says, "Marriage is give and take; *I* eat your cooking, so *you* do the dishes." (Mother and Marilyn fail to see the humour.) ...

LIFE'S LIKE THIS

Thursday, December 21, 1989, 8:45 p.m. Family has played Christmas music at Marrion Gardens, is congregating at Forsberg grandparents' home at #6, 3981 Nelthorpe, in celebration of parents' and grandparents' wedding anniversary. Family brings Margaret's laundry basket full of fruit and other goodies for grandparents. Parents had been torn between fewer gifts in a more professional arrangement, and more items in a more amateur arrangement; opted for latter. Grandparents overlook lack of esthetics, very appreciative of gifts (give laundry basket back to granddaughter), comment on how full living room is with seven grandchildren and parents; provide Christmas cake, tea and Grandpa's gingersnaps for guests. At Father's request, Mother plays carols for family. 9:30 Son-in-law arrives in uniform, with walkie-talkie murmuring messages discernible only to constable. Wolfs down dessert. Family's ears prick up as "Nelthorpe" comes over intercom. Complaint is relayed regarding noisy party in area. Family looks at each other uneasily, especially when complainant's address is given as #12 in complex. Constable tells switchboard he is in area, will check on problem. ... Returns to #6 with information that school across road is having a dance and neighbours do not appreciate the noise and confusion. Family is relieved.

Tuesday, March 27, 1990, 1:30 p.m. Mother is alone at home, napping in upstairs bedroom. Becomes aware of brisk footsteps near music room, accompanied by loud "YAHOO!" Enthusiastic shout decrescendoes at patio to "YAHOO!" and, still lacking response, to "YAHOO!" at back door. Mother, realizing something noteworthy must have occurred, makes her way downstairs to learn that eldest son has just taken first solo flight. Mother congratulates him, thinks to self that some things are better learned after the fact.

Saturday, August 25, 7:00 p.m. Toyota zips into French Beach campsite, disgorging eldest daughter and husband, eldest son, and huge, hyperactive dog (Igmore, Marilyn and Geordon's charge for a few weeks). Mother has just cleaned up after primitive supper for six other family members, is returning to campsite with pail of clean dishes and utensils washed at the tap (cold water) three campsites away. Thinks with longing of hot water and comfortable bed back in Victoria; views exuberant addition to situation gloomily. Musters what few hospitality skills she can to welcome newcomers. ... Later: Family surrounds campfire, talking and laughing, trying to contain Igmore's frenzied activity. Mother enjoys banter in glow of fire, dismisses earlier misgivings.

Saturday, October 20, 8:30 a.m. Twelve members of Lynden volleyball team, who have spent night bunked down in music room, plus three sisters and their two friends, plus one harried mother, are all getting ready to leave the house at 9:00 a.m.: American girls and one friend to PCS for volleyball tournament; family and other friend to join fourth sister at Elizabeth Elliott conference, which will be preceded by 10-minute violin prelude. All sinks and mirrors are in use. Air is thick with hairspray. Mother is relieved that brand-new volleyball uniforms which she laundered previous night appear not to have shrunk. Male members of family are not sorry to see group disperse, miraculously on time. Only casualties are luxurious towel and large make-up kit left behind.

Love and best wishes from the Hollands

Chapter 36: A Christmas Digest, 1991

EDITORIAL *by Louise*

Several geraniums survive in the garden, snowdrops are peeking through the soil, and a forlorn fuchsia, still producing the odd blossom, swings in the fall winds near the front door. The oak leaves congregate in piles where they were left two weeks ago when Mother traded a rake for a cortisone shot in her shoulder. And it is, unbelievably, December 14! Judging by the recent flyer-laden newspapers—yes, we're back on routes after a two-year break—it must be countdown until Christmas. We look past the tinsel and commercialism to the real meaning of Christmas, and thank God for the gift of His Son, our Saviour, and for the many gifts and opportunities He gives us each day. We send our love and best wishes to you and trust the end of 1991 finds you happy and well.

Nine regular regulars (our youngest five plus four young men) plus three intermittent regulars (Geordon and Marilyn; Michael) ensure that this place is rarely empty. Each "visiting" young person brings his own gift of personality, interests and ideas (and laughter), and our young people enjoy and learn from them and each other. This week we are saying farewell to Ian Lundman, who has just finished an eight-month work experience in Victoria towards a water engineering diploma; in January, we welcome back his cousin, Glen Halvorson, who completes his courses in mechanical engineering at UVic in April. Hugo Ciro, a high school classmate of Geordon's in Bogotá, and one of his groomsmen four years ago, works as a computer consultant and has graciously accommodated himself to the constant activity here. Jason Young, in first-year political science at UVic, and Greg Toews, in computer engineering at UVic, also fit in very well, water-fights and icing-sugar-in-the-bed episodes notwithstanding.

It has been our privilege again this year to provide music in several settings: weddings, church services, care homes, the opening of the new Baptist Seminary in Langley, and Sluggett Memorial Baptist's 100th anniversary celebration. Sluggett Memorial (Brentwood) is where I grew up. My first Sunday School teacher, Miss Doris Tickner, now in her 90s, still attends Central Baptist here in Victoria with our family. I remember crying, as a four year old, when I was invited to come into the Sunday School class. As a twelve year old, I learned to play the church's pump organ under the direction of the elderly pastor; I could hardly reach the all-important pumping pedals.

A special treat was having Hazel Page, an indomitable lady in her 70s, live with us for several days during the summer, entertaining us with stories of her linguistic work in the Far East. For many years, she was a missionary to tribal people in the Philippines, and more recently an English teacher in China. Our boarders and children were particularly impressed with her descriptions of the food she ate—and enjoyed—during her decades in the Philippines. Apparently flying ants pulled from the air and popped into the mouth are both crunchy and tasty! Hazel was given the highest award the Shanghai government gives to a foreigner for her contribution to the Chinese people.

We pass several milestones this year: one parent's entry into "prime time 55," the other's completion of her first half-century, and a 30th wedding anniversary. Bruce and I enjoyed a banquet and presentation at Government House in November, where Bruce received a framed 25-year certificate from Premier Harcourt and a handshake from Lieutenant-Governor Lam.

PREMIER HARCOURT PRESENTS 25-YEAR CERTIFICATE

PERSONAL GLIMPSES

Bruce continues to field a variety of social work calls, many routine, some increasingly ugly and sad. As the night-duty worker, he deals with the whole gamut of social problems, holding situations until the day workers can take them over. This may be why he is able to oversee this household so capably. In addition to the eleven of us who live here on a permanent basis, the dozens of music students who join us temporarily, the little children who sporadically come for babysitting, and Geordon, Marilyn and Michael, there are many other friends who wander into the activities here. While I teach, organize family music, and manage the family's little businesses (flyer distribution: our own 15,000 in November with other businesses' material included inside; Matt's Plants; Melody's Regal orders; and Melissa's Minding: house- and pet-sitting), Bruce keeps the crew well-fed, relying on a substantial repertoire of home-made soups, casseroles, and stews. He buys great quantities of food each week, and thanks God that we live in a land of abundant supplies. Leftovers are practically non-existent. With many willing and not-so-willing hands to help, food preparation is reasonably efficient.

Geordon and **Marilyn** whisk in and out of our home en route to a multitude of responsibilities. Geordon, as school liaison officer, works with Saanich students; lecturing against substance abuse and shoplifting is a major part of his work. He has also spoken in a variety of milieus: youth retreat, church lecture series, conference of lawyers in Vancouver. Marilyn, as half-time Youth for Christ worker, is completing her YFC internship programme, works in the schools, and conducts and manages the YFC choir, which starts touring in January. She also teaches private piano students and accompanies (and, in a pinch, conducts) the Police Chorus, and somehow manages, with Geordon, to help out with family concerts. They both take an active part at church as well, and wish, as we sometimes do, for elasticized days.

Michael, after driving delivery trucks for North Douglas Distributors for a year, became a summer worker at Camp Qwanoes, running the 240 h.p. Mastercraft for hours of water-skiing, carrying campers back and forth between camp and the ferry at Nanaimo in the bus, and playing his bass guitar for singsongs. After a $10,000 semester at Trinity Western University (aviation), he has decided to minimize future debts by picking up some courses in Victoria, and returning to the mainland for a one-year commercial license programme in January of 1993. Two of his sisters have paid him the ultimate compliment: Melody and Melissa have agreed to share Melody's room for four months, giving him Melissa's room, until another room is free.

Margaret [20] and **Melissa** [19] share a locker at Camosun College where Margaret is beginning an elementary teaching programme and Melissa an RN course. Both are finding the studies challenging and satisfying. Margaret gave a short lecture *en français* to her French class, using our 1/16th-size violin as a prop. She and Marilyn are playing violin in our church's Christmas cantata, an outstanding presentation. She joins Melissa in Sunday School teaching and Junior Church work. She and Melody spent the summer working at Camp Qwanoes with Mike. Melissa joined Marilyn and Geordon for a month in Cuba with YFC's Project Serve.

Melody [17] is in Grade 12, managing to fit in some academic courses around her volleyball responsibilities. In October she picked up a cast for her left arm in Emergency, after landing on her wrist instead of a more padded part of her anatomy. She is again working at the piano under Marilyn's direction. She and Mark have taken on

MELODY

an apartment paper route, which means only three or four early mornings a week for each of them. Melody shares her older brother's off-the-wall sense of humour and is usually near the centre of any boisterous activity.

Mark [14] has just written his Grade II Rudiments examination (required for practical music exams at the Grade VII and VIII levels) and hopes to do Grade VIII Violin in June, although his first love is sports. He is fortunate to have a violin teacher who is knowledgeable about hockey. Mark still plays the euphonium in the school band, running out to get a lift to band practice with his long-suffering band teacher at 7:25 a.m. twice a week.

Matthew [11] ambles through life, picking off A after A in his studies and quietly avoiding ultimatums given by the sister in charge of table-setting, dishes, making lunches, etc. He makes up advertisements on the computer for our flyer and has discovered that it is greatly to his advantage to deliver flyers by himself with Mother, as she shares her earnings with whichever children go out with her. Matthew's bank account fattened up during November's distribution and he managed to purchase a "ghetto blaster" (his maternal parent's least favourite item of furniture, next to the TV) which beams classical music into the upstairs quarters (a condition of its purchase). Matthew has taken up the trumpet in addition to piano and violin. He joins Mark in his love of volleyball and soccer, and his interest in professional hockey.

LIFE'S LIKE THIS

July 10, 9:00 a.m. Mother has been up until 3:00 a.m. putting final touches on July flyer; must have flyer original to business centre by 9:30 a.m. 9:15 a.m. Rushes into Saanich Centre parking lot, takes empty parking spot parallel to west end of Thrifty Foods. Parks as close as she can to right hand line; does not want to impede Thrifty's employees' access to end of building. Notices that a white car is parked very close to same line (with four-foot space on its other side.) 9:25 a.m. Mother returns to car, finds cheerful note on windshield: "Thoughtless, stupid parking." Glances over at white car to see woman driver sheepishly squeezing herself into driver's side. Walks over to driver, who wishes she could fade into upholstery, and asks if she put the note on windshield. Answer is affirmative, with comment that people with such big cars should allow more space. (Mother's car is minivan, fits in any SMALL CAR space in town.) Mother apologizes, promises to do better next time, returns to car, tears up offensive chit, and heads home, where she relates tale of woe to upstairs boarder.

July 12, 7:00 p.m. Mother parks car, a little skewed, a couple of blocks from church; attends special meeting. 9:00 p.m. Returns to car, finds note on windshield: "VERY GOOD INTELLIGENT!!! PARKING." Realizes boarder and cousin must have found car. Mother carefully places note in purse for future reference.

November 27, 4:45 a.m. Mother, getting a head start on flyer delivery, trying to keep ahead of November rains, is out delivering by streetlamp and moonlight. Enjoys early-morning fragrances, stillness, lacy birch trees dripping gold coins in the lamplight. Walks briskly up and down sidewalks and steps. **6:20 a.m.** Turns from mailbox into sudden glare of flashlight. Before panic sets in, is reassured by "Saanich Police. What are you doing?" Mother explains, tries to ignore group of squad cars surrounding her, and fourth one up street. Learns that a prowler has been reported in area: "17-year-old youth wearing a navy-blue windbreaker." Second policeman looks at Mother, comments, "Guess we didn't get our suspect!" Mother glances down at navy-blue sweater, wonders if early-morning walk has really been that rejuvenating.

SEEN AND HEARD ...

... Melody sitting quietly at the supper table until it is time for grace to be said, proffering her hand to Greg on the right side and Jason on the left (Family's custom of holding hands during grace originated many years ago, both to express affection for each other and to keep little hands out of the food. Jason has threatened several times not to hold her hand unless she is sure it is *very* clean. Sudden explosion indicates he is less than impressed with cold, clammy rubber glove she has put on in retaliation; resorts to long plastic fingernails another night.) ... Grandma Holland and Auntie Marilyn moving from their townhouses to a large home on Royal Wood Place, working to consolidate two households into one ... Melissa, in nursing uniform, racing at 6:40 a.m. down Saanich Road, across Quadra Street, and down Kenneth Street to Hodgson Place where Mother's car is parked (Mother promised her use of the car to get to hospital by 7:00 a.m. and, as happens more often than she cares to admit, totally forgot and took car out on paper route at 6:00 a.m. Melissa arrived at hospital at 7:02 a.m.; Mother's apologetic phone call was not really necessary.) ... Hugo, in business clothes, attaché case in hand, finding lunch Margaret has made for him in Little Caesar's double pizza bag (approximately 4' x 1 1/2'); cheerfully taking it off to work ... Margaret, Melissa and Melody preparing a "party-in-a-box" to send to Michael at Trinity for his 22nd birthday. Box is filled with streamers, confetti, junk food, miniature books and bubble soap, and is covered with photocopies of brother at different stages of his life; sisters speculate as to what response to gift will be ... Family playing at the Krellers' 50th wedding anniversary celebration in Parksville on September 21, sleeping on the carpet in the spacious new church, and rising at 7:00 a.m. to present mini-concert in both 8:30 a.m. and 11:00 a.m. services on the 22nd ... Family on way to performance in big van, bubbles streaming out back window over highway and little blue car following (Source of bubbles is third Holland offspring, recent recipient of diplomas from Conservatory and Camosun College; Toyota belongs to amused oldest sister and husband.) … Matthew, as a bike roadeo winner, receiving several prizes, including a very special jacket, from a familiar Saanich constable … Grandpa Holland's beautiful grandfather clock chiming every 15 minutes in our living room, a mellow, ethereal reminder of a much-loved and missed father and grandfather … a first-year piano class, who just happened to be in the room when the clock started chiming, listening to their piano piece "Chimes" for real … Michael buzzing Camp Qwanoes in a Cessna 152, acquiring current air time for his Trinity Western requirements … Margaret, flushed, receiving bouquets and accolades after her 90-minute graduation recital, a requirement for her Associate Diploma (Victoria Conservatory of Music) in violin performance and teaching … 28 slices of bread spread out on the counter for nine lunches, plus nine packages of cookies, plus nine pieces of fruit, five nights a week … Eleven *empty* clothes baskets resting briefly beside washer and dryer; second time during year that this high spot of Mother's domestic career has been achieved … Father driving down McKenzie Avenue, confronted by immense Saferway 18-wheeler manoeuvring its way out of testing station; realizing with a start that his eldest son is at the wheel and remembers that $150 road test was scheduled for this day … Later: Michael, greatly relieved, announcing that he received almost perfect marks; family jubilant! … Uncle Ed Robinson from Saskatchewan, treating Mark and Matthew to a hockey game at the Memorial Arena (Victoria Cougars vs. Regina Pats); the boys would have enjoyed it even if Victoria hadn't won!

Chapter 37: A Christmas Digest, 1992

EDITORIAL *by Louise*

Blessings and best wishes to you, our friends and family! We trust this Advent season finds you well and prospering.

"A man's life consists not in the **abundance** of the things which he possesses." (Luke 12:15)

Today's economy forces all of us to release our dreams (if we ever had them) of great material and financial gain, and that's good, as we realize just what is of lasting value. Many years ago, an elderly friend used to quote a verse from Proverbs where the writer prayed that he would not be so poor as to be forced to steal, and yet not be so rich that he would forget God. As we become older, and endeavour to pass on a value-system to our young people, we realize more and more the wisdom of King Solomon and of our old friend. We thank God for both the variety of modest opportunities that keep our chin above the water financially and for the strength and resources to take advantage of them.

HUGO AND TRACEY CIRO (AUGUST 1992)

From September of 1991 to this June, we enjoyed sharing our "hotel" with four young men: Glen, who has been with us for over four years and is now working on his Master's degree in Mechanical Engineering; Jason, in first year at UVic and now living in a castle—or two—in Paris, while he studies (colour his friends here *green!*); Greg, in second year Computer Engineering and now on a co-op term in Ottawa; and Hugo, working as a computer consultant, and courting and marrying Tracey (Tattersall, daughter of Norman Tattersall, the World Vision leader who was murdered in South America). A year ago, Hugo advised us that a Mac LC II with

ClarisWorks and a laser printer would be ideal for our printing needs, and time has proven him right.

When Michael returned after a term at Trinity, Melissa gave him her room and set up temporary residence in the (previously) most tidy room in the house (Melody's). Although much hilarity emanated from that room, after four months of such "close fellowship," Melissa escaped across town to board at Geordon and Marilyn's for six weeks and to study for her first year finals, and Melody was able to prepare for her Grade 12 exams in peace. Now the lunch-making chores (16 slices of bread instead of 28) elicit (a little) less negativism from the five lunchmakers.

As parents, we are very grateful for the loving, encouraging support we receive from our large church family at Central Baptist, for the education and spiritual training our children receive at Pacific Christian School, and for the opportunity for spiritual growth and service and outlandish activities that Camp Qwanoes (at Crofton) provides. At Central, an excellent pastoral team, in addition to teaching us Scriptural principles week by week, oversees a multitude of serving opportunities: helping some older friends with their business affairs and with moving into retirement centres (Bruce); organ/piano and Music Committee (Louise); Sunday School and Junior Church (Margaret and Melissa); sound system, occasionally (Mike); and violin/piano/bass guitar/euphonium (Marilyn down to Matthew).

Camp Qwanoes, under the able direction of Ken and Betty Bayley, is a home away from home for our family. In addition to intensive leadership training, Qwanoes offers strenuous service opportunities, and our teens and twenties come home at the end of the summer tanned, calloused, exhilarated, and, at times (especially after weekend retreats, where several days' worth of activities are crammed into a day and a half), exhausted. Parental eyebrows often rise when camp activities are discussed. Among the more bizarre are slug relays and contests (transporting slugs across the camp balcony; seeing who can get the most slugs to adhere to one's face), fire-hose water fights, and mud sliding and wrestling (and Mother wonders why there is a permanent film of fine sand in the washer and dryer during September). Melody, who counted a hockey card depicting the Canucks player, Cliff Ronning, among her prized possessions, received this threatening note: "MELODY—IF YOU EVER WANT TO SEE CLIFFY AGAIN, ATTEND CHAPEL WITH G.F. AND COME PREPARED TO PAY THE RANSOM OR IT'S THE ROYAL FLUSH FOR CLIFFY! ... WE MEAN BUSINESS." (The printing bore a striking resemblance to her older brother's.) Apparently the ransom wasn't adequate, and a video of the hockey card's demise into the septic system was shown in camp. In retaliation, an anonymous letter (composed in true gangster fashion of letters cut out of the newspaper), was sent to the camp pastor-speaker who was implicated in the "crime" with a return address of "Septic Field, Camp Qwanoes": "No one flushes Cliffy and gets away with it." There is an impending sequel to the saga of the abused hockey card, but it is shrouded in secrecy.

Melissa also had her difficulties with the Canucks, or rather, with one Canuck who shall remain nameless. She had been teasing a group of campers that she was this player's wife. To her chagrin, a few weeks later a video turned up at camp. Narrated by a programme director who had accompanied a camper to a Canucks training session on the Mainland—the camper had won the trip—the video showed the presentation of a very romantic card, with photographs of Melissa and some small children she babysat at family camp, to the hockey player. (A sister, fourteen months older and desirous of anonymity, took great pleasure in manufacturing the extravagant card, with the assistance of a younger sister.) During the quite lengthy interview, the hockey player (previously set up) confided that Melissa was indeed his wife, and said "hi" to her via the tape. Needless to say, the video was the highlight of the evening's entertainment at camp, and Melissa gives a new definition to the terms "embarrassed" and "blush" whenever it is mentioned. And she has developed a strong aversion to hockey rinks. *[In 2008, the BC government proclaimed December 17 as Trevor Linden Day, as tribute to his outstanding leadership and accomplishments as a hockey player, as well as for his extensive charitable work. The story above indicates that he must also possess a mischievous sense of humour!]*

Among the highlights of 1992 was our 30th anniversary gift: a week in Alaska organized and funded by seven young people, in cahoots with Auntie Harriet and Uncle Fred in Anchorage. Grandpa and Granny Forsberg accompanied us, and we all got a good look at the wilderness surrounding Anchorage (where Dr. Fred escapes from his clinic), and at the modern city itself. Granny was relieved to see that her daughter was not inhabiting the "boonies." Dropping into Anchorage through clouds, surrounded by breathtaking mountain ranges, was an exciting experience.

PERFORMING AT HUGO AND TRACEY CIRO'S WEDDING

At the end of August, the whole family provided music for Hugo and Tracey's beautiful wedding. Hugo's parents, as gracious as Hugo has always been, came from Colombia for the wedding. Mother and eldest daughter had managed to find four matching dresses on sale (the only four left and in just the right sizes), and their appearance at the wedding prompted a reference to the "Linen Sisters."

In October, the family had the privilege of providing nearly an hour of violin and piano music at Grandma Holland's church's 80th anniversary (Fairfield United; Grandma is one of the oldest living members). Grandma's friends were kind and appreciative, and a bonus to the evening was the introduction of the family to a high school classmate of Mother's who was happy to supply her new acquaintances with previously-unknown facts about Mother's youth. A good time was had by almost all.

PERSONAL GLIMPSES

Matthew [12 1/2] is in his final year of elementary school. He employs the same attitude of strategy to soccer and volleyball as he does to school assignments and newspaper and flyer delivering, with satisfying results. (Especially gratifying are the stereo—usually tuned to 92.1 FM—and the camera he bought with his earnings, after much catalogue scrutiny.) Matthew makes up advertisements for our flyer on the computer. He also practises violin, piano and trumpet with relatively little prompting.

Mark [15 and in Grade 10] is our only high school student. He has grown several inches in the last year and now looks down on most of his family. In June he completed the requirements for Grade VIII Violin, is now working towards the same level on the piano, and continues to play euphonium in the school band. Mark got some "hands-in" experience washing dishes at Red Robin's for several weeks. Sports activities are the high point of his week.

Melody turned 18 just a few days ago. She enlivens her classes at Sprott-Shaw with her wacky sense of humour. She enjoys her business courses and receives good marks. Judging by the amount of mail which leaves and enters this house with her name at the upper left corner or middle of the envelope, her course load cannot be too stressful. And the sign on her door—*World's Largest Phone Booth*—is well-placed. This fall, Melody, wearing her Paddington Bear hat and heavy gloves, transported load after load of oak leaves from the front of the property to the back, and planted dozens of winter pansies, to the accompaniment of Michael W. Smith and Whiteheart on her ghetto-blaster.

Melissa puts in long hours working towards her RN finals in August. Approximately 5' 8" tall and turning 20 in a few days, she was amused to hear how one of the very young piano students, whom she was helping, referred to her: "Mrs.

Holland, your *child* said to put a star on this piece." Melissa loves little children and has especially enjoyed her work in the mother-and-babe and paediatrics units. With her friend, Dawn, she is collecting household effects in anticipation of their batching together. She joined Margaret as counsellor at a recent youth retreat, where Mike drove the bus and played guitar, Marilyn was "speaker's wife," Melody washed dishes, and Mark was a camper.

Margaret [21 in October] is enjoying her full-time studies at UVic in the Education faculty. She works 24 to 28 hours a week at Ensign Motors as well, and babysits occasionally. For some reason, she cannot spare the time to keep on with her paper-route, so she has handed that duty over to another family member who enjoys the exercise but not the getting up at 5:30 a.m. every day. Margaret provides appropriate drawings, and also makes up advertisements, for our flyer.

Michael spends extended days driving trucks to the Mainland and up-Island. A youthful-looking 23, he finds that warehouse personnel look right through him when they go searching for his rig's driver. Michael plans to resume commercial flying lessons next fall. He spent the summer at Camp Qwanoes manoeuvring and maintaining the speedboat, driving the camp bus, and playing his bass guitar for singing. He recently went to hear Mozart's revision of Handel's *Messiah* and reported that the alto singer was a "major babe." (Mother felt that the evaluation, though employing a musical term, was somewhat lacking in culture.) Until June, Michael did the sound and light for Marilyn's YFC choir presentations, but has handed over that responsibility to Melody.

Marilyn and **Geordon** are leaving for two weeks in Caracas, Venezuela, on Boxing Day, with the aim of looking over missions opportunities there. We try to ignore reports of uprisings in Venezuela and are thankful our young people are in God's hands. Geordon continues as liaison officer within the Saanich elementary and secondary schools, with excellent response to his lectures on substance abuse and "stranger danger." He sings in the Police Chorus. Marilyn accompanies the Chorus, teaches piano half time, and works half time on the YFC staff. Both manage to keep a thoughtful eye on parents and grandparents, as well as providing guidance to brothers and sisters.

Louise is convinced there must be a way to do everything she would like to do, but finds her clocks allow her only 24 hours a day, and at least one-quarter of these must be spent in a horizontal position. Laundry, straightening up (both exercises in futility), supervising paper routes (four) and our little businesses (Melissa's Minding; Melody's Regal; Mark's Messages, the origin of our Shopping Opportunities flyer, 15,000 of which were distributed in November; and Matt's Plants), organizing musical programmes, and teaching, chip away at the day's allotment of minutes. She figures that anyone who can come in from an hour's paper-delivering, wind-burned and perspiring, to sit down and accompany her youngest child on a Telemann sonata, and then gather and transform an assortment of flowers and leaves from our half-acre weed patch into a care-home arrangement, has much to be thankful for.

Bruce has become more computer-literate over the past year, as he is required to record cases on the computer as soon as possible after dealing with them. His proximity to the computer keeps him office-bound for longer periods than previously as he cannot, for reasons of confidentiality, work on the computer at home. He continues to oversee the meal planning and preparation, involving other family members as much as possible. Now that there are only nine to feed, he has removed a leaf from our dining table. Much of his time is spent on family business and in helping several older members of our church congregation.

SEEN AND HEARD ...

... an edition of the *Cariboo Sentinel* (Saturday, June 17, 1865) sent down from Jason, who was working at a print shop in Barkerville for the summer: "MELISSA HOLLAND, Last Seen in the Company of Rich, Local Miner." ... "When I've finished 'O Canada', can I learn 'The Star Sprinkled Banner'?" (first-year piano student); "I'd like to play some pieces 'out of my mind'" (i.e., by memory, coined by a very young piano student, whose first memory piece was introduced as "Merrily We Go Rolling"; her music book says "Merrily We Roll Along") ... Grandma Holland napping each afternoon in the recliner, with McDuff and Tootsie asleep on her lap (McD. and T. are lovely, lively tabbies who have left the brambles at the back of Grandma's property where they were born, for a much better situation.) ... Melissa washing and washing and washing her hair and clothes after a Qwanoes muddy encounter of the worst kind ... Michael dwarfed beside his 48-foot trailer plus tractor ... Matthew receiving a silver medal notification for Grade V Violin ... Mark doing his part to ensure PCS's winning of the Island Junior Volleyball championship ... Mark out for 7:30 a.m band practice twice a week, for 7:00 a.m. volleyball practice once a week (Melody's days for their paper route) ... Georgia (Geordon's mother) graduating with a bachelor's degree in Nursing from UVic in June; Geordon graduating with a similar degree in Criminology from SFU; Glen graduating with his bachelor's degree in Mechanical Engineering from UVic ... Marilyn receiving her credentialling from YFC in Winnipeg, two years after she started the three-year course ... Melody graduating from PCS, resplendent in a blue satin gown sewn by Granny Forsberg (at the age of 85, in spite of cataracts, and under very bright lights—Granny's fourth Holland graduation dress; how fortunate her granddaughters have been!) ... Margaret, Melissa and Melody entering a beauty salon for the first time in their lives, in response to an Employment Opportunities ad (Their long hair was styled by competitors in a hairdressing contest. In spite of the ad's implied earning potential, they were not paid for their day in the parlour, and, on returning home, couldn't undo their coiffures quickly enough.) ... Margaret enjoying a History course given by a professor whose children were once in Mother's music classes ... Matthew sitting morosely behind his plant tables at a sale in June, becoming increasingly sanguine as the day wore on and dozens of his plants were taken off to new homes ... Margaret making her debut in church as children's choir director (Mother has unique vantage point on the organ bench, remembers when she first saw those graceful long fingers twenty-one years previous; prays—again—that her children's hands will always be employed in positive ways.) ... Michael, bass in hand, arriving late at the cantata dress rehearsal in work clothes, having driven down from Campbell River, to find CHEK-TV taping parts of the programme; turning his white T-shirt around to get rid of the pattern, and borrowing a jacket from a bystander, hoping the camera does not take in his jeans ... Michael, accompanied by Margaret and a friend, whining into the drive-in intercom at a darkened Kentucky Fried Chicken outlet: "We know you're in there"; rewarded, with much laughter, by an extra-large serving of chicken wings (Parents do not remember giving assertiveness training.) ... *On the paper route*: gorgeous, saucy Steller's jays, their iridescent blue flashing against the sombre oak leaves; the fragrance of a freshly lit fireplace; the pungent smell of damp leaves, mingled with the sweet scent of fir boughs, evocative of the deep forest; frosty grass, and leaves glistening in the moonlight ...

Love and best wishes from the Hollands

Chapter 38: A Christmas Digest, 1993

EDITORIAL *by Louise*

It is 10:00 p.m. on December 16, and I am propped up in my bed, surrounded by disjointed scribblings and the glorious strains of Handel's *Messiah*. In 27 years of compiling our annual Christmas Digest, I have never been so far behind schedule. With all the negative press Christmas letters receive, I had seriously considered letting 1993 slide into 1994 without comment, but promptings from family (particularly those of my Far Better Half, the resident traditionalist) and some friends (the ones who brew a pot of tea to sustain them as they wade through each year's offering) have motivated me to scribble some more.

The past year has brought increased business involvements which have eaten away at free time. Displaying what my family calls "A Bad Attitude"—as in "Someone here seems to have 'a bad attitude'"—I have determined to set aside more time to "smell the roses." Yesterday I cancelled classes and tagged along with our church's "Prime-Timers" (senior) group to the Chemainus Theatre for dinner and an excellent show; Bruce drove the van. This evening, he and I and Margaret (who is taking her practicum under one of PCS's elementary music teachers) and Melissa enjoyed Pacific Christian's Christmas concert at UVic Centre. And so I am wishing you a Happy New Year, rather than a Merry Christmas!

As the above may indicate, I am sometimes mildly frustrated by the inability to get everything done that I would like to do. A typical day starts at 5:15 a.m., when I hit the carpet. By 5:30 or 5:45 a.m., I usually have the van loaded with our 220 newspapers, to the accompaniment of classical music on CBC stereo. After half an hour of brisk walking by moonlight/starlight/streetlamp, or in drenching rain (sometimes), or high winds (rarely), or on icy sidewalks (terrifying), I rouse three other nightwalkers (Bruce, who does Mark's route; Mark, who does Melody's route; and Matthew, who does Matthew's route). After dropping off carriers and bundles, I complete Margaret's route and am usually finished around 7:00 a.m. Initial grogginess is replaced by a feeling of wellbeing as I travel up to six miles in a morning, up and down stairs, sidewalks and hills, leaving a trail of sensor lights shining in my wake. The hours between 7:00 a.m. and 4:00 p.m., when I start my teaching, are filled with teaching preparation and managing our family's little businesses: Shopping Opportunities, an advertising flyer that has grown from 500 in January of 1986 to 30,000 this past November; Melody's Regal orders, which she cannot handle from her new location; Matt's Plants (Matthew and I assemble and sell hundreds of plants during the spring and summer); and an occasional foray into Melissa's Minding territory, when Melissa is not able to check up on a house or feed a cat. (Bruce especially enjoys dealing with lonely felines who welcome both him and the food he dishes out!)

My frustration fades when I consider how privileged we are, to be able to live in the comfort and freedom this country affords; to be part of a loving family, a peaceful neighbourhood (most of the time), and a caring Christian community at church and school; and to be given the strength and opportunities to maintain this unwieldy household. God is good, and we thank Him for His gifts. It is the Christmas season, and we thank Him especially for the gift of His Son, our Saviour. We pray that our lives may be honouring to Him.

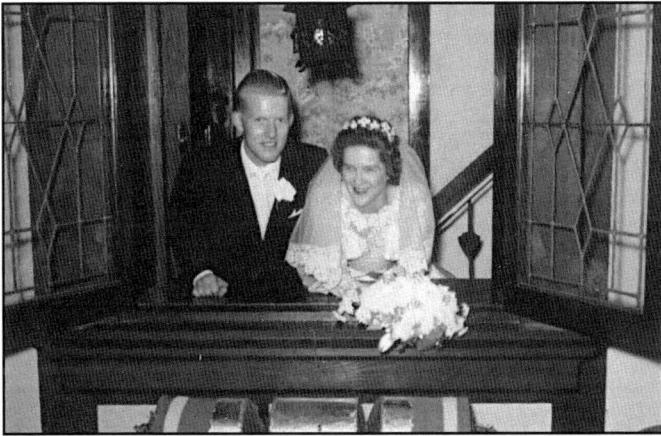

OLDE ENGLAND INN — DECEMBER 21, 1961

OLDE ENGLAND INN — DECEMBER 21, 1993

PERSONAL GLIMPSES

Bruce took a busman's holiday to Venezuela this summer, signing on as cook for this year's Youth for Christ Project Serve to Caracas. Although shopping for 24 people in a Spanish-speaking market had its moments, from all reports the menu did not suffer. And weeks of planning meals and accumulating provisions to take to South America had preceded the venture. Bruce's *real* job, in its 28th year, is after-hours emergency services, where he is responsible for all after-hours social work calls; child protection is his priority. His priority at home is catering (in both meanings of the word) to his family's needs, and he still finds time to lend a hand— or an ear—to some of our older friends.

He and **Louise** enjoyed a special outing at the end of August, after his return from Caracas. Spending three days in Vancouver, they visited with Joan Schmidt, Auntie Evelyn (Miller) and Cousins Ralph and Marilyn, as well as taking in a music workshop and *The Phantom of the Opera* (a Mother's/Father's Day gift from seven Ms).

Geordon and **Marilyn** moved into the lower floor of their house last spring, sifting through and paring down their possessions in anticipation of missionary work some time in the near future. In November they were accepted as missionary candidates to Venezuela, under our Fellowship Baptist Mission Board and Youth for Christ International. After directing a team of young people and leaders for a month in Caracas this summer, they feel this is the place of God's service for them. Geordon's experience here as school liaison officer and his and Marilyn's musical backgrounds could make a positive contribution to the families of Caracas. They both participated in our church's dynamic cantata, with Geordon singing, and Marilyn (with Margaret and Melissa) playing violin, but Marilyn ended up in a clinic between the third and fourth performances (2:30 p.m. and 6:30 p.m. on Sunday). The doctor took one look in her mouth and gave her a prescription for strep throat. After playing through the fourth two-hour session, she went home and crashed, and has spent most of this week in bed.

Michael's commercial flying instruction got off the ground a few days ago, after a two-year hiatus. Following several months of sixteen- and eighteen-hour days driving 18-wheelers to the Mainland and back, he was taken on as driver for three concert tours around North America, with the Christian "alternative music" groups Hokus Pick and Rhythm and News. After 45,000 miles on the road, as well as two months running the ski-boat at Camp Qwanoes, home didn't look too bad, and the family enjoys hearing of his experiences. Michael joined Rhythm and News in a chapel service at PCS recently, playing his bass guitar. His guitar provided an underlying bass line for the cantata; even his piano/violin/organ-oriented parents enjoyed it, especially where it provided a ripping introduction to "Go Tell It On the

Mountain."

Margaret continues with her training in Education at UVic, specializing in music. She conducts a children's choir at church, plays her violin in a variety of settings, and is learning to play the acoustic guitar. She asked to have her hours at Ensign Motors cut back from 28 to 16, and this has given her a little more breathing space. Margaret enjoys studying with Juli Serrano, a fifth-year student from Vernon whose mother, Anita Thorlakson, went through teacher training with Margaret's mother. She often helps Mark with his French, and Matthew with his violin.

Melissa received her RN in August and plans to start a BScN programme in January at UVic. After weeks of meticulous planning, she and her friend, Dawn Fletcher, spent five weeks in September and October driving 14,000 km to and from Quebec City, visiting family, friends, families of friends, and friends of friends, and receiving royal treatment. Her anxiety-prone parents (one in particular) needn't have worried: except for two speeding tickets (one each), the travelling was trouble-free, the car gave no problems, and the weather was untypically balmy, making shorts and sweat shirts the dress of choice. Melissa is now working for two home-care agencies and a seniors' care facility.

Melody completed her Sprott-Shaw course in April, and works full time at the Christian Book and Music Centre. In May she and Ruth Cave (Melody's co-worker at the Centre) decided to share an apartment three blocks from work. Although her family had mixed feelings about her "leaving the nest," Melody has proven to be capable and self-reliant, and continues to participate in family activities, including concerts. December 5, 1993, was a red-letter day for her as she celebrated her 19th birthday, and became engaged. She and Richard Stark plan to be married in April, and we all are very enthusiastic about our son/brother-in-law-to-be. Rick is active in our church as well as in YFC, and drives up and down the Island for Island Farms. Melody has sewn an enormous Christmas stocking for him, featuring dozens of little cows on a bright red background.

Mark and **Matthew** also celebrated milestone birthdays this year: Matthew's 13th in April, and Mark's 16th in September. Mark is in Grade 11, and participates in as many sports as he can manage, sings in the choir, plays euphonium in the band, adds his violin to family performances, and hopes to complete Grade VIII Piano soon. Last summer he took C.I.T. training at Camp Qwanoes. Matthew also expends considerable energy on the soccer field, as well as on the basketball, badminton, and volleyball courts. He and Mark spend hours playing roller-blade hockey on the church parking lot or at the Braefoot lacrosse box. Matthew makes up most of the advertisements for our flyer on the computer, as well as typing out an eight-page booklet each month for an air force squadron.

LIFE'S LIKE THIS

January 21, 7:30 a.m. Neighbour's car hits slick patch on Saanich Road, sliding across road into blackberry bushes, at only spot where ditch is not open, as Melody and Mother watch out front window. Fortunately, driver and passengers are only shaken up, and car is relatively unscathed. (Mother woke at 5:00 a.m. to the sound of rain, welcome after two weeks of snow and ice and falling. She didn't realize that the rain froze as it hit the ground, forming a treacherous glaze over half of her morning route. The papers were not all out until 9:30 a.m., and even then she fell. Dozens of accidents were reported all over Victoria, including an ambulance overturning three blocks from here.)

5:45 a.m. on a March morning Mother parks car on edge of diocese centre parking lot, counts out four papers in preparation for small hike up treed lane (Nelthorpe Street) to mailbox. Fragrances of musty blackberry vines and damp leaves and spicy wild rose bushes fill the air; crescent moon dangles over sleeping neighbourhood; city lights glisten off in the distance miles below. Mother revels in early-morning stillness, appreciates illumination from parking lot lights. Delivers paper up lane, walks width of parking lot and up behind Pastoral Centre to deliver two more papers, starts across pavement to priest's office with fourth paper. Wild area extends on her right up to townhouses on the top of Christmas Hill. Freezes in tracks as extraordinary hiss shatters the silence; stands motionless for a few seconds, trying to determine source of disturbance, but cannot detect activity either in buildings or in shrubbery. Quickly delivers last paper, makes way back to car, glad she delivered lane first. Wonders if sound was related to very large paw print she saw in snow up the lane a few weeks earlier. (Cougar had been sighted in the area at that time, but Mother was assured he wouldn't attack anything larger than a child.)

8:10 a.m. on another March morning Mother has spent almost two hours helping out on paper routes, has just had a bath and put her hair in rollers, when a frantic request from Margaret means she will have to drive up to the university. Slipping into sandals—it is cold and blustery—she puts on a long winter coat over a heavy Colombian sweater. She and Margaret rush to the car, and are unnerved by the sound of the engine. Mother has forgotten purse (therefore license and money) and hopes car will hang together until she makes it home again. Car coughs and snorts across McKenzie Avenue and onto Ring Road. Margaret ejects at MacLaurin Building and Mother shudders around curve past Student Union Building, car making horrendous noises. At intersection of Finnerty Road and McKenzie, car dies: no power, no lights—nothing. Motor does not respond; even hazard lights do not work. After thirty seconds of trying to will engine to life, Mother rips curlers out of wet hair, scrambles across lawn into Student Union Building looking for a free phone, passing bank of pay phones; finds one in depths of an office. Is reassured when Father says he will come for her. Disloyal vehicle has since been replaced by more cooperative model.

SEEN AND HEARD ...

...snowdrops poking up through crusts of dirty snow in mid-January; fragrance of *daphne odoratum* wafting through morning gloom ... Michael, phoning from Nashville: "Mom, the doctor says I need surgery." ... Mark in the BC Senior Boys finals for volleyball; in spite of practices and games three or four times a week, has managed to make the Honour Roll ... Michael, roller-blading for miles to a telephone at a campsite in Kansas ... Matthew, lifting his violin from rest position to perform at a recital, immobilized as his sweater refuses to relinquish his instrument (Turning his back on the audience, he and Mother try frantically and unsuccessfully to extricate the nail-like tuner from the wool. With a hefty pull from Matthew, the wool— fortunately not the violin—snaps, and the performance begins. And Mother thought she had seen everything in 20 years of violin lessons and recitals.) ... Melissa, with her December birthday the youngest in a class of 110, receiving her RN at the UVic Centre in August, cheered on by her friends in the balcony ("Way to go, Honeybee!") and by her mother and grandmothers on the lower floor (Bruce, Geordon and Marilyn, Margaret and Melody were in Venezuela; Michael, Mark and Matthew were at camp.) ... Michael, holed up in an Albuquerque motel for a week while the tour bus undergoes $5,000 worth of repairs (Hokus Pick went on ahead in a Ryder truck), deciding to phone home when he finds himself talking to the lampshade ... Marilyn, pictured with an impressive group of the city's "finest," on the front of a seniors' Christmas magazine (The Victoria Police Chorus sang for several Silver Threads groups in December.) ... Michael, alone, driving nonstop from Albuquerque, New Mexico, to Eugene, Oregon, coming down through the Siskiyou Pass (Northern California), yarding the tour bus to a grinding halt when the brakes fade—at 4:00 a.m.—in the pouring rain ... Tubby (Melody's not-too-clever but very appealing Siamese) batting away at Margaret's pigtail as she sits crosslegged on her bed ... Glen (our all-star boarder, halfway through his sixth year with us) receiving yet another trophy for his athletic achievements (He will not be pleased to see this in print.) ... Granny Forsberg quoted in the *Times Colonist* and interviewed on CHEK-TV, as the first teacher at the North Saanich School ... young student absent-mindedly removing his hand from music teacher's box of shiny stars; 20 to 25 stars adhere to pupil, who must have licked fingers, and who is now blushing furiously; Mother bites lip to keep from smiling ... Father preparing roast beef dinner for 31 in Caracas apartment ... Father bringing night-time frolicking to halt by threatening withdrawal of services the next day (cook only team member not "steamrolled" during month in Venezuela) ... Michael, tiptoeing across the light supports, high above the auditorium, as he helps set up for Rhythm and News concerts ... Mother sedately playing an organ prelude for the 11:00 a.m. service, suddenly aware of youngest daughter's exuberant presence at her left elbow (Family members knew for several weeks she would be receiving a diamond ring on morning of her 19th birthday, had managed to keep Rick's secret. Prelude continues, while Mother sneaks peek at sparkling jewel, comments on its beauty. Excitement rises as three sisters, long hair flying, dash behind organ to get their first glimpse of sister's treasure.) ... Glen, giving a presentation to government officials on a Real-Time Automatic Vehicle Sizing System, the result of research towards his Master's degree ... a grey squirrel sitting on a patch of moss just outside the kitchen window, holding an acorn daintily in its paws; has been entertaining the family and students for several weeks, scampering through the firs and oaks and along telephone wires [25 *years ago, grey squirrels were a novelty.*] ... Michael, re-orienting himself to the sky, practising spins and stalls under the watchful eye of his instructor ... Marilyn, as director of Project Serve in Caracas, receiving the news, after a 30-hour trip, that the dormitories where the team had planned to stay would not be available, and that all 24 of them would be living in a three-bedroom, three-bathroom, apartment for a month—possibly the lowest point in her YFC experience (The arrangement, though cramped, did have its benefits: savings in transportation time and finances; the opportunity to get to know each other *really* well; a dishwasher.) ... 30 YFC teenagers and leaders in the music room, living room and dining room folding and bundling nearly 15,000 of our 30,000 flyers for mailing (Our flyer has generated earnings for several groups and individuals, as well as giving our family considerable business experience.) ... Rick and Melody transforming potatoes into turkeys (Thanksgiving) and toilet tissue rolls into lambs (Christmas) in Junior Church ... Tubby curled up inside the dryer among the warm clothes, taking advantage of a phone call which interrupted the dryer's emptying ...

Chapter 39: A Christmas Digest, 1994

EDITORIAL *by Louise*

"Come now, let us reason together," says the LORD. "Though your sins are like scarlet, they shall be **white as snow**." (Isaiah 1:18)

It is December 3, and I am looking out of a second-storey window over a winter wonderland. Last night's snowfall has worked its magic. The firs droop slightly under their burden; the oaks, now leafless, are traced in white against a sepia sky, and any wayward garden debris has disappeared under a shining carpet. As a child, I was fascinated by the silence of the snow. After roaming over the miles of fields and through the acres of woods behind our home on West Saanich Road, I would sit quietly on a stump or log, watching the feathery flakes land noiselessly, accumulating in sweeping drifts. Occasionally, the subdued cheep of a chickadee disturbed the stillness. After a few hours, the blanket of white would be etched with tiny tracks, as mice and snowbirds (juncos) made their way from clumps of grass to shrubbery. The breeze shook the cedar and alder cones, dusting the snow with tiny seeds. And I would sit quietly, as I do today, lost in the beauty and peacefulness of the snow. The verse from Scripture reminds me of the true meaning of Christ's coming: "You shall call His name Jesus, for He shall save His people from their sins." (Matthew 1:21)

Our family sends our love and best wishes to you at this blessed time. We trust that 1994 has been happy and productive for you, and that 1995 brings God's best to you.

For our family, 1994's first special event gave us a new son. On April 16, Melody married Richard Stark, now our "favourite second son-in-law." Rick's involvement in our church's boys' club a few years back (when he took Mark and a friend up to Horne Lake to help build his cabin—we recently learned Mark hammered the rafters together); his bus driving for the Youth for Christ choir all over the Island and Mainland (he drives the Island Farms tanker truck up and down the Island, collecting milk from the farms); and his cycling activities with our "favourite first son-in-law" had given the family several opportunities to look over this prospective new family member. It was unanimously agreed that Melody was most fortu-

Ralph Steele

APRIL 16, 1994

nate to win the affections of such a fine, responsible young man, and we, in typically unbiased fashion, feel Rick has done pretty well, too. Rick and Melody and Bruce leave on January 10 for five weeks in Malaysia as part of a group to paint the Chefoo school for missionaries' children in the Cameron Highlands.

In June, Matthew passed his Grade VIII Violin exam, ending a twenty-one-year routine of weekly violin lessons. On November 13, he joined his brothers and sisters to play at Dave and Bette Vickers' 50th wedding anniversary in Nanaimo. This was a special privilege, as it was Dave who introduced Bruce and me to each other 36 years ago.

A highlight of our summer was meeting an outstanding gentleman from Kuala Lumpur, Subramaniam ("Maniam"), a sports journalist for the largest newspaper in Malaysia. Our friend, Berne Neufeld, in Kuala Lumpur with her group of high school students for work experience, phoned to ask if we could take any guests for the Commonwealth Games. (She served as team *attaché* for Malaysia when she returned to Canada. She confessed later that she had warned anyone coming to our place that there was to be "no smoking, no drinking, and no wild parties.") A handsome Tamil with expressive dark eyes, a black beard and flashing white teeth, Maniam quickly endeared himself to the whole family, with his gracious, appreciative manner. In the 19 days that he lived with us, we learned that he was a staunch Methodist, a leader in his church in Kuala Lumpur, and definitely not in need of the warnings our friend had, for our protection, given out. Bruce hopes to meet his wife and daughters when he goes to Malaysia in January.

This fall has been particularly happy, with six of our family under our roof, and the seventh, Melody, in and out with Rick. **Geordon** and **Marilyn** rented out their house and moved into our upstairs suite in early September. Little **Jordan** arrived on

September 19, transforming the rest of the household into instant grandparents and aunts and uncles. He was also welcomed by six great-grandparents, three on each side. Jordan, blue-eyed and blond, bears a striking resemblance to his mother and, by extension, to his mother's father. It goes without saying that he is a delight, and there are cheerful discussions as to whose turn it is next to hold and play with him.

DAVE AND BETTE VICKERS WITH JORDIE

At 2 1/2 months, he is approximately double his birth weight, so is a substantial armful; his cooing and smiles have even the most conservative members of the family babbling.

On December 30 (Marilyn's 27th birthday), Geordon, Marilyn and Baby Jordan fly to Costa Rica for seven months of Spanish study (for Marilyn; Geordon, brought up in a missionary family in Colombia, already speaks fluent Spanish), and then on to their work in Caracas, Venezuela. The last few months have seen them all over the province, speaking to many churches about their work with young people, and Geordon has also spoken to different service organizations and given interviews for *Saanich News* and CHEK-TV. They leave with much love and support behind them and, no doubt, a few tears.

LIFE'S LIKE THIS

On a wet mid-October afternoon Mother and a class of music students are discussing the week's assignments when the squeal of tires pulls her attention to Saanich Road. She watches in horror as a car spins across the road, its passenger side slamming into a telephone pole, and makes a complete turn, ending up in the bushes, facing the right direction on the wrong side of the road. Sonatinas and broken triads are forgotten as she races down to the house, yelling for Melissa, who is home on a break from her home-

MARILYN AND JORDIE

care. (Melissa has both her RN and industrial first aid certification.) What Mother doesn't know is that Melissa has Wee Jordan strapped to her, and Marilyn, upstairs, upon hearing the commotion, fears something has happened to the baby. Marilyn, Michael, Melissa, Mark, Matthew and Mother converge at the front door. Mother frantically describes what has happened. Mark unstraps Jordan from Melissa, who tears across the road. Mike calls 911. Melissa discovers, thankfully, that driver and passenger are not seriously injured and brings them into house where they wait, trembling. Mother returns to teaching. … Family's favourite constable, driving through intersection of Tolmie and Blanshard, hears report of accident in front of 4031 Saanich Road. Immediately assumes that family member has been hit trying to leave property; is relieved to learn accident involves only one car. Siren wailing, he makes his way to Saanich Road, where ambulance, tow truck and second police car and policeman on bicycle join him at scene. Michael later comments on the perplexity of accident victims who gave statement to a policeman who not only was dressed in civilian clothes—he had been chaperoning a group of student council presidents from high schools all over BC at the Empress Hotel—but who knew the tow truck operator, the ambulance driver, the police officers who arrived at the scene, *and* the people who live in the house where they were taken.

PERSONAL GLIMPSES

Michael is a flight test and written exam short of obtaining his commercial flying license, having accumulated the required number of hours aloft. **Margaret** is working through her final year in Education at UVic, which includes large blocs of practice-teaching. She (violin) and Mike (bass) joined **Melody** (violin) in five presentations of Central Baptist's Christmas cantata, a wonderful "gift to the community" that saw our church packed for each performance. **Melissa** studies toward her BScN, both at UVic and off-campus, and fills in empty spaces with RN and home-care shifts, and figuring out her next trip: England perhaps? Maybe Alaska? **Mark** and **Matthew** are in Grades 12 and 9 at Pacific Christian, and have completed a hectic volleyball season. Their band teacher, John Slofstra, picks them up three mornings a week for 7:30 a.m. band practice.

Bruce's office hours have been extended to seven consecutive days of ten-hour shifts (4:00 p.m. to 2:00 a.m.), so he arrives home at 2:30 a.m. seven days running, and then has the next week off. He spent most of two weeks volunteering for the Commonwealth Games, working in the stores warehouse at Heal's Range (known as Heal's Rifle Range when Grandpa Forsberg worked there 35 years ago). **Louise** tries to maintain a balance between her teaching (approximately 25 hours a week) and the demands of our little businesses, which provide a change of pace and activity. Propagating and potting plants (for Matt's Plants), keeping an eye on homes and pets (Melissa's Minding; duties are shared with Bruce and Margaret when Melissa is not available); making up and overseeing the delivery of Shopping Opportunities (which originated as Mark's Messages) four times a year, and managing, with Bruce's help, the orders for Matol and Regal, keep Mother on the go, and precipitate the occasional conflict in scheduling. Our resignations from the paper routes in May gave the family back several hours a week, which has greatly reduced the stress level.

SEEN AND HEARD ...

... Geordon and Melissa leading a Camp Qwanoes bike hike down the Oregon Coast in July: Geordon as speaker, Melissa as nurse; Geordon leading from the front, Melissa from the rear ... Mike accumulating air time by transporting family and friends to the mainland (Landing at the Vancouver International Airport for the first time in his tiny plane was a little unsettling, although his solo flight to California went remarkably smoothly.) ... Mark and classmates videoing updated version of the Good Samaritan as a class project: car moves slowly down Saanich Road, appears to hit pedestrian, who ends up sprawled over hood of car, much to consternation of passing drivers (and Mother, who comes upon scene at this point) ... kingfisher diving into neighbour's fish pool, re-surfacing with a brilliant orange fish in his beak, which he, perched on a nearby oak branch, proceeds to devour ... Melody driving herself and her bridesmaids in the Dart Swinger ("Mellow Yellow") up to Government House for pictures on her wedding morning, resplendent in her wedding finery and sunglasses ... Evita (Marilyn's cat) suspended over the upstairs bathroom window's edge, unable to get back in and terrified of falling out, meowing piteously ... Tubby (Melody's Siamese) hobbling around on a purple cast-bandage after surgery to repair a leg damaged by an unknown assailant (car or raccoon), recovering from near-death to typical rambunctiousness ... Evita and Tubby displaying the original meaning of the term "cat-fight" as territorial boundaries are crossed and fur flies ... PCS's senior volleyball team capturing the Island finals, earning themselves a place at the Provincial finals; Michael helping out with the driving to Prince George and getting to see Mark play ... a yelp from the upstairs suite as the new father discovers there are hazards in changing diapers on a baby boy (Mother-in-law had forgotten to warn him.) ... teams of young people collating and folding our latest flyer (35,000 copies) in preparation for mailing through Canada Post (Matthew does most of the computer work for the flyer.) ... Granny Forsberg, revelling in her newly-restored sight as cataract removal brought her eyesight from near legally blind to almost perfect (a satisfying situation, given her support of Operation Eyesight Universal for many years) ... Granny Forsberg and Grandma Holland participating in a baby-bathing and sewing skit at Melody's shower (Grandma gave each of our seven babies their first official bath; Granny has sewn dozens of garments for them over the years.) ... Grandpa Forsberg returning home with a policeman who had seen him take a tumble, refusing to go to the hospital, and making a very good recovery from what had been a serious fall ... Margaret spending hours interviewing Granny and poring over Department of Education files for her research project in Education History (Her report, which covered her grandmother's teaching career from 1925 to 1969, is entitled "One Typical Woman.") ... Matthew stepping out into the aisle to blast out "Trumpet Voluntary" on his trumpet, backed up by five violins (his sisters and brothers) and organ (his mother), as Melody, on her father's arm, follows her bridesmaids to the front (Matthew had broken his left wrist roller-blading, so could not manage the violin.) ... the Greater Victoria Police Chorus presenting Geordon and Marilyn with a large family Bible as a remembrance of their years together, Marilyn as accompanist and Geordon as Chorus member, at a sometimes-hilarious benefit concert held in Geordon and Marilyn's honour (The violins played for the generous offering and with the Chorus for one piece, and the new grandfather was coerced into singing with the Chorus for "Amazing Grace.") ... A beautiful Canadian flag waving over our front yard, a gift from our boarder of six years, Glen Halvorson, who used his mechanical engineering expertise to design, paint and erect a steel flag pole and supporting base ... Marilyn taking footage of the recent snowfall to look at in Venezuela ...

Chapter 40: A Christmas Digest, 1995

EDITORIAL *by Louise*

1995 could be called the "Year of the Trips," as Bruce, Rick and Melody headed to Malaysia in January for five weeks of painting the Chefoo School, a few days after Geordon, Marilyn, Jordan, the baby, and Evita, the cat, left for Costa Rica for Marilyn's term at the Spanish Language Institute. At her three sisters' suggestion, Louise accompanied her mother Anne Forsberg to Hawaii for a week in early March, a few days after Anne's sister Kaye Sparks passed away; the session in the sunshine was well-timed. Margaret completed her BEd in June and celebrated by visiting Geordon, Marilyn and Co. in Costa Rica the next month. At the end of June, Michael loaded our minivan with mattress, sleeping bag, fridge, cooler and food, and drove to Winnipeg for advanced flight training, and a dose of Winnipeg-in-the-summer. He referred to his campsite as "Little Van on the Prairie." Michael joined Margaret, Melissa and Melody at a wedding in Saskatchewan, and served as groomsman at another wedding in Prince George. Melissa is just completing her final paper for her Bachelor of Science in Nursing and has made arrangements to spend much of January with Marilyn and her men in Venezuela.

1995 is also the "Year of the Renovations" for our lower floor and an upstairs bathroom. The dark carpeting, drapes and kitchen cabinets chosen 24 years ago in the maternity ward two days after Margaret's birth have given way to lighter, pastel surfaces and window coverings, a boon to someone who routinely sets a black purse on the dark carpet and promptly loses or trips over it. The transformation demanded a complete emptying of cupboards, closets and drawers, a catharsis from which we are still trying to recover. We might get the rest of the boxes unpacked before 1996, but aren't counting on it. West Coast Decorating (Barry and Jeannie Arden) oversaw the entire project with much skill and patience. *[Jeannie is Louise's youngest sister.]*

PERSONAL GLIMPSES

Geordon and **Marilyn** are settling into their work in Caracas, after seven months in Costa Rica for Marilyn's studies in Spanish, prolonged negotiations in Miami for their permanent visa, and a flying trip back to Victoria from Miami in

September for Grandpa Rendle's funeral. Although tinged with sadness, this unexpected visit was a delight for the grandparents and assorted aunts and uncles here in Victoria. Baby **Jordan** had his first birthday party at his Rendle grandparents' home while he was here (September 19), in the company of three other babies. A sticky time was had by all. Due to Grandpa's passing, the visa applications were immediately released to the Venezuelan consulate in Toronto on compassionate grounds, and Geordon and Marilyn picked up the visas there on their return to Caracas, after only three hours of waiting, a small miracle in that the consulate in Miami had stalled for almost three weeks, and papers are not usually transferred for several weeks. In Caracas, Geordon has had many opportunities to speak on youth/family/drug issues, in their apartment complex, at local schools, with a government-sponsored anti-drug foundation, and at the national police academy. Marilyn works with a ladies' craft group, conducts children's and ladies' choirs, joins Geordon in youth work, and tries to keep up with a little blond whirlwind. They, and we, are grateful for the modes of communication available to us: e-mail, fax and even Fedex (in emergencies), in addition to the more traditional letters and telephone calls.

Michael has acquired considerable training (at $200/hour) beyond his basic commercial pilot's license. To fund his studies, he has been working at the airport, pumping fuel into planes ranging in size from the Cessna 172 through the Lear Jet to the Airbus A320. One of the more unsettling procedures is "hot fueling" the military Sea King helicopters, i.e., refueling while the engine is still running. He occasionally drives for Island Farms. Recently, he (on bass), along with Melody (violin), invested many hours practising for and performing in our church cantata (two dress rehearsals, five two-hour performances)—an excellent production.

Margaret is teacher-on-call for the Abbotsford and Langley school districts, outside of Vancouver. So far she has dealt with every grade from Kindergarten to Grade 12. We miss her very much, but are happy she is living in Surrey with the Harbuts, Geordon's aunt and uncle. There are four young men in the Harbut family, so mother Nola has been enjoying her new "daughter."

MARGARET, MICHAEL, MELISSA

Melissa may also leave home in the New Year, as she would like to work in paediatrics somewhere in Canada or the United States. We will also miss our "honeybee" if she, too, flies off. This year she has supervised the 4s and 5s in Junior

Church and often regales us at Sunday lunch with hilarious stories of the children's comments. She has also served as nurse at Camp Qwanoes several times.

Melody and **Rick** are thriving in their new-to-them bungalow not too far from here. Ten days after their move in late October, they came home from a Bible study to find their newly cleaned and organized basement under six inches of water: carpet floating, storage trunk sodden, Christmas gifts ruined. As a result, their front and back lawns look as if a giant mole has been at work, as the drainage system is exposed. Rick still drives for Island Farms, and Melody has left her job

THE STARK HOME ("MELLOW YELLOW" IN GARAGE)

at the Christian Book and Music Centre to work towards a piano teaching certificate. With her business training and experience, Melody gives efficient and much-appreciated help with our family's little businesses. She helps out with the young piano classes and shares her mother's delight in working with five and six year olds.

Mark graduated from Pacific Christian School in June and has been working full-time at Atlas Stereo and TV, helping within the store, and delivering orders all over the Capital Region. He usually works from Monday to Saturday, but manages to find a little time to develop his piano skills. He is taking lessons with Wendy Maggiora, as are Melody and Matthew. (Wendy has also worked with the eldest four in years past, and is known both for her excellent teaching and her unfailing patience.) Mark and Matthew enjoy floor hockey in a church league twice a week, and Mark usually manages to find the net more than once each game.

Matthew is in Grade 10 at PCS, and will be eligible to use the car keys in April. In his brothers' footsteps, he is a volleyball enthusiast. With band at 7:30 three mornings a week, and volleyball practices and games at least three afternoons, Matthew's fall has sped by, and his time at the piano has been somewhat abbreviated. Hopefully, he will be ready to take his Grade VIII exam in June. Matt won a math award last June and is now working at Grade 11 math. He also was put on an all-star team in a volleyball tournament, so his parents try to overlook the sometimes-dishevelled state of his room.

Bruce continues to deal with off-hours calls to the Ministry of Social Services. He serves on the board of Hope Resources, an organization which assists abuse victims, and on the Missions Committee at church, and oversees much of Marilyn and Geordon's North American business, including reloading and driving our/their

12-passenger van to Vancouver to be loaded into a container destined for Caracas. He had to make sure there was enough gas to get him to the dock, and yet arrive with an empty tank, so he carried a can of gasoline to ensure he didn't tie up traffic in the Deas Tunnel. He also keeps a watchful eye on some older friends and does most of the shopping and cooking. His expertise in this area sometimes brings extra responsibilities his way. Louise's high school friend, Clara Knight, catered tea for several hundred at both Marilyn's and Melody's weddings in 1987 and 1994. In October, her son, Byron, was married, and Bruce oversaw the serving of a roast beef dinner for 300. With son-in-law Rick's help, Bruce was able to track down the owner of the lot next door to Rick and Mel's cabin at Horne Lake, and purchase the lease. Bruce enjoys the peace and solitude of the lake.

Louise continues to teach piano at home and play the organ at church, both great privileges. June saw the completion of 35 years of teaching: seven years in the public schools, 28 in her own music classroom. With the help of family members and other young people, she supervises our small businesses. Last summer she escaped to the music room for hours on end to rewrite several of her piano courses, a welcome distraction from the clutter and confusion of house re-decorating. In March, she was elected to the Registered Music Teachers' Association executive, as secretary, and finds this new responsibility quite challenging and enjoyable. (She arrived at the first meeting, pencils sharpened, with a new minutes book she had been told to purchase. The old book, completely filled, was carefully stored with other R.M.T. material on a shelf in our office. To her chagrin, the president opened the meeting and then asked for the minutes of the last meeting. Louise has a history of turning beet-red when embarrassed and/or under stress, and no doubt the glow raised the room's temperature significantly. She had told her music students the evening before that it is better to take their music books to a concert and not need them than not to take them and wish they had.) She is also organizing the Toronto Conservatory's annual awards recital, for the fifth year. Matthew prints out the required letters and programmes. Louise usually plays organ for the worship team on Sunday mornings, often in company with Mark and Matthew (euphonium and trumpet) or Margaret, Melissa and Melody (violins) or Mike (bass guitar). At Grandpa Rendle's funeral in September, she was even able to play an organ-piano prelude with Marilyn. (It is doubtful if Granny and Grandpa Forsberg knew their 50-cents-a-week investment in piano lessons over 45 years ago would be multiplied in this way!)

We are thankful that our three grandparents, Grandma Holland and Grandpa and Granny Forsberg, all 88 years old this year, are available for wise and loving counsel. Grandma Holland lives with Auntie Marilyn, and both are on top of everything from the Grizzlies' latest exploits to the current political situation. She and Auntie Marilyn are always "there" for us, and we have appreciated this greatly.

Grandpa Forsberg is quite frail and a little forgetful, but usually manages to get out for his daily walk to McDonald's three blocks away from home. Granny Forsberg keeps a watchful eye on their many grandchildren, and still sews for the family. She misses her sister, Kaye, but is grateful for contacts with her children, grandchildren and great-grandchild.

SEEN AND HEARD ...

... Mark, handsome in his new teal blue suit, driving Rick and Mel's "Mellow Yellow" (a year or two away from vintage status) to his graduation ceremonies, a very special concession on their part ... Granny Forsberg, in her 88th year, soaking up the warmth on a Hawaiian beach in March, well-protected from the sun's rays by sun hat and towels ... Bruce and Rick and Melody careening around hairpin turns in the Cameron Highlands, Malaysia, wondering if they will ever see the streets of Victoria again ... Melissa informing mother and grandmother on arrival at Victoria airport from Hawaii, that Mother's (actually Melody and Rick's) carry-on was being sent home via Vancouver, after sitting in the Canada 3000 office for the week they had been in Hawaii (The carry-on had been left on the boulevard outside Honolulu airport in the excitement of greeting sister and brother and spouses. Daily inquiries to the airport's lost and found had not located the suitcase, which contained Mother's "best" things, plus a new book on piano pedagogy and two new Organic Gardening magazines. Needless to say, Mother was delighted, especially as the bag was part of the Starks' very good set of luggage.) ... a transformer across the street exploding into brilliant flames and sparks, simultaneously illuminating the neighbourhood streets and plunging the houses into blackness, accompanied by the roar of electricity gone berserk, a result of December's freezing ice storm ... Rick, submitting to a practice injection from Melissa, complaining that now he needed stitches ... Mother receiving and surreptitiously opening a small envelope from Margaret during the church service (Typically, envelope is decorated with calligraphy and flower sketches. Parents later smile when they learn friend who delivered letter from the Mainland wondered if ferry would leave without her while letter was in process of embellishment; scene is reminiscent of many over the years when the rest of the family were out in the car for school or church or a concert, with the straggler in her room making a card or preparing a gift for someone. Margaret's life has been filled with love, generosity and making things beautiful!) ... Granny Forsberg's trailer nestled under the cedar trees on our lot at Horne Lake, protected from winter storms by a wooden and aluminum structure designed and put up by Rick ... newly-carpeted living room filled with 35,000 of our flyers and 75,000 inserts to be collated into them, and several young people with flying fingers ...

Chapter 41: A Christmas Digest, 1996

EDITORIAL *by Louise*

December 1 If the oak trees have finally lost their leaves, can Christmas be far behind? Yes, they have, and no, it isn't! I have just read through all of last year's Christmas letters, and have been motivated to get started on our own. Bruce and I extend compliments of the Season to you and wish you God's blessing in the New Year.

We will be celebrating Melody's 22nd birthday today, as December 5 is crowded with many other activities. Around our table will sit Dad, Mom, Margaret, Melissa, Melody and Rick, Mark, Joel Mawhorter (our very compatible—it was suggested that these adjectives also be added: "wealthy," "brilliant," "young," "single"—boarder, a UVic engineering student from Prince George), and Jason Pohl (a young man who works with street children in Caracas). Matthew is in Kelowna for the provincial volleyball finals. Marilyn and Geordon and not-so-wee Jordie e-mailed that they would like to join us, but they are not scheduled to arrive back in Canada from Venezuela until December 17. Michael's work at the Vancouver Airport keeps him on the other side of the water.

This house continues to reverberate with the sound and activities of family, friends, students, acquaintances, and sometimes even strangers. Now that our young people are older and capable of entertaining guests on their own, we often do not even know who or how many are spending the night. Or, in the case of Mark's bedroom, who might be watching a video on his state-of-the-art TV and stereo system. He has transformed his room into a "bachelor's pad," and has a group of well-mannered friends who are welcome to wander in and out.

With Matthew's Grade VIII Piano exam in June, 25 years of music lessons have come to an end. I recently came across a tape from 1972. Complete with thuds, bumps and other extraneous noises, it features four-month-old Melissa cooing; 18-month-old Margaret chattering; three-year-old Michael quoting his Christmas concert verse: "Asyoucansee,I'monlythreebutIloveJesusandJesuslovesme" in three seconds flat, and then, after an exasperated sigh, repeating it at a more sedate tempo; and five-year-old Marilyn, also quoting her Sunday School poem and playing several little piano pieces. I reflect over Bruce's and my state of mind 24 years ago. When that tape was made, we couldn't foresee the eventual size of our family, or music lessons for seven children, or music lessons for seven children on two instruments. It was not until a year later that we were introduced to the violin, and now thousands of lessons and hundreds of concerts have come and gone. It is our prayer that our family will continue to use their musical training in the service of God and their community.

Until mid-August, our year had progressed quite normally. In late summer we received a phone call to see if our family would be interested in dealing with some "weeds" and preparing them for sale. To make a long story shorter, by the end of October we had sorted through, stalk by stalk, over 100,000 stems of the very best Canadian black-bearded wheat, and cleaned and bundled approximately one-third of that for sale, setting aside the less perfect heads for use as seed, and giving the stems to a local wheat-weaver who creates exquisite wall hangings with the stems, as well as with the complete stalks. The wheat was a shipment from Lethbridge, Alberta, headed to Spokane, Washington, and had been stopped at the border due to an embargo on Canadian wheat. The music room became a "barn" from Thursday evening to Monday morning for several weeks, as Mother and three daughters and a friend sorted and talked, and talked and sorted, with straw accumulating in bags, boxes and on the sheets protecting the floor, and Mother wondering to herself if the bundles would sell. A break came with a large order from Chintz & Company for their four stores (Victoria, Vancouver, and, ironically, Calgary and Edmonton); the floral manager commented that her supplier could not supply such lovely wheat. I often mulled over the many Scriptural references to wheat, right through the Old Testament to the New Testament's "fields white for harvest" (a motivation for our young peoples' mission work).

PERSONAL GLIMPSES

At 16 and six feet tall, **Matthew** looks down on most other family members. He has just taken out his learner's license, after returning from a trip with his French class to Paris. Matthew plays trumpet in the senior band, produces ads for our family flyer and publishes an air squadron's newsletter/booklet each month, plays volleyball and floor hockey, and is compiling stats for the school's basketball games. Matthew was given his Grandpa Holland's name (Norman), and seems to have inherited his skill in woodworking as well. He has produced a CD holder, boxes and vases, each made up of several varieties of wood, and has been working in his spare time on a boat in the shop at school for the last two years. He has programmed our computer to emit startling comments and alarming sounds when mistakes are made. I may be a nervous wreck by the time I have finished typing this; perhaps I should remind him that I have the keys to the car.

Mark is well into his second year of working 40 to 50 hours a week in a very congenial setting at Atlas Stereo and TV, and saving towards his eventual return to school. He works in the store and delivers and helps install sound systems and televisions. Mark has purchased professional gear for ice and roller hockey and plays both sports. One of the most amiable of our seven, Mark not only welcomes family and friends to share his room and equipment, but often ends up searching in Matt's room for shirts and pants, and occasionally realizes his clothing has made its way to Surrey, where another brother resides.

Melody and **Richard** continue to tackle the challenges of home ownership with energy and enthusiasm, and sometimes frustration. So far, the basement has stayed dry, in spite of a couple of very wet and windy storms. Their soil is mostly clay, but produced an impressive crop of vegetables last summer. The borders surprised them month by month with an abundance of flowers, a legacy from the previous owners. Richard drives the big rigs for Island Farms, both up-Island and to the Mainland, and has started his own small hauling business. He and his father replaced kitchen and bathroom linoleum, and he and Melody have painted several rooms. He encourages Melody with her piano studies—she passed Grade IX in June—and joins her in leading Junior Church, alternating months with Margaret. Melody helps me with a piano class, and works with a couple of young piano students. She also assists at two day cares in her area, and enjoys dealing with her many Regal customers.

Melissa has had a productive year. She took two trips to Caracas, Venezuela: one in January as her reward to herself for completing her BScN requirements, and the other in July as nurse, with a team of young people from our church who spent a month helping Geordon and Marilyn in their youth work. In June, she graduated from UVic and is now working on permanent night shifts at Mt. Edwards Court Care Home. Her knowledge of computers, enhanced by workshops in Vancouver, has enabled her to help set up and troubleshoot programmes for the care facility. With an eye to living on her own eventually, she has taken over some of the meal preparation, and is fast becoming a skilful chef.

Margaret passed the quarter-century mark on October 6. To celebrate the occasion, Melissa and her accomplice, Dawnmaree Fletcher, threw a party for her on the Causeway at the Inner Harbour, in front of the Empress Hotel. Family and friends converged at the party place, which Melissa and Dawn had decorated with balloons and streamers. The guest of honour, blindfolded, was ushered to the birthday bench and topped with a party hat. Melissa had baked a large cake, using three cake mixes, and covered it with an unusual topping concocted of both icing and coloured granulated sugar, to which coconut was added in an attempt to camouflage the gritty sugar. The entire cake, over 50 tasty slices, was shared with passersby, mostly tourists enjoying the fall sunshine, to the accompaniment of Melissa's "It's Margaret's birthday. Come and hug the birthday girl and get a piece of cake!" A face

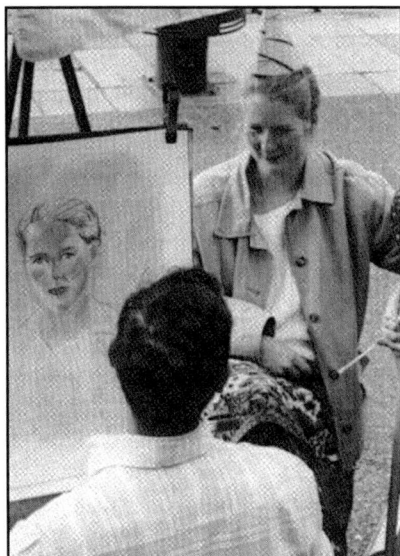

MARGARET'S 25TH BIRTHDAY

painter embellished Margaret's right eye with a multi-coloured arabesque, and an artist in pastels produced a beautiful likeness of the blushing party girl—both at no cost, as birthday presents. Margaret now has just over a year to plan for Melissa's 25th birthday.

After a year of living in Surrey with Nola and David Harbut, Geordon's aunt and uncle, in their spacious and hospitable home, and commuting to a variety of schools in Abbotsford and Langley as teacher-on-call, Margaret returned to Victoria during the summer to be near family, especially to her 89-year-old grandparents and Marilyn, Geordon and Jordie. On the Mainland, she had almost steady employment. Here she has been taken on by several independent schools, as well as the Victoria School Board, but has had only sporadic assignments. She is, however, building up a class of both violin and piano students. She assists me with two of my larger classes and participates in telephone surveys for the government. Margaret lives in a well-appointed basement suite at Auntie Marilyn and Grandma's home in the Royal Oak area, a wonderful provision for her. She finds herself in the Lake Hill area, more specifically at an address on Saanich Road, much of the time, and we are very happy for that.

Michael has been living with the Harbuts for most of this year. His transfer to the Vancouver International Airport gave him full-time hours and many contacts with flying personnel, and more recently he has been back flying and taking bass guitar lessons. His life took a devastating turn at the end of April, as a very special and loved friend was killed in a bizarre accident in the desert outside of Las Vegas. Mike had met Rachel Blythe Staton of Corona, California, when he was driving around North America three years ago with a Christian rock band. They kept in touch, and he flew his commercial cross-country flight from Victoria to Corona, where he stayed with Rachel and her family. In June of 1995, Rachel visited us for a week; for her 20th birthday this March, her parents gave her fare for another visit this June. Rachel had been living and working as a nanny in Las Vegas in preparation for her return to school in the fall. Mike was able to visit her there in February, and enjoyed a very special visit. On April 28, Rachel went hiking alone in an isolated area of the Valley of Fire state park. Four days after she was reported missing, a state trooper discovered the accident scene. Although the precise cause of the accident is unknown, the authorities determined that, after becoming stuck in loose sand off the main road, the engine or another component of Rachel's car overheated, causing a tremendous explosion and fire, killing her instantly. After exhaustive testing, foul play was ruled out. Michael travelled to California for the memorial service (held the day before Mother's Day), which was a beautiful remembrance of Rachel's many loves: her love of nature, her friends, her family, her love for God. Rachel was a gifted writer and had a special way with children. One of the most appropriate testimonies to her character was how much she loved and was loved by the many children she cared for over the years.

The Statons spent a weekend with us in August, and Dr. Staton commented that this was the most difficult experience of his life, and that Heaven had become even more of a reality to him. Our pastor has often said that while not all things that happen are good, "All things" *do* "work together *for the good* of those who love God" (Romans 8:28), and we have to trust God to bring something good out of this tragic experience.

It is now December 12, and I am back at this keyboard, chasing the cursor around on the screen and appreciating the ability of the computer to change and correct text instantly, as long as I discover my mistakes or omissions. And now on to Marilyn and Geordon, Jordie and Evita (their cat, who is coming home to stay).

Geordon and **Marilyn** are scheduled to arrive home next Tuesday; there is great excitement as last-minute preparations are made on two continents. Geordon and Marilyn were last home in September of 1995, for Grandpa Rendle's funeral. This time they are scheduled to stay in Victoria for several months, and we are looking forward to their living with us, as their own house is rented out. With an unlocked door separating our quarters from their suite, I suspect we will be the recipients of visits from a little person who is destined to be showered with affection by an assortment of grandparents and aunts and uncles. Geordon and Marilyn's time in Latin America has been filled with many learning and growing

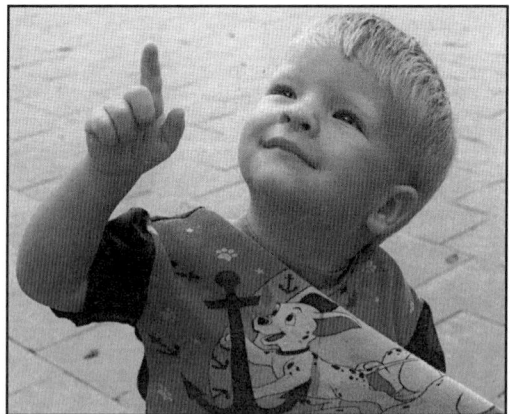

JORDIE WATCHING A SLOTH

experiences, as they (especially Marilyn) have adapted to a different culture and language, and they are finding it difficult to leave, even temporarily, people whom they have come to know and love. They thank God for the privilege they have had in encouraging young people to make life-changing decisions, and look forward to their return to Venezuela some time late next year. Geordon will be working on the Saanich Police force for the time they are home, and Marilyn has made no definite plans yet.

Bruce and I are again passing milestones this year, three involving the numbers 60, 55, and 35, but that's all I'll say about that! We are both busy and happy in our respective professions, and value the contributions to our family life from our caring, generous and wise parents, from our contemporaries who encourage us so graciously, and from our children, who assist us in family and business projects, and who guarantee that life is never boring. Bruce will probably take early retirement in the New Year, and we are looking forward to that. I hope to continue my piano teaching for many more years (d.v.). Where else could I put on sparkly earrings and a brooch and have someone (a very active four year old in my beginning music class) exclaim, "Mrs. Holland, you look so bee-*yoo*-ti-ful!"? Bruce is on the counselling and missions committees at church, and on the board of Hope Resources. I am on the music committee, usually play the organ on Sundays, and am completing my second term as secretary for the Registered Music Teachers (131 members in Victoria). Our family flyer (35,000 copies four times a year, covered with advertisements from our own and local businesses) demands many hours, and almost every family member helps me in some way or the other with it. And our other little businesses: plants, house/pet minding, Matol, Regal (Melody's), and now, wheat, ensure that hands are not idle.

LIFE'S SOMETIMES LIKE THIS

March 31 Father and Mother are at the Caracas airport, having spent three weeks visiting daughter, son-in-law and 18-month-old grandson. Their many activities included a shopping trip to Makro, Venezuela's version of Costco, where Mother discovered demerara sugar packaged in lots of twenty 500-gram bags, at an excellent price. Over mild protests of husband, Mother has purchased a bundle of twenty bags and packed them into her suitcase. Son-in-law takes luggage off for processing and is asked to come to side room where he is detained for several minutes. On his return, parents learn that X-rays suggested Mother's suitcase could be filled with drugs.

December 10 (*Happy Birthday! to nieces Cindy and Sonya, sisters born exactly 13 years apart*) Mother looks for excuse to go for a walk, decides to deliver flyer information to customer several blocks away. Dons padded winter coat and woollen gloves, happily strides down Saanich Road to crosswalk at Quadra. Eyes two lanes of traffic approaching on other side of road; stands back on sidewalk to await their passing. To her surprise, both lanes come to a halt. Mother looks left to closest two lanes and is startled to see that, they, too, have stopped. Cars stretch down both sides of road as far as can be seen. Mother hurriedly steps into crosswalk, feeling very conspicuous. Halfway across, drops letter onto damp pavement, desperately tries to retrieve it, hampered by thick gloves and long, bulky coat; is very conscious of four lanes of traffic waiting patiently. Spends next three blocks musing on how a few moments can transform one from a comfortable anonymity to a most uncomfortable spectacle.

SEEN AND HEARD ...

... Cousin Tara joining Granny Forsberg in celebration of their mutual birthday on August 3, in the exuberant company of her mother, two aunts and three cousins ... *Department of Wish I Hadn't Said That:* Mother's query: "What will happen to all that wheat if no one buys it?" Father's answer: "Oh, he'll probably have to take it to Hartland Road and pay to have it dumped"—a statement guaranteed to bring action from his frugal, nature-loving spouse, who could not bear to think of the destruction of 24 large (cubic 1.25 metre) boxes of saleable wheat ... Grandpa Forsberg explaining how wheat was planted and harvested on the prairies 70 years ago ... Matthew, back to the net, tipping the volleyball over into a hole in the opponents' defence, instead of setting it up to a team-mate for the expected spike ... Rick driving the tanker, or float, in Island Farms parades in Victoria, Oak Bay, Esquimalt and Sidney, accompanied by Melody, supervising children on the floats ... Joel, older brother to Jared and Joshua, after noting how his host family refers to the seven Ms as "M1," "M2," etc., attaching a sign to his bedroom door: "J1" ... a newspaper article saved by the North American son-in-law while his inlaws were in Venezuela, entitled "Do 90s guys long for old-fashioned girls?" which contains this interesting statement: "A few decades ago, bobbed hair was considered indecent, but playing the piano increased a woman's marriageability." A notation has been added to it: "This is how Mom Holland snagged Dad Holland." ... Caracas, a city of contrasts: tropical heat downtown, more moderate temperatures on the outskirts; modern apartments everywhere, hundreds of thousands of red clay tenements stacked on top of each other in the *barrios* (slum settlements), extravagantly wealthy homes; multi-lane highways (no speed restrictions), cobblestone alleyways barely wide enough for one car, used as two-way streets; dilapidated trucks and buses bringing workers in from the *barrios*, luxury autos nosing their way into traffic ... Margaret, Melissa and Melody assembling Creative Memories albums of their photos, all with captions and decorative shapes, under the direction of their good friend, Karen Harmsworth ... Mother's bulletin boards covered with dozens of music-motif Christmas cards collected over the past 30 years ... Four tiny sand dollars on the windowsill, a memento of three blue-eyed pixies (Kimba, 8, Willow, 7, Belle, 2) and their brand-new brother, Abram, who stayed in our suite while their father, Phil Meagher, worked on his Master's degree at UVic this summer (Mother Sherri took advantage of their time away from Fort MacMurray to explore Victoria, with her very well-behaved little entourage.) ...

Chapter 42: A Christmas Digest, 1997

EDITORIAL *by Louise*

It is 4:05 a.m., the house is uncharacteristically still, and the computer and I are the only ones stirring. Bundled in a heavy dressing-gown and Bruce's sweater, with a blanket on my lap—the furnace will rumble into action in another two hours—I am yielding to a rare bout of insomnia. At 1:00 a.m., a strange sound woke me up. Several seconds of ferocious snarling culminated in a loud thunk as a hapless creature met its doom, probably on our laundry stand in the back yard. Then— silence. I expect to find a dead bird, squirrel or cat when I go out later this morning; I am not going out to check now. I could not identify the attacker, but I suspect either a raccoon or an owl. For the last three hours I have lain awake, mulling over the tumultuous events of this past year, and finally decided I could be more productive in a vertical position. (Later: the night's misadventure is still a mystery; I found no fur or feathers in the back yard. Perhaps an owl or hawk carried off the evidence.)

The Christmas letter I wrote thirty-one years ago also started early one December morning. The imminent arrival of our first baby accounted for that sleeplessness. When I look back over the intervening 30 years, I can only marvel at God's goodness to us as a family.

We could call this "The Year of the Annas." Not only do I have three students named Anna, but Granny Anna Forsberg, in company with Grandpa Hjalmar and Grandma Olive Holland, celebrated her 90th birthday, and her granddaughter, Melody, presented the family with dear little Anna Phyllis on November 21, named after little Anna's great-grandmother and Richard's grandmother. Baby Anna is a delight, and is bringing much joy to the family.

PERSONAL GLIMPSES

Geordon and **Marilyn** returned from Venezuela last December and were booked to return permanently to Caracas on September 15. They did return to Venezuela for two weeks in September to renew their visas, but were forced to delay their permanent return until March 31 when Marilyn learned she is, happily, and contrary to her gynecologist's predictions, pregnant. Her medical plan would not cover the cost of childbirth in Venezuela, so we are happy to have our time with them extended for another few months. Geordon and Marilyn are "missionaries-on-staff" at our home church, in addition to their work with Youth for Christ; Geordon completes his term as interim Executive Director on December 31. In April his parents returned from Nicaragua due to Georgia's excruciatingly painful shoulder. A tumour was removed, and radiation administered, with a temporary slowing of what was diagnosed as melanoma, allowing Georgia and Don to travel to Penticton in August to watch Geordon complete the Ironman Triathlon. The malignancy reappeared in the lungs, and moved very quickly, taking the life on November 25 of a brilliant, caring woman who was devoted to serving others as a missionary in both Central and South America. It has been difficult, as Georgia's friends, both to accept her death and to watch her husband and sons struggle with the loss. Their acceptance of God's will has been an inspiration, but it is a hard experience. Little **Jordie** (three in September) tumbles through both storeys of this house, bringing merriment with him, and that helps to brighten the dark winter days.

Michael continues to share the Harbuts' home in Surrey. He rises at five most mornings to make lift-off at six, as he flies with Navair into many smaller towns in southern BC with bank mail. He is accumulating flying time, especially on the runs where weather makes landing at his designated destinations impossible and he has to touch down at another airfield and then return when the weather cooperates. He augments his flying income by refueling aircraft of all sizes at the Vancouver International Airport, and recently dealt with Air Force One and Air Force Two in Vancouver for the APEC conference. We miss him here at home, but he is busy with a group of young people from the church he attends (Panorama, a Mennonite congregation), and plays both bass guitar and violin (fitted with a pickup) in the church's worship services. Although he still grieves Rachel's loss, he is coming to terms with it.

We miss **Margaret**, too, as she left us abruptly in August to take up a teaching position at a school for missionaries' children in Caracas. She is working with a small Grade 4 class, and teaches music and physical education to other grades in the school as well. It will be her first Christmas away from the family, but she has wonderful friends down in Venezuela who will help make up for that. Her future plans are uncertain, as the school administration would like to keep her down there. We would love to have her back on this continent, but that is not for us to decide. Margaret is presently in Caracas on an expired visa, and plans, with another teacher in the same predicament, to fly to the island of Bonaire in the next few days (mid-December) to have it renewed. (She e-mailed to say she was spending some time in "Borneo," which caused her parents some consternation; when questioned as to her destination, she acknowledged the typo and commented, "Where is my head?") Most communications from Margaret are upbeat, for which we are thankful, as she is perhaps our most loyal homebody.

Melissa reaches the quarter-century mark in December, but Margaret's threat to repay her for last year's 25th birthday on the Causeway, where Melissa invited passersby to "hug the birthday girl and have a piece of birthday cake," will probably not be carried through, with Margaret so many miles away. Melissa continues to work the night shift at Mt. Edwards Court Care Home, and oversees computer training and troubleshooting. She has been accepted for a course in International Nursing in Ontario, and leaves us for four months on January 16. She hopes to take her three-month practicum in Cuba at a later date. Melissa was stranded in Mt. Ed when the "Snowstorm of the Century" hit Victoria last December 29, dumping four to five feet of snow, and immobilizing the city for several days. She and two other staff members cared for the 85 residents, relying on advice by phone from the regular cook, stranded at home; as the day wore on, other workers gradually filtered in to the facility, and Melissa was able to leave after almost 24 hours of supervising. Melissa and her friend, Dawnmaree Fletcher, headed up a 10-day bike hike for 20 bikers down the Oregon Coast last summer. On a preliminary trip, they scouted out the campsites and activity resources, and then planned each day's mileage, activities, and food. Camp Qwanoes sponsored the bike hike and was happy to have it come in under budget. Melissa has served many times as camp nurse, and is now on the Camp Board. A highlight of her year was a trip on her own to Ontario and Massachusetts, where she fell in love with the Cape Cod area. Her parents were glad to have her back safely.

Melody and **Richard** are delighted with their tiny twig on the family tree! **Anna** has already brought the family much happiness. Rick continues as foreman at Island Farms, driving the 18-wheelers up-Island and to the Mainland. He has built a cozy room in their basement, as well as a 9' x 9' room in our carport to store Margaret's possessions while she is in Venezuela. Melody assists me with five music classes and hopes to get back to her own piano studies in the near future. She helps with our family businesses and oversees her own thriving Regal business.

Mark continues to work at Atlas TV and Stereo, helping out with sales and delivering and setting up equipment. He appreciates the Hordyks' integrity and generosity, and has learned a lot about business and work practices from them. He and several friends took a trip to Disneyland last spring, and were bumped twice on their flight home, which netted them each two free trips anywhere in North America where the airline flies. In September, he flew to Miami on one ticket, and paid to fly from Miami to Caracas so he could stay with Margaret and Marilyn and Geordon for the two weeks they were in Venezuela to renew their visas. Unlike his sisters, Mark had never been on an overseas Project Serve, so this was a broadening experience for him. He and his friends are also travelling to Disney World in Florida in January, before his second free ticket expires. Mark has been helping out each week at the

Juvenile Detention Home with a sports programme sponsored by YFC and this has also been instructive. He and Matt put in a strenuous roller blade hockey season last spring, cheered on by a variety of family members, including their Granny Forsberg.

Matthew has just returned from the Volleyball Provincials in his last games of high school volleyball. In tournaments leading up to the finals, he was put on the All-Star team twice. With graduation in June beckoning, Matt is involved in several fundraising activities, including delivering telephone books, with his father as assistant. He continues to make up ads for our flyers and types and formats a monthly newsletter for an air force association, as well as tackling the odd computer job. He has almost talked his parents into the purchase of an even more versatile computer. He is quick (and wise enough) to assist his technologically-disadvantaged parents in becoming more knowledgeable and comfortable in front of the monitor. June of 1998 marks the completion of seventeen years of association with Pacific Christian School; Matthew will be our seventh graduate. One of his teachers is considering making a T-shirt that proclaims, "I taught M all!" We have very much appreciated the privilege of our children's attendance at PCS, and trust that Matt and his siblings will be a credit to the school and its principles of living from a Christian perspective.

Bruce is almost certain he retired from the Ministry of Families and Children last March, but his time seems just as full as it was before then. He sits on three different committees or boards, and keeps an eye on the business affairs of several of our older friends, as well as dealing with the day-to-day needs of this household. We usually have eight to twelve around our table once a day, and Bruce's culinary prowess is greatly appreciated. He organized beautiful receptions in our home for Granny Forsberg's 90th birthday in August, and for Grandma and Grandpa Neale's (Geordon's grandparents) 60th Wedding Anniversary in September.

Louise continues to enjoy her music students, and has classes or private lessons parts of six days a week. She recently overheard Bruce comment that he and Louise weren't free just to take off whenever they wanted because Louise "is still working." That was a new concept for her, as, before now, she has not regarded "teaching" as "working"! Sunday finds her at the organ, often in the company of piano and an assortment of other instruments (strings, flutes, horns, etc.), as part of the team which leads the congregation in worship. She was elected president of the Victoria Registered Music Teachers in January, an honour which carries considerable responsibility. Fortunately, she has an excellent executive around her, including a very knowledgeable and helpful past president, Wendy Maggiora. She also manages the family's little businesses. Bruce has taken over several of Melissa's Minding clients, and Melody helps out with the flyer (most recent edition 40,000); Louise in turn helps her with her Regal business. Some of Louise's happiest times are spent digging compost (of which we have much) and leaves (of which we have many) into the garden, which, over a few months, produce many wheelbarrow loads of friable soil for potting up Matt's Plants.

LIFE IS SOMETIMES LIKE THIS

Saturday, December 21, 1996 Father and Mother are celebrating their 35th wedding anniversary and have been promised a quiet night out. *Chez Marguerite* (or should that be *Casa Margarita*?), Margaret's spacious suite in Grandma Holland and Auntie Marilyn's home, has been transformed into a restaurant, with a table set for two, and candles and flowers throughout the room. Two young men, towels draped over their left arms, serve the three-course meal, solicitously inquiring as to their guests' comfort and wishes. Violin music emanates from behind a partition, mingled with some giggling, and is replaced by soothing music on the stereo, as the chefs (Marilyn, Margaret, Melissa) and waiters (Mark, Matthew) tiptoe off into the night, leaving their parents to finish the gourmet meal and watch a movie on TV.

Thursday, March 20, 1997, Father's last shift before retirement Family decides (unknown to Father) to escort him home into retirement. At 12:30 a.m., Margaret knocks on window of building and is invited in, waits while Father takes one last look around the office and checks to see that computer reports are up to date. Rick and Melody, Mark, Matthew, Geordon and Marilyn, and Mother wait in parked cars for Father and daughter to exit building. Mother has been persuaded to replace teaching dress with long (opaque, and decorated with a discreet amount of lace) black caftan under her heavy, long winter coat, as children remind her of second meaning of "retiring." Following children's instructions, and feeling more than a little foolish, she carries Father's pajamas folded under one arm and a handful of helium balloons in her other hand. Children had hoped to talk Father into changing into pajamas before he leaves office, but fortunately, Father's conservatism stands him in good stead, and he leaves his place of employment respectably attired. Is surprised by presence of family, gets behind wheel of car for drive home, preceded by two other family cars. Makes way along Blanshard and is startled by siren and flashing lights as police car pulls him over. Officer comes to window, comments on Father's speed, and asks if he has received any speeding citations recently; Mother checks to see that coat buttons are done up. Father, dismayed, is sure he was not speeding, and replies that not only has he recently paid a fine for driving 63 km/h in a 50-km/h zone (on another stretch of Blanshard, on a quiet Sunday morning as he returned home from church to organize lunch), but that this is not a pleasant way to end his last night at work. Asks officer how fast he was going; receives answer, "62 km/h." Officer returns to police vehicle. Father and Mother sit quietly for several minutes. Officer reappears at window, hands Father ticket, which Father reluctantly takes. Officer suggests he look more closely at it, and Father notices message:

HAPPY RETIREMENT! By this time, rest of family has surrounded car, and one son-in-law (who collaborated with his former colleague in the prank) greets him gleefully.

Friday, April 18 Stranger comes to front door to retrieve wallet that Matthew has found in a phone booth at a shopping centre. Asks Mother for Matthew's name, and then wonders if he could be related to a social worker named Bruce Holland. Mother assures her that this is the case, and guest goes on to relate her high regard for Bruce. Mother smiles, knowing that surprise retirement party the next day will involve not only family and friends, but colleagues from Ministry for Families and Children, and that his children have had magnets made up expressing a sentiment they have heard many times over the years: "Count Me Among The Privileged... I know Bruce Holland! 1997 © Holland Children & Associates." Bruce's responsibilities extended across the Capital Region out to the Gulf Islands, up the Malahat, and out to Port Renfrew, a huge area which often necessitated his calling for help from local police and RCMP, and his family sometimes grumbled that they couldn't go anywhere without being identified as Bruce Holland's children.

Monday, August 18, 8:30 p.m. Margaret and Melissa are leaving the Bankonins' beautiful home in Broadmead after a 24th birthday party for their friend, Chris Bankonin. They, with nearly 20 others, have enjoyed a happy and hilarious time, but Melissa has to get home to rest for her night shift. Their friend, Heather Burns, ahead of them, notices what appears to be steam or smoke in the garage she is passing. She runs back to ask the family if something is in the dryer. Older brother, Harvey Bankonin, opens door to garage to discover flames; yells for guests to get out. Melissa runs up to parents' bedroom, where Mrs. Bankonin is looking for a card in which to put a gift for Margaret's work in Venezuela, tells her that house is on fire; Mrs. Bankonin and Melissa grab three pictures from the bedroom as they run out. Other guests, shoeless, flee to street and watch in horror as "dream home" (which Mr. Bankonin had designed) and years of family remembrances disappear into smoke in less than ten minutes. Mrs. Bankonin overrides Margaret's reticence and insists she accept gift (cardless); Mr. Bankonin tells reporter that he is thankful everyone got out safely.

SCENE IN PASSING ...

... Matthew, smiling a gleaming white for the first time in two years, as his top braces come off for Christmas ... note on kitchen chalkboard beside Hydro bill (well over $200/month): *"Turn down! Shut off! Shower with a friend! The Management"* ... printed below previous note: "In order to save electricity, I have unplugged the refrigerator." (Second note is unsigned, but suspicion is on electrical engineer-in-training—Joel Mawhorter, our boarder—who obviously is acquiring useful information in his courses at UVic.) ... Marilyn, beautifully "great with child" (a friend's evaluation), leading the choir each Sunday as interim choir director; Geordon, singing enthusiastically in the choir in spite of the shattering loss of his mother, whose lyric soprano voice graced many a service, both here and in Latin America ... a bright red telephone, fitted with Mother's photo on the dial, painted and decorated by her handyman son-in-law [Richard], a "hot-line" for "Mme. President" (Mother's head goes spinning whenever the dial is activated.) ... Mother and four daughters at a ladies' retreat; daughters, in spite of their violin contributions, proving to be among the most zany in the group. ... "Cows" decorating Grandma Holland's lawn, with an accompanying message: "Have you *herd* that it's Olive's 90th birthday?" ... case-room nurse by phone to Mother/Babe unit of hospital: "Mrs. Stork and her baby are ready to come." (Blushes when she realizes what she has said; Melody's married name is St*a*rk.) ... Melody arriving home one recent Sunday after lunch at our place, to find her house filled with Rick's family and friends,

REGISTERED MUSIC TEACHERS ASSOCIATION "PRESIDENTIAL PHONE"

waiting to give Melody and Anna a surprise baby shower (Melody and Anna were overwhelmed by the generous assortment of gifts they received. At least Melody was overwhelmed; Anna slept quietly on a series of laps.) ... two ambulances out front, four paramedics in our living room, Marilyn seated calmly on chesterfield, wired for racing heartbeat (230 beats per minute); trip to hospital results in injection which brings rate down in four seconds to 40 beats, which then rises gradually to 80 (Doctor says condition, which has precipitated several such incidents this fall, is not serious, and can be remedied with minor surgery after the baby is born.) ...

Best wishes and love to you from all of us. May your 1998 be blessed and fulfilling!

Chapter 43: A Christmas Digest, 1998

EDITORIAL *by Louise*

Compliments of the Season to our friends and family! You are among God's very good gifts to us, and we are thankful for you. We extend to you our love and best wishes, and trust you might find something interesting on these pages. In common with most families, ours has experienced both joy and sorrow, and we praise God for His guidance and peace throughout the year's experiences.

After co-existing happily with us for 15 months, Geordon, Marilyn, Jordan, and Joshua left for Caracas at 6:00 a.m. on March 31. After 10:00 p.m. that evening, I received a call from James Bay Lodge to report that Grandpa Hjalmar Forsberg was very low, in the last stages of Alzheimer's Disease, and that I should come quickly. After phoning

my brother, Eric, I made the 15-minute drive to the home, arriving a few minutes after him, and our father died less than ten minutes later. Although his passing brought sadness to the family, we were thankful he did not have to suffer any longer. All five of us children (including Harriet, from Anchorage) were able to support each other and our mother at his memorial service. Dad was buried in the family plot in the peaceful burial ground of Holy Trinity Church, Patricia Bay, just west of Sidney.

Hjalmar Emmanuel Forsberg (1907–1998)

MY DAD [*written June 2019*]

My father, Hjalmar Emmanuel Forsberg, was born in Minot, North Dakota, the son of Swedish immigrants who had immigrated to North America a few years earlier. The family moved to a farm in southern Saskatchewan, and the family grew to 14 children.

Hjalmar often reminisced about life on the farm—the expanse of the prairies, the winter cold, the relief as spring brought rising temperatures, the fragrant wild rose of summer, and planting and harvesting with horse and plough.

During the Depression years of the 1930s he "rode the rails" to the coast, eventually obtaining work on Vancouver Island. He met and married my mother Anna and settled down with his rapidly expanding family on a small farm on West Saanich Road, 15 miles from Victoria. He made an extensive renovation to the small tearoom on the property, placing kitchen windows low enough that his children could see the garden and watch the passing traffic.

This was during World War II and Hjalmar found work at the munitions plant on James Island, which we later learned was both dirty and dangerous. He joined the air force in the early 1940s and trained as a chef at the military camp in Kamloops, where he was scolded for not having gone farther in school; his IQ had tested at a very high level. He later worked as custodian at Prospect Lake Elementary School and developed a jam-making business at home, displaying a colourful variety of jams, jellies, marmalades and butters on a stand in front of our home. An excellent cook, he built up a clientele of customers from the many tourists who passed our home on their way to Butchart Gardens and even mailed jars of jam to customers in California and Texas. The newspaper of the day carried an article on his little business, accompanied by a photograph of him and his two eldest daughters.

Hjalmar became cook on one of two tugboats owned by Island Tug & Barge, which meant he was away for days at a time. During that time we received news that a cook on a tugboat had drowned, and my mother was very anxious until she learned it was not our father.

Closer to retirement, my father became groundskeeper at Heal's Rifle Range, a job he enjoyed—revelling in the opportunity to work outdoors, sharing his habitat with the deer and other smaller animals of the area, and being free to set his own schedule.

In retirement, my parents for many years spent the winter months living in their trailer in Arizona. My father no doubt related the wide-open spaces of the desert to the prairies on which he had grown up.

My siblings and I remember a sometimes-impatient, sometimes-nonconforming, but loyal father who took his children to play on softball and basketball teams and prepared delicious meals for the family. I remember dancing the polka and schottische with him on the burgundy linoleum in our living room, and square dancing with him at the community hall. His favourite songs were "Life in the Finland Woods" and "On Top of Old Smoky," which I would play for him on the piano. He would entertain/annoy us with his off-key rendition of "Swanee River," often as we were struggling to wake up in the morning; he was always up before we were.

His grandchildren think with fondness of his ginger cookies with icing in the middle, of him braiding their hair, of sandpaper chin rubs, of watching baseball with him, and of his fondness for candy which he all-too-willingly shared with them.

I remember the pink wooden doll buggies he made in the early 1950s for my little sisters Peggy and Jeannie—a labour of love.

He has been gone for 22 years now, and I still think wistfully of the activities we shared, his love of nature and gardening, and the enjoyment he found in his grandchildren's antics.

PERSONAL GLIMPSES

Marilyn and **Geordon** continue to work with young people in Caracas, establishing a chapter of Youth for Christ for Venezuela. Most of the youth come from relatively affluent families, and it has been a challenge to motivate them to think beyond themselves, so their recent involvement in prison ministry, singing and speaking in the youth prison under Geordon and Marilyn's leadership, has been encouraging. At the national level, there has been much interest on the part of pastors and youth organizations in the resources that YFC can offer, and several have expressed a willingness to form a YFC board for Venezuela. A team of 14 young people from Central Baptist spent the month of August in Caracas, living in Marilyn and Geordon's apartment, reaching out into the surrounding neighbourhood, and conducting a youth camp in an isolated area two hours away. Jordie (pardon me, **Jordan**—"I'm *four* now") goes to a Spanish preschool five days a week, and has become fluent in Spanish, entertaining his parents (one with a lifetime of Colombian Spanish, the other with textbook Spanish acquired partly from her studies in Costa Rica) in Venezuelan Spanish, with its clipped word endings and abbreviations. **Joshua Michael**, at ten months, is very active and determined, and appears to have inherited a strong and wiry physique. Auntie Margaret sometimes comes out second-best in a battle of wills with her tiny nephew. Geordon returned to Victoria in early June to visit with his father for a few days before Don's marriage to Sharon Thompson, a lovely widow whose friendship with Don and Georgia (Geordon's mother) has extended over the past thirty-five years. Geordon's trip was a gift from friends. Although there is still much heaviness surrounding Georgia's death, the family is happy that God has provided for Don in this way. When Geordon returned to care for Jordie, Marilyn and Joshua flew up (largely on air miles) for a heart procedure: an ablation, where the misfiring electrical circuit inside the heart was dismantled, putting to an end the episodes of tachycardia when the heart raced over 200 beats a minute. We thank God, and the medical professionals, that the day surgery was successful, and Marilyn has not experienced any more arrhythmia. On December 12, Geordon's brother, Andy, and Stephanie Heslop were married at

Central. Geordon did not feel he could leave Caracas to attend this momentous event (several years in the offing!), due partly to the expenses involved and the Christmas programmes with the young people in Caracas, but mostly to the unsettled political conditions surrounding Venezuela's recent elections. He could not leave Marilyn and the children on their own in case violence erupted and ex-patriates were forced to leave the country. Staying in Venezuela on December 12 was very difficult for him and Marilyn, and those of us who were fortunate enough to attend the beautiful wedding (Andy in MacKenzie kilt, Stephanie in white velvet with MacKenzie tartan draped over her shoulder, anchored with a gorgeous "plaid" pin) missed the family very much.

Michael continues to fly cargo runs out of Vancouver into smaller towns both on the Mainland and on the Island. One job is hauling newspapers from Vancouver to Nanaimo in the middle of the night (usually two or three trips, depending on the size of the papers). For the past few months he has been "pilot-in-command" which means he has full responsibility for his flights, and sometimes flies on his own with his cargo. The extra responsibility has positive results financially, although not to the extent that those of us rooted to terra firma might assume; it is not until pilots fly for regional airlines that salaries rise to a living wage. Michael has learned to budget carefully, and whittles away conscientiously at his student loans.

Margaret returned for a second year at Academia Cristiana Internacional de Caracas. She enjoys her teaching and sharing time with Geordon and Marilyn and her little nephews. She drives Jordie and some other children to school each day. Jordie entertains her on the hour-long trips with stories recited verbatim, repeated continuously, with his parents' inflections ringing through the recitations: "This is the story of the three little pigs who built their houses and went out into the world to seek their fortunes. ..." Margaret plans to return to Victoria in June, hopefully to a teaching position.

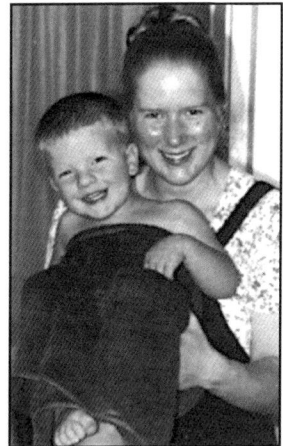

MARGARET AND JORDIE

Melissa left us for four months last January to attend a course on International Health at Seneca College in Ontario. She returned to Victoria via a three-week stopover in England to visit relatives, who treated her royally. Bruce's cousin, Andrew Hollingsworth, manages Alton Towers, Staffordshire's mix of Butchart Gardens and Disneyland, and Melissa was given free run of the tourist attraction. Another cousin's family, the Ian Hollingsworths, prepared a nine-course meal for her, accompanied by handprinted menus. Needless to say, Melissa's at-home-in-Victoria siblings were a little envious of their travelling sister. Melissa has arranged her work schedule to allow volunteer time up at Camp Qwanoes, and she took over directing

AUNTIE VI HOLLINGSWORTH AND MELISSA

the Jasper-Lake Louise bike hike in July, serving also as girls' counsellor and camp nurse. Each week she and several friends meet for a prayer breakfast in our living room, and she whips up a batch of cornbread or muffins for her guests. She has spent the last several months housesitting at Uncle Eric and Auntie Wynne's home while they lived back East, where Eric supervised work on the pipelines. She did not mind rattling around in that large house by herself, or leaving for shift work at 10:30 p.m. or 6:30 a.m. in the dark. Fortunately, her maternal parent's forays out into the gloom to deliver papers for so many years have made her less susceptible to worry. Melissa is heading for three months of nursing in the rural areas of Venezuela on January 18 to complete the requirements for her international health course.

Melody is also leaving for Caracas on the 18th, with Baby Anna, to spend some time with all three sisters and to renew her acquaintances from her YFC trip in 1993. Her trip is the gift of several friends and relatives who overheard her "My name is Melody and if I could I would…" response at the Thursday morning Women Connecting Bible study. She completed the statement with "go with Melissa to visit my other sisters in Venezuela." This once-in-a-lifetime opportunity is a lovely instance of the caring and sharing that occur within our church family. **Richard** will be keeping the stay-at-homes company, working with Island Farms and studying for his computer course. He will miss his "little punkin," but knows her cousins and aunts and uncle will be delighted to have her visit with her mother. (Bruce and I wonder if the reason two sisters are still single is that they haven't found men to match their brothers-in-law, both of whom are loving, devoted, sensitive and generous husbands and fathers.) Melody continues to help me with my music classes and is a top Regal representative on the Island, and **Anna** is a one-year-old delight who "talks" incessantly and is almost ready to walk without holding on to chairs, tables and legs.

Mark is still at Atlas Stereo & TV, and lends his technical expertise to friends and relatives. He plans to take some courses by open learning in January, with the eventual goal of teaching, probably in the area of athletics. He is out most

MELISSA, MARK, MELODY

nights with some youth activity, as youth leader at Lambrick Park Church. In last spring's altercation between neighbourhood rowdies and his youth group, he and his fellow leaders refused to fight; one member of his group was badly hurt in the scuffle and hospitalized, and Mark ended up with a neck bruise. The fracas received both press and TV coverage, with Mark acting as one spokesman. He will be witness in a court case in January. Mark joined Melissa and Melody in the strings section for our church's outstanding Christmas cantata. He and Matthew have taken over the upstairs suite, and are getting a taste of batching, albeit on what their older siblings consider a rather limited scale. We have the pleasure of their company for supper, and take responsibility for their lunches, and Matt has the use of a family car, and the odd white shirt receives motherly ministrations, etc., etc. In their defence, it should be noted that their financial contributions help ensure we all can continue to live in this "hotel"; their parents occasionally threaten to down-scale to smaller quarters, but that would leave four young men (including our exemplary boarders) and Melissa out on the sidewalk, and at least one parent would be desolate at the prospect of leaving her half-acre nature sanctuary.

Matthew projected his parents into yet another stage with his graduation from Pacific Christian School in June, the seventh and final family graduate (at least of his generation). He and a friend each escorted 1.5 young ladies to grad; the two took and shared expenses for three young ladies, perhaps a variation on the "safety in numbers" theme! He is high scorer for a church floor hockey league, and feels quite left out when he returns to watch the PCS volleyball team in action. Matthew works almost full time at Atlas Stereo with Mark, and appreciates his good fortune in obtaining work so easily. He is also considering more academics, but is undecided as to an appropriate course of study. His graduating As should give him some latitude in that area. For the last six or seven years, he has done the computer work for our family flyer, and the family consults him when computer problems arise.

As is so often the case, **Bruce**'s enjoyment in retirement has been tempered both by the heavy demands made on him by family and church commitments, and by the chronic discomfort resulting from a mid-January fall. After several days of flu, he collapsed to the floor, fracturing a vertebra. Twenty-one days in hospital was a new experience, after 30 years of working with no sick leave, and after 50 years of no hospitalization! He was feeling well enough in July to assist Melissa by driving the bus for the bike hike. Unfortunately, the bus gave in to old age near the Columbia Icefields, creating the challenge for Melissa of arranging everyone's return home; she managed somehow, and on budget. This misfortune also meant Bruce had to crawl into a pup tent for the remainder of the trip, after his previous "comfort" on the bus. The bus, $400 worth of towing later, still rests somewhere in the Rockies. Bruce looks forward to more time savouring the tranquillity of Horne Lake in 1999.

As I arrange this information and my "take" on the happenings here, I think back to our first Christmas letters of over 30 years ago, written by hand first, and then carefully typed on my high school graduation gift, a portable Remington Rand. This year I am typing at a computer that moves *very* quickly, and scrolls through several pages a second when all I want to do is move up or down a quarter page. My family is gently pulling and pushing me into the 20th Century, and now the 21st looms menacingly! This fall, with Melissa away most of the time at her uncle's home, I have been on my own with my five men: Bruce, Mark, Matt, Joel and Angus, a contrast to the years when this was a distinctly feminine household. Our 59th and final flyer edition went out at the beginning of December, completing ten years of production (up to 50,000 at a time), and I am revelling in the freedom of not having to organize another one. Our family has gained much experience from the project (originally designed to provide them, and eventually several others, with material to deliver), and it has generated considerable income for those who have helped with assembly and delivery. I am completing my second year as President of the Victoria Registered Music Teachers, and have again been supported by an incredibly cooperative and competent executive. My own teaching is a continuing source of satisfaction and, at times, minor frustration, as I work with a variety of ages and stages at the piano. It is very gratifying to share in the pleasure that students experience as they become increasingly proficient at the keyboard.

SEEN AND HEARD ...

... Geordon frantically chasing a garbage truck down the streets of Caracas in an effort to reclaim the black garbage bag full of Santa's gifts for Jordie's preschool (Leaving the bag beside the van where Santa was getting changed, Geordon had crossed the street to talk to another parent. Realizing moments later that the bag containing 30 presents had disappeared, and catching sight of the garbage truck rumbling down the street, crushing garbage as it went, Geordon retained his Ironman status as he galloped behind the truck, yelling for it to stop. Thankfully, he was able the retrieve the bag before it was inhaled by the crusher. Marilyn cannot tell the story without dissolving into peals of laughter.) ... a summer newspaper article featuring two 91-year-old friends examining their 1925 Victoria High School year book (Anne / Anna Forsberg and Olive Holland had attended Victoria High School for three years together, but Anne, who served as housekeeper and nanny to earn her

GRANDMA HOLLAND, GRANNY FORSBERG

way through high school, had not been able to afford the year book's 50-cent cost 73 years ago. When she and Olive attended a tea at Vic High in May, they learned that a laser copy could be made, and Anne finally received her high school annual. The *Times Colonist* carried a beautiful photo of the Holland children's two grandmothers beside an upbeat story entitled "Grad of 73 years ago finally gets yearbook."
December 18 Olive is in the hospital with a broken hip—healing well, with pin—and shoulder injuries sustained in a recent fall. Anne still manages very well on her own, and is careful to use her walker when she travels the two blocks to Safeway or the bank. Both maintain a lively interest in current affairs, especially those of family, and entertain us with their sense of humour.) ... Mother on portable keyboard, four daughters on violins, providing two hours of music in garden at Father's old home

THE SEVEN

(from 1945 to 1965), for neighbour's garden wedding (June 24th date allowed Marilyn to participate, as her heart procedure took place on the 17th.) ... a red-breasted nuthatch bullying the tiny gray bushtits and chickadees away from the piece of suet hanging outside our dining room window (Although not much larger than the others, he manages to intimidate them and they scatter as he zooms in to feed.) ... Granny Forsberg faxing to Anchorage, Caracas, Vancouver and several ad-dresses in Victoria; appreciates receiving news "hot off the press"... Mother pruning multitude of blackberry vines on lowest terrace, cutting them into foot-long lengths and composting them in garden (Vines had overtaken huge pile of oak leaves—(12' x 15' and nearly 3' high—which had decomposed into powdery soft leaf mould and has also been shovelled into gardens.) ... Mother wearing rain hat, working for a couple of hours in November rain with plants on concrete pad at back, musing on mother-in-law's comments from many years previous about those who "don't know enough to come in out of the rain" … Matt and Mother working on November flyer until 4:00 a.m.; Matt due at work by 9:00 a.m. … our newest boarder, Angus Kellett, from Prince George, practising piano several hours a day as he works towards his Associateship in performing and teaching at the Victoria Conservatory (Mother enjoys calling out at suppertime, "Time to get off that piano, Angus"—a contrast to piano-related comments of the past 20 years!) … our other boarder, Joel Mawhorter, crawling through attics and under the house, setting up cable modem to allow continuous high-speed access to the Internet, and to free up regular phone lines (Joel possesses many admirable traits, including the willingness to take innumerable phone calls and make sure the right party gets the appropriate message—in time.) … Melody (in Victoria) talking to Michael (in his plane near Penticton); Marilyn (in Caracas) talking to Michael (in Kamloops), all by cellular phone … Marilyn and Margaret, self-described "second-hand queens," delighted to find a consignment store in Caracas …

Chapter 44: A Christmas Digest, 1999

EDITORIAL *by Louise*

At the end of November, I enjoyed a long read through 1998's Christmas letters and cards, with the intention of "priming the pump" for our own 1999 mini-book. My plans were, however, pushed aside by a series of circumstances, less-than-efficient time management, and more recently, a distressing family emergency. I console myself with the realization that a late Christmas letter is not going to cause any of its recipients undue inconvenience, if indeed they give the matter any thought! I do hope your Christmas was happy and that your New Year will be filled with blessing and joy.

December 20 I have just returned from an invigorating two hours of delivering Regal catalogues for Melody. Because they are nearly expired, and because of Melody's substantial discount, she picked them up at no cost and is able to give an attractive discount to prospective customers. Problem: How do you deliver hundreds of catalogues with two tiny children? Solution: Ensure the children's grandmother loves the fresh air and walking. *So...* Mother/Grandmother Holland has enjoyed several mornings out in Victoria's beautifully mild winter. At the risk of appearing to brag (which I plan to do), I will describe some of the December gardening marvels in the part of Victoria where I walked: tuberous begonias a little bedraggled but still blooming outside; wanda primroses covered in magenta blossoms; shrubs (cotoneaster and pyracantha), laden with orange and red berries; licorice ferns rising from cushions of emerald moss; flowering cherries making an early appearance; snowdrops, daffodils and grape hyacinths poking through the damp soil; pink, blue and white blossoms on escallonia, California Lilac and Mexican Orange (*choisya ternata*) shrubs; golden pot marigolds (calendula); and a still-unidentified shrub on our property set to bloom. A factor in the purchasing of our tiny house in December of 1966, the fragrant shell-pink blossoms have not disappointed us for the past 33 years.

When Bruce and I were married thirty-eight years ago, my three sisters sang the hymn "God Hath Not Promised." Over the years, many of the words have rung through my consciousness and these days, as my beloved sister, Peggy, lies in the hospital in critical condition, the words take on heightened meaning: "God hath not promised skies always blue, flower-strewn pathways all our lives through" (although I have been blessed with many "flowers" in my life); "God hath not promised sun without rain, joy without sorrow, peace without pain ... *But* God hath promised strength for the day, rest for the labour, light for the way, grace for the trials, help from above, unfailing kindness, undying love." *[Copied from the hand-printed score that Harriet, Peggy, and Jeannie sang from, which has yellowed in the piano bench for nearly 40 years.]* It is distressing to think of my "little sister" of over 50 years, with her enormous talents and capabilities, restricted to the confines of a hospital bed and hooked up to a variety of life-support machines. We are grateful that such technology is available and live one day at a time, praying that God's will be done in this crisis, and if possible, she be returned to us, whole.

December 24 With three of our own young adults at home (Melissa, Mark, and Matthew), and three students (Joel at UVic, Angus at the Victoria Conservatory, and Luke at Pacific Christian School), Melody and Richard a five-minute drive away, Margaret a three-minute walk away, and Michael an 11-minute flight (plus 20-minute car ride) away, and the almost-daily influx of music students, our home is rarely still (or tidy). Today our three students have returned to their homes for the holidays and Melissa is housesitting, so the four bedrooms adjacent to ours are temporarily unoccupied. This means *I have the bathroom all to myself*, as Bruce is in the habit of using the downstairs facilities. Some of us find happiness in small things.

PERSONAL GLIMPSES

Last February **Granny Anna Forsberg** moved quickly to answer the door and collapsed on the kitchen floor. An hour later she had managed to drag herself to the bedroom phone. Her message, "Louise, I think I'm in trouble," did not overstate the case. The position of her right leg led to the ambulance attendant's immediate diagnosis: broken hip. Four days after surgery in Vic General (by Dr. Calder, whose boys I taught 20 years ago, assisted by her own GP, Dr. Forster), she was moved to the Jubilee for what was projected to be another three or four days of rehabilitation. Six weeks later, after suffering with pneumonia, hives, thrush, congestive heart failure, a weight gain of 22 pounds in two days due to fluid retention, and an uncharacteristic loss of appetite, she was allowed to leave the hospital into our care. We did what we could to make her comfortable, with the assistance of a variety of health care workers (therapists, nurse, social worker) and by the end of one week, she was talking about going home to her condominium! Exactly two weeks later she did just that, and insisted she could manage on her own. With frequent monitoring from here, she gradually gained strength. Our concerns for her wellbeing were alleviated when our niece, Tara, an RN who specializes in geriatric care, volunteered to share the condo with her. With the exception of a few weeks when Anna was on her own and managing very well, Tara has been keeping an eye on her grandmother. Anne (Anna) gets around in the condo unaided, but does take her walker when she covers the two blocks to Safeway and her bank at Shelbourne and McKenzie. She and I enjoy frequent phone conversations and she, in company with her friend and our other (great-)grandmother, **Grandma Olive Holland**, maintains a quick wit and appreciation for life. Both turned 92 this year. Grandma Holland, unfortunately, is more restricted, due to Parkinson's disease. Although medication has effected dramatic improvement, mobility is still a problem. Auntie Marilyn cheerfully supervises Olive's care, with some respite from care workers (not without problems due to the many changes that have occurred within the home care system over the past year), sister Shirley, and Bruce. Marilyn's loving faithfulness is an example for the rest of the family.

On June 25, **Jordan** [4] and **Joshua** [1 1/2] accompanied Auntie Margaret home for a whirlwind eight-day visit, returning to Caracas with Uncle Mark and a youth team from Lambrick Park Church. With two aunties (Margaret, Melissa) on site serving as nannies, and another aunt and uncle in the near vicinity providing a playmate with their daughter, Anna [just over 1 1/2], the two Js had a busy time with their North American family. **Marilyn** and **Geordon** and the two little boys—Jordan would not appreciate the "little"—are in their new home in Caracas, a Youth for Christ house that they are renovating for their ministry. The house is very large and contains two rentable suites and rooms for assembly and offices, but had been stripped by the previous owner of anything that could be sold. Several dump trucks of garbage had to be removed from the property. Geordon's parents, Don and Sharon, spent a month helping with the move. A dozen or more young people joined them for their first weekend in the house, and life shows no sign of slowing down. (For two months in the fall we enjoyed hosting Nahualt and Carlos, 19 and 18 respectively, leaders in the youth group, here in Victoria.) The terrible flooding nearby has claimed tens of thousands of lives. Geordon has been taking supplies in their 4x4 over the mud to accessible areas, maintaining contact with Marilyn by cell phone. There is the threat of disease, with so many bodies trapped in the mudslides, and the horror of bodies that have been carried into the Caribbean by the slides now washing up on the beaches.

Michael continues to fly out of Vancouver each day, now as the captain of the Mitsubishi MU-2 (a light twin-engined turbine aircraft), flying courier freight. Some days he flies as far as Fort St. John and Smithers; other flights take him to the Interior and Coast, and even Victoria and Nanaimo. Apparently Castlegar and Terrace present special challenges, and vague references to poor weather and occasional mechanical difficulties filter through to our pilot's mother. We are proud of Mike's tenacity in achieving his flying goals, and pray for him every time we hear a plane overhead (and, in my case, any time I see any of the trucks he used to drive in

Victoria: Cur-Quin, North Douglas Distributors).

It is a treat to have **Margaret** back in Victoria, after two years in Venezuela. She and a friend, also a teacher on call, are sharing an apartment half a block from here on Quadra Street. This allows her quick access to either spare car or ride and the occasional meal. Margaret has been substitute-teaching at Burnside School three days a week for two months in the area of music. With the regular teacher's return after Christmas, her teaching opportunities again become more precarious. She has left many friends and some family in Venezuela, and is dealing with reverse culture shock. Margaret and Melissa played their violins in the orchestra for our church's Christmas cantata, and help out with youth activities at our church.

Melissa thrives on travel by plane, car, and bike. In January, she, Melody, and little Anna flew to Caracas for time with Marilyn and Geordon and Margaret. Melissa was completing the practicum for her international health course, in the more rural outskirts of Caracas, and did not return until April. For three weeks before she came back, she worked in the jungles of Ecuador, in the area where five missionaries were killed by the Auca Indians over forty years ago. During the summer, Melissa and Dawnmaree Fletcher

MELISSA AND A "FRIEND"

directed two ten-day bike hikes, the first on the Olympic Peninsula, the second down the Oregon coast. Bruce helped with the driving on the second trip and had the unnerving experience of becoming locked in heavy traffic on a bridge near Portland. A semi-trailer had overturned, so he and his van-load of young people waited for several hours in pelting rain for the traffic to clear. In November, Melissa and Matthew drove Dawnmaree to her new home in Iowa. Their two weeks and 8,500 km took them through Washington, Oregon, Idaho, Nevada, Arizona, New Mexico, Texas, Oklahoma, Kansas, Missouri, Iowa, Minnesota and North Dakota in the United States, and Manitoba, Saskatchewan, Alberta and British Columbia in Canada, and they enjoyed good weather all the way. Between excursions, Melissa nurses at Mt. Edwards Court Care Home as well as the General and Jubilee Hospitals.

Richard and **Melody** presented the family with a wonderful gift on September 21, a dear little brother for **Anna**, born nine days before "big" (Uncle) Michael's birthday. **Michael Ron**—Ron is his Grandpa Stark—was a reasonable weight at birth (8 pounds, 6 1/2 ounces), but is an arm-numbing 16 pounds at three months. Baby Michael's arrival has been unsettling for his older sister, who alternates between great affection for, and perplexed annoyance with, the amiable intruder. (I have always had a soft spot for the "old" baby, having dealt with six of them! "Old babies" need lots of TLC.) Richard is now working inside the plant at Island Farms, with an occasional shift behind the wheel of a tanker, which allows him a more predictable schedule. His truck-driving days sometimes extended into 14 hours or more, often under very uncomfortable driving conditions. He is also studying towards a business and administration certificate at UVic. He shares childminding responsibilities with Melody, allowing her to help me with some music classes and to carry on her Regal business. Melody's three-week trip to Venezuela was another highlight of her year.

Mark, after four years of working full-time, has returned to school with the aim of becoming a teacher, probably in the area of physical education. He is studying part-time and receiving very good marks, a not-uncommon scenario with the highly-motivated "mature" student. Most Fridays and Saturdays he continues to work at Atlas Stereo & TV. Mark cannot speak highly enough of the Hordyks' business practices and ethics. Mark and a classmate collected information and photographs of Swan Lake to fulfill the assignment of producing a web site dealing with the Swan Lake Nature Sanctuary. Matt designed the page, which should be available soon under the auspices of Camosun College. It is very attractive and informative, with Mark's photography and his and his partner's research. In September, Mark and Matthew escorted their Venezuelan friends through the Rockies to Banff, Jasper, Lake Louise, and the West Edmonton Mall.

Matthew, our only teenager and that for only four more months, continues to serve as our computer resource person, and is frequently consulted when computer problems arise in this household or over on the mainland. Even his two siblings who are the happy owners of Mac PowerBooks are impressed by their "little" brother's expertise and knowledge. Matt is taking a leave from regular work (his choice), to pursue his own projects. Room and board funds come from an apartment paper route and from odd jobs, including computer assignments, around home. With an excellent academic background behind him, and scholarships languishing in his bank account, he may choose to re-enter the area of organized education some time in the future, but he has the freedom to do "his own thing" right now. He joins his two brothers in spoiling his little niece and nephews, and plays with Mark in the Sports Trader roller hockey league. Their team, the Pilons, topped the league last year.

Bruce spends much of his time supporting family projects and activities. It is not uncommon for him to run out to the ferry or airport two or three times in one day (an hour round-trip). Or to whip up a meal for 16 on a Sunday (8 to 12 the rest of the week). Or to unload a carload of filled grocery bags at least once a week, with smaller runs in between. Bruce serves as secretary of our church board, which means paying close attention at the meetings and spending hours at the computer at home, assembling minutes. He also chairs both the membership and counselling committees. His "*No, Anna*" has the same positive effect similar pronouncements had during the years when our own children were little.

Louise views our unkempt half-acre as her all-purpose environment. With a ten-second commute to her music room, she can enjoy the dozens of students who work with her each week. A gap between classes might be filled with a housework project, or some meal preparation, or a quick "garden fix" when she tidies up plants for sale. Mornings are often spent outside digging in compost and potting up perennials. Oak leaves, buckets of peelings from the kitchen, and plant debris are dug into the garden, and our soil is rich and productive. In spite of sales of hundreds of plants (in aid of youth work), our soil supply has not dwindled. Several evenings recently have passed in proof-reading Mark's essays, and she has learned a fair amount about the situation in Quebec, and the attributes of our beautiful Swan Lake. Her third year as president of the local branch of the Registered Music Teachers has been rewarding, as her executive again is very self-motivated and capable. Boredom is still not a problem.

SEEN AND HEARD …

… Melissa's amaryllis stretching 24" in a month, now with four extravagant scarlet blooms on one stem, and another lot of buds showing promise on a second stem—her (and our) first experience with this flower … our church's beautiful like-new Hammond 926 organ, which Louise is allowed to play each Sunday, a musically satisfying challenge … Mark sporting slightly streaked hair, Matt blonder than blond; their sisters maintaining their long hair in its natural state … a Nature Lovers 1982 calendar which has been serving us again this year, as the days fall on the same dates (A gift from Phyllis Ellis, widow of the British naturalist, E. A. Ellis, who wrote the text accompanying the varied photos of British wildlife, it is a reminder of our trip to England 20 years ago with six children, five violins, eight suitcases, one stroller and one diaper-bag—Mark's; Matthew arrived the following year.) … a description of our household in September and October: "two parents, two daughters, two sons, two boarders, and two Venezuelans," our version of Noah's Ark … 16 sleeping throughout the house the night before Carlos and Nahualt left; tearful farewell on the lawn the next day … Bruce and Louise fretting that Carlos and Nahualt might miss their 5:00 a.m. check-in time at the Vancouver International Airport, with their luggage plus two extra suitcases full of gifts for our Caracas family; Mark and two alarm clocks accompanying them across the water to Richmond *[Thanks, Cousins Marilyn and Ralph, for bedding down our young men for their short night of sleep.]* … daily faxes from Granny Forsberg to reassure us she is up and well … four-year-old Jordie wishing Grandma a Happy Birthday and then politely asking Grandma if she would like to speak to *her* "child" (Marilyn) … a note from a six-year-old piano student:

"Dear Ms. hollen I am sorry I said oh, veary interesting. I'm sorry I've been rude." (Louise had been explaining something to her class when this little sweetheart suddenly interrupted with, "Oh, *very* interesting!" no doubt taking the opportunity to try out a new phrase she had heard; unfortunately for her, her mother was in the waiting room and overheard the exclamation, which resulted in the note a week later.) ... little Anna shushing her mom when she came into her room; it was not until Melody looked under her blanket and found a row of "sleeping" dolls that she realized that Anna had been paying close attention to Mommy and the new baby ... Joel crawling around under the house and through the attics, trailing blue wiring and wiping away elderly cobwebs, adding a couple more computers to the computer system in his room that serves as a hub for the household's e-mails ... Angus filling the house with brilliant scale passages from a Bach Prelude and Fugue, and thunderous chords from a Beethoven Sonata ... Luke (Stones, a short term boarder) good-naturedly accepting ribbing about his "jewellery" of choice: a paper-clip on a chain around his neck (Landlady suggested perhaps that was how he held his life together.) ... Louise potting hundreds of perennials during the summer, in the company of two or three neighbourhood cats, a squirrel or two and a couple of chatty nuthatches ... Carlos, Nahualt and Matthew raking oak leaves, under the benevolent dictatorship of an older sister ... Baby Michael, at six weeks, cooing and smiling for several minutes as his mother held him in front of her; sharing our delight with dear friends, Frank and Alice Peters, also parents and grandparents several times over, who were equally entranced with this display of early communication ... a young child's response to our pastor when he asked the children at Children's Corner how their Christmas had been: "Well, I got *two* things from my three-thing list." ... Margaret labelling dozens of iridescent snowflakes and brass Christmas ornaments for her music students, her generosity reminiscent of an entry in our 1981 Christmas letter when she returned from the church bazaar up the street, laden down with multiple gifts for both family and house ...

JOSHUA, ANNA, JORDIE

Chapter 45: A Christmas Digest, 2000

The message of Christmas: JOY TO THE WORLD!
The Lord is come—to give us life, and that more abundantly.
Our response: O COME LET US ADORE HIM!

EDITORIAL *by Louise*

I sometimes have started our annual letter with a comment on the oak leaves that blanket our property at this time of the year. However, I am pleased to report that most of them, thanks to Matthew and an older student, have been raked into a huge mound at the back of our lot, replacing the enormous pile from a year ago which has been dug, basketful by basketful, into our garden beds. That project was completed by the end of July, and by mid-August, heat-dried leaves were already starting to fall. *C'est la vie.* The squirrels, bushtits, chickadees, nuthatches and neighbourhood cats keep me company as I dig, and many gallons of beautiful soil have been produced to nourish hundreds of Matt's Plants.

This has been a year of changes, with our very full house gradually emptying to the point that only five people (Matthew, our boarders Sarah and Joel, and Bruce and I) share the above address. Angus Kellett gave an outstanding piano graduation recital in June and has moved closer to the Conservatory. We enjoyed hosting our Venezuelan "son," Omar, from February to August, as he studied English at UVic. His parents Farouk and Nancy, sister Nur, girlfriend Stephanie and her sister Jennifer joined Omar for the month of August. Farouk and Nancy stayed at Grandma Holland and Auntie Marilyn's home; Nur lived with Melody and Rick for August and September; and Stephanie and Jennifer joined Margaret. With Marilyn, Geordon, Jordan and Joshua here from June 8 to September 21, and family and Venezuelan friends congregating on the patio near the fence, the neighbours must have thought there was a Spanish invasion at 4031!

A relatively empty house does not, however, mean a lack of activity here. Margaret and Melissa share an apartment just behind us, and they flit in and out several times a week. Melody helps me with some of my classes, and I assist her with her Regal business, so she and Richard, Anna and Michael are also here on a regular basis. Mark moved to Vancouver for school in June and is bunking in with

Michael in the Marpole area until next April, so we, unfortunately, see less of them. I still have the pleasure of working with dozens of students from the age of four to eighteen, and am constantly reminded of the special gifts each child and teenager brings to our relationship. And a few days ago, Phoeun and Phaly, two young Cambodian men who attend our church, have joined the household until they can get established on their own in Victoria.

Last Christmas our family was very distressed at the condition of my sister, Peggy, who was, on December 22, given a 1 to 5% chance of survival. Her lungs appeared totally destroyed, and she was on 100% oxygen via a ventilator for several weeks. We thank God that He spared her, and she was released from hospital three months later, weak but mentally alert and able to breathe almost normally. She was supported by much prayer and love from many quarters and, while struggling with the pain of fibromyalgia, is grateful for the good things each day brings.

Our mothers, both 93, continue to share their wisdom and love with us. Both are frail but mentally alert. Granny Forsberg broke a second hip in October, but came through the experience very well, all things considered. Our niece, Tara, continues to keep an eye on her, and her Granny benefits from both Tara's loving disposition and her expertise in caring for the elderly.

PERSONAL GLIMPSES

Marilyn and **Geordon** returned to YFC House, Caracas, and their work with Youth for Christ Venezuela in September with little **Jordan** [6 in September] and **Joshua** [3 next February], and have hosted two groups of Canadian supporters already. In October, three young men from Victoria, working into the evenings, spent a week filling their large kitchen with a wonderful array of cupboards; previous storage had consisted of a few shelves, a table and boxes. In early December, a team of 17 from Abbotsford and Victoria painted the outside of YFC House and some rooms, replaced most of a complicated and dangerous electrical system, and completed several other renovation projects. On December 22, 15 members of our church are leaving for two weeks in Caracas with the intention of helping out both with renovations and with a youth camp which already has 150 young people registered. YFC House is large (8,000 square feet); ideal as a headquarters for youth work in a city where hundreds of thousands of young people live; includes office space, a small auditorium, two apartments, and living space for Marilyn and Geordon; hosts at least 100 people each week; and is in need of much repair and renovation. The Rendles are very grateful for those who share their vision of youth work and are willing to join them in making this vision a reality.

Michael's year has been eventful, with training on the Metro III in Newfoundland earlier this year in preparation for flying with Provincial Airlines, and flight training in Arizona at the beginning of November for his new job with Canada Jet Charters. He is now flying the Lear 35, a light business jet, for charters and medical evacuations. His first flight transported three doctors from Edmonton to Anchorage to pick up a heart, then returned to Edmonton for the implantation. In January, Michael made a "gear-up" landing at Victoria International Airport in his MU2 when the landing gear failed to extend as he approached Terrace. Later on this spring, his Metro was struck by lightning, causing $300,000 worth of damage. Mike is sharing his bachelor pad with Mark, and this is a positive experience for both.

Margaret continues as teacher-on-call in the Victoria public and independent schools, and tutors at the READ Society. She has been on the Search Committee for a new senior pastor for our church and works with Melissa as a youth sponsor and Sunday School teacher; she also serves on the YFC board. Margaret managed a trip to Venezuela in April to touch bases with friends and family, and enjoyed visits here in Victoria with her American friend from Venezuela, Leslie Bucher, in March and July.

HAVE VIOLIN, WILL TRAVEL!

Melissa is on the Missions Committee at church, is a youth sponsor, and serves as board member for Camp Qwanoes. This summer she and her friend Dawnmaree led their fourth bike hike, under the auspices of Camp Qwanoes, down the Oregon Coast. Geordon was speaker, and Melody's husband, Richard, and sister, Margaret, served as counsellor and support staff respectively for the 10-day camp. Melissa manages to accommodate trips in between shifts as nurse in both acute-care hospitals and at Mt. Edwards Care Home. During the summer, she attended a ten-day conference of Nurses Christian Fellowship International in Edinburgh, Scotland, preceded by sightseeing in Ireland, Wales and England. She has just returned from two weeks in Halifax, where she visited with her good friend and colleague, Sandra Loewen. Melissa will likely be applying for a position at the children's hospital in Halifax. On her Saturday flight home from Halifax, Melissa was able, during a stopover at Toronto, to take in a friend's wedding; visit in the afternoon with another friend, formerly of Victoria; fit in an IKEA shopping trip; and still be in Victoria by ten o'clock the same evening. (Her room-mate tattles that she was not at her cheerful best on Sunday morning.)

Melody and Richard continue to experience the joys and frustrations of childrearing and home ownership. Little Anna [just turned three] keeps them on the run, and Baby **Michael** [15 months] amiably toddles from one adventure to the next. Richard works on a more regular schedule at Island Farms, and takes a business administration course at UVic in the evening. (And he gets *very* good marks.) He recently built a room at a friend's warehouse and now he and Matthew are constructing a second bathroom in his own basement. Melody is responsible not only for her own two little ones, but for two or three others who require lunch-time or after-school care. She has had her best year ever with her Regal business, and enjoys her contacts with her many customers. Twice a month she joins other young mothers (and ladies of all ages) at Central's Women Connecting, where she organizes help for new mothers and families with health problems. And she keeps her hand in at the piano by helping out with a couple of Mother's piano classes.

Mark is fulfilling a dream of several years to become more proficient in film-making. Still unattached and not tied down with family responsibilities, he felt this was the time to enroll at the Vancouver Film School. His tuition for ten months makes regular university fees appear paltry in comparison, so brother Mike's provision of room and board is greatly appreciated. The film school is situated in a rather seamy area of Vancouver, and has drawn students from all over the world; Mark is gaining another perspective on life. Thankfully, his Christian faith, although expressed unobtrusively, has gained the respect of his classmates, and at least one potentially volatile assignment has been sidestepped because Mark had earlier taken a stand on a controversial issue. He is happy to have been chosen as cameraman for the two most recent class projects.

Matthew keeps himself occupied with a variety of activities, many of them computer-centred. Most recently he has worked on two websites that should be of interest to those who care about the less fortunate: Fair Trade Concepts, and Level Ground Trading. The latter site outlines Hugo Ciro's coffee company which imports containers of quality coffee beans from small-scale farmers in his native Colombia. Not only are the farmers given fair value for their coffee (which, incidentally, is sold as gourmet coffee under the Café San Miguel label), but their community receives help with schooling and other community services. Matt also put together a video featuring Victoria and our church and its activities, to be given to prospective pastoral candidates, and another one of some church families preparing for Christmas, which was projected on a screen during a choir selection in the cantata. Melody and Rick appreciate his help both with babysitting and with building projects, and we are grateful for his efforts on this expanding (or so it seems) property. He rides his newly-purchased bike wherever he can, and plays both floor and roller hockey.

Bruce and **Louise** have almost completed their 39th circumnavigation of the sun together, and thank God for the gifts of family and friends, home, church, and opportunities to use the talents and resources they have been given. Bruce serves as secretary to the church Board of Management, and chairs the Christian Counselling Service and the Membership Committee. Louise provides organ music as a small part of an extensive and uplifting music ministry at church, teaches part of six days a week, has just completed a fourth term as Registered Music Teachers president (or chief delegator, as she views herself), and spends as much time as she can outdoors, working with an increasingly varied assortment of flowers, herbs and shrubs.

SEEN AND HEARD ...

... Margaret reading over Mother's shoulder as Mother assembles family letter, laughingly requesting that several sentences be deleted from her account. Mother respects directive, selects "too-much-information" material, and regretfully presses delete button ... all seven junior Hollands with two spouses and a girlfriend at Cousin Tracy Forsberg's beautiful wedding in Blue Mountain Baptist Church on August 5 (It was great to be all together again, and the hosting cousins were very gracious towards this rather large group of guests. Granny Forsberg, 93 two days previous, enjoyed the festivities, staying in a hotel overnight with Bruce and Louise and Margaret.) ... Mark receiving 50 out of 50 for a website dealing with Swan Lake that he and Matt worked on for a course at Camosun College ... note from our very positive boarder, a commentary on Bruce's culinary abilities: "That meal was outrageously good!!! Thanx. Luke"... Bruce and Louise spending a night at Luke's family home on Pender Island, perched above the ocean, with spectacular views of the BC ferries churning from Tsawwassen to Swartz Bay and back, with Luke's parents spoiling their visitors "outrageously"! ... Joel introducing his fiancée, Rose Fetherston, which means his five-year tenure in this establishment comes to an end on May 11 (We will miss his quick wit and courteous company.) ... Bruce giving out baking tips at a Women Connecting meeting at church ... Louise displaying some of Matt's Plants at another Women Connecting gathering ... a circle garden 14 feet in diameter, surrounded by a 30" stone wall and mounded with wheelbarrow loads of compost and soil, filled with hundreds of flowers in honour of eldest daughter's visit this summer (Marilyn had suggested years ago that circle should be used for flowers only, not the vegetables that parents usually plant.) ... Grandma and Jordie planting two kinds of lettuce, swiss chard (both very successful: still harvesting in December), basil, beans, parsley, cucumber and carrots, all identified with signs printed by Jordie. ... Omar signing in at barber shop (Barber notices Saudi Arabian name, asks Omar for surname. Barber recognizes "Alireza" as well-respected family in his native Saudi Arabia and gives Omar free haircut. Omar's father, born in Saudi Arabia, moved to Venezuela in 1960; Omar gains new appreciation of "small world" concept.) ... delightful seven-year-old piano student sharing riddle with teacher: "Why is 10 afraid of 7; give up?" Teacher and child share a laugh when student happily gives answer: *"Because 7 8 9!"* "Seven is an odd number, right? Do you know how to make it even; give up?" *"Take off the 's'."* ... a lovely couple from England unexpectedly taking up residence here for a week after the wife had emergency gallbladder surgery, cutting short their 17-day, 40th anniversary trip to Canada (Alan Chambers, nearly 80, cheerfully accommodated himself to this quite Canadian and rather busy household after requesting a place to stay in a phone call to our church. His wife Beryl arrived three days later and spent the rest of the week recuperating before their flight home to their worried children. Beryl shared birthday honours with Margaret on October 6: Beryl 73, Margaret 29. We could not have wished for more gracious, grateful guests. Note re. October 6: we have also just learned that our new Cambodian friend, Phaly, was also born on this date.) ... Excerpt from e-mail from Melissa in Great Britain this summer: "Currently I am being hostelled in a lovely castle that overlooks beautiful green fields full of sheep— and Loch Lomond! Absolutely gorgeous! And tomorrow I shall be hiring a cycle to ride over to the west side of the lake along the West Highland Way—should be a wee bit of fun, don't you think?? Had a brilliant time in Ireland, though the sun didn't really shine the whole time I was there. ... I did a bit of cycling in County Donegal (favourite little piece of Ireland) and think that I will have to go back and cycle the whole west side of that Island (maybe next year's bike camp??) ... Melissa on Edinburgh street among spectators out to see the Queen; singled out by the Queen for a short chat ... Margaret, with face, hair and clothes covered in bright blue and yellow paint, after helping young people paint out their roomy lounge in church basement; appearance the result of encounter with another youth sponsor, Liz Willock ... three-year-old Anna pirouetting around living room as Melody plays Bach Prelude, propelling Mother back nearly 30 years to when another tiny girl twirled gracefully around the same room, singing, "Snowflakes drifting, gently drifting," as Mother played the piano ... Dainty alpine strawberry plant bearing exquisite pure white flowers, tiny green berries, and two ruby-red oval-shaped berries, all at the same time, in mid-December ... Margaret and Melissa playing violin for Central's glorious Christmas cantata *Welcome to Our World* in which choir, drama team and orchestra joined forces to share the Christmas message with the community ... Steve Morrison, Matt's best friend and our fourth "son," surreptitiously (he thinks) carrying box of Timbits to orchestra under cover of Father's coat (Unfortunately, neither he, a violist, nor the violinists, who had commissioned the treats, had thought to bring along hand-wipes for sticky fingers, much to the flautist's dismay.) ...

LIFE'S LIKE THIS

... **Tuesday, January 12** Venezuela is still reeling from December's devastating floods, when 50,000 to 100,000 people were buried in mudslides on the outskirts of

Caracas. Melissa, tired and frustrated, arrives at Simon Bolivar airport after four cancelled and then rebooked flights and two missed connections. No one has been able to meet her at the airport (45 minutes away from Caracas), due to the flooding. She discusses her predicament in broken Spanish with a taxi driver and, given her limited finances, decides to make her way up to the city on a public bus. With no access to a phone, Melissa cannot let Marilyn know she has finally arrived, and prays for a phone as the bus lumbers towards the city; is dismayed to find the bus terminal is simply a spot off the side of the road under a bridge, with no phone in sight. Melissa is stranded alone in a city of 6,000,000, responsible for two 70-pound bags full of medications. Slowly descending from the bus, she is startled and then overjoyed to hear her name called by Nahualt, a member of Marilyn and Geordon's youth group (who lived with us for two months a year ago). Although he did not know when Melissa would be arriving or where she would be, he felt he should check out the bus "station," just in case. He was going to wait for only one or two buses and, as Melissa says, "There I was on the *first* one. God was at work away ahead of me!"

... **Monday, January 18** Michael has left Smithers for Terrace in his MU2 but cannot land because landing gear refuses to come down. Handing over the controls to his co-pilot, he struggles to lower gear manually, with no success. His company advises him to fly to Vancouver where he orbits for 15 minutes, again attempting unsuccessfully to release the gear. Company instructs him to proceed to Victoria, where he circles to burn off excess fuel and consults with company maintenance engineers. Several more attempts to release the gear are unsuccessful. Tower personnel confirm that right gear door is shut, and Michael executes a gear up landing, emerging with co-pilot through a window as he, partner and plane are foamed with fire-retardant. (Although the incident was televised on local TV, with emergency vehicles and flashing lights surrounding the plane, his parents were not informed about it until the next morning. His aunt had heard a news bulletin stating that a plane was having difficulties over the airport, but did not realize it was Michael. Mother taught blithely on, and Father worked on the computer, neither aware that their eldest son was circling over Sidney. Company officials commended Michael for his expertise, and his parents thanked God for his safety.)

... **February evening** Mother is teaching after-supper class. Evening is chilly. Mother decides another cup of hot tea would be pleasant; leaves class working on theory while she returns to kitchen to see if there is some leftover tea. Tea is gone. Mother returns to classroom. ... Several minutes later, door opens and Father enters room, carrying tray with small pot of fresh tea, milk and a cup. Student comments, "Your husband sure is kind to you." Mother agrees, and tells class that she has been able to teach for so many years because husband has always been so kind and helpful. (Mother's note: Probably best lesson taught that evening!)

... **Thursday, February 17** Margaret is substituting in an inner-city Grade 2 class where a little boy has brought his violin to "show" to students. Child gravely explains to Margaret and classmates how violin works, and plays a few notes. Margaret listens respectfully, and, as performance wavers, turns to piano to accompany "Lightly Row," whispering "E 2 2, 3 1 1, A 1 2 3 E E E" as support. Child finishes piece, turns to Margaret incredulously: "*You* know that song, too!" Margaret brings out and tunes old violin from storage room; asks if student would like her to play violin with him. Student is ecstatic to be performing with teacher—a "magic moment" for Margaret.

... **March 12, supper time** Omar, our gentle and polite guest from Venezuela, has been immersed in English for several weeks. Family is eating supper, with the usual bantering and chatter, when Melissa, attempting to cut up a piece of beet, accidentally flips a piece off her plate on to the tablecloth. She expresses frustration, and Matthew and Mark flash the "L" sign at her (index finger up, the thumb straight out to make an "L" for "Loser"). ... Margaret, late from tutoring, sits down to eat, and a piece of beet flies from her plate, too. Immediately Omar flashes the "L" sign to her, and the table bursts into laughter. Obviously, Omar is learning the important subtleties of the English language and Canadian behaviour.

... **March 23, excerpt of an e-mail from Michael (on course in Newfoundland)**: "I'm sitting in the rental car at Cape Spear, which is the most eastern point in all of North America. The wind is rocking the car, but it's cozy inside and I have the radio on playing classical music (piano-cello duet) so I feel very civilized. Not to mention having a laptop perched on my knees! (Just announced who the cellist was—Yo Yo Ma! Gotta love CBC.)"

... **Tuesday, December 5, 7:10 a.m.** Mother and Father have just left weekly 6:00 a.m. prayer meeting at church, and decide to drop in at nearby Mt. Edwards Court Care Home where Mother has, yet again, left behind her raincoat after helping Melody with her Regal display on Saturday. Mother receives code numbers via intercom, punches in numbers, and enters hallway. Five or six medical personnel peer out from nursing station at her. Mother, a little intimidated, states that she has come for coat. Teasing reply, "Oh, we gave it away to a charity," does nothing to alleviate Mother's discomfort at having interrupted staff meeting. After several other comments, Mother finally brings out "big guns": "Do you know Melissa Holland?" "Oh yes." "I'm her mother." Statement transforms atmosphere, which gives way to very positive comments about Melissa, ending with, "We know Melissa—we live vicariously through her!" Mother makes way to lower floor, smiling, and rescues coat.

Chapter 46: A Christmas Digest, 2001

EDITORIAL *by Louise*

October 8 Thanksgiving Day, an appropriate time to start our Christmas letter, especially as today promises to be the "lull" before the (happy) "storm." Margaret is getting married in 19 days! Many projects have been completed in preparation for this joyous event, but much needs to be done to ensure everything comes off smoothly. More will be written about the long-distance cyber-romance that has tied up computer and telephone for the past few months. And a few weeks from now, an after-the-fact report can be given!

In company with our fellow North Americans, we find our Thanksgiving coloured by the tragic events of the past few weeks. We are probably the most fortunate people on the face of this tortured planet, living on a beautiful island in freedom. And yet we too must accept that we are not exempt from the trials and tribulations of the rest of mankind. As I look out on our yard, rapidly disappearing under the annual leaf fall, with geraniums blooming cheerfully, moss and licorice ferns greening up as the rains return after the summer drought, and chickadees, nuthatches, and squirrels co-existing in apparent harmony, I am grateful for such tranquil surroundings and can only pray that such peace be extended to those in more troubled areas.

November 10 It is *so quiet!* Our 40-foot warehouse has been re-transformed into a living room as Chris and Margaret's bags left for Indiana, and Marilyn and Geordon's belongings returned to Caracas. Margaret's teaching friend from Caracas and now Indiana, Linda Cummings, graciously slept in this room on the hide-a-bed, surrounded by other peoples' stuff. Mike slept on the hide-a-bed in the music room waiting room, and all other rooms were filled. Our table has shrunk to seven or eight, down from 15 to 20, and Bruce can't say he is unhappy about that!

December 15 For the past few months, we have had the inestimable privilege of hosting our new pastor, Leigh Robinson, and his daughter, Sarah, as they have made use of our upstairs suite. Leigh and Sarah have left us for most of December as Leigh fulfills speaking engagements in Africa. They return to Victoria on December 22 with wife and mother, Irene, and daughter and sister, Julie, who has just completed her high school studies in Johannesburg. Our congregation has thoroughly enjoyed our new pastor's forthright yet courteous manner, his excellent sermons, and his wise, compassionate counsel. We will miss the Robinsons when they find their own home.

Our Christmas wish for you is that you experience the love, joy and peace found in the One whose birthday we are celebrating, and that 2002 brings you much satisfaction and many blessings.

PERSONAL GLIMPSES

Because much of this letter will be devoted to the happy event we could not have anticipated a year ago (so far, we have had weddings only every seven years, so have to make the most of this one!), Personal Glimpses will be very fleeting. **Geordon**, **Marilyn**, **Jordan**, and **Joshua** share YFC House, Caracas

MARGARET SURROUNDED BY HER SIBLINGS

with a constant stream of guests, including those using the house as a meeting place, young people who spread up on to the spacious roof at youth events, and North American visitors who are interested in their work. As Youth For Christ director for South America, Geordon has spent time this year in Porlamar and Maracay, Venezuela; Germany; Colombia; and Argentina. An unexpected treat for the family was their two weeks in Victoria for Margaret's wedding. ... **Michael** continues to fly the Lear jet for business charters and medical emergencies and has recently spent two

weeks in Texas training on the Citation jet. We are thankful he is still close enough to come home for a few days every so often. ... **Margaret** is acclimatizing to a new life in a new country. And her new inlaws, warm and gracious, have promised to help take care of our "pearl". ... **Melissa** (our "honeybee") has flown to Halifax, many miles away. She is nursing at

MICHAEL, OFF-DUTY, SHOWING HIS PLANE TO HIS PARENTS

the children's hospital in Halifax, and has purchased a brand new split-level house (half of a duplex, with three bedrooms that have already accommodated a variety of guests) in Dartmouth. Melissa is taking an active role in the youth work at the church she attends, and rumour has it that she and her friend, Dawnmaree, plan to lead yet another bike hike in the United States next summer. ... **Richard** and **Melody**, with **Anna** and **Michael**, share their busy lives with us, as they live only five minutes away from here. Melody assists with music classes, and Mother helps her with her Regal business. Richard is working full time at Island Farms, and studying at Royal Roads University, with the aim of completing the final two years of a commerce degree in 2003. He also helps out with financial matters at our church. ... **Mark** and **Matthew** spent the summer months at Camp Qwanoes filming the incredible variety of activities, editing the hours of material

MICHAEL AND ANNA

into videos for the campers to take home at the end of each week. Mark made use of his year's training at the Vancouver Film School, and Matt complemented Mark's skills with his computer expertise. Both are attending Camosun College part time, and live at home. And their parents enjoy their company. ... And the parents? **Bruce** shops for and prepares meal after meal; helps several elderly friends; transports his most appreciative mother-in-law to medical appointments; tries to keep on top of the Canadian business of his "American" and "Venezuelan" daughters; as secretary, types out minutes for the church board; and wonders how he filled his time before he "retired." ... **Louise** is completing her fifth (and final) year as president of the Victoria Registered Music Teachers Association, and continues to share music with a wide variety of students, including beginners aged four (*"Please* can I play 'Merrily We Roll Along' again?"), fifteen ("Wow, this is *so cool*, Mrs. Holland"), and seventy-eight ("My wife and I just *love* being able to play the piano"). With Margaret providing both motivation and initiative, she has been sifting through 40 years of teaching material, so experiences "nostalgia interludes" every so often.

SEEN AND HEARD ...

... Mike spending several days in basement, attic, and rooms between, drilling through walls 60, 30 and 17 years old (original house, two renovations) to install new computer/telephone wiring, setting up family for most communication eventualities ... Louise distributing 2,000 Regal brochures for Melody at the end of August, to most townhouses over a wide area of Victoria; taking note of the variety of gardens inside the front gates, many most innovative, colourful and often fragrant (After receiving the diagnosis of dermatomyositis in May, Louise is grateful to be so well and active with—so far—no interruption of teaching or gardening activities, thanks to the prayer support of family and friends, and to appropriate medical intervention.) ... Matt flying to Caracas to gather material for a documentary he has been asked to make for an international school's fund-raising, returning with several hours of filming, editing it into a 20-minute presentation ... Mark graduating from his course at the Vancouver Film School with a certificate of excellence; friend Tanya and brother Mike sharing in evening's festivities ... Matt's 21st birthday lunch, with the expected nine to twelve around the table swelling to 21 (appropriately) by the time the meal is served: a happy, rowdy time ... Louise receiving a bicycle night light for her birthday, so she can garden in the dark ... a very special piano rendition of "Happy Birthday"

for Grandma by a six-year-old grandson, relayed by telephone from Caracas in the middle of June ... the same grandson responding in November to Grandma's question as to what he thought of his mother and her sisters and brothers playing their violins together with Auntie Margaret at her wedding: "It was great, and you played the piano very nicely, too, Grandma." Seven-

CLEAN COUSINS!

year-old diplomacy! ... Mike, headquartered in Vancouver, flying up on Friday night from San Antonio, Texas, where he was on a training course, for Margaret's wedding Saturday, returning on Sunday ... two sons-in-law and a son-in-law-to-be singing a new version of "Down By the Old Mill Stream" at the wedding rehearsal dinner: "Right on the world wide web, Where I first met you, At that cute address of m3holland@yahoo; It was then I'd seen that you'd be my queen; You were 29, my Canadian find, right on the world wide web." The amplified version included, "Right on the web *(not in person but the web)*, Where I first met you *(not her but you)*, At the cute address *(not a chat room but address)*, Of m3holland@yahoo *(not aol but yahoo)*; I began to sweat *(not relax but sweat)*, As the letter was sent *(not delayed but sent)*, But you wrote me back *(not in front but back)*, Though it took too long *(not short but long)*." ... Cousin Ralph Steele assuming, for the third time, the stress of photographing a Holland daughter's wedding ... Melody and Dawnmaree driving with Melissa from Victoria to her new home in Halifax; Melody later returning to Halifax for two weeks, using a gift plane ticket ... Anna (four in November) and Michael (two in September) phoning grandparents with the help of the speed dial ... heart-stopping Indiana Jones-type footage on Mark's demo reel which indicates that second son has been up in stunt plane to film action on the ground a few feet below plane, another incident that parents, thankfully, learn about after the fact ... Sarah Ephgrave, our diminutive boarder, redecorating her bedroom in Wedgwood blue and white, after living with the previous boarder's choice of battleship grey for over a year ... Melissa's luggage receiving intense scrutiny as she goes through airport security on her return to Halifax (Dozens of Matt's Plants have been stuffed into her carry-on bag, to resume their lives on the other side of the country.) ... Melody balancing demands of family, household, boarder, and business, maintaining her status as a Diamond Regal representative ... Our boarder of five years, Joel Mawhorter, leaving us for Vancouver in May with his new wife, Rose Fetherston, just in time for Margaret's temporary return home ... little Anna climbing up onto the huge "throne of God" (a prop from the Christmas cantata) on the church stage behind the storyteller's back, instead of sitting with the other children preparing to leave for Junior Church ...

LIFE'S SOMETIMES LIKE THIS

May 11 Mother moves 40-litre bags of potting soil into place for plant sale by half-dragging, half-lifting. **July 7** Mother wants to take remaining two bags to back yard. Tries to move them, with no success; soil seems to have transformed itself into concrete, and bags will not budge no matter how much effort she puts into lifting. (Muscle weakness is part of dermatomyositis.) Coerces Matthew into carrying them to back yard. **July 16** Dermatologist prescribes prednisone. **August 8** Mother is tidying back yard and wants to move bags again. Leans over to pick first one up, lifts it to chest level, carries it to other side of yard. Repeats process with second bag. Gains an understanding of why steroids are banned at athletic events.

May Chris Bucher, here for a month to visit Margaret and her family, researches engagement rings with Margaret, "in case" their relationship becomes more serious. **June** Relationship heats up, but there is still some uncertainty as to whether this American-Canadian liaison will be made permanent. **July 5** Chris phones Margaret's father, asks for her hand in marriage, receives a resounding vote of approval. Chris tells Father that he plans to fly up from Indianapolis on Saturday, be picked up at the airport by the jeweller with the ring, and surprise Margaret. Exciting news is transmitted almost immediately by Mother, over Father's mild objections, to maternal grandmother and sister in Halifax and brother in Vancouver, and to sister in Victoria who relays message to sister in Caracas, all of whom are equally delighted but have to keep quiet for two long days. Mother knows that future relationship with son-in-law may depend on her silence, so manages (just) to keep lid on secret. **July 7** Margaret has been working for days on family garage sale, has just spent 10 hours organizing and selling hundreds of items. Is given message that Chris will be contacting her around eight that evening. After barbecue supper at

Melody's, arrives home just before eight to wait for Chris's call, does not realize that Melody has set video camera on piano to record imminent drama. Sits wearily on couch, listening, eyes glazed, to Mother discuss merits of piece of music on other piano. Is galvanized into action by "I'm here for the garage sale," whirls around to confront someone she has assumed is still in Indiana. Family enjoys moment, discreetly withdraws.

A MODERN LOVE STORY

OCTOBER 27, 2001

Four years ago Margaret Holland left for Caracas, Venezuela, to teach at an international school. During her two years there, she met a young woman who had been sent down from YFC USA to work with Marilyn and Geordon Rendle. Leslie Bucher (pronounced "booker": "boomer" with a "k" instead of an "m") came from Indiana to visit Margaret in Victoria during 2000 and, after her second visit, strongly urged her big brother Chris, a civil engineer with missionary aspirations, to marry Margaret. This is Chris's response to this startling ultimatum: "… I mean, what's a guy supposed to do, just start writing to a girl that he's never met? It seemed too weird, so I continued to just plod along and tried to ignore the nagging thoughts of Miss Perfect out there, building igloos or sewing walrus hides, or whatever they do up there in Canada. Finally, after several months of unsuccessfully removing the thought of her from my mind, I gave up and decided the best way to 'meet her' was to write an e-mail (a real 'new millennium' relationship, eh?). … I must have sat in front of the computer for a couple of hours trying to get going, before finally deciding on a satisfactory introduction and then launching into a lengthy, descriptive saga about my thirty-one years of life on this earth. A total of four hours after first sitting down to write, with trembling finger I hit the 'send' button and wondered what in the world I had just done. She made me sweat for what seemed like a month before I got a response. ... She actually wanted to continue writing this goofy American guy. Well, to make a long story short, writing turned into phone calls, phone calls into visits (boy, was the first visit ever nerve-wracking!), and I even spent the month of May living nearby her at her parents' place in Canada. Finally, on July 7, I surprised her by flying up to her home and asking Margaret to be my wife! We both believe that the Lord has brought us together. ... I'm still astounded that what began as 'cyber-penpals' has led into wedding vows. I guess my little sis knew what she was talking about." She did, and October 27, 2001 (Bruce's 65th birthday), was an occasion of great celebration, overseen by our new pastor, Leigh Robinson, whose fate it has been to sit at our dinner table as wedding plans swirled around him. Our church sanctuary was filled with many of Matt's Plants and decorated by Louise's classmate from high school days, Clara Knight. Larry Skaggs, our good friend and principal cellist with the Symphony, provided a prelude of unaccompanied Bach suites and "Salut d'Amour" (Elgar) during the signing of the register. Bob Overman, our church's

MARGARET AND ATTENDANTS

minister of music, arranged the setting of the 23rd Psalm traditionally used as the wedding processional in the church in which Chris grew up. He and the rest of the Chamber Choir (nine solo voices) sang the Psalm *a cappella* as the attendants and bride entered the sanctuary, a very moving start to the ceremony. Margaret's attendants, three sisters and a sister-in-law (the matchmaker), were dressed in fall colours and carried radiant bouquets of gerbera daisies and peruvian lilies. Three-year-old cousins Anna (flowergirl) and Joshua (her partner in mischief) supported each other as they reluctantly made their way to the front, ahead of the bride. Joshua promptly climbed up on father Geordon's lap and slept away the ceremony; Anna took her nap during the reception. Pastor Robinson led the service, and former Pastor Ernest Kennedy led in prayer. Highlights of the reception included tributes given by Geordon, master of ceremonies, for Margaret, and by Curt and Dana, Chris's brother-in-law and sister, for Chris, and a happy account by Leslie of the beginning of this romance, and her assurance that because *she* had peace about the relationship, it was sure to work! A wonderful tea was served by ladies from the church, under Barb Dicker's direction; pies, the groom's favourite dessert, were included on the menu. The seven violins sang out with melodies from 15 and 20 years ago, and the reception ended with an entertaining slide show ("'A' you're adorable, 'B' you're so beautiful," etc.) depicting Chris's and Margaret's lives from babyhood to the present, put together with the help of the computer by Mark and Matt. And our Margaret/Maggie, the new Mrs. Bucher, has been whisked off to the United States, leaving behind her igloo and walrus hides, and taking up residence with our very special American son-in-law in Indianapolis.

MARGARET LEADS VIOLIN ENSEMBLE AT HER WEDDING RECEPTION

Chapter 47: A Christmas Digest, 2002

EDITORIAL *by Louise*

December 2 It's early in the morning, and I hope to get out watering the plants when the day warms up. "December 2" and "watering the plants"? Yes, this is Victoria, and I have been out gardening over the past couple of weeks in a summer dress. And yes, this is remarkable even for Victoria, and also a little unsettling as far as our water supply is concerned, as our recently-enlarged reservoir is far below capacity at present.

We send our love and best wishes to you, our family and friends, and pray that you will have a meaningful celebration of our Saviour's birth, and know the blessing of God in the New Year.

2002 has flown past, filled with much joy and some sadness. We are thankful for God's peace as we said good-bye to our beloved Granny, Anna Forsberg, on September 28. My mother, and many of her belongings, moved into our suite upstairs at the beginning of August. She had been in considerable pain from osteoarthritis before her move, and her fine mind was deteriorating. Over the next few weeks, she became increasingly forgetful and required assistance with every aspect of living, and yet she never complained or asked for anything; we had to keep checking to see if there was anything we could do for her. It was a privilege to share her last few weeks with her, and the family is happy that she was able to die in her own bed, peacefully, with no apparent discomfort. I miss her very much, as we had almost daily contact for much of my life, and she was always very interested in, and supportive of, her expanding family and my teaching and music activities. And just before her eyes closed for the last time, she was able to glimpse the most recent addition to the family, Richard and Melody's Eric Matthew Stark, a dear little brother for Anna and Michael, named after Great-Uncle Eric and Uncle Matt. (Now Uncles Mike, Mark and Matt each have a namesake in the next generation.)

PERSONAL GLIMPSES

Marilyn, Geordon, Jordan [8], and **Joshua** [4] have just welcomed a team from Victoria to YFC House Caracas. The team completed many projects during their ten days in Venezuela, from repairs to painting to plumbing to computer upgrading. Marilyn's father provided meals for the group and enjoyed his time with his South American family. Geordon and Marilyn manage a household of seven young people, two of their own and five for whom they serve as house-parents. Dozens of young people stream through YFC House each week, participating in both organized and casual activities. A national director for Venezuela has been appointed and a Youth for Christ board has been established over the past few years, and YFC has become a welcome component of the youth scene in Caracas, as Geordon gives leadership training to other youth leaders in the city. Geordon travels quite extensively in his role as Regional Director of Latin America for Youth for Christ International, and has just returned from giving a seminar at The Cove (Billy Graham Evangelistic Association) in North Carolina, USA. He has also started his Masters programme in Leadership and Training at the Royal Roads University here in Victoria. (The wonders of technology, especially e-mail!) The Rendles plan to return to Victoria next summer after the birth of their third baby, due at the end of April. Last August, the family made a surprise holiday trip to Victoria, as other vacation plans had fallen through, and this gave them the opportunity to have final visits with Granny.

Michael has moved to Winnipeg, where his new company, Keewatin Air, has its headquarters. As I write this, he is flying as co-captain of a Learjet 35 on a medical flight to England, his first intercontinental experience. Later, Mike described a landing at Keflavik, Iceland, as one of the worst he has ever experienced, due to very bad weather conditions—this from someone who manoeuvred his way into treacherous airports at places like Castlegar and Terrace for years, whose Metro sustained $300,000 worth of damage from lightning, and who made an (intentional) gear-up landing at Victoria International Airport a couple of years ago. This is yet another incident his parents were blissfully unaware of until after the fact. Michael has found a comfortable tenth-floor apartment and looks forward, at last, to furnishing it to his own taste. Michael acquired many money management skills (a euphemism for thrift) during his years of training and less-remunerative flying. He has already experienced cold and wind, and there are still several more Winnipeg winter months to live through. Michael also spent pleasant hours visiting with his grandmother before he left Victoria's benevolent climate.

YAY CANADA!

Margaret and **Chris**, a.k.a. "The Lovebirds," have just bought a brick house in a reclaimed area of downtown Indianapolis. Chris works as a civil engineer at Alt & Witzig Engineering Firm, and Margaret teaches at the International School of Indianapolis where lessons are given in English, French and Spanish. Chris and Margaret spend much of their free time in house renovation and repairs, and look forward to settling in on February 1st. They also serve as youth sponsors at College Park Baptist Church. In June, after Margaret was cleared to cross the border legally, they visited here and had some good times with Granny. Margaret and Granny were very close, as they discussed teaching issues and worked together on sewing projects. Margaret wrote a research essay on her grandmother's life when she was at UVic, even accessing government archival records, including class registers, from the 1920s. Before they left in June, driving a U-Haul truck full of Margaret's furniture, Margaret and Chris bought plane tickets for another visit this Christmas, and we are eagerly anticipating their time with us.

YAY USA!

Melissa is also "way far away" across the continent in Dartmouth, Nova Scotia. She serves as youth sponsor in her church, and works with Inter-School Christian Fellowship at the local high school. She recently asked for some music books so she could use her piano and violin skills more fully. (Mom was quick to respond to the request!) She shares her home with another nurse, who, unfortunately (!), could not fit her piano into her downstairs bedroom and therefore has to keep it in Melissa's living room, and Melissa looks forward to playing piano duets with her. Melissa nurses at the children's hospital (known by its initials IWK, as the full title, Isaak Walton Killam, seemed incompatible with its purpose). Melissa also spent a relaxing holiday here in July, and had several happy visits with Granny. Melissa has been infected by the gardening virus, as she enthusiastically plants her unlandscaped lot with a variety of flowers, herbs, strawberries, and shrubs. (Mother assures her that there is no cure for this malady.) An assortment of Matt's Plants, transferred both by mail and in Melissa's luggage, have taken up residence in Nova Scotia.

Richard and Melody count sleep-deprivation as their greatest enemy, with both new baby responsibilities (Melody) and school assignments (Richard) disturbing and/or eating into rest times. Richard is preparing to graduate with a business degree from Royal Roads next August. He is also working full time at Level Ground Trading, the thriving fair trade company which produces San Miguel coffee. Level Ground supports students in the small Colombian village where Hugo Ciro, who started the company, grew up and where the San Miguel coffee beans originate. Richard, as operations manager, finds his job both challenging and exhilarating. Melody worked in the office at Level Ground for several months before little Eric arrived, and still maintains her Regal business. She helps me with piano classes each

Wednesday. Along with the unpleasantness of her third Caesarean section, she had a large, unexplainable growth in her nose removed a few days after Eric was born. Three days ago, little **Anna** [five on November 21, and now in Kindergarten] came down with a most impressive and uncomfortable case of the chickenpox. (Melody's comment on this development: "If we can live through this, we can live through anything.") **Michael** [three in September] jealously searches in vain for comparable spots; he may get his chance in a couple of weeks! Anna and Michael are enthralled with their little brother who, at two months and fifteen pounds, is rapidly leaving his first wardrobe behind.

MARK AND MATT AT CAMP QWANOES

Mark and **Matt** live quite separate lives within our home, but are often found together consulting on video and computer techniques, and participating in as many sports as they can fit in. They spent a second summer filming and editing weekly videos at Camp Qwanoes. Both are taking courses at Camosun College, Mark in criminal justice and Matt in general studies. For many years, our family had subsisted without cable TV, but Ms 6 and 7 became aware of a special deal which includes both TV and computers PLUS continuous music through the TV. With five young people living here and several computers in use, the parents capitulated, and the two initiators smile smugly when they crank up the TV on the lower floor to provide classical music in the background. (And the smiles are wider as they sprawl in front of the tube upstairs to watch hockey.) In September, Mark edited a video for Central Baptist's 75th Anniversary. He also prepared two videos for Geordon and Marilyn's work, and has several other projects on the go. A year ago, for our fortieth anniversary, he put together a video including not only dozens of family photos from the past 40 years, but also live footage of Bruce and me 35 years ago. One segment is from Christmas Day, 1967, when Bruce and I were opening a wonderful gift from his parents, a bathroom cabinet which soon-to-be-Grandpa Holland had constructed in secret for the downstairs bathroom in our 750-square-foot house. Marilyn was born five days later, and the cabinet is still in use. (As is another cherished gift, our wedding piano which Bruce's parents gave us. After forty years of use and abuse—hundreds of pupils, thousands of hours—we are getting that piano rebuilt and refinished, using part of my mother's gift to me. We have been blessed with caring parents/grandparents on both sides of our family.) Our anniversary video also includes a sequence of seven violinists playing excerpts of pieces from three or four different stages of their lives, ending with a few bars of their performance at Margaret's wedding a year ago. Sniffle time for Mom!

With so many young people in and out of our home, including the dozens of students who share time at the piano with me each week, it is easy to forget that Bruce and I could be in the rocking chair and slippers set. Life is very full. I spent August and September caring for my mother, and since her death, have passed many hours poring over her writings and organizing her belongings, a bittersweet process. In November, Bruce spent ten days in Caracas cooking up a storm, and, with those who travelled with him, was impressed by what our eldest and her husband are attempting, successfully, with the Lord's help and blessing. Bruce had a very amicable relationship with his mother-in-law, and probably feels her loss almost as keenly as I do. In scanning 2002's calendar, I noted an unsettling number of doctors' appointments, mostly mine. At least seven doctors have been involved in dealing with dermatomyositis and carpal tunnel syndrome, and I am thankful that, although most auto-immune diseases carry pain and/or fatigue with them, I feel remarkably well and energetic most of the time. Bruce and I are grateful for a medical system that can give such assistance. I, especially, thank God for the 100% healing in my hands and wrists. Carpal surgery in April dealt with a right hand that had been numb for five months; the right thumb had become quite crippled and the longterm outlook was not too promising. However, the left hand and wrist have returned to normal without surgery, and only a rather unattractive scar gives evidence that there ever was a problem with the right hand. Never have I appreciated the abilities to write, type, and play the piano and organ as much as I do now.

For several months in 2001, we were privileged to share our home with our pastor, Leigh Robinson, and his daughter, Sarah. Last December, Leigh and Sarah returned to South Africa to touch bases with their beloved congregation in Johannesburg and to bring Leigh's wife, Irene, and second daughter, Julie, back to Canada. For three months the four of them lived in our upstairs suite; for part of that time son Jonathan, and wife Nicky, joined them there, and we had a comfortably full house, with South African and Canadian accents mingling happily. In April, the Robinsons moved into their new home just three blocks from here. We especially appreciated their love and support at the time of Granny's death; Granny spoke often of her regard for our pastor as she listened each week to his sermons on tape, and, after meeting Danish-born Irene, said she would be happy to take her into our family!

We have welcomed three other fine young people into our home. Caner Budakoglu, an engineering Masters student from Turkey, had been living with Melody and Richard. Caner prepared a magnificent Turkish meal for two Turkish friends last Saturday, and Bruce and I, and Mark and Matt, were invited to share in the feast. Holly Darkes, just out of high school and also an excellent student, is studying for her Associateship at the Victoria Conservatory of Music (the same programme Marilyn took 16 and 17 years ago), so we again have the pleasure of enjoying advanced piano repertoire. Holly grew up in the Northwest Territories, and wishes she could go skiing every day. Steven Morrison, Matt's classmate and fellow athlete at PCS during their high school days, has taken the last upstairs bedroom, and co-exists amiably with the other four. Although he has been holding down two jobs for several months, he plans to return to UVic for some courses in January. Steve plays the viola, and generously contributes his talents to worship teams and cantatas at our church. We are very fortunate to have the company of such beautiful young people.

LIFE'S LIKE THIS

December 25, 1968 Father, Mother and Baby Marilyn, five days short of her first birthday, arrive at Great-Granny Hansen's home, where Granddad and Granny Forsberg are living. A delivery van, marked *Scott Piano*, also turns into the driveway, and Mother's parents are perplexed at the strange events. Bill Scott and his helper open the van to reveal a beautiful, brand-new, little Sherlock-Manning piano, a replacement for Granny's piano, which is in the family home on Gladstone Avenue. Granny is delighted with the gift, and says she will put Marilyn's name on it, so that she can have it when Granny does not need it any more. ... **August 1, 2002** Granny's furnishings arrive at 4031 Saanich Road, and the piano is set up in the living room. ... **November 30** Granny has been gone for two months, and Mother decides to have pianos tuned. Remembers Granny's promise to put Marilyn's name on piano, checks back of piano, sees no name, assumes label has fallen off. Piano-tuner opens up top of piano, revealing bold black printing: "For Marilyn Louise Holland with thanks to her parents, Love from Granny." The next day, Mother finds Christmas gift card attached to old masking tape that piano tuner must have retrieved from inside of piano: "To Mom and Daddy Love from Bruce Louise Marilyn" with a special note to Grandad: "No, you can't eat off it, Daddy, but we hope you *both* will enjoy it." Mother wishes she had known earlier what had stayed hidden in the piano for 34 years; she and Granny would have had a chuckle over it a few months ago.

July 6, Church of Our Lord Anna and Michael are at boarder Sarah's wedding, acting as flower girl and ring bearer. Procession makes way to front of church. Bored, Michael unties ribbons, and rings roll around on carpet. Attendant picks up rings; Melody re-ties them

MICHAEL AND ANNA

on pillow. When rings are requested, Michael is asleep on his father's lap. Anna takes them up and explains very carefully to the minister that her little brother is asleep, so she is bringing up the rings. Congregation and minister wait patiently as she gives lengthy explanation.

September 20 It is Friday afternoon; the sun is hot, the traffic heavy, as Granny and Mother take a stroll around the Saanich/Quadra/McKenzie triangle. Wheelchair bumps over sidewalk, tilting at driveways; makes side trip across Quadra during break in traffic to check out yard full of huge sunflowers. Granny comments later that wheelchair ride was best part of day. Mother is thankful to have such a happy memory.

SCENE IN PASSING ...

... Anna distributing "frinkles" and "farkles" over the icing on Caner's birthday cake ... Father and Mother enjoying 40th wedding anniversary celebration, with delicious meal at Richard and Melody's home,

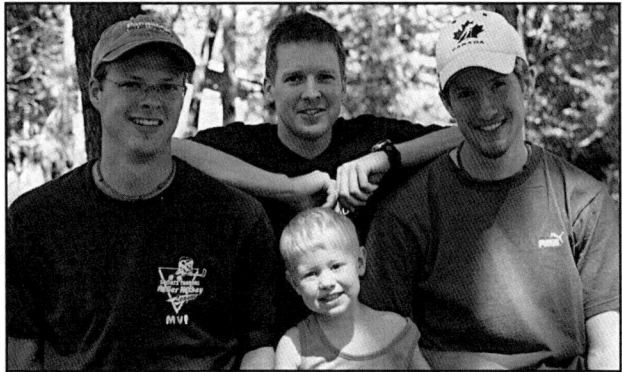

MARK, MIKE AND MATT, WITH NEPHEW MICHAEL

and three very special gifts: anniversary video, portrait of seven very special young people, and watercolour of house painted by talented neighbour, Benita Blundell ... Mother selling huge bundles of lunaria (money plant) and shoo-fly plant to the florist ... Matt flipping pancakes and baking cornbread to help ease the famine while family chef is in Venezuela ... a couple of days later, Holly presenting an appreciative group around the supper table with two cookie sheets of delicious pizza ... Margaret and Chris crossing the border with their huge U-Haul truck, on their way to Indiana, amazed and relieved that they are not asked to open it up ... Baby Eric and family featured on CH TV, as owner of Thrifty Foods announces gift to the paediatrics wing of the hospital ... Father and Mother browsing through antique stores, shocked to see that one dealer is asking $295 for an oak chair with original, tattered leather upholstery, identical to family chairs, which have long since been re-upholstered with naugahyde, increasing their durability and probably reducing their value (Father paid $65 for nine chairs, round table, and buffet forty years ago. Parents learn that oak is quarter-sawn and design is Arts and Crafts. Family has always appreciated furniture's indestructibility and now eyes it with even greater respect.) ... Bruce, en route to Caracas, carrying a large ham and block of cheese in his carry-on, pleased that customs officers do not ask him to open his case ... Mother, holding Granny's arms, encouraging her to stand up, with no success ... Mother suggesting she could get Father to help, whereupon Granny bolts upright … both having a good laugh at example of extrinsic motivation … Mother, in earlier months of year, sorting through boxes and shelves of papers, children's schoolwork, etc., filing and discarding; comes across forgotten diary from early 1973 with entries: Michael [then 3 1/2]: "Mommies shouldn't take toys away from children."… Michael gets "upsited" when M3 bothers him. … Michael's response to question, "What's new at your house?" "A flashlight." (The correct response: "Melissa.") … Mother finding a Mother's Day card from 1983 which explains why Margaret is always on time for activities: "Happy Mother's Day! Things I should do for you: **M** - do my MUSIC; **O** - OBEY you; **T** - do what I'm

TOLD; **H** - work HARD until a job is done; **E** - get up EARLY in the morning; **R** - be READY when we go somewhere." … Grandma Holland, at 95, enjoying the Canucks' success in hockey, maintaining an interest in family and world affairs, and feeling the loss of her friend of the past 80 years (Her loving, supportive attitude towards our family, and Auntie Marilyn's interest and kindness have been among our family's greatest gifts.) … Mother cancelling Granny's name from charitable organization mailing lists (to date, has sent 24 notices upon which she has, sadly, printed "deceased") … Baby Eric smiling and cooing, bringing much joy to this large family, especially at the time of year when we remember the Baby of Bethlehem, who came to be our Saviour …

GRANDMA HOLLAND—CANUCKS FAN

Chapter 48: My Mom

Tribute given at Memorial Service, Central Baptist Church, October 2, 2002:

Anna Ingeborg Forsberg was born on August 3, 1907, to Christian and Ingeborg Lorenzen, Danish immigrants who had settled on a homestead in Pilot Mound, near Winnipeg, Manitoba. Her older sister and brother had perished shortly after her parents arrived from Denmark, so she was given her sister's name, Anna, a name which is found several times in the family history, and which has also been given to a great-granddaughter. Anna's artistic talents were nurtured by her early life on the prairies, where her parents and aunts and uncles created exquisite crocheted, knitted, embroidered and sewn articles. She told of the underwear, lovingly embroidered, made from flour sacking, and

KATRINA AND ANNA

of the flourishing gardens her mother tended on the homestead. During this time of the First World War and anti-German sentiment, Anna's family referred to her as "Anne," in an effort to camouflage her family's European origins, and that name, and "Annie," were used until more recent years, when the original "Anna" made a return.

When Anna was 12, her family, which now included her sister Katrina (Katie) and brother James (Jimmy), moved to the Sidney area, due to her father's deteriorating health. Her father, a skilled and prosperous auto mechanic in Manitoba, turned to farming here on the coast. Chicken farming was not a good choice for someone with tuberculosis, and his

ANNA INGEBORG FORSBERG

death three years later was perhaps the most heartbreaking event in Anna's life. Her father had instilled in Anna a love of learning, and at that time, at the age of 15, she was working as a nanny and housekeeper for a family in Victoria while she attended the only high school in the area, Victoria High School. During her high school years, due to her responsibilities at her boarding home, she had no time for socializing, but she did make the acquaintance of Olive Taylor, a classmate who lived in Victoria, and who befriended this shy young girl from the country. Thirty-four years later, when her daughter and Olive's son married, they resumed their friendship, and have enjoyed each other's company for the past 43 years.

ANNA AS BRIDESMAID

During her time at Vic High, Anna was allowed to visit her family in the "wilderness" of Sidney once a month, and told of carrying eggs from the farm back to her employers in Victoria and, at one point, having the bag break, scattering eggs across the intersection of Blanshard and Yates Streets, where the street car had carried her. After her father's death, she continued her high school education at Vic High, living with two other families, and then attended Victoria Normal School for teacher training. Her first posting was to Fraser Lake, in BC's northern wilderness, where she spent two of the happiest years of her life. Her mother's insistence that she return to Sidney brought an obedient response and she returned home, unhappily, to a job in that area. For many years she lived with, and helped to support, her hardworking mother. In 1940, she married our father, Hjalmar Forsberg, a handsome Swede who had migrated to Victoria from Saskatchewan during the Depression.

SCHOOLTEACHER AT FRASER LAKE

Over the next 6 1/2 years, five children were born to Hjalmar and Anna: Louise, Harriet, Eric, Margaret and Jeannie. It was not easy for Anna to move from her secure, well-established teaching career to the project of raising five children, but she rose to the challenge and became an expert homemaker and seamstress, a loving and concerned mother, and a model of frugality.

Family finances were not always reliable, so when Louise was eight, Anna went back to substitute teaching, and two years later was hired by the Saanich School Board as a full-time teacher at Brentwood School, where she taught at the primary

JEANNIE, PEGGY (MARGARET), ERIC, HARRIET, LOUISE, HJALMAR, ANNA (1963)

level for the next 18 years. In 1970, she had a fall at school, damaging her back and ending her teaching career. This was one of her life's biggest disappointments, as by now her children were all married, and she derived much satisfaction from her teaching. For the last 32 years, she made the best of retirement life, creating articles

PAINTBRUSH IN HAND

of clothing for her children and grandchildren, painting, and following with keen interest the activities of her five children, 17 grandchildren and 12 great-grandchildren. Her children's homes display samples of her skill with needle and paintbrush, and her love of beauty has been passed on to her family. She and Hjalmar spent several winters on the desert of Arizona, where she made new friends and took several art courses.

Although Anna had always had an association with the Christian faith, in the Anglican tradition, her attendance at Parkdale Evangelical Church during the 1970s brought her to a strong faith in Christ, and she was baptized as a declaration of that commitment. Her faith in God and reliance on His grace and strength characterized her life in later years, as she faced the increasing physical and mental challenges of old age with a positive attitude of gratitude to God for all He had given her. She often spoke of lying awake at night, praying for members of her family. Those who dealt with her in her

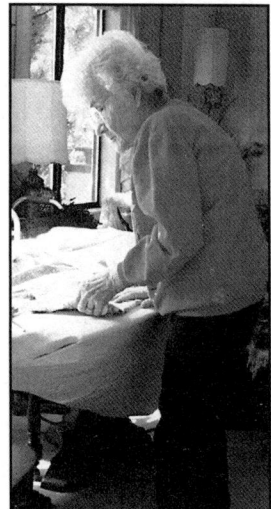

CHOOSING MATERIAL FOR YET ANOTHER SEWING PROJECT

last few weeks were impressed by her uncomplaining spirit and her appreciation for the least small kindness. As her life drew to a close, she could still respond with enthusiasm and affection to those who came to see her. Her love of colour and design were still evident in her last days, as she discussed many of her sewing projects and handled several items of clothing she had made over the years.

ANNA AND DAUGHTER HARRIET

A special gift to Anna over the past three years was the companionship of her grand-daughter, Tara, a geriatric nurse, who shared her condominium. Tara ensured that Granny was showered with affection and care; Granny kept all her little notes, and often spoke of Tara's thoughtfulness to her. Tara's aunts and uncles are grateful for the peace of mind Tara's efforts gave them during this time.

As a family, we are thankful for the privilege of enjoying our mother's love and support for over 60 years, but her death has left a large void. We are glad she has been released from pain and infirmity. We know she is in a far better place, but already we miss her keenly. We trust we have learned from her lessons of faith, love, patience, frugality, tolerance, generosity, a love of natural beauty, and an appreciation of what is truly worthwhile, and will continue to practise these attributes in our own lives.

ANNA AND SON ERIC

Memories of my Granny
by Marilyn Rendle

Anna Forsberg wasn't just my Granny. She was a daughter, sister, wife, sister-in-law, mother, aunt, teacher, grandmother and great-grandmother–all over a span of 95 years! What a heritage of relationships. I count it a privilege to have known my Granny right into my own adulthood. She wasn't just a distant blood relative but a vital, integral, involved part of my formative and adult years.

I vaguely remember the apartment on Irma Street, the house on Vernon Avenue and then, of course, the townhouse on Nelthorpe, within walking distance of our family home and Swan Lake, as well as the condominium on Shelbourne, and finally the little suite that was home to us on several occasions in years gone by. Wherever Granny lived, we were always welcomed with open arms. Even in these last few years, as great-grandchildren descended upon the Forsberg household, there were little toys set out on the coffee table to keep busy little hands occupied.

Thinking back over the years, I remember the family gatherings with Granny and Granddad, aunts, uncles and plenty of cousins. I remember a couple of "girls only" overnight shopping trips to Port Angeles when the dollar was in our favour, and our big family trip a few years later to see Granny and Granddad in Quartzsite, Arizona, spending a few days at Disneyland along the way. I remember Granny's patience and flexibility with my somewhat gruff, impatient granddad. Whether it was preparing the motor home on a moment's notice to head to Arizona, or going golfing, she went along for the ride, trying to keep the peace by being a cheerful companion.

I remember the matching outfits for the Holland children, my high school graduation dress, my college graduation recital dress and bridesmaids' dresses—all made by Granny. She was always frugal, but designed her creations with extravagant love. When I got married, I often stopped by with a full bag of mending or ironing to be done. She was always willing to help and often ended up doing the majority of the jobs, as her expertise took over.

I remember with fondness late-night talks visiting with Granny—while Geordon worked night-shifts—enjoying some kind of goodies that were always out on the table for visitors. Grandpa's dark ginger cookies with icing in the middle were one of my favourites. Chatting about everyday activities, big events, and philosophies of life with Granny was always fun. She listened patiently but also joined in—when asked—with experiences she had lived through.

I remember how much she loved her family. Her photo albums included every family member and their important stages. She lived through the good and the bad and observed as her family did the same, wise enough to let each one work through their own issues, reaping their own unique consequences —always quietly supportive along the way.

I remember how giving she was with her

ANNA AND GREAT-GRANDDAUGHTER ANNA STARK

time, her possessions, her resources. Whether it was helping sew for a preschool, make cloth dolls for little children, or contributing to Operation Eyesight, she was willing and ready to pitch in as she could.

One of the reasons it was hard to say goodbye seven years ago to head overseas was leaving our family and especially our grandparents. Granny, always supportive, was concerned that our little boys would keep their English intact and hoped to see us as often as we could make it back. I'll always remember calling her when we finally landed in Venezuela. It was her birthday, August 3, and we had arrived after being in Costa Rica for seven months learning Spanish! Even being so far away she managed to keep in touch, faithfully sending us Christmas cards and even the occasional fax (imagine a 90+ year old operating a fax machine!). She was fascinated, and maybe even a little intimidated, by new-fangled technology like a VCR or a fax machine, but was willing to learn if it meant she could keep in touch with her family. Personal videos were especially enjoyed.

Amazingly enough, our little boys have been able to be back once a year since we left and we have enjoyed our fair share of time back in our home country visiting with family, too. This last impromptu visit in August was especially significant as we shared Granny's little suite with her and saw her every day. Though she was in incredible pain at times, she enjoyed it when family members would pop their heads in, smiling and welcoming them as much as she could. We are sad to lose her, but our loss is heaven's gain. We know that she is at peace now, and that knowledge comforts us until we see her again.

Chapter 49: A Christmas Digest, 2003

EDITORIAL *by Louise*

Greetings of the Season to our family, friends and any acquaintances who would like to wade through our 38th Christmas letter! We thank God for you all and pray that you, too, will experience the peace and hope that come from trust in the Saviour, whose birth we celebrate at this time.

As I write this, we are happily anticipating an influx of family members from Indiana (Chris and Margaret), Halifax (Melissa) and Winnipeg (Michael). With Marilyn and Geordon already here from Venezuela, and Melody and Richard nearby, and Mark and Matt upstairs, the family will be together for the holidays.

Bruce and I enjoy the company of our youngest sons as they share our upstairs suite, and our three UVic students, Caner Budakoglu (from Turkey, completing a Masters programme), Steven Morrison (Matt's classmate through high school), and Angela Alba, whose sessions at the piano fill the household with beautiful music. (At last Bruce gets to hear Chopin's *Fantasie-Impromptu* as it should sound.) Richard and Melody (Anna [6], Michael [4], Eric [1]) and Geordon and Marilyn (Jordan [9], Joshua [5], Jolyn [7 months]) drop in and out several times a week and we enjoy keeping tabs on their activities.

For 37 years we have watched helplessly as millions of Garry oak leaves descend on our unmanageable half-acre each fall, and, in spite of constant composting, we have fretted over our inability to keep the yard tidy. No more. Representatives of the Habitat Acquisition Trust enthusiastically applauded our efforts at recycling the leaves, along with hundreds of buckets of kitchen scraps and garden debris, into heaps of beautifully friable and fertile soil. They also outlined strategies for making the property even more bird- and butterfly-friendly, and advised leaving some leaves in borders (!) to provide nutrients for plants. So now we are "environmental stewards," making a small contribution to the wildlife corridor that runs between Swan Lake and the Blenkinsop Valley. Flocks of bushtits, pairs of downy woodpeckers, chickadees, sparrows, wrens, robins and nuthatches entertain us as they peck away at our bird feeders, scattering seeds which are eagerly devoured by black-hooded juncos on the ground, and by the occasional frustrated squirrel who cannot get a toehold on the feeders.

The year since my mother died has had its sad moments, as I even now revert to the patterns of years past, thinking that I will share this idea, or that anecdote, with her, and having to remind myself yet again that this will not happen. For years I would come down from my classroom, make several lunches for the next day, and then relax into an hour's conversation on the phone with my mom, as she patiently listened to me and shared the fun and frustrations of my life. She used to say she lived vicariously through the lives of her children, and our conversations were often punctuated with such comments as, "It's 10:32, Louise. We've been talking for 35 minutes and you've got to get your sleep." She had frequent naps during the day, but, as always, was concerned for her children's welfare. And then we would chat on for another half an hour. I miss her input into my life, and am thankful that much of the void is filled by her grandchildren and great-grandchildren, who frequently visit and share meals with us, and by the music students whom I am privileged to teach.

My mother left her autobiography and diaries, as well as writings and personal effects belonging to her Aunt Anna, who died in 1951. Aunt Anna, born in 1870, emigrated from Denmark in the early 1900s to a homestead in Saskatchewan, and her diaries, written mostly in German, detail both the harshness and the beauty of her new life. I would love to write a book, perhaps entitled *Two Annas*, but that may have to wait for another lifetime!

Bruce and I were enticed out of our routine and from our comfort zone twice this year, as we visited Chris and Margaret in Indianapolis last March, and Michael in Winnipeg and Melissa in Halifax at the end of September. It was good, and reassuring, to have a peek into their situations.

PERSONAL GLIMPSES

Although **Marilyn** and **Geordon** were scheduled to come back from Venezuela in June, they hurried out of Caracas in January due to the threat of civil war and the possibility that Marilyn would not receive adequate care during the remainder of her pregnancy. Naturally, we were overjoyed to have them home early, and to hold **Jolyn Eva Marie** soon after her birth on April 27th. Geordon is working on his Masters in Leadership and Training at Royal Roads University, as well as supervising Youth For Christ work in Latin America via telephone and e-mail. In September he, Marilyn, Jolyn and Mark spent three and a half weeks in Latin America, touching bases with YFC chapters in several countries, including an international conference in Brazil. Geordon, as Regional Director for Latin America, was pleased that all of his Latin American directors were able to attend the international conference, where representatives from over 80 countries met to worship God and share ideas on their work with young people. Jolyn's parents figure their wee daughter was held by at least 300 pairs of arms; Jolyn's grandmother flinched at that figure, but must admit that her youngest grandchild did not appear to suffer from so many contacts. (Geordon's comment to the director from Rwanda, a large black man who would have loved to take Jolyn home with him: "You can take her if you can prove to immigration that you are her father!")

Michael has left his flying job in Winnipeg, and looks forward to what the new year will bring. Every member of his extended family is delighted that he will be back in Victoria, and his brothers especially look forward to more time with him, starting with a father/sons marathon domino session at Christmas. This past year found him flying to Russia, the UK, France, and all over North America, in a Learjet 35, repatriating injured or sick travellers. The exhilaration of projecting a small and powerful airplane across 500+ miles of terrain or ocean in an hour, often at 45,000 feet, was offset by the times spent alone in hotels or in his apartment, wishing he could have more time with his family on the West Coast. Matt flew to Winnipeg on December 10 and the two of them drove a heavily-laden U-Haul truck, Mike's car perched on a trailer behind it, across the prairies and through the mountains, while Mother prayed fervently!

Margaret and **Chris** arrive here December 22, and we look forward to chatting up a storm. Chris and Margaret purchased a well-built but derelict brick house in Indianapolis's inner city eighteen months ago. Although the 1884 house is sound structurally, it and the property had been abused for years, so they gutted and have completely renovated the house, combining upstairs and downstairs apartments into their own living quarters, and keeping a third apartment (1,100 square feet) at the back of the house for rental. The original

CHRIS AND MARGARET'S HOME IN INDIANAPOLIS

owners would be happy to see the building restored so beautifully. Chris continues to work as an engineer on a highway project, and Margaret teaches Grade 5 at the international school.

Melissa nurses half time in Halifax, and serves as youth ministry co-ordinator at First Baptist Church half time. With probably 18 years' involvement in youth work, first as camper and youth group member and then youth sponsor, Melissa enjoys her new role and brings her positive attitude and enthusiasm to this new assignment. Melissa's main interests continue to be nursing, youth work, gardening and travelling (not necessarily in that order).

Melody and **Richard** have endured a gruelling year, as Richard has completed his studies, as well as working full time. Both have dealt with the demands of three small children, one of whom—a sturdy blond, blue-eyed replica of his grandpa 60-plus years ago—has not been the most cooperative baby on the block. Hopefully, 2004 will be less stressful. Richard works within sales and operations at Level Ground Trading, and has made his contribution to the wonderful success Level Ground has enjoyed this year. Level Ground won the Ethics in Action Award for small- to medium-sized BC businesses. Melody oversees the activities of **Anna**, **Michael** and **Eric**, continues to help me with my piano classes, and deals with her many Regal customers. She and Marilyn played their violins in the Christmas cantata.

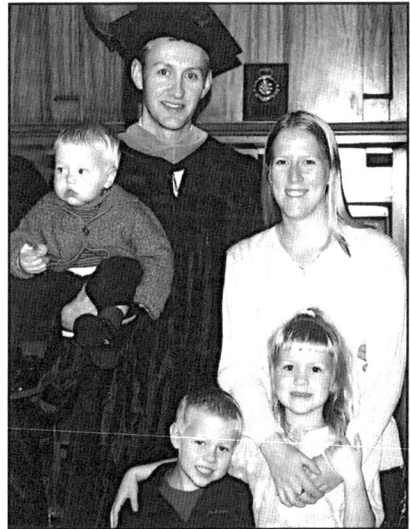

BACHELOR IN ENTREPRENEURIAL MANAGEMENT

Mark and **Matt** live independently in their bachelor pad upstairs. Guests often join them in front of the TV for hockey games, movies, video games, etc., including their young nephews and niece who race up the side staircase to hang out with Uncle Mark and Uncle Matt and Uncle Steve, as soon as they enter the house. Mark is completing his second year in Criminology, pulling in high grades, and managing to produce several videos. He is not sure what his next step will be, but we are in no hurry to see him move on. Mark had a wonderful time videoing and editing YFC activities in South America, producing a documentary that could be taken home by the delegates to the international YFC conference in Brazil. Matt works as bookkeeper and Internet Technology person for Level Ground, and has spent weeks developing computer business forms which should save the company many hours of work. Matt joined Mark, Marilyn, Steve and his mother Christie, and me, to provide music for a wedding in July.

LIFE'S LIKE THIS

Summer 2001 Melissa has moved to Halifax. Her friend and bike hike co-director in years past, Dawnmaree Fletcher, is camping with a group of young people in Banff National Park. A young Swiss couple, camping nearby, mention that they are biking across Canada and will be in Halifax a few weeks later. Dawnmaree suggests that they stay with Melissa. Melissa is happy to put them up, but must work for most of the week that they are there. To her delight, not only are the couple exemplary house-guests, but Melissa arrives home each evening to the fragrance of a wonderful supper prepared by her guests! The young couple plan to tour the

Maritimes and return to Halifax, so Melissa gives them her house key, as she will be in Victoria during their second visit. ... **August 2002** Melissa receives word from her Swiss friends that they are expecting a baby, due on December 30th, and Melissa comments that the baby should be born not on the 30th, Marilyn's birthday, but on December 23rd, her birthday. ... **December 23, 2002** Melissa receives an e-mail from Switzerland to inform her that a little girl was born that morning, and they are naming her "Melissa"! ... **May 2003** Melissa travels to Europe, stopping over in Switzerland to meet her adorable namesake; is treated to a wonderful week's holiday by her generous host and hostess.

    Tuesday, August 12, 2003 Richard has just completed his BComm in Entrepreneurial Management, and is looking forward to a break and some quality time with his family. He and Melody, with five-year-old Anna, three-year-old Michael, and 10-month-old Eric, visit with Michael in Winnipeg. Uncle Mike takes the family on several outings, and Richard and Melody begin to unwind. ... **Thursday, August 14** Family arrives in Toronto from Winnipeg on way to Halifax. Temperature is a humid 40+ degrees, and the children are fretful. Auntie Margaret is in Halifax waiting to see the family; leaves for Indianapolis on Monday. Melody eagerly anticipates visiting with her sisters, and the children can't wait to see their aunts. ... It is 20 minutes before the flight leaves for Halifax, when the lights suddenly dim. ... A couple of phone calls home inform parents that family is stranded in the airport, as power has failed. Family is not allowed to access luggage, and food—and diapers—are in short supply. Parents and eldest sister pray that some help will come along for family. ... Richard and Melody strike up conversation with Dutch couple travelling to BC with their two-year-old son. Within minutes, Melody discovers that Annemeik shares her off-the-wall sense of humour and Richard suggests to Marc that couple stay in the Stark home in Victoria, and tells them where key is. ... The two couples spend the first night in the airport, sharing food and child minding responsibilities, the second sharing a hotel room, and the third back at the airport. ... **Sunday, 3:00 a.m.** Margaret and Melissa pick up weary and bedraggled family at Halifax airport. Melody had hoped to join Margaret and Melissa on violins for church, but family heads straight for bed. ... **Monday, September 1** Family arrives back in Victoria, is greeted by their Dutch friends who share their home with them for another few days. ...

    Friday, September 26 Father and Mother disembark at Halifax, are greeted enthusiastically by their Nova Scotian daughter. Mother realizes that a lady who looks like Mrs. Law from Victoria's Big Barn Garden Centre is in fact Mrs. Law. She and her daughter, Alice, who went to school with Melissa, enjoy several minutes of conversation, along with Alice's fiancé and Mr. Law. Alice Law has not seen Melissa since elementary school, although Mrs. Law often asks about her, so the meeting was very pleasant for all concerned. ... Mother comments on mild temperature and benevolent wind that blows continuously. Melissa assures her that weather is unseasonably warm, and casually remarks that a hurricane warning is in effect for the weekend. ... Mother and Father enjoy Saturday visiting with Melissa, and on Sunday attend both morning services at her church where she welcomes the congregation, makes announcements, and leads in prayer at the beginning of the first service, and plays her violin in the second service. Wind continues; church is uncomfortably warm. ... After lunch with other youth leader and family, Father and Mother decide to explore nature sanctuary up the road from Melissa's home, while she attends planning meeting at church. Parents return from walk laden down with wild apples (Father), and an assortment of flowers, leaves, berries, cones and birch bark (Mother). Sky darkens ominously, rain sprinkles, and wind picks up. ... For next several hours, wind builds. Around eleven o'clock, Hurricane Juan hits, full-force. Melissa's house (one side of a two-storey duplex) shudders in the darkness (which becomes even darker as occupants discover power is off), and there are cracks and bangs off in the distance. Melissa and parents lie on beds, wondering if and when roof is going to fly off. Mother covers ears to block out incessant roaring. ... Sleep comes three hours later, as wind gradually abates. Roof remains on top of building. ... Early-morning stillness is quite disconcerting after days of incessant blowing. Melissa and parents later learn that wind blew in gusts up to 230 km/h, two people were killed, half a million trees were uprooted across the area and into Prince Edward Island, and there was considerable property damage. At least two explosions could be attributed to neighbours' barbecues smashing deck railings on their way to the grass below. Melissa's power and phone connection did not return until after parents left four days later, necessitating candle-burning and early bedtimes, and day excursions to outlying areas where the power was not affected. (Nurse Melissa's description of her house, its white vinyl siding plastered with shredded leaves and other debris: "It looks as if something has vomited on it!")

SEEN AND HEARD ...

... **Jordie** [then 8] and **Josh** [5] whipping the puck around on the concrete slab, a *déjà vu* experience for Grandma, who remembers Uncles Mark and Matt doing the same thing at the same age, 18 years earlier ... Anna choosing which garden ornament should go to Auntie Melissa and which should be kept for herself and Mommy: "I like this one best, so I'll give it to 'Glissa." ... Grandma Holland (now 96) and Auntie Marilyn sharing their home with the Rendle four/soon-to-be-five for three months ... Louise rescuing several varieties of plants from imminent destruction as tradesmen trample the yard around Chris and Margaret's new/old home; potting up what appear to be violets (learns that they covered themselves with dainty purple flowers a few weeks later), asters, day-lilies, and nepeta; wonders who planted them, and how long ago … meltdown and replacement of five appliances, and installation (after 36 years) of new furnace which does not belch oil fumes, hopefully ensuring an extension of our tenure in This Old House … Mark, Matt and Steve and team-mates accepting roller hockey trophy as they win the crucial game by two points scored in the last few seconds, proudly observed by parents, siblings, nephews, and nieces (They had been raised to a more challenging division for the finals, so the win was doubly sweet.) … their volleyball team winning intramurals at UVic in April and November … Melissa roused from slumber at 2:30 a.m. between Germany and the Czech Republic, as officials remove her from train because she does not have a visa (a new requirement), a huge disappointment, as she

MARK, FRIEND STEVE MORRISON, MATT, AND THEIR FANS

had planned her trip around the music festival in Prague, and had friends in Prague waiting to take her to the opera … large photo of baby Eric, bottom lip protruding,

ERIC, UNHAPPY

attached to the Stark fridge, with inscription: "It's not fair! Mommy won't get up with me at five o'clock every morning." … Geordon tumbling over his handlebars as a taxi turns into the Juan de Fuca Rec Centre in front of him, rolling on the ground as he lands (a reflex move from his police training of years back), weeping as he sees his dream of running his second Ironman evaporate (He had planned to run in memory of his mother, Georgia, who passed away six years ago, and to raise funds for the final payment of the YFC House in Caracas. Thank God that, except for a fractured tibia that required several weeks to heal, he was not badly injured.) … Melissa playing violin solo with no introduction at large Remembrance Day service, startled as keyboard accompaniment is several semitones lower (Unknown to accompanist, keyboard pitch had been lowered for the singing of "O Canada.") … Bruce and Louise enjoying tour of Winnipeg, pumpkin ice cream, and extraordinary Winnipeg Symphony performance of Viennese music in company of eldest son; and spectacular Halifax

Tattoo and trip to the Tangled Garden (and several other gardens) with third daughter ... Melody leaning over, weeding front border, with back facing street; jerking upright as lady mail carrier states, "Here's a letter that matches your butt." (Melody is wearing high school Pacific Christian School track pants with *PCS* on backside; letter is from PCS.) ... Mother raking leaves from front pond during summer drought, notes exquisite little nuthatch clinging to concrete side, sipping stagnant water with tiny beak, less than a foot away ... Mark and Matt running computers and video cameras during Central Baptist's Christmas cantata, communicating with each other via headsets and intuition ... Matt making a 40-kilometre detour around accident scene in Alberta on side roads in 14-foot U-Haul truck plus car trailer, and inching over the Coquihalla Highway in heavy snow, lights on, in company of other large vehicles creeping down the treacherous slopes (Older brother gives his driving skill high commendation.) ... Father preparing supper for eight to twelve most days, making shopping forays several times a week ... Mother thanking God for the gifts of such a helpful husband and such compatible house-mates ...

Chapter 50: A Christmas Digest, 2004

EDITORIAL *by Louise*

December 10 What is green and creamy white, intensely fragrant, and started blooming on December 1? More hints: It usually blooms around Easter, and is a symbol of resurrection. Yes, it is an Easter lily, found growing in a heavily composted patch of earth in our back yard this fall. In a pot, it has been decorating our patio entrance for the last few weeks, a fitting reminder of the new lease on life the patriarch of the family is enjoying after bypass surgery on November 23.

This is the family matriarch (her brother's designation) writing, with far too few days remaining between now and Christmas. It is a typical winter day in Victoria: gloomy, damp, mild, with the occasional flash of sunshine. Pink blossoms cover several bushes and trees which apparently have not consulted the calendar recently. As has been the pattern for the last 38 years (and probably many before), this property has blanketed itself in Garry oak leaves, a reminder of its origin as a Garry oak meadow.

As I type, the patriarch/Grandpa is building a log house with his two youngest grandsons, Michael and Eric Stark, who keep the grandparents company two days a week while mother Melody works at the La-Z-Boy Furniture Gallery. The Lincoln Logs have survived from Grandpa's childhood, through a complete generation, to a new generation. Grandma totally approves of such creative play. (Grandma and the TV have never got along too well.)

December 31 It is New Year's Eve, and the snowdrops are blooming. The past three weeks have flown by in a blur, as birthdays (Melody's, Melissa's, and Marilyn's), wedding anniversary, two funerals, a wedding, and Christmas have woven themselves amongst preparations for the Rendles' return to Caracas on January 4. Chris and Margaret arrived on the 20th, and return to Indianapolis on January 5.

We hope you had a happy Christmas and will have a New Year filled with the things that truly matter.

PERSONAL GLIMPSES

Bruce (Grandpa) has received a fresh start, healthwise, as an angiogram on November 18 led to bypass surgery November 23. We thank God for the incredible support of praying friends and family, for skilful medical personnel, and for the fact that this surgery took place before, rather than after, heart damage had occurred. As is his custom, Bruce oversaw the preparation of Christmas dinner for 18, and invited almost as many for lunch the next day after church to eat up the leftovers. (He had prepared special dishes, one each day, for several days ahead.) He hopes to get back to his work on the church board (as secretary) and on the membership committee, as soon as possible in the new year.

Louise ("Grandma" to seven little people, "Mom" to seven—or more—larger people, and "Mrs. Holland" to quite a few music students) is very happy that her greatest supporter has come through his recent ordeal with flying colours. She continues to teach and, with Bruce, manages the Regal business which Melody built up over 19 years, starting as an 11 year old on her paper route. Many gallons of wonderfully fertile composted soil nurture the variety of plants she grows in support of youth work. Each time she plays organ or piano, she thanks God that hands, in spite of dermatomyositis and carpal surgery, still function normally. Her only complaint is that the day is too short.

Geordon and **Marilyn** hurried out of Venezuela two years ago, a few months before Jolyn was born, with two little boys: **Jordan** and **Joshua**. They are returning imminently with twice as many children, with the addition of little sisters **Jolyn** in April 2003, and **Joy Emma Louise** in September 2004. They are just completing the enormous project of distributing their belongings to their storage shed, friends' homes, thrift shops, the dump, and (surprise!) our home, as their house will be rented out for the next two years. Geordon hopes to complete his Masters degree shortly after his return to Caracas, and Marilyn hopes to survive! Geordon has spoken (and sung) in many settings while in Canada, as has Marilyn, as well as studying at Royal Roads University and supervising Youth For Christ activities in Latin America via conference call, e-mail, and the occasional visit to South America. Marilyn has also made good use of her piano and violin skills. Jordan [10 in September] passed his Preliminary Rudiments exam in May, and his Grade IV Piano exam in August. Joshua [6] has mastered several piano pieces. Jolyn [1 1/2] is an entertainment committee of one, and Joy [3 1/2 months] is well-named, with a very sunny disposition.

Michael is, as he puts it, "between jobs," as his company declared bankruptcy a few weeks ago. He has been hanging out with his brothers, sharing computer expertise, and helping with maintenance work on this property, an effort greatly appreciated by his parents. Although Mother wasn't too happy with him up on our multiplicity of roofs—she adamantly refused to let Father get up there—he did clean out all the eaves troughs and figured out how to get the water off the music room's flat roof.

Chris and **Margaret** have added a beautiful, old-fashioned, wrap-around porch on the front and side of their inner-city home in Indianapolis. Chris exploited his knowledge of soil engineering, as truck-loads of dirt were spread over the large lot. Neophyte gardeners, he and Margaret planted all kinds of shrubs and flowers. The neighbourhood, in the process of reclamation, welcomes the many improvements to what had formerly been a handsome brick house built in 1884, but derelict when they bought it. Chris works as an engineer for the state

BEAUTIFUL PORCH IN INDIANAPOLIS

department. Margaret teaches in a private school just a block away from their home. With a wide range of abilities and behaviours, the inner-city children present her with many challenges and some satisfaction.

Melissa divides her time evenly between paediatric nursing and youth leadership in Halifax. In January she travelled to Bolivia to mentor her former boarder in a mission project for young adults, and in May attended a youth seminar at the International Baptist Theological Seminary in Prague, Czech Republic. She spent ten days of her holiday time here at the beginning of November, and then returned a week later for three days around her father's surgery. Recent plans to spend two days on her own in New York over the New Year's weekend were thwarted by poor weather conditions and too many travellers. Her parents were not unhappy with the change in plans.

Richard and **Melody** have made a large corner of their basement into a wonderfully efficient office. Now both floors of their homey bungalow are fully utilized, with much credit due to Rick's building expertise and Melody's organizational abilities. Completion of the office project was directly related to Richard's leaving for 12 days in Colombia (i.e., according to Richard, he couldn't go if he didn't get it done). While he was gone, Melody painted the basement, with help(?) from their three little ones. Richard continues to work in sales at Level Ground Trading, and Melody spends two five-hour days bookkeeping at La-Z-Boy Furniture Gallery.

Mark received a diploma in Criminal Justice from Camosun College in the spring, and spent a second summer working for Customs. He spends much time on his computer, editing and producing videos, using footage taken in a variety of settings. His most recent assignment is producing a video for Level Ground Trading. He coached a volleyball team at Pacific Christian School, and he often joins Steve and Matt for roller hockey, floor hockey, and volleyball. Mark hopes to spend some time in Venezuela in 2005 taking footage for YFC Venezuela and immersing himself in the Spanish language.

Matthew continues to arrange squiggly patterns on his computer into user-friendly forms for Level Ground Trading. He and his brothers have joined the many computers in this household into one network, and Matt can access these, and his work computer, from his bedroom, which means he really doesn't have to leave his bedroom to get his work done. His Canadian brothers-in-law gave him a couple of special gifts at Christmas relating to this scenario, but this writer does not have the liberty of sharing what they are. They did, however, generate much hilarity. Matt enjoyed his week at the Apple conference in San Francisco, thanks to Level Ground's sponsorship.

SEEN AND HEARD ...

... Eric [2] standing spread-eagled, inviting Grandma to crawl between his legs; Grandma refusing invitation as gracefully as she can ... Joshua (Grade 1) unenthusiastic about visiting his new baby sister, Joy, in the hospital; doesn't want to miss any time at school ... Joshua winning $1,000 worth of Famous Player movie passes for a drawing of Shrek he entered in a contest ... Auntie Marilyn bushwhacking the wilderness behind her home, chopping down and stacking four-inch thick willow trees, under the watchful eye of (Great-) Grandma Olive Holland (98 in March 2005) ... Louise, having just proofread a friend's biography, addressing an e-mail "Marry Christmas," not noticing it until friend made a reply ... Melissa shopping with four nephews [10, 6, 5, 2] and two nieces [7 and 1 1/2], receiving quizzical glances as she manoeuvres troop through Beacon Hill Park and McDonald's, responding in the negative when asked if they are *all* hers ... Geordon a dashing figure in his new-to-him $500 tuxedo jacket, purchased for $6 at the Salvation Army store; his wife wearing dragonfly earrings and brooch, and an attractive long skirt decorated with dragonflies, the jewellery gifts from family, the skirt also from the Sally Ann—off to a birthday supper at Millo's (with a gift certificate) ... Mark flying to Colombia with brother-in-law Richard, for 12 days of filming Level Ground coffee plantations and fruit and coffee processing plants, and participating in presentation given by students supported by Victoria coffee company ... handing over new and expensive cameras to flight attendant at beginning of flight to South America ... arriving in Bogotá to find cameras and luggage have disappeared … thankful when all cameras and luggage, plus an unidentified suitcase which he and Richard will not touch, are available 24 hours later … family reading "fortunes" from Chinese cookies at Father's birthday supper (Louise's "Cherish home and family as a special treasure" quite appropriate, as is Jolyn's, 1 1/2 on Grandpa's birthday: "A welcome change is about to happen.") … Geordon, Jordie and Josh running the "Bridgemile" on Canada Day in Halifax, exactly one mile across a bridge that spans the Halifax Harbour … Geordon running three miles: once with Josh, then back to the beginning, then running it again on his own! … Geordon "winging" it as words for solo in cantata did not come up in correct order on prompter screen at back of auditorium; conductor and orchestra frantically trying to follow him … Boarder Angela Alba, runner-up at 2004 Provincial finals, giving a stunning recital for Louise's students, performing Chopin's *Fantasie-Impromptu* and Liszt's "Tarantella" with panache … Bruce and Louise having lunch with Regal personnel from Mississauga and Victoria, discussing many aspects of Regal business with President across table from them, and Vice-President of Marketing at Louise's left elbow (Louise gives President and Vice-President copies of 1957 Christmas letter from founder of Regal company, which she found among her mother's belongings. President comments that founder, William S. McCartney, was a "fine Christian man"; she was delighted to receive copy of letter. Letter was received by Louise, as a teenager, when she pedalled her bicycle through Brentwood area, taking Regal orders.) … Steve Morrison, our other boarder, practising his viola with his three "sisters" (Marilyn, Margaret, Melody) on their violins for a New Year's offertory …

LIFE'S LIKE THIS

Christmas Day, 2003 Exclamations of delight and expressions of gratitude fill grandparents' living room as family open gifts. Grandmother takes package from daughter, becomes aware of sudden lull in family chatter. Puzzles over gift tag which says, "To Louise From Bruce," as she knows grandfather did not receive her name for gift exchange and printing does not look familiar. Opens gift, blinks at less-than-edifying message on brand-new orange sweatshirt, original price-tag still attached; blushing, glances in disbelief at husband, who sits innocently across room. Family dissolves in gales of laughter. Perpetrators of prank found item at thrift shop and decided to have a little fun at grandfather's expense. … T-shirt, still unworn, hangs at back of grandmother's closet. *[While I still cannot bring myself to type out the shirt's message—something about gardening without adequate clothing and getting some colour—I must confess that I smile as I think of my mischievous son-in-law's delight when he happened upon the item in the thrift shop, and saw the potential for setting up his father-in-law.]*

February 10, 2004 Louise is leaving Adrienne's Restaurant at Mattick's Farm with sister and decides to show her, as the salesman had demonstrated, how the button on the key ring works to locate her new van in the parking lot. She presses button, appropriately labelled "Panic," and horn starts honking frantically several car-lengths away. To sister's delight, incessant racket continues as Louise keeps pressing button in futile attempt to make sound stop. She runs to van, fumbles it open, trying to tune out din, searches all over dashboard to find something to make it stop. Sister finds an electrical outlet knob, pulls it out, and sound, mercifully, disappears. … Louise has not pressed button for last 10 months.

July 12, 1:00 p.m. Baby Eric [almost 2] has been put in playpen for afternoon nap. Grandma, Anna [6] and Michael [4] arrange themselves on bed and floor mat for their siestas. Anna exclaims that she just loves being at Grandpa and Grandma's house and could stay here forever; she especially loves sleeping on the floor. Michael says he isn't going to sleep; he just wants to lie there and watch the hands on the clock move. Anna comments that they should stay here for at least 100 days. Michael, lip quivering, replies incredulously, "But that's a *WHOLE WEEK!*" Anna cheerfully informs him that it is, actually, longer than a week.

August 8, 9:40 p.m. Father and Mother are quietly reading the paper. Phone rings: Mike is calling from Williams Lake. He will be arriving at Victoria International Airport in 45 minutes; would they like to see his plane? He also mentions that patient is their friend of nearly fifty years who is coming to the Jubilee with heart problems. … Twinkling light off in distance rapidly transforms itself into elegant Learjet 31, touches down on tarmac, jets shrieking, and taxis near fence where parents stand. Pilot waves from cockpit, smiling, as he guides plane towards waiting ambulance. After getting permission from patient, asks ambulance personnel if parents can speak to patient. Parents have a quick visit with friend as he is transferred to waiting vehicle. … Parents drive to viewing spot near airport to watch Lear blast off for 12-minute flight to Vancouver. As jet disappears, parents are aware of peace and quiet of airfield. Only sounds are chirps of crickets and plaintive "kill-dees" of killdeer flying across the fields. Mother thinks of parents, grandparents, aunts and uncles who came to this area from the prairies nearly 85 years ago, and who lay buried in the Holy Trinity cemetery on the other side of the airfield, just blocks away from their first west coast homes. … As a child, Mother referred to the "Pat Bay Airport," and decides, upon return home, to research the airport on the internet. To her surprise, she learns that the airport, after serving as an air force base since 1940, became an international airport as recently as 1959. Her family would have had access to the huge field for many years before it became an airfield. Mother also learns that during World War II, 10,000 servicemen were trained at Pat Bay, with 100 losing their lives in training accidents.

Christmas Eve Good cheer fills Rendle living room as family open gifts after candlelight service.   Louise opens youngest son's gifts to her: gardening gloves, deluxe hose spray, a variety of handcrafted items from Ten Thousand Villages, chocolates, a gift certificate for 20 iTunes, and one last item that perplexes Mother, who turns to donor for explanation. Matthew turns the computer on his lap towards her, exposing image of computer desk at home, which appears to have a strange computer sitting on it.   Mother assumes Matt has superimposed computer photo over photo on laptop but he assures her that new computer is in fact sitting on computer table at home.   Unknown to easily-distracted parents, eldest and youngest sons managed to install upgrade computer, which had been downloading files from old computer in eldest son's room for a couple of days, when parents left early for church service. Webcam is relaying picture of iMac from Saanich Road to Murray Drive.

Chapter 51: A Christmas Digest, 2005

EDITORIAL *by Louise*

It is a typically damp, dull November evening on the West Coast, and the power-that-is has just suggested I get working on this year's Christmas letter. That is not really a problem, as, even though much has remained the same (daily provision for physical and spiritual needs from a faithful God, stimulating company of young people, myriad activities, an abundance of oak leaves on our property), the past year has brought many changes.

Bruce and I extend our love and best wishes for a blessed 2006 to those who patiently make their way through these paragraphs—the 40th Christmas letter to leave our home.

PERSONAL GLIMPSES

Marilyn and **Geordon** had a rocky beginning to 2005, with their return to Venezuela in January. The apartment they had hoped would be theirs did not materialize, so for several months they lived in another missionary family's apartment when that family returned temporarily to Texas. Not only were they living out of suitcases, with the owners' belongings all around them, but they had left Venezuela two years earlier with two children, and returned with four, two of whom were (are) tiny. They have been in their own apartment for a few months now, and are feeling more settled. Geordon's work with Youth for Christ International keeps him away from Caracas for days at a time, but he is very helpful with the children (even diapers), housework, cooking, etc., when he is home. And their maid, Eva, whose name is part of Jolyn Eva Marie's (as well as Great-Grandma Holland's), much to Eva's delight, provides help three times a week. Marilyn's administration skills are

RENDLE FAMILY

well-utilized, as she works with women's and youth study groups, organizes Geordon's schedule, oversees the family's financial affairs, provides music in a variety of settings, and keeps a close eye on the children and their activities. Political unrest in Venezuela may force their move to another South American country in the near future, as Geordon can handle many of his work responsibilities from anywhere in the world with conference calls and e-mail. In May, Geordon completed his Masters degree in Leadership and Training from Royal Roads University, e-mailing chapter after chapter of his thesis back to Canada for proofreading and

UNCLE MARK WITH RENDLE CHILDREN

input from his faculty advisor. Many hours, some very frustrating, were spent on this project, and Geordon is grateful to the mother of his children for her support at that time. (Geordon's comment: "AMEN!") He insisted that Marilyn join her sisters in Indianapolis in November for a few days of sister-bonding, and managed their household for 13 days without Mommy. **Jordan** [11] and **Joshua** [7] have readjusted to their respective classes at Academia Cristiana Internacional de Caracas. **Jolyn** [2] and **Joy** [1] bask in the adoration of their parents and big brothers. And Grandpa and Grandma miss them all. There are plans for some time in Victoria next June, after 18 months in the southern hemisphere.

MICHAEL ON THE ROAD

Michael's air ambulance job evaporated late in 2004, as his company went into bankruptcy. After a few weeks of driving for Pepsi-Cola this spring (12-hour night shifts, during which, as he says, he "resigned three times each shift"), he decided to take advantage of the opportunity to travel. Gearing himself up for any exigency, he took off on his motorcycle (a 1997 BMW R850R), travelling from Vancouver to Halifax, touching bases with friends along the way. After a few days in Halifax visiting with friends and Melissa, he headed south to

Indianapolis to hang out with Chris and Margaret, and was well on his way to California when he received an invitation for an interview with CanJet Airlines on September 9. With an abrupt, albeit welcome, change of plans, he made the more-than-3,500-kilometre trip from Independence, Missouri, to Vancouver in four days. Along the way, he received an interview date with Air Canada Jazz on September 4.

He has accepted a position flying the Boeing 737 with CanJet in Halifax, necessitating a coast-to-coast move, and recently completed ground school in Miami.

Margaret and **Chris** also experienced a major life change on October 19 when our fourth granddaughter, beautiful **Victoria Ann**, became the newest blossom on the family tree. Victoria was a little reluctant to enter

MARGARET AND CHRIS

this cold, unfamiliar world, and, as a result, her mother spent many hours in discomfort, and ended up with an emergency C-section. That unpleasantness is becoming a

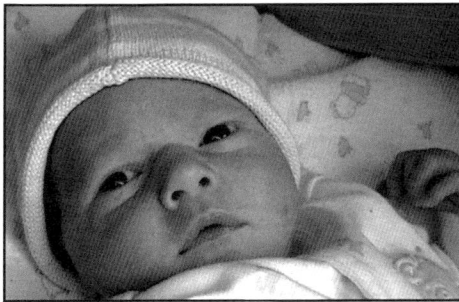

VICTORIA ANN BUCHER

distant memory, as little Tori gives much joy to her family, and Chris and Margaret can barely remember the time when they were on their own. Chris has put in fencing around their double lot: a tall wooden fence around the back half, and a wrought-iron one around the front half, greatly enhancing their old brick home. Chris continues his work as civil engineer with the highways department; he recently passed his Professional Engineering examinations. Margaret resigned from teaching in June, and is enjoying her new role as mother.

Melissa, still half-time youth pastor at First Baptist Church in Dartmouth, and half-time paediatric nurse at the IWK Health Centre in Halifax, continues to fill her days productively. We refer to her as our "Honeybee with Altitude" as she flies from project to project. In April and May, she accompanied another pastor and a social worker to the outskirts of Kenya for two weeks, visiting missionaries from her church and providing medical seminars. In July, after

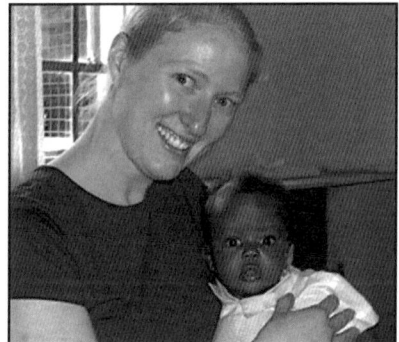

MELISSA IN KENYA

cheerfully hosting her parents for two extra days due to a fog-in, seeing them off at 6:00 a.m., and working an eight-hour shift at the hospital, she flew out to London in the evening, just after the first bombings, and on to Croatia and Bulgaria, to liaise with other camp workers in the European Baptist Union. In August, she travelled with brother Mark and another youth worker to inner-city Boston with her junior high group. Mark's videos highlight the young people's activities with children, and their satisfaction with their accomplishments.

Melody and **Richard** and their brood continue to lead busy lives. Richard has moved into the position of sales manager at Level Ground Trading. Melody works as bookkeeper at La-Z-Boy two days a week, and **Eric** [3] keeps the grandparents company during those days. Melody also helps with a piano class each

STARK FAMILY

week, and assists with her mother's Regal and plant projects. **Anna** [8] and **Michael** [6] join Grandma each week for piano lessons, play soccer, and participate in BMX racing. Richard and Melody have just completed a major kitchen renovation, resulting in much more efficient use of their kitchen area.

Mark's travel record almost matches Melissa's, as he has been capturing and editing reams of video in several settings. Last December, he went to Colombia for two weeks with brother-in-law Richard and Level Ground's CEO, Hugo Ciro. He spent the early weeks of 2005 producing both long and short versions of Level Ground's coffee-growing activities in Los Andes, Colombia, and its implementation

MARK IN BOSTON

of fair trade. March to May found him in Caracas, Venezuela, living with a Venezuelan family and with sister Marilyn, trying to learn as much Spanish as he could, and interacting with young people with whom he has worked on Project Serves over the years. Posters advertising his videography seminar were beamed back to Victoria for his family's interest. After visiting Chris and Margaret in Indiana, he accompanied Melissa and her youth group from Halifax to Boston, producing a couple of videos, one for the church and another for the youth group. He also spent a week in August filling in as videographer at Camp Qwanoes. More recently, he coached the Senior Boys volleyball team from Pacific Christian School, guiding them to city and island championships and on to the provincials.

Matthew spends a lot of time in front of the computer, both at home and at work. He has completed three years at Level Ground, working up an order management system for the company, and troubleshooting when computer problems arise. He participates in roller hockey, floor hockey and softball, sometimes with Mark and Steve. He and Mark still batch in the upstairs suite and we have the privilege of their company for supper

MATT CELEBRATING HIS BIRTHDAY

most evenings. Matthew joined Mark behind video monitors for our church's four Christmas concert performances, providing a constant flow of images to the large screen suspended over the stage.

Bruce and **Louise** thank God for good health and the opportunity to enjoy family, church and business activities. Bruce retains his status as chef *par excellence*, and Louise works with many music students, pots and sells plants in support of youth work in several settings, and has ridden, with Bruce, the Regal roller-coaster, as, after 77 years, the Regal Greetings & Gifts company went into receivership on August 3. Although Louise had, as a teenager, sold Regal products door-to-door, the Regal business had been Melody's for 18 years, starting with a catalogue distribution on her paper-route when she was eleven years old. With the pressures of three small children and a part-time job, she handed the business over to her parents almost two years ago, and they maintained it as one of the more active Regal businesses on the Island. After purchasing 1,000 catalogues on August 2, they were dumbfounded to learn of the company's bankruptcy a day later. The warehouse was closed for August and September, and re-opened for the month of October, during which time many Regal products, and new customers, were acquired as stock was liquidated. For the month of November, large shipments were received from the main warehouse in Mississauga, and now that, too, has closed. It is strange, and yet freeing, to see this chapter of our lives coming to an end.

SEEN AND HEARD …

… Michael [6 in September, and new at BMX racing] deliberately waiting until competitors have started; taking after and passing them … Louise snapping wooden handle of her favourite shovel, wondering if it's a sign she should give up her plants project; deciding, after 7.5 seconds of contemplation, that the answer is no (is presented with shiny new shovel a few days later by partner-in-yardwork) ... a wooden seagull from Nova Scotia, attached to top of gate, spinning its wings in the breeze; giving new meaning to the expression "getting nowhere fast" ... four-year-old student's description of his music teacher: "She has white hair at the front, black hair at the back, and wears pretty dresses with flowers all over them." ... Louise, wearing one of her two-part "pretty dresses," startled, as the skirt suddenly dropped to her ankles, though not half as startled as her piano student (thankfully a woman, who also dissolved into gales of laughter) ... skirt ascending even faster than it had descended, and safety pin ensuring it stayed there ... Steve Morrison, our boarder and friend of many years, receiving his Bachelors degree from UVic in May, a tribute to much effort and perseverance ... Joshua, enjoying a pajama party with father Geordon in the hospital in Caracas after an emergency appendectomy, and, a couple of days later, taking part in a school play, where the cast landed on top of him; his mother, on the verge of a heart attack, relieved to see him emerge from the pile of bodies none the worse for the experience ... gas price in Caracas: less than 5 cents Canadian a litre; graffiti on city walls: "Gringos go home" ... Bruce and Louise spending nine hours overnight in Newark airport, trying to sleep on chairs with interlinked arms which could not be made into any semblance of a bed, at end of 24-hour trip from Indianapolis to Halifax ... Grandma, in Victoria, examining grandson Jordan, in Caracas, at the Grade V Piano level, via webcam; faxing his results to him a few minutes after test ... Kassi Lloyd, our newest boarder, from Port Alberni, driving back and forth over the Malahat from one home to the other, experiencing a steep learning curve as she adjusts both to her new living environment, and to the demands of university ... enthusiastic comment from mother of young person in Melissa's youth group to Mark, after viewing video of Halifax youth group mission to inner-city Boston: "Mark, ... you have a gift for 'capturing the moment.'" ... Newly-found scrap of paper on which the following is written: **May 4, 1976, 8:45 a.m.** Mother is practising the violin with Margaret. She notes Michael out of corner of eye, holding organ lesson notebook and pen. Suggests sternly that Michael put book down. **May 5, 1976, 10:00 a.m.** Mother is at organ lesson. Teacher opens notebook to record assignment, says, "I see someone has written you a note." Mother looks, sees Grade One printing: "I love you m," feels like 1 1/2 cents. (Mother has located assignment book with printing, still feels remorseful almost 30 years later!) ... In mid-November, Aunts Marilyn (from Caracas), Melissa (from Dartmouth), and Melody (from Victoria), descending on sister Margaret (in Indianapolis) to check out their newest niece, visit, and give advice to the new mother (Grandmother's counsel to her three travellers was to be sure their hostess got enough rest, but she suspects that did not happen.) ... Angela Alba, in fourth-year piano performance at UVic, filling the house with the beautiful sounds of Bach, Beethoven, Rachmaninov, and other masters of music … Little Jolyn "feeding" her doll the same way Mommy is

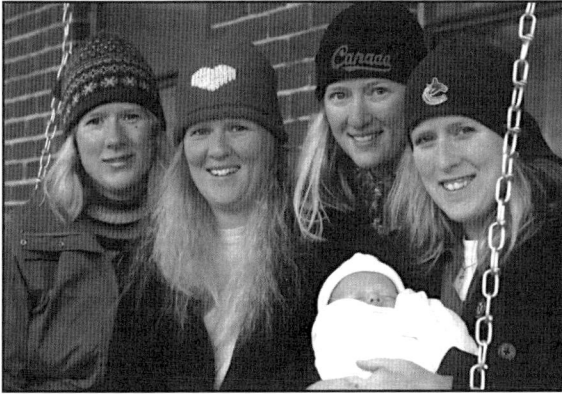

A NEW MOTHER, THREE AUNTIES, AND BABY VICTORIA

feeding baby Joy; reminding grandmother of similar scenario 36 years ago, as recorded in 1969 letter … Grandson Michael (then 5) telling the Emergency Room doctor that he was hit by "Chinese wood" (He had, while running from living room to kitchen, slipped on the hardwood floor, and crashed into the china cabinet.) … Jordan and Joshua receiving an offer of a substantial discount on their tuition at an international school in Buenos Aires, should they move to Argentina, a partial confirmation of a move the family is considering … Little Eric reminding his grandparents that it is his naptime, bounding off to a playpen where he beds down for a couple of hours … Louise emerging through a crowd milling around inside the Victoria court-house, eyes straight ahead, after hearing welcome message from court clerk that she is dismissed from jury duty, set to begin just as her September classes were scheduled to start; nervous that someone might have a change of heart and call her back, relieved that six weeks of uncertainty are over … Mike's description of his first landing in a Boeing 737: "A passable first landing, we will live, and the aircraft can be used again." … Grandma Holland, at 98, enjoying her son's birthday party in October; Auntie Marilyn providing a beautiful luncheon in honour of her big brother … redwing blackbirds joining their smaller cousins at the bird feeder, unwelcome but very beautiful … Richard, installing weatherstripping around back door, in response to plea from father-in-law, who has just received $600 and $800 oil bills … Anna, Michael, and Eric spending hours in their cardboard playhouse (a large stove box acquired from a neighbour by their grandfather) … Mark, way out of his comfort zone, speaking to an attentive women's mission group at our church about his experiences in South America, and showing some of his

ERIC, MICHAEL, ANNA

video work … Mike and Matt enjoying each other's company on a trip to Seattle to

MATT AND MIKE

watch the Seattle Mariners baseball team … discovery that Great-Grandma Forsberg (Louise's grandmother, named Lovisa) was born on March 25, 1880, in Sweden, and Great-Grandma Taylor (Bruce's grandmother) was born March 25, 1880, in Ontario; similar to discovery over 40 years ago that both Holland and Forsberg parents shared the same wedding date, December 21, which became their children's wedding date as well … sister revealing at Sunday lunch that a comment card evaluating the church Christmas concerts referred to those "precious camera-men"; brothers saying, "Thanks, Mom," and Mother stating that while she is capable of writing such sentiments, she didn't … Eric accompanying Grandpa to the daily fill up of the bird feeders, partly in an effort to distract him from mother's departure for work …

LIFE'S LIKE THIS

Saturday, December 10 Grandmother is in living room, pricing dozens of Regal products for upcoming sale, babysitting youngest grandson, who has amiably been arranging items in boxes, "helping" Grandma. Grandma suggests he get into pajamas, and he proceeds to get changed for bed: "*Don't wook*, Grandma!" Grandma says she won't "wook," continues printing labels, musing on child's sense of modesty. Suddenly grandson exclaims, "WOOK, Grandma!" Grandma looks, expecting to see little body covered in flannelette; is taken aback to see both clothes *and* pajamas on carpet, and young cherub clapping with delight … Experience projects grandmother 22 years backwards, as she remembers a couple of Christmas letter entries involving a young child of exactly the same age and gender, who replaced "l" with "w", and who enjoyed the summer sun and refreshing water sprinkler, *au naturel* (Christmas Digest, 1983).

Afterword: First Edition

Late August 2006

I am sitting in our family room. The Indian plum trees outside the window radiate green and gold as the sun shines through them. Chickadees, sparrows, nuthatches, downy woodpeckers and purple finches flit from trees to feeders to fence, gorging on seeds and suet. Golden *rudbeckia* and crimson, yellow and orange *crocosmia* fill pots throughout the yard, and the Grandpa Ott morning glory glows in sapphire and ruby tones as it climbs toward the sun. Bruce has gone out to assist his recently-widowed aunt, and I am alone with my thoughts.

Over the past several months, not only have I been immersed in the thousands of words which precede these, and the memories and emotions which they prompt, but I have reread my mother's autobiography and sifted through hundreds of family photographs. I am reminded of my Danish grandmother's influence, especially her love of flowers, my mother's encouraging guidance, especially in the areas of music and education, and my father's sometimes nonconforming perspective towards life, and I am grateful for my heritage. I have, at times, to pull my thoughts away from the past and into the present.

This summer has been a wonderful family time. Geordon and Marilyn and their four children stayed with us for six weeks, a hiatus between their move from Venezuela to Argentina. Their presence here provided motivation for siblings to visit from Halifax (Michael, Melissa) and Indianapolis (Margaret and Chris, with baby Tori). For several days in mid-summer, fifteen of us shared

MARILYN AND MICHAEL ON PORCH OF PLAYHOUSE, 1972

these living quarters, with frequent visits from Melody's family, which brought the total to twenty—communal living at its best! In preparation for this influx, Richard and Melody renovated and repainted the backyard playhouse that Grandpa Holland built nearly 35 years ago out of scrap lumber from our first renovation. With curtains sewn by Auntie Shirley, and hanging baskets assembled by this generation's

Grandpa Holland, the little house provided a happy congregating place for the cousins. Jolyn [3] and Joy [nearly 2] often sat on the porch in small chairs, "watching the world go by." And Jolyn's exclamation, "This is my favourite house in the whole world!" made her aunt and uncle smile.

At the beginning of this book I referred to our stage of life as "The Best is Yet to Come." As Christians, we believe that is our longterm prospect. Yet in August of 2006, the immediate future beckons pleasantly, with our young boarders returning here to university and our home,

RENOVATED PLAYHOUSE, 2006

a full slate of music teaching, and a new cabin on Horne Lake (Bruce's dream come true), waiting to provide recreation and relaxation for family and friends.

My mother often spoke of lying awake at night, praying for her children and grandchildren. She has been gone four years now, and her mantle has passed on to me. I, thankfully, rarely suffer from insomnia, but during the day I often find myself pleading with our Heavenly Father

THE CABIN AT HORNE LAKE

to protect and guide my children and grandchildren in His ways.

And now—on to 2006's letter!

Louise

Chapter 52: A Christmas Digest, 2006

EDITORIAL *by Louise*

October 1 A flicker, passing through our area in migration, calls off in the distance. A Steller's jay, glistening in the sun, screeches just outside the window, intimidating the tiny bushtits, chickadees and nuthatches into keeping their distance. Oregon juncos, blackhooded, venture back into the feeding area, nibbling on seeds spilled from the bird feeders. Licorice ferns, prompted by the fall rains to throw up dozens of fresh new fronds, shine emerald-green in the October sun.   It is nearly Thanksgiving, and the fall sunshine bathes the yard with its benevolent warmth. And, predictably, the oak leaves have started carpeting the borders, sidewalks, driveway and grassy areas with their crunchy compost-to-be. It must be time to start yet another Christmas letter, the forty-first to leave this address.

2006 has been a year of special dates reached and goals met. The writer of this missive is still in a state of mild disbelief as she, starting in July, opens a welcome cheque from the government each month; her much better half also reached a milestone, as his seventh decade completed itself. And both peer back 45 years to their wedding ceremony, wondering at the swift passage of the intervening years, and thanking their Heavenly Father for His gracious oversight of those years. In

THE BEAUTY OF HORNE LAKE

preparation for an influx this summer of four family members and their families (Mike from Halifax, Melissa from Dartmouth; Margaret, Chris and Tori from Indianapolis; and Marilyn, Geordon, Jordan, Joshua, Jolyn and Joy from Caracas), the Victoria three (Melody and Richard, Mark, and Matt) assisted the parents in spiffying up the yard, and refurbishing the playhouse constructed by Great-Grandpa Holland 35 years ago. As well, the cabin at Horne Lake became a reality under the capable direction of contractor Brian Neufeld.

In June we said farewell to Angela Alba, who returned home to Prince George, and in August, to Steve Morrison, who has moved out on his own. In September we welcomed sister and brother, Charlene and Steve De Vries, from Duncan. Charlene is working towards a nursing degree at Camosun College, and Steve joins our other boarder, Kassi Lloyd, at UVic. Kassi's goal is medicine, and Steve's is opera, but he is backing that up with a degree in Music Education. Charlene plays flute (ARCT gold medal) and piano, and Steve plays violin and bass guitar, and sings with the university chorus and in Pacific Opera Victoria. So our house is still full of music!

At the back of a rarely-opened cupboard, I recently found a bag of nearly 100 letters written from me to my parents between 1963 to 1966, when Bruce was back at school, and I was teaching school in Vancouver. My mother had saved them for me, but I do not remember rereading them during the past 40 years. So that I did. It was a strange experience to picture myself at an age younger than any of my daughters are now. These letters would not have been written if phone rates had not been, comparatively, so high. In one letter I comment that Bruce says I should write a letter, and not phone; in another, I refer to my sister, also living in Vancouver at the time, as an "extravaganza" because I learned she had phoned home to Victoria! My daughters were impressed that I actually played second-base and pitched in a baseball league, and that I used to do most of the cooking (these were pre-children and pre-violin days), and much sewing (this was before my mother took over as family seamstress, sewing both for me and for her four granddaughters). As youth sponsor, I was required to join a team for a pie-eating contest. The team had to consume a whole pie a bite at a time, with hands behind backs; I had seven turns. (Knowing my propensity for "germlessness," my family was amused by this account.) And here is a description of my first driver's test: "May 3, 1964. I'm quite proud of my driver's license. After all, it's not everyone who can get one in only 6 3/4 years! [I was 22 3/4.] My examiner was the crabby one who had failed Lillian [another primary teacher] the first time, and he didn't smile the whole time. I got so rattled after I got parked on a hill (couldn't get going, car got stalled three times— something to do with the emergency brake) that he told me to take my hands and feet away from the controls ('Please, Mrs. Holland, PLEASE, Mrs. Holland'), and gave me a talking-to about how well I was doing and that I shouldn't be nervous, etc., etc., so I guess he wasn't completely inhuman after all. I took the exam at 4:30

[in Vancouver traffic]."

November 27 SNOW—lots of it! How beautiful! How treacherous! Several inches have fallen on Lotus Land (a.k.a. Victoria), paralyzing traffic and precipitating many fender-benders. Tree branches litter the ground; Matt's car has skewed itself across the driveway, blocking the family car—no great problem, as neither parent would be so foolish as to attempt leaving the property today. Music students are calling to say they will not be able to make their lessons. It seems an appropriate time to get back to this year's Christmas letter. We extend our wishes to you for a happy Christmas and a New Year filled with God's blessing.

BRUCE AND LOUISE

PERSONAL GLIMPSES

Bruce and **Louise** continue in their respective professions (social work and music teaching), although Bruce, theoretically, has been retired for nine years. Bruce is out almost every day, assisting family and friends and/or shopping for the large meals that he serves most evenings. Louise teaches approximately 20 hours a week, which allows time for digging, composting, potting up plants for sale, often in the early hours of the day, and managing the dwindling Regal inventory. Both are grateful for their association with Central Baptist Church and the opportunities presented for service and spiritual growth.

Geordon and **Marilyn** have settled well into their new home and Youth for Christ work in Buenos Aires, Argentina, and are

RENDLE FAMILY

re-acquainting themselves with the contents of the container they left in Caracas, Venezuela, several months earlier. After an anxious first week or two, **Jordan** [12] and **Joshua** [8 1/2] have adjusted happily to their new school, Asociación Escuelas Lincoln, and **Jolyn** [3], and **Joy** [2] keep their parents busy and entertained. Jordan completed Grade VI piano, and Rudiments I this year, and Joshua finished the Grade II level. Jolyn possesses the strongest will that her grandparents and parents have experienced. The following was written while Geordon and

JOLYN

Marilyn were away for a five-day staff conference in Princeton and the Holland grandparents were holding the fort: "… Jolyn is very strong-willed and independent.   Today, after an unhappy episode, I [Grandma] asked her if Daddy ever got cross with her: 'Yep.' Mommy? 'Yep.' Both affirmatives were followed by a melt-you smile! She and Joy sing much of the time, and usually play well together. When Joy cries for no apparent reason, Jolyn will announce, 'I hit Joy.' Joy just loves 'Jojo,' and continually mimics her. … Last night I told Jolyn she couldn't wear her flannelette pajamas to bed [temperature was in

JOY

high 20s], so she talked Jordie into helping her get them on. She had the grace to look guilty when I commented on the situation, and poor Jordie felt badly; he didn't know I had said no. I wanted to take them off (long sleeves, long legs, neck as high as it can go; thick, waist-length hair), but she set up such a howl I couldn't. Before I went to bed, I checked up on the girls, and the

JORDAN AND JOSHUA

pajamas were damp with perspiration, so off they came while Jolyn was asleep. Both girls slept in diapers only, and, in the heat of the upstairs bedroom, that was enough. Her father says Jolyn will be the CEO of a large company, and the rest of the family will work for her!"

Michael leaves in early January for Dubai, United Arab Emirates, where he will fly the Boeing 777 as First Officer. His family is aware of the tremendous hurdles he has overcome to reach this goal, and are very proud of his determination and tenacity—and thankful for his abilities.

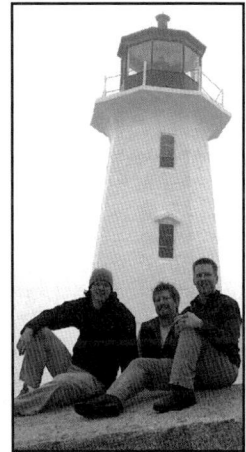

MARK, MATT, MIKE

Chris and **Margaret** and little **Victoria** [1 in October] will join us from Indianapolis for the holidays on the 26th, and our family Christmas meal is scheduled for the 27th. In a few months, Tori becomes "Big Sister," as a second twig or blossom is added to the American branch of the family tree. Her mother now has dual citizenship, as she was sworn in as an American citizen a few months ago, in the supportive company of her husband and

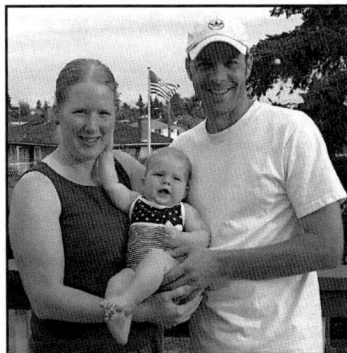

CHRIS, MARGARET, TORI

parents-in-law. Margaret has become an enthusiastic member of the MOPS (Mothers of Preschoolers) group of her church. Since March, Chris has been enjoying his new job as a bridge inspector/construction project manager with The Schneider Corporation, a private civil engineering consulting firm.

TORI

MELISSA

Melissa continues to maintain a split schedule, nursing half time in the children's ward in Halifax, and serving as half time youth pastor in her church in Dartmouth. With the resignation of the other half of the pastoral team, she is attempting to maintain the youth programme on her own, with volunteer help, until the church can find a full time youth worker. Her plans beyond that point are nebulous, but we would not be unhappy to see her return to this side of the continent. Her trip to Caracas in August with eight of her high school young people was a highlight of her year. She and Marilyn played their violins at the top of Mt. Sion, grateful to the young people who cheerfully carried not only the violins, but also little Jolyn and Joy, up the mountain.

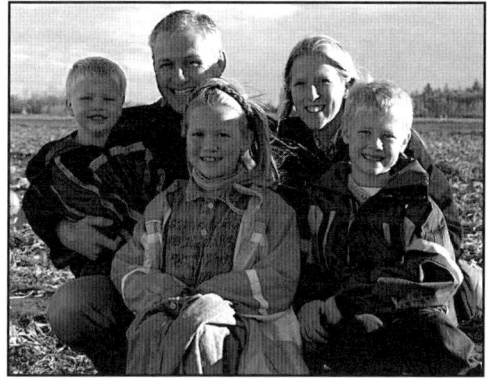

STARK FAMILY

Richard and **Melody** and children help Mark and Matt keep an eye on the family homestead in Victoria, and the new cabin at Horne Lake. Rick, handyman extraordinaire, generously takes on fix-it projects here and at the lake; Melody utilizes her considerable organizational skills both in her own home, and her parents'. Rick continues as sales manager at Level Ground Trading, and is gratified to be part of a growing business. **Anna** [9] and **Michael** [7] take piano lessons with Grandma each week, and **Eric** [4] occasionally comes to visit Grandpa and Grandma, but not so frequently now, as his mother works from home. Last year's Christmas letter ended with a story which included Eric's exclamation: "*Wook*, Grandma!" Early this year, Grandma wrote to his mother at work: "Eric just decided he would like to put that artificial poinsettia on the table. I said that was OK, so he removed the candles from the ceramic tray—Grandma helped

ERIC

when she heard the clinking of glass against pottery—and set the bright red flower, flanked by fuchsia-coloured candles on either side, in the centre of the (mainly mauve) tray.   Clapping his hands, he said, 'People eat – eat – eat, and *wook – wook – wook!*' I imagine so!"

Mark is back at school, working on the third year of a degree in geography at UVic. With a certificate from Vancouver Film School, a diploma from Camosun College (Criminal Justice), and several forays into Latin America in his background, he may have trouble figuring out his course of action when he graduates in 2008.   Using his skills in photography, he has made striking posters of unique buildings in downtown Victoria for a class project. He spent four months this spring at Capernwray Bible School in Costa Rica, working

MARK

on his Spanish and studying Scripture. As has become his habit, he made up a DVD of his experiences in Latin America, including the trip he and other students made into the jungle to help refurbish a school and build some additional classrooms. He accompanied Melissa and her group of high school students to Caracas in August, a different experience for them both, as Geordon and Marilyn were now in Argentina.

Matthew is completing his fourth year at Level Ground Trading, working in the area of computer technology, and troubleshooting computer problems. He has spent many hours this fall assembling his mother's manuscripts into book format, patiently enduring yet another revision and yet another photo. He and Mark take a break from their back-to-back computers by playing floor and roller hockey, and volleyball. In August, he accompanied Mark to Halifax to visit with Mike and Melissa, as Mark worked with Melissa on preplanning the Caracas trip. He joined Richard and Mark for three days of staining the cabin at Horne Lake, and has worked on several other

TOGETHER AGAIN

cabin-related projects.   Living under the same roof as we do, but quite separately from us, our two youngest sons are very good company for their parents, and for the other young people who share our home.

SCENE IN PASSING ...

… newest member of family dragging his master up hill and down dale, at the end of a leash: Shadow, a year-old black American spaniel, Louise's gift to Bruce, and the first dog to share this property with us in 40 years … Michael's description of his 2005 Christmas: "Christmas was actually very enjoyable all things considered. I had a nice evening with Melissa before she left, went to the *Messiah* and then opened a few presents. I worked from the 23rd to the 27th, spending the nights of the 24th and 25th in Toronto. It was a lot of fun; if I hadn't been working I would have just been home alone, but I had a really good crew and we made the best of it. The captain, about my age, had bought us all Santa hats (two pilots + three flight attendants). So we wore those all day. Try to picture five elves in airline uniforms parading through Toronto's Pearson airport. The security folks loved it, and it sure makes it easier to stick together as a group when you can see red hats bobbing along in a crowd. One thing I have always liked about aviation is that by and large the people in the industry are usually pretty interesting. Not always easy to get along with, mind you, but rarely dull." ... Great-Grandma Holland celebrating her 99th birthday in the company of children, Shirley (and Jack), Bruce (and Louise), and Marilyn ... Louise, proofreading Mark's essay on "elites" (those who set the agendas in politics, business, etc.), and deciding she and Bruce do not belong in that group ... Margaret regarding plastic surgeon with some apprehension, as he meticulously, and successfully, removes "beauty spot" mole from below her left eye ... Melissa, working in her garden, assisted by a couple of young people from her youth group who had been expelled

AUNTIE MELISSA WITH
JOSHUA, JORDAN AND ERIC

from school temporarily; Melissa in court, trying to support several young people who are there for drug, robbery, and vandalism charges, but who seem to value the youth programme at her church; Melissa and Mark and Halifax youth group stranded in New York overnight, just when the Orange and Red Alerts came into effect ... a new book made up of 40 years of Christmas letters, *"Hey, there's no violin in this case!"*, a gift to seven wonderful children and their extraordinary father ... Matt painstakingly formatting that book; Mark filling a violin case with family photos to produce a cover ... Jolyn in the raspberry patch with her cousins: "I picked just the red ones, not the greem ones." ... a story compiled by Joshua's Grade 2 class in Caracas, starring two main characters, named by Joshua: a little boy, Mark, and a dog, Matt (Joshua's mother commented to her two youngest brothers,

JORDAN

JOSHUA

"You are loved.") ... Mark digging out grass and weeds in area around play house, sifting soil for Mother's use, shovelling many wheelbarrow loads of clean pea gravel over area ... Wild Easter lilies blooming in their usual spot on one side of our fence;

JOLYN AND JOY

chocolate lilies decorating a secret place on the other side, behind an Indian plum shrub—probably there, unnoticed, for the last 40+ years ... Rendle and Stark cousins furiously pedalling their little bikes and trikes around and around on the concrete pad beside the play house ... Marilyn welcoming her Qwanoes camp director of 26 years ago, Janet "Thumper" Anderson, to Caracas, where a team from Qwanoes has come to observe camping, Latin American style (Mother's mind returns to that summer, when eldest daughter, then 12, unexpectedly was required to learn the 55-page accompaniment for a camp cantata in the few days before camp, notching up her sight reading skills several degrees in the process, and giving her the confidence to accompany Central's senior choir for the "Hallelujah Chorus" that December.   Mother also remembers that daughter, the youngest in that senior camp, and the only camper capable of managing the piano accompaniment, was also the only camper who failed the swim test.   That fall, with characteristic resolve, Marilyn joined little

MICHAEL   ANNA

beginners for swimming lessons, quickly moving through the different levels. Her mother proudly recalls her sitting serenely on the edge of the pool with her much-younger classmates, determined to become a swimmer.) ... Camp Qwanoes marking its 40th anniversary in a joyful celebration which filled Central, and included footage from the 1966 camp session where Bruce, as the camp's first cook in a very rustic setting, is seen ringing the dinner bell, and serving food ... Margaret's description of our tiny fourth granddaughter's antics: "On the way home from Chris's

TORI

grandparents, she started playing peek-a-boo by herself—pulling her blanket verrrrryyy sllowwly down her face until just her eyes were peeking over. We'd say, 'There you are!' or 'Peek-a-boo!' and she'd burst into big smiles and giggles.   So cute!" (And the distance between Victoria and Indianapolis widens.) ... bittersweet farewell to family trailer as young family from up-Island purchases 29-year-old vehicle, delighted with its condition (thanks to Richard's and Melody's efforts); parents thankful that nine-year-old violinist and seven-year-old pianist, and their parents, will enjoy the little house on wheels ...

Chapter 53: A Christmas Digest, 2007

EDITORIAL *by Louise*

October 20 I sit in the tranquil coziness of our cabin at Horne Lake, disturbed only by the ticking of a clock, the gentle lapping of the lake against the shore a few yards

GRANDMA OLIVE HOLLAND ON HER 100TH BIRTHDAY

in front of our shelter, and the scratching of a leaf rake, as Bruce gathers up golden leaves released by the broadleaf maples that glow throughout the more sombre firs and cedars. It is easy to feel near to our Creator-God in such idyllic surroundings, and the old hymn "How Great Thou Art" is never far from my thinking.

This year (June 16), Bruce lost his loving mother, Olive Eva Holland, I lost a wonderful mother-in-law, and our children lost a great friend and supporter. Olive was 100 on March 26, and had lived a full and productive life, thanks in large part to the faithful care of her daughter, Marilyn, for nearly 25 years. It was Melody's, Mark's, and Matthew's privilege to play Grandma's favourite hymn "In the Garden" on their violins at her memorial service. My mother-in-law was a gracious, highly-principled woman who made a huge impact on our family, and we thank God for giving her to us.

We were also saddened in recent months by the sudden deaths of two cousins, both in their 30s: Eric Scriver, my sister Harriet's son; and Joseph Barlow, my sister Peggy's stepson.

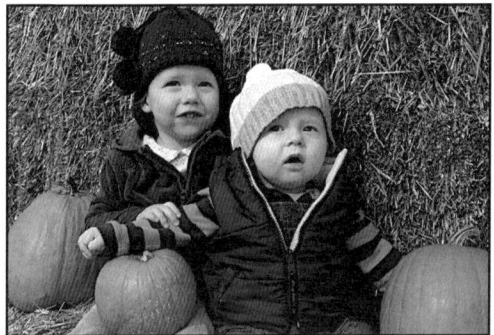

TORI AND JONATHAN

Members of our family crisscrossed at least two continents in 2007: Louise to keep Margaret company in Indianapolis for two weeks after the birth of her second child in March; Bruce and Louise to Buenos Aires for nearly three weeks with

Rendle Grandchildren

Marilyn and her family at the end of August (travelling on Geordon's air miles); Michael back and forth from Dubai to the Maritimes several times to visit his sister and friends; Melissa to Argentina with a team of 15 young people for two weeks; Matthew to South America, with Hugo Ciro, to learn more about the sources of Level Ground Trading's coffees and dried fruits, with a nine-day stopover in Buenos Aires on his way back; Mark to Indianapolis during reading break in November; and Melody and her family to Buenos Aires for several weeks at Christmas. According to a high-end tourist magazine *Condé Nast*, the most favourable tourist cities in the Americas are Vancouver (3rd), Victoria (2nd), and Buenos Aires (1st). Having lived in or visited all three cities, we would have to concur with these evaluations; Buenos Aires is indeed interesting and beautiful.

November 28 Bruce and Melody spent the last week of October in Halifax, in surprise visits to Melissa. Realizing that Melissa would probably appreciate family support in her time of transition, Marilyn arranged, via Geordon's air miles, to send her father and sister to be with Melissa during her last "official" week as nurse and youth pastor. Melissa was, of course,

Stark Grandchildren

delighted to greet first her father, then her sister a day later, and they were happy to be able to help her with her packing. The church honoured Melissa in several settings, the first of which was a seniors' tea where she had been asked to play her violin. Her friend, who had picked up her father from the airport, decided it would be wise to let Melissa find out that her father was in the audience before, rather than during, her performance.

PERSONAL GLIMPSES

Geordon and **Marilyn** are into their second year in Buenos Aires, and are grateful both for the service opportunities that have opened up in that

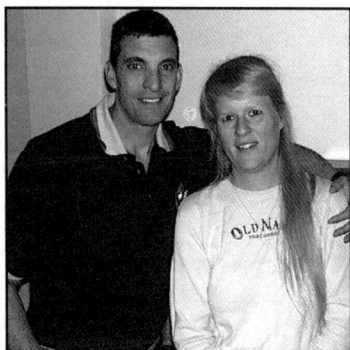
Geordon and Marilyn

city, and for the more agreeable setting for bringing up their family. Geordon travels thousands of miles each quarter, touching bases with Youth for Christ national directors and programmes in several Latin American countries, while Marilyn supervises a household of four young children plus two young people who live with the family and work with them in their ministries: Halima O'Brien from Central Baptist in Victoria (September 2006–June 2007) and Shauna Brown from Cloverdale (September 2007–June 2008). (Shauna is the daughter of Brian and Betty Brown, Geordon and Marilyn's mentors from over twenty years ago.) This is in addition to hosting the teams of young people who come to assist in their work. Marilyn works as one of Geordon's administrative assistants on a half-time basis, and shares leadership of the youth group at their church. She also keeps an eye on **Jordan**'s and **Joshua**'s musical development, with a small assist from her children's grandmother via video chat on the computer. (Never would Grandma have thought ten years ago that she would be giving piano lessons to students a continent and a half away!) In addition to hosting several other guests and the family members mentioned above, the Rendles were able to enjoy time with both sets of grandparents in one year as Don and Sharon Rendle travelled to Argentina for a couple of weeks in November. Geordon had a difficult experience a few weeks ago when his back pack

MIKE AND BOEING 777

was stolen. Although running shoes, credit cards, shaver, etc., were taken, he was most distressed by the theft of his journal, and of his mother's well-read and marked Bible. (November 25th marked the tenth anniversary of Georgia's death.) We are thankful that no physical harm was done and that the family continues to be blessed with good health and safety.

After a strenuous and challenging three months of training on the 777, **Michael** has been flying out of Dubai for several months now, revelling in his more flexible timetable and also in the attractive income he finally is receiving. His long flights (some 14 hours) are counter-balanced by days off where he is able to fly back to Canada, usually the east coast, for visits. He enjoyed Melissa's two-week stay in November.

Chris and **Margaret** and little **Victoria** (Tori) welcomed sweet, good-natured brother **Jonathan Clark** into their home in March. Chris is currently acting engineer for the city of Shelbyville, 40 miles south of Indianapolis, and Margaret maintains a warm, loving home for her three. The Bucher family has been very concerned over Chris's sister Leslie's recent surgery, when what was thought to be "only" a sinus polyp actually turned out to be hiding a substantial cancerous tumour that narrowly missed her brain. (Leslie is the sister who suggested to her big brother six years ago that he marry Margaret, whom he described as "Miss Perfect" up in Canada, with her "igloos and walrus hides"). A ten-hour operation appears to have been successful, but there will still be much recuperation and therapy in the future.

MARGARET, TORI, CHRIS, JONATHAN

Melissa is readjusting to life on the

MELISSA

West Coast, as she has left hospital, church, house, and, most important, friends and colleagues in Nova Scotia, to pursue a new course. 2007 found her accompanying young people to youth retreats in New Brunswick and PEI, to an orphanage in Kenya, and to a slum area in Buenos Aires. She will probably work in paediatrics here until she gets her bearings. Needless to say, her family is very pleased at the prospect of seeing more of Melissa.

Richard and **Melody** have capped a busy and productive year with a five-week session in the sun. They arrived in Buenos Aires on Melody's birthday (December 5), after nearly 30 hours in transit. Richard, as sales manager at Level Ground Trading, has had a part in the company's growth this year, and Melody has her perspective on life expanded as she types out transcripts of interviews. **Anna** [10, in Grade 5] is becoming a lovely young lady who enjoys her music, reading to her brothers, **Michael** [8, in Grade 3] and **Eric** [5, in Kindergarten], and soccer. Her brothers also play soccer and Grandma is privileged to have a session with all three of them each week for music.

STARK FAMILY

Mark reached a milestone birthday this year, completing his third decade. In his final year of a bachelor's programme at UVic, he is considering various options. His heart is in Third World development, working with those less fortunate. On weekends during the school year, he serves as a custom's officer at the Canadian-American border, and he works on video projects as time allows. Mark enjoyed his trip to Indianapolis, visiting with sister Margaret and brother-in-law Chris and observing niece Tori's latest gross motor skill development—the gallop, and baby nephew Jonathan's favourite pastime—the jolly jumper! Margaret and Chris were thrilled that Mark was able to experience a few of these fleeting, precious moments with them.

MARK AND NEPHEW JONATHAN

MATT

Matt is completing five years with Level Ground Trading where part of his job description, according to him, is to "keep things running" in the computer area. Every so often he gets a distress call at work from home, and his parents watch with fascination as their computer responds to his commands from miles away; usually the problem is solved in a matter of seconds. He enjoyed his weeks in Colombia and Bolivia, becoming more informed about Level Ground's work in those countries, and his side-trip to Argentina and Uruguay, where he visited with his eldest sister and her family.

With Great-Grandma's passing, **Bruce** and **Louise** have become the "older" generation, but are still enjoying their respective activities: Bruce as Grandpa, Dad, chief shopper and cook, and companion/counsellor to elderly friends, and Louise as Grandma, Mom, piano teacher, potter of plants, and manager of the family's little businesses. They extend a wish for God's blessing in 2008 to their acquaintances, friends and family.

LIFE'S LIKE THIS

March 18 Mother is packing for 12 days in Indianapolis, where she will help Margaret, Chris and Tori after the birth of Jonathan on March 12. Packs warmer slacks and blouses, sweater and mittens in preparation for cold Midwest March. Is pleased that summer heat and humidity will not be the problem it has been on other visits. As an after-

JONATHAN

thought, throws in cotton T-shirt and slacks in case rain and snow allow her to work in the yard. ... **March 19** After arrival in Indianapolis, learns that Indianapolis is in the throes of a record-breaking heat wave—30 degrees Fahrenheit above normal March's 30s and 40s. ... Spends free time making three garden beds, layering leaves and kitchen trimmings conscientiously saved in containers through winter by son-in-law and daughter, with heavy clay soil. Digging activities confined to daybreak and dusk. Son-in-law activates air conditioner indoors to keep mother-in-law comfortable.

July 30 Mother and Father are watching second-last play-off roller hockey game, a little tense. The teams are well-matched, and Mark and Matt's team may not come out on top. If the Pilons win this game, they will receive cup; if not, a third game will decide their fate. ... Outcome in overtime is 7 to 6, in the opposing team's favour. ... **July 31** Mother and Father are again at rink side, Mother especially nervous with well-padded bodies hurtling against each other and at protective plexiglass around rink, and the excitement of a close game. Pilons take an early lead, and Mother relaxes. ... Game heats up as opponents score several goals; parents a little apprehensive. ... In last five minutes of third period, opposing team scores to tie game, which thrusts weary teams into overtime. 40 seconds into overtime, sudden goal brings explosion from opponents' fans; Pilons droop in disappointment as championship evaporates. ... Parents congratulate exhausted, perspiring sons on excellent match and leave arena for less stimulating projects.

December 3, 11:00 p.m. Parents head for bed, after setting three alarm clocks of dubious reliability for 4:15 a.m. Starks must be out at airport by 5:00 a.m. for flights to Argentina. As is her custom, Mother tosses and turns, wide-awake, wondering if at least one alarm will wake them up, praying for safety of precious son-in-law, daughter, and grandchildren as they leave on exciting adventure, and listening to incessant downpour on roof. Cannot get rid of "Let It Snow! Let It Snow! Let It Snow!" which she had been sharing with older student earlier in evening. Extra arpeggiation, grace-notes, and altered rhythms and harmonies run through her mind. Water cascades over edge of eavestrough just outside bedroom window, clattering onto concrete below. Mother finally drifts towards sleep, is jolted back into consciousness by wailing of sirens and thundering of emergency vehicles. Fire trucks roar into night a block away on McKenzie Avenue. Ten minutes of shrieking sirens and honking horns do nothing for Mother's insomnia; Mother sure she can smell smoke through open window. Rain decreases. Mother, owl-eyed, tries unsuccessfully to sleep. **1:55 a.m.** Mother hears movement in other side of upstairs, realizes son must be toiling away at essay. Dons dressing-gown and slippers, pads through door to suite, discovers son has just finished essay and would appreciate proof reading. Son e-mails essay downstairs, where Mother prints it off, spends next half hour learning about Bolivia's indigenous people and their economic struggles, and the role of deforestation in those struggles. **2:30 a.m.** Mother returns to bed where Father, as is his habit, continues to sleep peacefully beside her. Mother listens to patter of rain on roof, checks clocks at regular intervals, startles out of bed as first of three clocks rings alarm at 4:00 a.m. ... Phones daughter, who is just waking up as well, and day is underway.

SEEN AND HEARD ...

... glittering red and silver earrings for Grandma, a gift from Anna, one which Grandma will wear with pleasure (Anna had earned some "dollars" in Sunday School for the Sunday School "store" and spent them all on gift for Grandma—"the only ones there, Grandma"; how fortunate Grandma is!) ... Seven-year-old Michael, after spending the afternoon with his brother and grandparents while his mother and sister went to a reception: "Grandma, this is the best time we ever had at your place. Grandpa gave us a popsicle; you gave us two cookies and yogurt. We got to watch both a baseball and a hockey game, and play on Webkins, and they only got to go to a party!" ... little Eric carrying on an earnest conversation with Grandma,

ERIC   MICHAEL   ANNA

after a discussion on "peelings" (carrots) and "peels" (oranges) ... Grandma: What am I going to do with the peelings? Eric: You're going to put them in the compost. G: What will happen to them? E: They'll turn into dirt. G: That's right. What other word do we use for "dirt"? E: "Soil." G (with a double-take): How did you know that word? E: You told me. G: When did I tell you? E: You were down at the circle garden and you told me. (At least one of us has a good memory.) ... young student to his piano teacher, after less-than-polished performance: "It's because your piano is a lot different than ours; ours is black." ... student's brother, a few weeks later: "I can do it at home, but I can't do it here—the keys are too bouncy." ... a *Pearls Before Swine* cartoon in which a little brain, which has escaped from its owner's head, is conversing with another cartoon character who has just asked, "There are more of you escaped brains running around?" The brain's answer resonates with Mother: "Yes, we tend to escape during prolonged periods of television viewing. Most people don't even notice we're gone." ... a happy visit with Howard and Doreen Hutt from Scarborough (Doreen gave group piano teaching courses 40 years ago in Victoria. At 81, she still leads music festivals and teaches piano classes, and has just republished her class method book.) ... Mark receiving a letter from UVic; assumes it to be information regarding his student loan, discovers a scholarship cheque—a President's Award based on his academic standing ... Michael's description of his trip from Toronto to Windsor: "I had just booked an economy car but they didn't have any so they gave me a free upgrade to a new Dodge Charger...hilarious. I felt like a gangster. It wasn't really 'free' what with the increased fuel consumption but it was nice to have the power and size on the 401 which is not *that* far off some of the roads in Dubai." ...

JOLYN   JOY

Grandma playing "You Are My Sunshine" on the piano while **Jolyn** [4] and **Joy** [3] sing like little bells beside her, Joy gently "playing" the keys beside Grandma (As a teenager, Louise regarded this song, one of her father's favourites, as both appealing and a little melancholic; in this setting 50 years later, has similar response to piece.) ... Chris leaving a note for Margaret after discovering Cheerios and magnetic letters in both of his work boots: "Do we have mice, or an 18-month-old?" ... note on outside of envelope addressed to Melissa, in Victoria, from friend Donna Christiansen, in Dartmouth, whose extraordinary kindnesses to Melissa over the past few years have been much appreciated, regarding Melissa's move back to Victoria: "I'm still not happy, but I'm cooperating." (Part of that "cooperation" was a huge bouquet that could hardly fit into the largest vase in this household, timed to arrive on the day Melissa flew in to Victoria International Airport.) ... Jolyn and Joy dancing under the church's magnolia tree, picking up handfuls of translucent mauve petals "to give Mommy" ... Jordie and Joshua playing roller hockey with Uncle Matt in Buenos Aires ... Jordie and Joshua racing across the field after the soccer ball, participating in what Google calls Argentina's "national obsession" ... Bruce and Louise enjoying Faith Baptist's 50th Anniversary celebration for a weekend in May, renewing ac-

JORDAN   JOSHUA

quaintances with friends from over 40 years ago (Photos of a spindly 20-something Bruce being pushed off the diving board after a kangaroo court judgment at youth camp brought back memories of many good times and much hilarity from our three years in Vancouver.) ... Margaret, hobbling around after a foot operation, no match for her fleetfooted little daughter ... Mike at the controls as the 777 takes off for New York from Dubai, carrying his sister, Melissa ... a large raccoon washing some food in the pool in front of the living room, ambling along the edge, stripping and eating berries from the cotoneaster bushes, and sipping water

MICHAEL SITTING ON SAND DUNES IN DUBAI

from the pool ... lively chatter around the supper table as two sons (Mark and Matt) and three student boarders (Charlene De Vries, in nursing, her brother, Steve, in music education, and Charlotte Robertson, in first year general studies) share the day's activities ... Tori and Margaret decorating the bathroom mirror with 37 whipped cream kisses, on Chris's birthday (Cleanup was a little difficult.) ... Tori "helping" Margaret by emptying out the laundry baskets, leaving a trail of socks, shirts and pants behind her, sporting clean clothing on her head and around her neck, most frequently her father's boxers or her mother's "unmentionables" ... father Richard appearing at daughter Anna's classroom door with a bouquet, taking her out for a surprise lunch on her 10th birthday ...

TORI

Chapter 54: A Christmas Digest, 2008

EDITORIAL *by Louise*

October 29 A table below a bay window in our cabin serves as a desk, as I utilize the light streaming through a cleared section of our wooded lot. Our cabin, though cozy and comfortable, may have to wait many years for the amenity of electricity, and we now depend on daylight, or gas lanterns with fragile gauze mantles, and, on occasion, a generator. The cabin is wired for electricity, but the majority of the lake dwellers fight against the intrusion and ecological damage electricity will bring. Rising and setting with the sun has its charm! At least it does in the summer time. At the end of October, that means 12-hour nights.

Although it is drizzling, it appears that the sun is shining, thanks to the incredibly yellow leaves still attached to several maple trees sharing the neighbour's property with firs and cedars. Occasionally a leaf detaches itself from its parent and dipsy-doodles leisurely down to join its companions on the ground.

We are here to close the cottage for the winter. It is very quiet deep in the forest around Horne Lake, several logging-road miles away from the nearest town (Qualicum), and it appears that we are the only ones on the lake today.

Bruce is chopping wood for the stove below. The propane heater behind me in the living/dining room area refused to come on this morning, although it did take the temperature from near-freezing to 70 degrees Fahrenheit last night. The weather is unseasonably mild, so we are still quite comfortable, and the heat from downstairs should warm up the cabin floor.

This break from the regular routine gives me time to reflect on

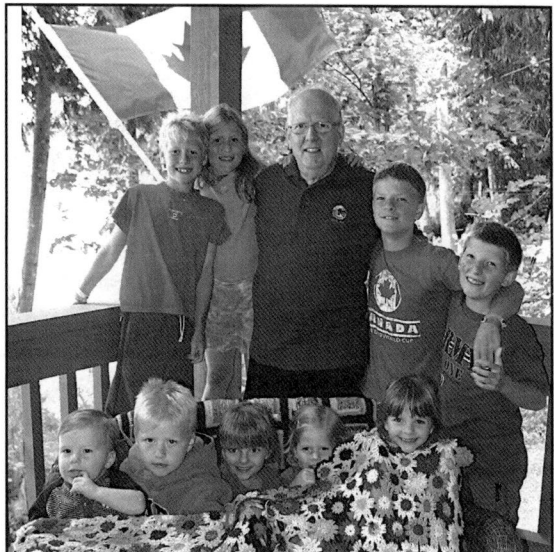

GRANDPA WITH NINE GRANDCHILDREN AT HORNE LAKE

what 2008 has brought to us and our family. We have again been reminded that God oversees our lives: "For I know the plans I have for you," declares the Lord, "plans to prosper you and not to harm you, plans to give you hope and a future (Jeremiah 29:11)," as we live through times both happy and sad. The positive episodes far out-number the negative, but a very sad event this year did cast a shadow over us: the death this summer, at the age of 32, of Margaret's maid of honour and sister-in-law, Leslie (Bucher) Aschliman, the "match-maker" who suggested seven years ago to her brother Chris that he marry Margaret. Several horrendous surgeries and treatments to deal with a brain tumour, and the fervent prayers of a host of friends and family were not enough to keep this beautiful mother of a two year old with us. Leslie's husband Tyson maintained a blog for several months that bore an incredible witness to their mutual faith and submission to the will of God, as well as glimpses into the

turmoil of body, mind and soul that such a trial brings. Our hearts go out to Margaret's American family at this time.

NEW STARK HOME

December 8 By the end of December, four of our children will be in homes new to them. Chris and Margaret are moving from Indianapolis to Salem, Oregon, in December. Melissa has moved into her newly-renovated Royal Woods condominium at 1009 McKenzie, two half-blocks from here. Richard and Melody took ownership of a larger home on Hartford Green in the Lake Hill area, still only five minutes away from us, but in another direction. And Matt has just moved into his own condo which he has renovated with brother-in-law Richard's capable support. Matt's ad-dress is 1005 McKenzie, the sister building to Melissa's. (Our children delivered the *Times Colonist* newspaper into these condos for many years.) Although we had noth-ing to do with the choice of housing, we must admit it is great to have these new homes within walking distance of This Old House, and These Old Folks.

A year ago a collection of letters written over a period of forty years was pub-lished as *"Hey, there's no violin in this case!"* In the introductory chapter, safety pins are mentioned, in relation to a skirt worn by the writer, a teenager at the time, who had secured the hem of her skirt, temporarily, with safety pins. The subject of pins comes up nearly 50 years later, in reference to a long skirt, again worn by the writer (no longer a teenager), which suddenly yielded to gravity, descended very quickly and ascended even more rapidly, and was then fastened in place with safety pins.

What wasn't included in the book was an episode described thirty years ago, as the writer shared life with her mother, holidaying in Arizona: "This morning Margaret wore that pink dress with the pinafore that you made for Marilyn. It wasn't until we were coming down the walk into the house after church that I noticed she had a row of little gold pins holding together a foot-long gash several inches up from the bottom of the pinafore. To my greater consternation, I discovered that she had torn it just before we left, and had 'fixed' it herself. I just wonder what the congregation thought as she and her four siblings entered the service to the strains of their mother's organ music. One's pride certainly takes a beating at times!"

For the past few weeks I have had the privilege of working with nearly a dozen instrumentalists preparing Christmas music for inclusion in Christmas programmes at church. I had arranged several of the pieces for my own children over 30 years ago, and it has been somewhat nostalgic hearing them in a different context. I was reminded of some excerpts from old Christmas letters, printed earlier in this book: on **December 31, 1978** (p. 77), toddler Mark (supposedly that year's letter writer) describes Melody's violin debut with her four older siblings; on **November 29, 1979** (p. 84), at the other end of the same letter, Mark comments on Melody rehearsing "Silently Night"; and a year later, **November 30, 1980** (p. 106), the new baby describes the Christmas activities, including a reference to his siblings' performance of "Gesu Bambino," and ending with: "We hope that you, too, will have a joy-filled Christ's-Birthday celebration, and a blessed New Year. Love, Matthew."

Twenty-nine years later, this is also my wish for our friends and family.

THE FAMILY

PERSONAL GLIMPSES

Geordon and **Marilyn** were here from Buenos Aires for two months this summer. The anticipated respite from their activities in South America somehow did not quite materialize due to a variety of circumstances, although it was wonderful to

RENDLE FAMILY

have them here! The month prior to their leaving for Canada was spent in dealing with the aftermath of a house robbery [story in Life's Like This] and each Sunday they were in Canada they spoke at supporting churches here, on the mainland, and in Alberta. As well, Marilyn made four several-hour visits to emergency rooms in Saskatoon, where the family was attending the annual Canadian Youth for Christ conference, and Comox, before a kidney stone was removed by surgery. Geordon continues to oversee YFC work in Latin America and Marilyn supervises a very busy household while contributing administrative and musical skills both at church and with an international youth group in their community. **Jolyn** [5] has joined her older brothers in the study of the piano. She is also attending Lincoln School with the boys, leaving **Joy** [4] to finish her final year at the wonderful preschool, Global Garden, in their church. This is the first time the little girls have been separated.

Michael flies out of Dubai, the hub of the Middle East, all over the world as a first officer for Emirates Airline. He was pleasantly surprised this spring to receive an extra 14 weeks' pay as his 2007 share of the airline's profits. His thoughts often stray back to his roots on the West Coast, and we enjoyed his visit at Christmas. As is his practice when he is on this side of the world, he checked

MIKE IN COCKPIT

up on the old homestead, resulting, after consultation with his brothers, in some upgrades to his parents' computers, stereo and telephone systems.

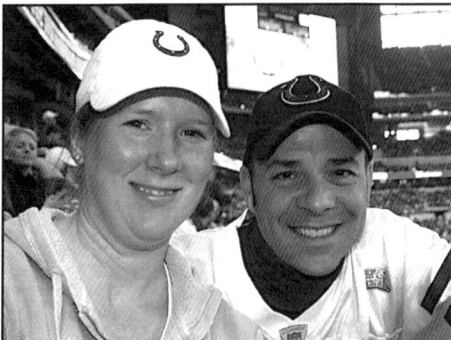

MARGARET AND CHRIS

Margaret visited us for two weeks this summer, with toddlers **Tori** [3] and **Jonathan** [1 1/2]. **Chris** joined them for what was planned to be a second two weeks, but returned to Indianapolis the next day when his sister's condition worsened. He was able to spend the last three days of her life near her; in spite of her weakness, she smiled at him when he reminded her that he had a wonderful wife

JONATHAN

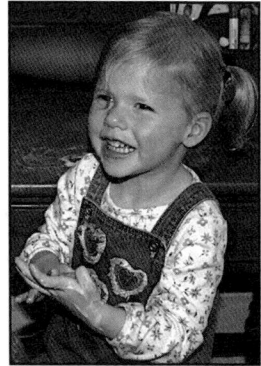

TORI

and children, thanks to her, and she was welcome to say, "I told you so." *[The Stark five, Michael and Melissa later travelled down the west coast to Salem, Oregon, where they helped the Buchers unpack in their new home.]*

Melissa has made a comfortable new home for herself in her condo, filling it with family and friends on the occasion of her father's birthday in October. She nurses in the paediatric unit at Victoria General Hospital, and has committed ten hours a week to working with the youth at our church, a project to which she brings much experience and enthusiasm. Her flexible schedule has allowed her to lend a hand in different settings, including a two-month trip which included Indianapolis, where she visited with Margaret and her family, and Argentina, where she babysat her Rendle nieces and nephews while their parents were in South Africa for the YFC General Assembly.

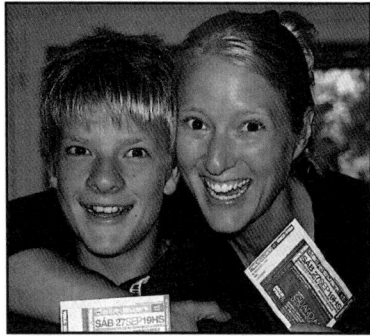

MELISSA WITH JORDIE

Richard and **Melody** are enjoying their new location near Braefoot Park, within walking distance of Lake Hill School, where **Michael** [9] and **Eric** [6] follow in their mother's footsteps of 25 to 30 years ago. **Anna** [11] is in a Grade 6 French immersion programme at Cedar Hill Middle School, and Michael and Eric drop by for music lessons each week; we enjoy the whole family's company at Sunday lunches most weeks. Richard is manager of sales and marketing at our favourite coffee company, Level Ground Trading. Melody fits in hours of typing interviews around the family's many activities.

MELODY AND RICHARD

MARK GRADUATING WITH BACHELOR OF ARTS IN GEOGRAPHY (DEAN'S LIST)

Mark plans to make our suite his home for the next little while, and is happy to have the extra room for his filming equipment, with Matthew's departure. He spent November and most of December in Quebec taking advanced training for work. After travelling to South Africa to film the YFC conference, where approximately 100 countries were repre-sented and half of the delegates were young leaders, he stopped off in Dubai to visit with brother Mike, who then served as first officer on his flight to Johan-nesburg. Mike and he joined sister Marilyn, already in Johannesburg, for an overnight visit. Mark and Matt maintain their involvement in sports, playing roller hockey year round, and softball in the summer; Melissa joined them in a volleyball tourney, helping ensure they won in their division.

MATT IN INDIANAPOLIS

Matthew, in his sixth year of computer work at Level Ground, is gratified by the company's continu-ing growth. His condo renovations presented a steep learning curve, and a large investment of time, and he is now taking on the challenge of cooking for himself.

SCENE IN PASSING ...

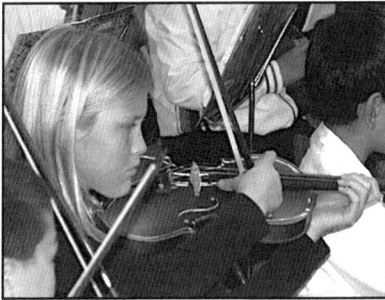

ANNA PLAYING THE VIOLIN

... Anna on newly-purchased flute, Michael on violin, both showing Eric, at the piano, how he can play his song ("Hot Cross Buns") with them if he moves from E-D-C to B-A-G ... **Jordie** [13] and **Joshua** [10] book-ending their summer in Victoria with piano exams at the Grade VIII and Grade IV levels, taken a day after their 27-hour trip from Argentina, and theory exams (Rudiments II and Preliminary Rudiments) two days before they left Canada (All exams were passed comfortably, and Grandma is a little poorer—happily so—as she backs up the commitments *[bribes?]* she made last spring to her young pianist-entrepreneurs.) ... Matthew painstakingly assem-bling IKEA cupboards and drawers and shelving units, ap-plying baseboards and other trim, and painting, and paint-ing, acquiring a most attractive new home, and enhanced carpentering skills, in the process ... Melody returning to a cool and damp Victoria from an exciting 10-day visit to Michael in hot and dry Dubai ... Mark graduating from UVic with a BA in geography, with distinction and a place on the

ERIC

Dean's List ... Auntie Marilyn providing shelter for the five Starks for a couple of days, when the previous owner could not leave the new house in time ... young beginner sliding to right edge of piano bench, performing "Twinkle, Twinkle, Little Star" in the piano's highest register, informing teacher that stars are very, very high, so he wanted to play the highest notes ... Bruce and Louise rattling around in their part of the house, with Andrew Rokeby (fourth-year microbiology student at UVic) and Steve De Vries (third-year music education student, also at UVic) keeping them company ... grandson Michael accompanying the school choir on "Ode to Joy," first at the school concert, and then on A-Channel TV ... Mark rearranging the suite to suit himself, replacing the back-to-back computers (his and Matt's) with a kitchen table ... Richard rebuilding a large section of our fence, providing surfaces for squirrels, birds and cats to perch on (usually not all at the same time!), and a launching pad for the many birds who feed at the suet and sunflower feeders, an almost continual source of entertainment ... Sign brought home from Halifax by husband last year: "I can only please one person per day.

MICHAEL

today is not your day. tomorrow doesn't look good either" (wife is unsettled as much by the standard of English as by the sentiment expressed); sign purchased by wife (with husband's amused acquiescence): "My husband said if I buy any more plants he would leave me ... Sure gonna miss that man!"

LIFE'S LIKE THIS

December 24, 1961 Bruce and Louise return from three-day honeymoon at Point-No-Point, for Christmas Eve gathering at the Holland home. Louise, standing beside beautiful wine-red velvet curtains in living room, watches snowflakes drift gently to garden below, entranced by the beauty and peacefulness of the scene. ... **October 1971** Parents Bruce and Louise are rejoicing in birth of third child, have just finished huge renovation, tripling size of tiny cottage. Carpeting and curtains have been chosen, but decision has not been finalized re. living room drapes. Mother asks if red velvet drapes could fit budget. Father not sure, but both decide to invest $400 in heavy, lined red velvet curtains for three large windows, to be installed by Parkers' Draperies and Antiques. ... **January 1972** Mother plays rhythm class song "Snowflakes Drifting, Gently Drifting" on the piano as eldest child, five, pirouettes around 40-foot living room. Huge snowflakes descend lazily outside large window, framed by warm burgundy drapes. Time stands still, as mother and child give themselves over to the beauty of the moment. ... **November 1995** Lower floor of house is showing wear and tear contributed by seven children, dozens of music students, and several boarders. Parents decide to renovate, and more pastel colour scheme leads to removal of aging curtains. Youngest daughter takes piles of drapes, some faded along edges, one showing cat damage, and has two made into shorter curtains for bedrooms in home. Over next few years, Mother considers having long velvet dress made for self, but realizes that she does not have the 5' 10", 120-lb. frame to do such a garment justice. Curtains continue to languish on daughter's shelves. ... **October 2007** Youngest daughter has brainwave: Why not make Holland granddaughters red velvet dresses? Contacts friend Pat Robbie, seamstress extraordinaire, and project is underway. Melody washes material in hot water, and Pat starts cutting out four different dresses, in four sizes. **December 21, 2007** On her anniversary, as instructed, Louise opens parcel given to her previous Sunday by Pat. Is somewhat puzzled by spacious red velvet bag, decorated with black handles and trim. Father assures her enigmatically that she hasn't seen anything yet! Later, son Mark presents Mother with framed photos of four cherished little girls, ranging in age from ten down to two, each dressed in an elegant red velvet gown, trimmed with black satin and ribbon. Mother is overwhelmed by daughter's ingenious scheme, and by the exquisite results of friend's efforts.

January 2004 Geordon, Jordan and Joshua have just eaten at the Dairy Queen in Courtenay with Grandma and Grandpa Rendle. Hurrying over to the train station nearby, they settle in for the beautiful, snowy ride down to Victoria. 45 minutes into the ride, Jordan suddenly realizes he has forgotten his retainer, wrapped in a serviette, at the DQ. No one on the train has a cell phone! Geordon goes up to the conductor, asks to use his train radio and phones Marilyn. She calls Grandpa Rendle and he makes the drive back to Courtenay from Union Bay, digs through the DQ garbage can and finds the retainer. The DQ staff, seeing Grandpa's embarrassment, comment, "Don't worry, sir, this happens *all* the time!" **March 2008** Having just completed a seven-day Project Serve trip with a team of 22 to Chile, Marilyn and the four Js are making their way through Customs in Argentina. Joshua realizes with dismay that his retainer has been left on the plane's meal tray, wrapped in a serviette. Marilyn rushes to the airline counter to ask if she can re-board the plane. An agent offers to look through the garbage for it and brings it back to a very relieved boy. Their frazzled mother's comment: "Both boys were close to the same age (9 or 10) at the times of

JORDAN

JOSHUA

these incidents.   Guardian angels must work overtime at this lifestage!"

Monday morning, April 14 Mother has seven plant sale notices to deliver to neighbours. After delivering first six, crosses McKenzie Avenue to give one to customer at #5, 3981 Saanich Road. Lady's name and #5 are marked on envelope. Unfortunately, Mother's mind wanders and, absentmindedly noticing red mailbox just outside of townhouse complex, she drops notice into mail chute, realizing immediately that unstamped, unaddressed—except for "#5"—envelope will end up in undeliverable area of post office. Later phones customer to invite her to sale. **Thursday morning, April 17** Telephone rings, lady from #5 asks, "Can you guess what came in my mail this morning?" She and Mother marvel at thoughtfulness of mail personnel who took time to see letter was delivered, without even stamping "postage due" on it. **Friday, April 18** Flowers, ground covers, grasses and shrubs spread over circular driveway in preparation for sale. Brisk morning sales are overshadowed by gathering steel-gray storm clouds. Violent hailstorm hits after lunch, which sends plant seller indoors for the duration, hoping that Saturday's weather will be more congenial. **Saturday, April 19** Gardener wakes up to eerie stillness: no bird songs, no children playing outside. A peculiar brightness fills the room. Mother tiptoes downstairs, looks out windows, is confronted by winter wonderland: firs, oaks, shrubs, driveway—and plants—covered by three inches of white fluff. Feathers of snow continue to fall. Plant-potter is delighted with beauty, in spite of damage to sale prospects.

Saturday, May 10 (Geordon's birthday), Buenos Aires Geordon, Marilyn, Jolyn, Joy, Shauna Brown (an intern living with the Rendles for nine months), and Miranda and Amy (members of the church's youth group) are returning from a happy graduation

JOLYN

recognition ceremony at the church. As Geordon parks the van, the others enter the house and are unsettled to hear loud shouts directed towards Geordon outside. Four robbers, two carrying guns, demand that they enter the house with Geordon; one hits him on the head with the butt of his gun. After locking the women and girls in a bathroom, they take Geordon to each room of the house to show them where the valuables are. Although there are not many items of high value, the thieves ransack the place, taking laptops, iPod, some appliances, wedding rings, video projector, video camera, Geordon's passport, credit cards and National Identity Document, backpacks, soccer bag, and cell phones. As they leave, they lock Geordon in the tiny

JOY

bathroom with the other six, pull the telephone lines out of the wall, and speed off in the family van. One of the teenagers has a cellphone hidden on her, and when the men have gone, a phone call is made to friends who have a house key and come to let the family out.

[Our first knowledge of this trauma came two hours after it occurred, when Marilyn phoned late Saturday night and started the conversation with, "We're all OK, Mom." She told the above story unemotionally, and apparently was able to fulfill her Sunday responsibilities at church the next day. On Wednesday, in discussing the situation, she commented that she must have been in shock on Sunday, because she was very weepy and emotional on Monday and Tuesday; by Wednesday, she was more herself again. One of the saddest losses was the grandmothers' wedding rings, one from Granny Forsberg on Marilyn's side of the family, the other from Grandma Neale on Geordon's. It took weeks to clean up the mess, and

MARILYN IN SOUTH AFRICA

even longer to come to terms with irreplaceable losses, such as Marilyn's three heavily-marked calendars (taken in her backpack), material on the computers, and perhaps, most important, the emotional damage that such an invasion leaves in its wake. We are thankful that a bad situation did not turn worse, and that no one was seriously hurt.]

Wednesday, November 19   Mother welcomes young student, almost seven years old, to piano lesson. Child walks purposefully into the music room, music books under his arm, and regards a piece of music on the piano. Says, with considerable authority, that the piece could be played "Adagio," or perhaps a little "Prestissimo," (pronounced "presteessimo") or even "Allegro." Somewhat taken aback, teacher asks him where he had learned those words—she certainly hadn't taught them—and he replies that his school teacher had been talking about them. He then adds "Presto" and "Moderato" to his list, and proceeds to explain what they mean. He is correct, and is able to recall them two weeks later. (Lesson to teachers and parents: children are capable of a lot more than we sometimes think they are.)

Chapter 55: A Christmas Digest, 2009

EDITORIAL *by Louise*

October 16 Today my father would have been 102. I often think of him and my mother, and wish they were both here to share in my family's life. But time goes on, and the years fold into each other seamlessly.

It is early on a rainy Victoria morning, and I have been working at the computer for some time now. The furnace has come alive, and our household should soon follow. I expect our lovely young Japanese piano teacher, Sayoko Kobayashi, will be the next person I see, followed in short order by our long-term boarder, Andrew

LOUISE AND BRUCE

Rokeby, in fifth-year studies at UVic, and then Diego Olivera and Allen Gomez, our temporary boarders, tourists from Mexico. Bruce deserves to sleep in, but probably will be up soon as well. Mark, the only other family member to live here (in our suite), is currently on a three-month trip to South America, so that part of upstairs is very quiet.

November 11 We have just returned on this bright, sunny day from the Remembrance Day service at Saanich's cenotaph. Overseen by crows congregated on the municipal hall's roof, and by seagulls circling overhead, we, in the company of a large crowd of Saanich residents, were reminded of the great sacrifices others have made for the freedoms we all too often take for granted. I was struck by the power of the hymns which were sung, "O God Our Help in Ages Past" and "Abide With Me", songs that reach into the depths of human experience and need. In a time of great insecurity, it is reassuring to remember Who, according to the hymn and Scripture, has been our Help in time past and is still our Hope for the future.

In late September 2008, our special missionary friend, Hazel Page, passed away at the age of 91, after a lifetime of service to God in the area of linguistics. Hazel spoke in over 20 languages (but, as she would say, "only one at a time"); her biography, written by Carol Ferguson, is appropriately titled *God's Mimic*. Hazel was known both for her generosity and her frugality. This latter quality resulted in a houseful of items to be dealt with, as very little was thrown away. Bruce, her executor, has taken his responsibility seriously. After months of sorting through things in her home, he set up a room here (referred to by the family as "Hazel's room") to continue the winnowing process. In addition to household items and souvenirs of her years of translation work in China and the Philippines, there were many boxes of papers, all of which Bruce is dealing with, paper by paper. Tiny diaries, written in immaculate microscopic script, have been discovered, as well as handwritten dictionaries of the previously unwritten tribal languages she transformed into writing. A small scribbler from 1930 surfaced, filled with her older sister Florence's descriptions of a summer camping trip she and their mother took. In great detail, and in beautiful handwriting, Florence, 15, records the activities of each day (swimming, hiking, boating, working on "fancywork"), as well as the meals she and her mother prepared. There are lists of supplies (curling iron, parasol, hand cream, embroidery thread, pen, pencil, notebook, ink, blotter, etc.) and expenses (including groceries: 1/2 dozen doughnuts—15 cents; two bunches of lettuce—5 cents; one dozen eggs—25 cents). "Mama's luxuries" include two cones (on five occasions)—10 cents; three soft drinks—15 cents; motor boat ride—25 cents; merry-go-round—25 cents, and several other items. Florence died of typhoid fever two years later, and Hazel managed to protect this little book for 76 years. Bruce also found a miniature jam jar which held nine white bean seeds. Not knowing how old or viable the seeds were, I planted them along the edge of a garden plot, where their lack of vitality would not be noticed. To my surprise, each one germinated and grew into a robust vine, producing dozens of 12- and 14-inch pods, the last of which were dried and saved for next spring. These seeds are perhaps a symbol of Hazel's productive life.

December 27 Days imperceptibly lengthen, snowdrops poke through, Indian plum buds fatten, and the promise of a new year beckons to us. We wish you God's most excellent blessings in 2010.

PERSONAL GLIMPSES

RENDLE FAMILY

Marilyn and **Geordon** and the four Js live in Buenos Aires, working with Youth for Christ, Geordon as Americas Area Director (responsible for North, Central, and

South Americas, and the Caribbean), with Marilyn as his part-time assistant. At Geordon's urging, Marilyn has undertaken a Master's programme in Leadership and Training at Royal Roads University, working online except for three-week residencies in Victoria at the beginning and end of her years' work. In the preliminary course her marks were higher than the B required for entry into the programme—no doubt a reflection of her life experience! **Jordan** [15], **Joshua** [nearly 12], **Jolyn** [6], and **Joy** [5] all attend the same school now. They are active in sports, especially soccer, and spend some time at the piano, with a little encouragement via internet from Victoria.

MICHAEL

Michael is well into his third year of flying Boeing 777s in the Middle East. He has a ringside seat to Dubai's excess, extravagance and beauty, and, now, its difficulties in paying off its creditors. He looks down from his 32nd floor apartment into 14 lanes of traffic; the incredible Burj Dubai, at half a mile in height the world's tallest skyscraper, casts its shadow over his apartment block's swimming pool. Although e-mail and iChat allow us to visit with him, it was very special to have him stay with us for two weeks in October.

Margaret and **Chris**, with **Tori** [4] and **Jonathan** [2 1/2] are making a new home in Salem, Oregon, since their move to this side of the continent on New Year's Day.

BUCHER FAMILY

Chris works with the Federal Highway Administration as a civil engineer, and Margaret provides a welcoming home for him and their two little ones. A new Bucher Baby is arriving at the end of March.

Melissa continues to gather air miles, and kilometres on her odometer, as she travels both on youth projects (housebuilding in Mexico), family visits (Argentina and Oregon), and excursions to the Maritimes to touch bases with colleagues and friends from her six years in Dartmouth. Her nieces and nephews in Buenos Aires, Salem, and Victoria love to hang out with Auntie Melissa. On December 14th she left on a two-month trip which includes Argentina, South Africa, and Dubai. Her parents wonder if her name—Melissa means "honeybee"—has something to do with her affinity for flying. Melissa divides the rest of her time between paediatric nursing at Victoria General Hospital and youth work at our church.

Melody and **Richard**, **Anna** [12], **Michael** [10] and **Eric** [7]—numbers their grandmother can hardly accept, although she has watched these grandchildren grow up near-by—are prospering at home, work and school. Richard manages sales at Level Ground Trading, and Melody transcribes interviews, and both support their children in their many activities. This year they bid a sad farewell to Mellow Yellow, the 1971

LAST DAYS WITH DODGE SWINGER

Dodge Dart of their early marriage (which Melody drove to Government House 15 years ago in all her wedding finery for picture-taking)—such are the priorities of family life!

MARK IN PARACAS, PERU

Mark is returning imminently to Victoria after his time in South America. Cameras and laptop in hand, he has already shared several extraordinary shots of places he has visited. As he crisscrossed the continent, he renewed contacts with friends in Venezuela, Colombia and Argentina, and spent some time with his eldest sister and her family in Buenos Aires. Since graduating from UVic in 2008, Mark has been working full time with the Canada Border Services Agency at the Victoria border crossing.

Mark's younger brother and sports pal, **Matthew**, has made a comfortable home for himself in his condo, continuing to renovate as time allows, and learning many new skills in the process. Matt's efforts around this property (raking the ubiquitous oak leaves, putting up the Christmas lights) are much appreciated by those here who would prefer not to spend all their free time on the end of a rake, and who should not be up on ladders or roofs. Matt spends his official working hours at Level Ground's computers, either tweaking his order management system, or troubleshooting.

Bruce and **Louise** continue to keep an eye on their expanding family, enjoying the privileges of accumulated years without some of the responsibilities of years past. Visits from family

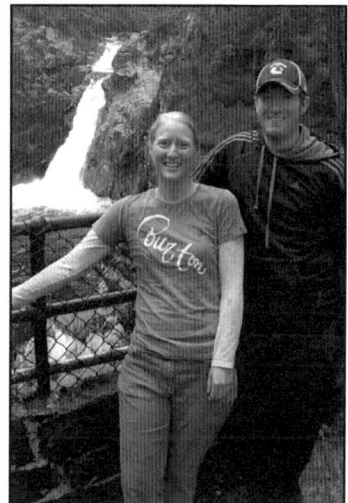
MELISSA AND MATT

members from Argentina, Dubai and Oregon speckled the calendar, and a reciprocal trip to Oregon meant they got to see the Buchers on their own territory, and experience the state fair, the magnificent Oregon coast, the children's museum, a magical carousel in a municipal park, as well as a very pleasant day with Louise's sister Harriet and husband Ed in Hood River. Bruce spends much of his time assisting friends, acquaintances and family in many practical ways, the most noteworthy of which is probably in the area of cooking and baking. Louise is in her 50th year of teaching, the last 43 on a bench to the right of her piano students—a great privilege. Propagating and selling plants in support of youth work gives her an excuse to dig in the dirt and enjoy the outdoors.

SCENE IN PASSING ...

... the bird feeder gang: the little nuthatch bullying the even daintier bushtits, house wrens, and chickadees; the purple finch, with his dipped-in-raspberry-juice head; the large northern flicker displaying his red under-feathers as he grasps the suet feeder, gorging on enough food to supply several of his smaller relatives; black-hooded juncos and orange-eyed towhees foraging among the licorice ferns for tidbits dropping from the feeders; sparrows sitting thug-like along the fence, waiting for a chance to displace the flock of chickadees ... two brothers preparing to play their duet in music room: "Three, two, one—go!" (reminiscent of Margaret's "One, two, buckle-my-shoe" introduction thirty years ago to a duet she and Melissa were performing) ... alarming news from contractor who is set to replace rotting 4 x 4 at bottom of greenhouse wall of glass: all 4 x 4s are infested with termites, except for one closest to house ... rebuilt greenhouse filled with tender perennials, surrounded by Suntuf (corrugated polycarbonate) walls and roof, basking in warmth of sun as temperatures dip to freezing ... iridescent green hummingbird frantically zooming around just under the ceiling of greenhouse, refusing to come low enough to exit through door, resting occasionally on the hook of a hanging basket (After trying, unsuccessfully, to coax the little creature out with a broom and then a leaf rake, Mother sets geranium with red bloom in doorway in the hope that bird will be attracted to it; returns an hour later to find greenhouse empty except for plants.) ... mother Melody supporting Lake Hill and Cedar Hill's activities as book room organizer, field trip driver, fundraising and classroom

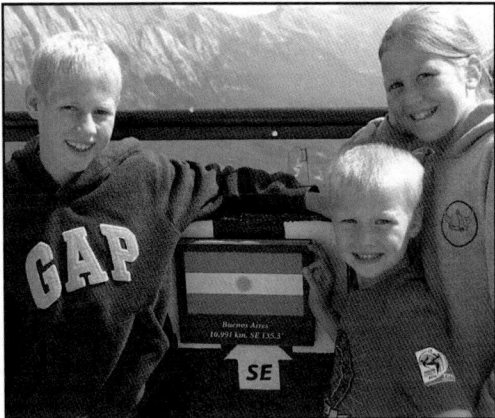

MICHAEL, ERIC AND ANNA

coordinator, and audience for beginning readers, maintaining an exercise routine as she accompanies Michael and Eric to school most mornings … Michael chosen as Lake Hill School's representative at the Olympics torch run … Anna playing the part of young teenager with attitude in church's dinner theatre production (Grandma hopes she will return to her normal sweet self by next morning.) … Bruce and Louise spending a few happy days at Horne Lake in the company of Bruce's sisters Shirley and Marilyn, and brother-in-law Jack, the first time in 50 years that all three siblings have vacationed together … second printing of *"Hey, there's no violin in this case!"* … Bruce babysitting American grandchildren (Tori and Jonathan) in Oregon, after harrowing bus, taxi and train trip from Victoria to Salem via Vancouver (Victoria bus forgot to pick up passenger, who had confirmed reservation and was waiting for nearly a hour on Vernon Avenue, resulting in missed ferry and terrifying $64 taxi ride from Tsawwassen into downtown Vancouver where Seattle bus was waiting for frazzled traveller.) … Grandpa cutting section of Tori's hair in an effort to remove toy fire-engine, motor still running, which had become entangled in locks … Auntie Melissa babysitting her Bucher relatives in Oregon while Chris and Margaret travel on business trip to Washington, DC … Grandma enjoying video of Tori and Jonathan playing "Tap-a-Tap-a-Tap" with rhythm sticks via computer, remembering years of rhythm classes with her own and others' small children … snowberries (waxberries) beside the path to the house glistening in the winter twilight (beauty appreciated 80 years ago when Holland grandparents were married on December 21: wedding photo shows newlyweds under trellis covered in snowberry branches) … cotoneaster rehderi brightening up a sodden November with its apricot- and amber-coloured leaves … Michael surveying left-over *per diem* money from countries into which he flies: Chinese yuan, Japanese yen, Swiss francs, British pounds, Thai baht, Indonesian rupiah, South African rand, Australian dollars, Euros, Malaysian ringgit, Sri Lankan rupees, Philippine pesos, Singaporean dollars … Melody filling in for strings teacher at Lake Hill School's Christmas concert, as she lends stability to string ensemble with her violin, later receiving accolades for her work at the school (Her mother's mind wanders—as is sometimes the case—back 30 years as she remembers Melody, in Kindergarten, and her four older siblings spread across the stage in front of the curtains, violins in hand, providing interlude music during scenery changes.) … squirrel's death-defying acrobatic performance 30 feet up in oak trees (Three grey squirrels are chasing each other through the canopy of oaks over Mother's head, when one suddenly takes a flying leap to what he discovers is a very unsubstantial branch. Holding on precariously, white tummy fur waving in the breeze, he desperately, and successfully, grabs for foothold a few inches higher.) … Matt (from 1005 McKenzie) and Melissa (from 1009) sharing the condo swimming pool with an assortment of relatives, including nieces and nephews … Eric wearing his watch to school, reassuring his teacher, who had suggested he take it off so it wouldn't distract him: "It won't distract me. I just look at it every minute." ... cotoneaster leaf, 2" long, shiny side down, downy side up, carrying a precious cargo of one little dandelion head and two tiny daisies, floating at the edge of the pool (Grandma wonders which cherubic grandchild leaned over to put this miniscule ark into the water, risking a dunk in three feet of water) ... Grandpa and Grandma on first cruise, which took them to the metropolises of Vancouver, Seattle, Port Angeles, Victoria and Port Alberni (Louise would rather have been home digging compost and potting up plants but grudgingly had to admit she had a good time; Bruce is wondering where he can sign up for another one.) ... pair of exquisite golden-crowned kinglets accompanying Bruce and Louise in early January on walk around Christmas Hill through remnants of December's snowfall ... Mark scoring eight goals, assisting in one more; Matt putting in a goal and making nine assists in Puck Hogs roller hockey game (After over 20 years of playing together, these brothers operate by intuition!) ... Matt chosen in November for All-Star team ... Richard and Melody and children working in the rain at the mission station at Esperanza (on the northwest coast of Vancouver Island)—a productive if not always comfortable use of their Spring Break ... huge owl swooping soundlessly into oak tree outside kitchen at twilight, turning its head almost 360 degrees to keep an eye on its surroundings (and, no doubt, potential nourishment) ... Father Chris to two-year-old Jonathan: "Why did you just do what I asked you not to do?" Response: "Because I didn't listen and obey." (Grandmother and mother bite lip to keep from smiling.) ... Margaret and children and their grandparents picking blackberries in rural Salem, Tori with purple mouth and tongue ...

JONATHAN AND TORI

LIFE'S LIKE THIS

Monday, May 25, 11:15 a.m. Grandma is set to listen to granddaughter Jolyn's piano pieces. Jolyn is in Buenos Aires and Grandma is in Victoria; lesson is transmitted through computer's video camera. Jolyn wants to show Grandma a trick first. Placing feet and hands on both sides of a door frame, she "walks" up the frame like a spider, touches the top, and drops to the floor; Grandma is appropriately impressed. Jolyn then takes her place on the piano bench and plays "The Ducks" and "The Pretty Butterflies," with mother Marilyn sitting beside her, occasionally prompting: "two-eighths, quarter, two-eighths, quarter." Jolyn leaves to play outside and Joshua takes her place, eager to share his Grade V exam programme with grandmother, especially his Beethoven sonatina, which he has mastered and memorized over the past couple of weeks. Lesson is going well, when a shriek startles both Joshua and Grandma. Grandma hears Jordie's desperate call for mother, and piano lesson comes to an abrupt halt. Jolyn has fallen on arm on trampoline, is in great pain. Arm is twisted; Marilyn will have to take her to hospital nearby for help, leaving Jordie and friend Seth in charge of Joshua and Joy. (Father Geordon, on a 16-day trip to Venezuela and Colombia, is visiting with his parents in Tolu, Colombia, at a prison ministry conference, and has just commented how thankful he is that things have run smoothly at home in Argentina while he has been gone; is looking forward to return home next day.) … X-rays illuminate breaks in both radius and ulna bones in right arm. Marilyn contacts Geordon, who is able to comfort Jolyn on computer screen. Marilyn phones family doctor who advises her to ask for top paediatric orthopedic surgeon to operate on arm. Hospital orthopedic surgeon is quite willing to work with specialist, who is coming from town 30 minutes away. … Marilyn accompanies stretcher towards operating room. Anesthetist asks how she intends to pay for his services; cash will be required. Paediatric cardiologist makes similar demand. Marilyn rushes home to collect money, returns to hospital to find Jolyn coming out of operating room, her bones aligned with two long pins. Marilyn asks surgeon as to fees, is told not to worry. She can pay when her insurance sends her the money; her family doctor has made him aware of the special work she and her family are doing in Argentina, and he is in no rush for payment. Marilyn is grateful for his kindness. …

Tuesday, May 26, 4:30 p.m. Grandma is teaching young student the same pieces Jolyn performed the previous day, working out rhythm: "two-eighths, quarter, two-eighths, quarter." Becomes more prickly as lesson progresses. Student, gifted musically, is taking lessons "because Mommy wants me to, and Grandma is paying for the lessons, but I don't want to take them," and has not prepared her assignment well. Teacher tells student about granddaughter's painful experience previous day, and student's expressive brown eyes darken with concern. Lesson finally completed, teacher escorts child to door, and is startled by student's farewell: "Mrs. Holland, tell the little girl that your student Sally [*name changed*] wants her to get better soon. No, just tell her that one of your students wants her to get better soon." Teacher, touched by child's generosity, replies, "Thank you, Sally. I will tell her that my student Sally wants her to get better soon." (**September 25** Jolyn breaks same arm, at the wrist this time, in failed attempt to grab playground rings; requires cast but no surgery.)

Chapter 56: A Christmas Digest, 2010

EDITORIAL *by Louise*

November 3 Mark's upstairs suite at 4031 Saanich Road is empty; likewise, the condo at 1009 McKenzie, and its partner at 1005 McKenzie. The home on Hartford Green has temporarily relinquished its parents; the mother of the family on Elflein Street, Buenos Aires, has also left home for a few days. Two other siblings, Mike in Dubai, in the midst of advanced flight training, and Margaret in Oregon, caring for a beautiful baby and his sister and brother, and their parents in Victoria watch the excitement from a distance, wishing they too could be part of the action. The action? Two days from now, Mark, currently in Pisco, Peru, is marrying Margeliza Escobedo, a lovely young Peruvian he met in South Africa two years ago. (Although Mark has travelled several times in South America over the past few years, he did not meet Margeliza in Peru, but rather in Johannesburg, where she attended a YFC International conference in 2008. Mark had been asked to document this meeting of young leaders from all over the world, and to prepare a DVD for them to take home.) Melissa, Matt, and Richard and Melody have left Victoria on flights to Lima, Peru; Marilyn is travelling on Geordon's air miles from Argentina. Several violins are also making the trip. This is probably the first time in 40 years that there are no Holland children in Victoria!

NOVEMBER 5, 2010, IN PERU

November 6 We have received beautiful photos of the happy couple, one after their civil ceremony on the 4th and the second after the real wedding on the 5th. We look forward to enjoying the hundreds of photos stored on at least five cameras that travelled to Pisco (five hours from Lima), and no doubt the groom himself will put together yet another wedding documentary, with his own bride in the starring role!

November 21 We are enjoying the company of our young Panamanian boarder, Plinio Antonio (Tony) Ruiz, who is attending UVic's school of business. My students and our boarders reflect Victoria's growing multiculturalism. At present I have more students of Asian origin than I do of any other ethnic group. These children with Chinese, Filipino, Vietnamese and Indo-Canadian backgrounds bring their unique gifts to our relationships, as have our boarders, who have included young people from Colombia, Turkey, Venezuela, Mexico, Japan, and now Panama.

One of our first non-Canadian boarders was a young man from Colombia who came to share in Geordon and Marilyn's wedding 23 years ago. Hugo Ciro had attended high school in Bogotá, Colombia with Geordon, whose parents were missionaries working in the prisons of Colombia. Don and Georgia Rendle had a great impact on Hugo, and their example of serving those less fortunate and more vulnerable no doubt influences Hugo's life to this point. Thirteen years ago Hugo and three other Christian friends formed Level Ground Trading, offering San Miguel coffee from Hugo's home town in Colombia. A large share of the profits from this venture has been invested in the education of children from this village. Since then the company has sourced coffee from several other areas: Bolivia, Peru, Tanzania and Ethiopia, and considerable funding has been contributed to education and health care in these areas as well. Hugo travels frequently to each country to ensure the quality of the coffee, much of which is organically grown, and to get to know the coffee farmers; hence the company slogan: "We shake the hands that pick the coffee." *[2019: "We shake the hands that farm the land."]* As observers, we have been delighted to note both the company's growth and its numerous awards, several in the area of ethics. And the young man who left us to get married to Tracey Tattersall in 1992 continues to pour his energies into this Direct Fair Trade company. We are happy that our son-in-law Richard Stark and son Matthew make their contributions day by day within the company.

PERSONAL GLIMPSES

Marilyn and **Geordon**, **Jordan** [16], **Joshua** [almost 13], **Jolyn** [7] and **Joy** [6] look forward to another year and a half in Buenos Aires before their return to Victoria in the summer of 2012. Geordon travels all over South America and, to a lesser extent, North America, as he supervises the work of Youth for Christ in those areas. Marilyn, working halftime as his administrative assistant, has just completed the first

RENDLE FAMILY

year of her Master's programme at Royal Roads University. Her studies in leadership are focusing on "practical ways to increase the engagement of collaborative partnerships between YFC Canada and other chapters worldwide." For those less familiar with YFC, she included this description in her final essay: "Youth for Christ is an international non-governmental organization (NGO) with over 46,000 full time, part time and volunteer staff in over 100 nations of the world connected by a shared vision, using diverse programmes in local settings to reach young people around the globe with a message of hope and purpose." She and Geordon recently hosted a meeting of local Christian leaders to discuss the formation of a YFC board for Argentina in the near future. Their recent trip to Caracas brought great satisfaction and praise to God, as they shared in the celebration of the 10th anniversary of the founding of Venezuela's YFC board. Jordie and Joshua play soccer and roller-blade hockey and work at their music studies, Jordan as an International Baccalaureate student in Grade 11 at Lincoln School, Joshua at the Grade 7 level in both school and piano. Jolyn and Joy also attend the same school, in Grades 2 and 1 respectively. Although their mother has been hard-pressed to keep on top of their piano studies, they usually have something new to share with Grandma via webcam most Wednesdays.

MIKE

Michael continues to fly 777s out of Dubai for Emirates Airlines. He has just completed a gruelling study programme in preparation for three Command Development Training flights and a crucial interview which he completed in early November. He will soon begin ground school towards the position of captain. We enjoyed his visit with us at the beginning of December, and while we wish he did not live halfway around the world, we are glad that technology usually gives us quick access to him, wherever he is on the planet.

Margaret and **Chris** do not wonder

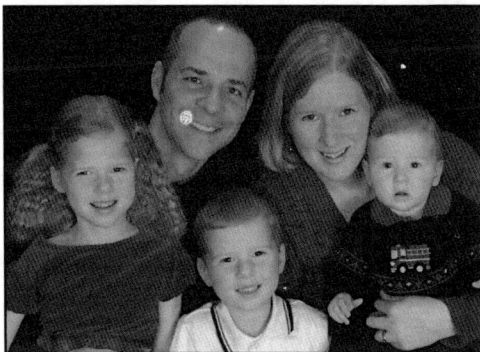
BUCHER FAMILY

why 2010 has passed so quickly. After a very uncomfortable pregnancy, Margaret presented the family with **Justin Robert**, over nine pounds in weight, on March 29. Margaret's discomfort extended into the first three months of Justin's babyhood, as Justin was reluctant to conform to the family's sleeping schedule. For the last several months, however, he has been a model baby, sleeping up to 12 hours a night. **Tori** [5] and **Jonathan** [3 1/2] love their not-so-little brother. In the spring, Chris and

MELISSA WITH CUB IN SOUTH AFRICA

Margaret supervised the building of their new house in Salem, and moved in at the end of June. Chris still enjoys the Pacific Northwest. As Operations Engineer for the Oregon Division of the Federal Highway Administration, he oversees the funding of roadway and bridge construction projects for Central and Southwestern Oregon and travels over these areas inspecting projects and holding contracts accountable.

Melissa has recently embarked on a Master's programme through the University of Edinburgh. In between working with young people, studying and travelling (in alphabetical order: Argentina, Chile, Dubai, Nova Scotia, Oregon, Peru, South Africa, Venezuela, Zambia, and Zimbabwe), she takes shifts in the paediatric unit at Victoria General Hospital. We are glad she lives only two half-blocks away, on McKenzie Avenue, and can drop in every so often, sometimes to add her compost materials to the large composting area in our backyard, other times to pick flowers for decorating her condo. Because she lives on the ground floor, she is able to nurture flowers, herbs, and some vegetables on her two patios, and against the wall of the building (the latter area fortunately screened by the property's landscaping).

Melody and **Richard** and **Anna** [13], **Michael** [11], and **Eric** [8] have managed to fit in school, work and music responsibilities around their various excursions. Melody manages a comfortable and productive household, occasionally typing out transcriptions for a local businessman, and Richard makes an excellent contribution to Level Ground's growth in his capacity as Sales

STARK FAMILY CONTRIBUTING TO AN
EXCELLENT HUMANITARIAN ENTERPRISE

Manager. The whole family took an extended spring break, travelling to Mexico to build a house for a needy family and enjoying some of California's tourist attractions, and Richard returned later to work on another house with a team from our church.

A hot week at the Gleaners in the Okanagan resulted in huge quantities of dried vegetables to be sent to less prosperous nations. Richard and Melody left the children in the care of the Stark grandparents for two weeks in November as they holidayed in Peru and took in brother Mark's wedding.

Mark and **Margeliza** have set up housekeeping in Pisco, Peru, and are planning to return to Victoria in February or March. We had the pleasure of Margeliza's company last spring when she came to Victoria to

MARGELIZA AND MARK

visit Mark and his family.

Matthew is holding up his end of the roller hockey programme here in Victoria, with his line-mate's sojourn in Peru, recently completing their team's 22nd "season" in 15 years with a divisional championship (including back-to-back five-goal games), as well as participating in various indoor and outdoor volleyball leagues. He, as the second of the "little boys" of 25 years ago, was best man at Mark's wedding ceremonies. Matt prefers to remain mostly in the background, but is very quick to respond to family requests for help, especially in the area of computers. His computer expertise allowed him to purchase a ticket for Peru later than his siblings, and at a

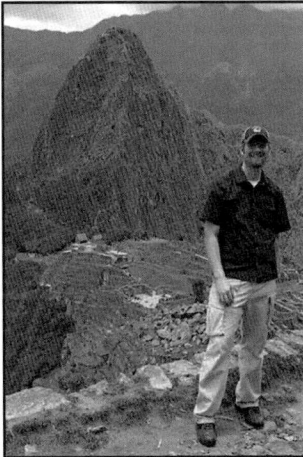

MATT AT MACHU PICCHU

lower price; he works one day a week from home and was able to deal with computer problems at Level Ground from both Peru and Argentina. Matt's dry sense of humour sometimes takes the family by surprise. He no doubt is happy to retreat to the quiet of his condo after work or a session at the family home, and has nearly completed renovations, as well as decorating the walls with his own photos.

Bruce and **Louise** continue to enjoy the in-

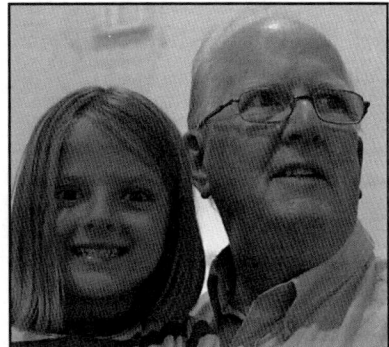

BRUCE WITH GRANDDAUGHTER JOY

teractions with family, boarders, piano students, plant customers, and friends. Bruce has been dealing with the affairs of older friends and family, Louise more with younger family and students. In early September Louise was enticed on to a cruise ship travelling to Alaska; she and Bruce enjoyed the break from routine. Both were saddened by the deaths over the past year of two extraordinary violin teachers who gave our family such a fine musical foundation: Dr. Elfreda Gleam on December 31, 2009, and Frona Colquhoun on March 14th of this year.

SEEN AND HEARD ...

... Jolyn and Joy smiling around matching two-tooth gaps (just in time for "All I Want for Christmas is ...") playing Christmas carols December 22 on the piano for Grandma via Skype, in their bathing suits (33 degrees outside), with the Christmas tree blinking in the background ... Geordon and four friends ascending Mount Aconcagua in January: a three-week undertaking, with a successful summiting and Geordon's comment after the fact that he probably wouldn't have attempted it if he had known how hard it would be (the climb is raising funds towards a YFC centre in Colombia) ... *an indication that some members of this family spend an inordinate amount of time at their computers*: On December 21, 2009, at 11:09 p.m., Mike sends out challenge to family as to who can respond most quickly with the correct answer to his question ($1 prize): "What is wrong with this (caption in Dubai newspaper)?" Caption: "Canucks loose game ..." With the exception of Mark, who is on his way home from South America, Mike's siblings respond: Melissa, from Argentina—11:11 a.m.; Margaret, Oregon—11:13 a.m.; Melody, Victoria—11:14 a.m.; Matt, Victoria—11:16 a.m.; and Marilyn, Argentina—11:17 a.m. There was some discussion as to who really won, as Marilyn's and Melissa's answers came from the same house at the same time, although from different computers. Mike gave Marilyn an honourable mention (50 cents), sympathizing with unpredictable internet servers in foreign lands ... Joshua scoring seven goals and 14 assists over four games in a recent roller hockey tournament in Mar de Plata ... Eric assembling Anna's new keyboard and bench with no advice or help from anyone; Michael and Eric changing Auntie Melissa's tire, under their father's supervision ... new piano student (6) set to play "Criss Cross Buns" (teacher thinks that is not an unreasonable re-titling of "Hot Cross Buns") ... Tori [4], naming the letters of the alphabet, coming to the end: "In Victoria we say 'zed,' but in Salem we say 'zee.'" ... Jordie, in Victoria, playing on his uncles' roller hockey team, at 15 only half the age of most of his team-mates, winning their approval as he puts in several goals, to the delight of the three generations of family members watching the games; in his final game, his hat trick goal was set up by passes from Uncle Matt and Uncle Mark, our version of the Vancouver Canucks' Sedin twins. *[Mark's description of this exciting goal: With the team heading out on the*

powerplay, a Sedin-esque goal from the right point (Matt), to the right face-off dot (Mark) to Jordie at the left side of the net who quickly put the puck to the back of the net for his hat-trick goal in his fourth game with the big fellas. The look on his face was worth more than the price of admission.] ... Matthew, visiting in Buenos Aires after Mark's wedding, playing roller hockey with his nephews ... several family members, after hiking to the peak of Machu Picchu in Peru, echoing brother-in-law Geordon

JORDAN WITH HIS TWO UNCLES

that had they known how difficult it would be, they might have remained at the bottom ... seven years spent in primary classrooms, printing charts, decorating bulletin boards with coloured papers and pictures, over forty years ago; years of Sunday school and junior church handcrafts; an inability to throw away any useful and/or pretty scrap of paper or greeting card; a summer sort-through of cards spanning fifty years, and the saving of many beautiful card fronts = the start of a new tiny hobby/business, Beauty Reclaimed, and the making of dozens of cards in support of the Canadian Foundation for the Children of Haiti ... multi-tasking at its most innovative: Melody, on her way home from a trip to the bank to pick up a substantial sum of American money for her brother in Peru, serving cupcakes at the school fair, her camera strap looped around her ankle, ensuring that neither her new camera nor the cash that has joined it in its case, is removed from under the table ... Anna and Michael participating in school choirs and band, and assimilating the French language at Cedar Hill Middle School ... Anna, Michael and Eric entering Grandma's music room with varying degrees of enthusiasm for the weekly piano lesson ... Tori bringing Mommy's "knee pads" to her, after baby Justin has been fed; Jonathan enjoying a "wunch" date with Daddy (and trying to feed Curious George the way Mommy feeds Justin); Justin lighting up the room with his one-tooth smile—an amiable 22-pound charmer ... a waterfowl, paddling sedately across Horne Lake, trailing a tiny and expanding wake on the glassy surface ... two stubby stumps, all that remain of a couple of maple saplings between our property at Horne Lake and the neighbour's; no doubt the neighbour now has a more pleasing outlook from his property ... Marilyn and four children trapped for 20 hours in the airport at Buenos Aires at the start of their trip to Venezuela, landing in Caracas 40 hours after leaving their home ... Geordon making a 70-hour return flight from Caracas, observing violence and robbery close up during layovers, thankful that Marilyn and family got home safely ... Pilot son's tongue-in-cheek response to mother's request to children for information regarding their travels this year: "Well, according to my logbook, in 2010 I travelled to Hamburg, Karachi, New York, Tehran, Shanghai, Guangzhou, Birmingham, Singapore, Brisbane, Houston, Mumbai, Beijing, Sydney, Colombo, Glasgow, Kuwait, Vienna, Los Angeles, Melbourne, Doha, Perth, Jakarta, London, Delhi, Cairo, Dammam, San Francisco, Amsterdam, and Munich, some of them multiple times. I also went to Toronto, Seattle, Vancouver and Victoria on personal travel."

TEN GRANDCHILDREN

LIFE'S LIKE THIS

Mid-September lunchtime Louise, at dining room table, notes wasp crawling sluggishly along window sill. Makes mental note to despatch it as soon as lunch is finished. ... Wasp drops to floor, crawls slowly out of sight. ... Louise feels sensation on leg, assumes slacks are responsible, glances over to where she last saw wasp, immediately realizes its disappearance might be related to movement on ankle; grabs pant cuff but not soon enough. Searing pain results in several hours of swelling, a few days of itching, and determination to be proactive next time venomous insect invades territory. ... **Several days later** Louise is standing on elevated circle garden, pulling out tomato plants. Suddenly aware of burning pain on upper leg; realizes wasp must have climbed up on inside of baggy gardening

PLANT SALE

pants. Is restrained from tearing off slacks by proximity of townhouses on both sides of back yard. Knows wasps can sting more than once, frantically rolls up pants from bottom. Wasp flies out, but not before placing stinger firmly in ankle on way past.

December 25, 1967 Bruce and Louise open large parcel from senior Hollands, delighted to find arborite-topped cabinet for bathroom, constructed surreptitiously by Grandpa to fit exactly into narrow room, replacing old pedestal sink. Over next few days, Grandpa Holland installs new sink and cabinet, just in time for birth of granddaughter Marilyn on December 30. **July 9, 1976, 8:30 a.m.** Annual letter contains one of the writer's favourite stories, regarding eldest two children and their involvement with the sink (p. 46). **November 1995** Lower floor of enlarged home (little house quadrupled in size by additions in 1971 and 1983) is renovated. Contractor assumes that bathroom cabinet is to be replaced, but sentimental mother requests that old cabinet be retained; does not notice what happens to old sink. **May 2010** For several months, metal plug has not cooperated, and water leaks out of sink in spite of plug. Now piles of towels on shelves under sink are soaking wet, with pieces of rust and metal strewn across them: sink bottom and pipe have disintegrated. ... Matt removes sink, replacing it with new model. Old sink is consigned to dump, but not before Mother notices date on bottom: *July 1967*. Cannot believe that this is the original sink which has submitted to 43 years of usage in a very busy household.

Chapter 57: A Christmas Digest, 2011

EDITORIAL *by Louise*

Best wishes to our friends, neighbours and family for a 2012 filled with God's blessing! By the time you get this (or have the time to read through it), the busyness of Christmas will be behind us. But the Gift of Christmas, our Saviour, will continue to guide us into the future.

50TH ANNIVERSARY

For the past couple of weeks, our family's attention has focussed on the past—to be precise, on December 21, 50 years ago, on the anniversary of both Holland and Forsberg parents—when the writer joined hand and heart in marriage with a man destined to become the father of their seven children. These children, now aged 31 to 44, gathered here mid-December to give their parents an incredible weekend of celebration. A reception for family and friends who had attended our wedding and others who do not attend our church was held in the little church where we met, followed by a reception for friends at our church (Central Baptist) after the service on December 11, and a family meal at Vista 18 in the evening. A special gift to us (and apparently to others) was the sound of seven violins in the church service that day. And two nights were reserved for us at Point-No-Point, where we spent our honeymoon 50 years ago. We ourselves could never have dreamed up such an exciting finale to 2011!

Earlier in the year, there were other reasons for rejoicing: the welcoming into our home of our beautiful daughter-in-law from Peru, and a few months later, the delight in our newest grandchild, named after his uncle Matt and both grandfathers. In May, our eldest son made a move to the left (captain's) seat of the 777, and in December our eldest daughter was released from two years of academic commitment as she handed in her final Master's project to her superiors at Royal Roads University.

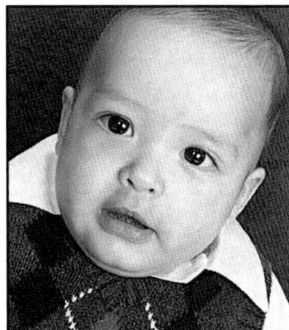

MATTHEW BRENDON ELI HOLLAND

Our household is enriched by the presence of our sterling boarders. Steve De Vries teaches music and gifted students at Arbutus Middle School, and Morgan Kinahan (just out of high school, from Chemainus) studies in a sports programme at Camosun. They, the trio at the other end of the upstairs, and the rest of our family in Victoria, weave in and out of our activities here—guaranteed to keep us a little younger.

Not only are the elderly-weds somewhat taken aback at reaching the 50th milestone, but their respective birthdays this year brought them another unsettling pair of numbers: 75 and 70. As have many before them expressed, they too ask, "Where did the time go?" And they exclaim, "Great is Thy faithfulness!"

RENDLE FAMILY

PERSONAL GLIMPSES

Geordon and **Marilyn** and family—**Jordan** [17], **Joshua** [almost 14], **Jolyn** [8], and **Joy** [7]—are preparing for a move from Buenos Aires to Victoria at the end of June, leaving much of their heart in South America. Geordon's position as Youth for Christ Director of the Americas means he can work from any area in North or South America. Eldest son Jordan's graduation from high school appears to be a fitting time for a return to Canada. While we have admired and supported the Rendles as they headquartered in Latin America, we must admit the prospect of having them closer is very appealing. The family is relieved that Marilyn has completed her Master of Arts in Leadership, and her parents are proud of her tenacity in doing so.

Michael has also reached his goal of several years, and now sports four gold stripes on the arm of his flight jacket. He continues to fly all over the world for Emirates Airlines.

MIKE

His very full schedule entitled him to a three-week break in December, and he used much of his time to upgrade his parents' computer and other electronic equipment. (His brothers keep an eye on the electronics between visits from Dubai.)

Chris and **Margaret**, with **Victoria** (Tori) [6], **Jonathan** [4 1/2], and **Justin** [1 1/2], drive up from Salem, Oregon, whenever we can entice them here. Tori happily reads in both English and Spanish (is in Spanish immersion at school), Jonathan enjoys sleeping in the clothes closet at Grandpa and Grandma's, and Justin takes pleasure in suc-

BUCHER FAMILY

MELISSA WITH HER SWISS NAMESAKE

cessfully hiding himself in little spaces, as well as depositing small (and sometimes important) items in hard-to-find places. (Grandpa has still not found the portable phone after the last visit.) Chris's work with the federal highway system has shifted to central and southwest Oregon, which brings him to the coast, an area he, with his roots in the Midwest, finds especially appealing. Margaret continues to keep the home fires burning, a difficult challenge for several weeks in June and July due to foot surgery; her father spent two of those weeks cooking and getting well-acquainted with his very sweet American grandchildren.

Melissa continues in paediatrics at Victoria General Hospital, both as nurse and in a variety of supporting roles. She travels to South America and Oregon to provide a little respite for her sisters and families. The Rendle and Bucher nieces and nephews join their Stark cousins in Victoria in their great affection for "Auntie Melissa," as do her parents, who have learned that she was the main organizer of the anniversary celebrations. Melissa is working towards a Master in Clinical Education through the University of Edinburgh.

Richard and **Melody** continue to facilitate family activities and celebrations. **Anna** [14], **Michael** [12] and **Eric** [9] attend three different schools (Reynolds, Cedar Hill, and Lake Hill), and are active in sports and music (and French and Spanish), so Melody's gift for organization is in constant use. She works part-time at La-Z-Boy as an administrative assistant. Richard employs his managerial skills at Level Ground

Trading, and is pleased to report that business has been at record levels—good news for those in developing countries who receive fair prices as well as community development from Level Ground.

STARK FAMILY

Mark and **Margeliza** (Margie) are the proud parents of **Matthew Brendon Eli**, born July 22. The grandparents delight in experiencing this newest grandchild, as he and his parents live in the upstairs suite. Although there are days when the generations do not see each other, little Matthew is usually brought down in the evening to say good-night to his doting grandparents. Mark is currently on parental leave from work, and he and

MARGIE, MARK, BABY MATTHEW

Margie are anticipating a trip to Peru in the New Year so little Matthew's Peruvian family will have an opportunity to meet him.

Matt participates in baseball, volleyball and in-line hockey, in between his work responsibilities at Level Ground, where he oversees his order management system and keeps the computers running efficiently. He recently accompanied Grandpa down to Oregon, when

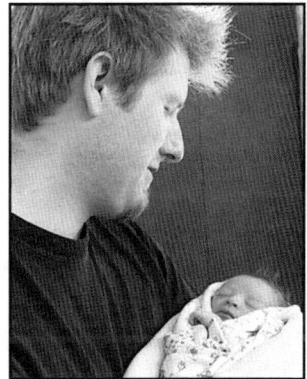

TWO MATTHEWS

both Grandpa and Uncle spent a weekend caring for the Bucher children, while the parents celebrated a 40th birthday.

And the grandparents? The patriarch enables the matriarch in her several endeavours (teaching piano, working with plants in support of young people, making/recycling cards in support of an Haitian orphanage, and, whenever possible, joining her partner in some of the household responsibilities). As this is being typed, a splendid Christmas meal is gradually appearing in the kitchen to her right, so it is obvious which of the grandparents is labouring over a hot stove. ... The typist has just emerged

BRUCE AND LOUISE

from the dishpit, and following an interlude of playing Christmas carols on the living-room piano (such musical reprieves a lifelong form of enjoyable procrastination), and some work at the computer, is now motivated to help set up a table for 20 (maybe 22? maybe 24?) guests. Both grandparents are involved in Bible study groups, one as facilitator for an evening group, the other in a morning group where she has had the positive experience of studying Proverbs in depth. Now to apply so much wisdom!

ANNA, MICHAEL AND ERIC

SCENE IN PASSING ...

... Eric accompanying school recorder ensemble on "Eric's Song" (actually entitled "God is So Good," and so announced by narrator) ... Anna on flute, Auntie Melissa on violin, providing background music at church's breakfast for the homeless ... comment to Marilyn by member of her cohorts at Royal Roads during February's residency, after her group made a presentation: "Your violin solo was heavenly on Monday morning. It really struck the heart and soul of many as that song ["Danny Boy"] and as the violin can do. Well done!" ... Grandma waking from a nap to discover pair of red shoes dangling from the doorknob, a gift from Grandpa who had observed she found her new black pair very comfortable ... little Justin using an older sibling's plastic cup to obtain a drink from the toilet, while parents are preparing for grandparents' anniversary celebration ... re-discovery of

JORDAN AND JOSHUA

Great-Grandpa Forsberg's jam stand notebooks, filled with hundreds of customers' signatures from the 1950s (Hjalmar, trained as a chef, sold a great variety of his jams, jellies and marmalades to customers passing our home on West Saanich Road on the way to Butchart Gardens; many American states and several Canadian provinces are represented) ... Rendle family supplying music at church service in BABS Care Home in Buenos Aires; Stark family serving in programmes at Central Care and Mt. Edwards Court in Victoria: continuation of family programmes from years past, although Grandma does

JOLYN AND JOY

not remember the previous generation doing gymnastics as part of the entertainment (grandson Eric enjoys displaying his mastery of handstands, much to the delight of his elderly audience) ... 69-year-old sister's birthday card to year-older sister: "Jesus loves us, this I'm told, even though we're really old ... In spite of wrinkles and false teeth, He sees the young soul underneath!" ... Tori and Jonathan forming a quintet with their Canadian cousins in Victoria, singing "Can a Little Child Like Me...thank the Father fittingly" in the Thanksgiving Sunday evening service ... the featured sweets for Mark and Margie's reception in Victoria: M&Ms ... *Question*: What is worse than leaving for a doctor's appointment with a large red velcro hair roller attached to the elbow of a bulky-knit sweater? *Answer*: Arriving home to discover roller attached to arm, and realizing that curler, just out of owner's range of vision, has accompanied owner throughout morning excursion ... **The Emotional Life of a Piano Teacher**—*wry humour*: student has made her painstaking way through four lines of a Bach minuet, assisted by teacher's frequent suggestions and corrections; noting repeat signs, cheerfully asks if teacher would like her to play passage again (teacher's response is gentle negative) ... *frustration, part 1*: student has forgotten assignment book from which teacher takes information about previous lesson and determines course of current lesson; new assignment written out on sheet of looseleaf paper in the hope it will find its way into assignment book by next lesson ... *frustration, part 2*: student has left crucial piano book on instrument at home after last-minute practice session; teacher may or may not have duplicate copy at hand ... *delight*: student has memorized eight-page Haydn sonata, presents teacher with buoyant, fluent performance ... *frustration, part 3*: student possesses considerable musical ability, has managed to fit 30 minutes of practice—once—into previous week's activities; lesson becomes second practice session of week ... *elation*: student has, after weeks of effort on technical requirements (scales, chords, arpeggios, etc.), brought technique to a proficient level; shares with teacher that he really enjoys being able to play so quickly and well (teacher muses inwardly that "quickly" and "well" do not always correlate) ... *frustration, part 4*: student returns from holidays with 1/4" nails projecting from fingertips, skates from note to note (or plays with flat fingers); teacher makes emphatic demand that scissors or clippers be employed before next lesson ... *satisfaction*: student with developmental difficulties has laboured for weeks on set of pieces, enjoys playing them as duets with teacher ... *attitude of prayer, as in "Lord, give me patience"*: student insists on playing F natural throughout piece, even though key signature at the beginning of each line displays F#; consistent reminders half a beat ahead of each controversial note gradually bring compliance ... *delight in students' artistry*: weekly sticker on front of practice record, chosen from eclectic mix of stickers on teacher's tray, gives insight into student's thought processes, as stickers are organized into random collages, or symmetrical design, or groupings of specific subjects (animals, cars, flowers, etc.) ... *gratitude*: for the privilege of interacting week by week with a variety of personalities, and levels of motivation and ability ...

LIFE'S LIKE THIS

March break Newlyweds from Peru have settled into suite in western half of upstairs. Bucher family from Oregon are ensconced in other half. Parents startled to learn that four-year-old son Jonathan has made his way during the night through door dividing two areas, crawling into bed with Uncle Mark and Auntie Margie.

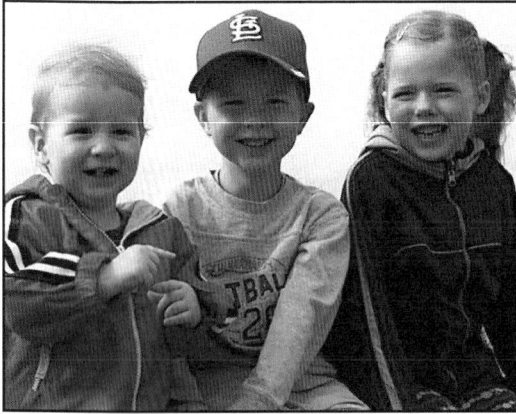

JUSTIN, JONATHAN AND TORI

Early summer Tori brings home four sunflower seeds from preparatory visit to new school, in anticipation of fall attendance. Plants them lovingly with assistance from Auntie Melissa. Two sprout and continue to be showered with affection until Bucher family leaves for two-week vacation in Illinois. Next-door neighbour agrees to water seedlings. E-mails from neighbour to mother Margaret give day-by-day progress reports and convey concern for success of sunflower project. Temperatures hit 80s and 90s; sunflower plants wither. Neighbour purchases two well-developed plants from nursery, replaces shrivelled plant corpses. Youthful gardener returns, is ecstatic when she catches sight of her plants. Neighbour and mother, feeling a little guilty, do not share behind-the-scenes drama with child.

December 4, 2011 Son-in-law Geordon has taken wife Marilyn to airport in Buenos Aires for flight to Montreal, where Marilyn will participate in YFC national staff meeting on way to parents' anniversary celebration in Victoria. Comments in phone call to father-in-law that as he was speaking from Argentina to gathering in Montreal several hours later, it was somewhat surreal to see his wife walking into the boardroom; Father-in-law comments that it was like the day 53 years ago when his wife-to-be first walked into the little church where she had been invited to play the piano, and he knew she was *the one*. *[The writer of this looong letter is shamelessly including this little story only because of the significance of this year!]*

Chapter 58: A Christmas Digest, 2012

EDITORIAL *by Louise*

November 11 It is Sunday afternoon, Remembrance Day. A piano concerto fills the cabin at Horne Lake, courtesy of the CBC; a warmth radiates throughout the rooms, thanks to a propane heater in the corner. It is peaceful and calm inside, a little less tranquil outside, as the cedar branches sway gently in the wind. The morning lake's tints of palest blue, visible through a curtain of wet snowflakes, have given way to multiple shades of gray, the water now dimpled by raindrops.

We again remember with gratitude the sacrifices of those who have given us the freedom to sit in such comfort and safety. This is Armistice Day, but it is also Sunday, the Lord's Day, and we thank God as well for his many gifts to us, both temporal and spiritual.

I have reread last year's Christmas letters and our once-in-a-lifetime 50th Anniversary cards, and am reminded of the generosity of friends and family, not only last December, but during the past year.

If at times we appear distracted or not entirely on top of things, it could be advancing years, and/or it could be the side effects of trying to keep tabs on our expanding family: two of our children by Skype as well as by their visits to Victoria, and the other five who live within minutes of us here in Victoria. Eight grandchildren in Victoria and three in Salem, Oregon, add spice to the mix, and our three boarders provide glimpses into the world of today's young adults. Steve De Vries teaches music in the Victoria school system, Jasmine Montgomery-Reid takes general studies at Camosun College and trains with the Camosun Chargers basketball team. Brandon Fyall, grandson of Lily Milljour from our church, is in the culinary course at Camosun. Many mornings start with Brandon's shower at 6:00 a.m., in preparation for his classes at 7:30 a.m., Mark's (in the upstairs suite) at 7:00 a.m. for work at 8:00 a.m., Margie's at 7:30 a.m. for classes (English at Camosun) at 8:30 a.m., and Jasmine's later on during the morning, depending on her schedule. Two days a week, our PhD student from the mainland, Isaac Kim, makes use of the downstairs shower. And this writer, whose bedtime often straddles midnight, lies in bed, dimly aware of all the clean people she hears leave her house! She and her partner of nearly 51 years approach the day in a more leisurely fashion, he to shopping and cooking responsibilities, she to plant and teaching activities, both to household chores.

December 24 It is Christmas Eve, and this writing project is obviously not going to be finished before Christmas. Although there are kind friends who ask around Christmas time where the letter is, we have observed its lateness does not bring about any great suffering! So… less stress, more pleasure in the task. May your 2013 be filled with many blessings!

PERSONAL GLIMPSES

MATT

Matthew quietly maintains the order management system he has developed for Level Ground Trading, and ensures that the company's computers work efficiently. He, along with the rest of the family, is enjoying his little namesake. We enjoy having our youngest son just two half-blocks away from us, a great convenience when computer glitches arise here. Inline hockey, volleyball and softball continue to be major interests.

MARGIE, MARK, MATTHEW

Mark and **Margie** and little **Matthew**, now 17 months old, keep us company, living quite separately in the upstairs suite here in the home where we have spent 46 of our 51 years together. Mark continues to keep a watchful eye on those who cross the Canadian-American border. Margie is very appreciative of aunts, uncles, nieces and nephews who have kept little Matthew company while she is at Camosun upgrading her English; the babysitters are happy to have some Matthew-time. The grandparents receive at least one visit a day from their youngest grandchild, and are very willing to work or read with a powerful baby monitor on the counter when the parents need to go to an appointment or shopping, and the baby is asleep.

Melody's work at the La-Z-Boy Furniture Galleries is much appreciated, judging by her co-workers' accolades. (Her mother is not surprised, having worked with her for

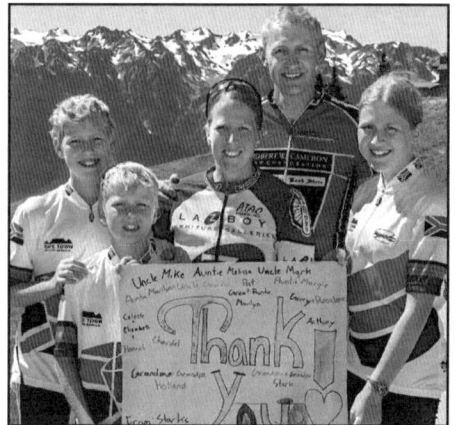

STARK FAMILY

several years in our little family businesses.) **Richard** continues to oversee Level Ground's continuing growth, and with Melody, to support **Anna** [now 15, at Reynolds Secondary School], **Michael** [13, at Cedar Hill Middle School], and **Eric** [10, at Lake Hill Elementary School] in their various athletic, musical and academic ventures. Three weeks in South Africa last March allowed them not only to visit friend Dawnmaree (Fletcher) Philip and her family, originally from Victoria, but gave them some up-close experiences with the face of poverty in that country.

MELISSA AND A SPECIAL BIRTHDAY

Melissa nurses in the paediatric section of Victoria General Hospital, as well as overseeing nursing students from Camosun and UVic who are completing a practicum in the paediatric area; maintains an interest in the young people at our church and in our family; and is completing her Masters in Clinical Education through the University of Edinburgh. She and as many family members and friends as she can convince to come are planning a walking trip across Spain after her course is finished.

Margaret and **Chris**, **Tori** (Victoria) [7], **Jonathan** [5 1/2], and **Justin** [2 1/2], live tantalizingly close (ferry ride + six hours' drive) to us in Salem, Oregon, and were able to make four trips up to see Margaret's family this year. Chris and Margaret have chosen to enroll Tori and Jonathan in an inner-city Spanish immersion school, and both are thriving. Margaret's teaching background allows her both to evaluate the

BUCHER FAMILY

quality of the children's education (which to date has been very good) and to help out in unobtrusive ways in the classroom. Chris continues to monitor highways and bridges over a large area in Oregon.

Michael is completing his sixth year flying for Emirates Airlines in Dubai, the last two as captain. That statement now carries much more meaning for his parents as they flew to Dubai at the end of November to have a look at the "greened" desert on the other side of the world. The 14-hour flight was made easier in the first-class accommodation that Mike provided for his

UNCLE MIKE AND MATTHEW

pampered parents, who were also treated to tours of the quite amazing city that has arisen over the last 41 years on the desert. Michael's maternal parent often voices reservations regarding excess and extravagance, but admittedly found many things to interest her in this city of superlatives, including the 60-storey Millennium Tower where Michael lives (32nd floor); its neighbouring apartment blocks which feature unusual architecture, especially the 180-storey Burj Khalifa (formerly the Burj Dubai), tallest in the world; the lush tropical vegetation sustained by desalinized sea water; the huge malls, one containing a ski hill, another a regulation-size hockey rink; the variety of Arabic dress seen in the malls, including the women in a variety of coverings, from eyes-only visible to full face exposure, from black head-to-toe to coloured burqas; shopping in the modern supermarket; cooking and sharing meals in Mike's apartment; and best of all, several days of having our eldest son to ourselves!

Marilyn and **Geordon** and family are gradually settling into the home they left 17 years ago, a physically demanding and emotionally draining procedure, as possessions stored for those years and items acquired since must be sorted through, and their work with Youth For Christ and family demands must still be addressed day by day. Marilyn spends approximately half time serving as one of Geordon's assistants; Geordon works at least full-time as Americas Director, field-

RENDLE FAMILY

ing e-mails, Skype and phone calls from all over North, Central and South America, and travelling to conferences in the same areas. **Jordan** [now 18] is in second year drama studies at Trinity Western University; **Joshua** [nearly 15] attends Grade 9 at Reynolds Secondary with cousin Anna, in Grade 10; **Jolyn** [9] is in Grade 4, with **Joy** [8] in Grade 3 at Lake Hill Elementary, where cousin Eric Stark also attends Grade 5. The grandparents' home on the north end of Saanich Road provides temporary shelter (and a piano for practising) for the girls after Joshua has been taken to Reynolds for 7:50 soccer practice twice a week; they can enter Lake Hill only after 8:19 a.m.

Bruce and **Louise** continue to savour each day and its variety of activities. It is great to be able to share this property with family, friends, boarders, and students, and to

LOUISE AND BRUCE AND THE BURJ KHALIFA

enjoy the natural wonders on this little patch of Garry Oak meadow. We are thankful for these blessings. And we are thankful, too, for this year's excursions: in February to join Louise's brother and wife in their winter home in Arizona, and in November to Dubai.

LIFE'S LIKE THIS

February 5, 2012 (letter to children and grandchildren): "Hello all, I just thought I'd tell you about a strange experience I had on the way to church this morning. Our radio had been set at 98.1, which is an American equivalent of CBC. An announcer was interviewing a young violinist, and we came in where he said to the young man that he understood he and his family did a lot with music, and that he had heard that this young violinist helped his younger brothers with their music. The violinist said yes, he spent about an hour a day with each of his brothers, and that it was a great experience to have some one-on-one time with each in turn. (Father plays piano, as does a sister. Not sure about the mother.) Anyway, the announcer asked what the family did, and the violinist answered that they played in all sorts of places as a family, and especially enjoyed playing in care homes for the 'lonely' and 'forgotten.' His parents said that music was a gift to be shared and not to be used for 'self-glory,' but for the glory of God. He added that J.S. Bach often used to write 'For the glory of God' on his compositions. (He had a little bit of a German accent, and the name 'Bach' was pronounced the way it should be!) It was quite a wonderful interview, and I said to Dad/Grandpa that we had had our sermon for the day, and should turn around and go home. (We didn't.) … Then this young man played a Beethoven concerto, a huge and beautiful piece, accompanied by a skilful pianist. It was just as if someone had pressed a button, and I started to weep, totally unexpected and a little embarrassing. I was not unhappy, but the gorgeous music, after what the young person had said, took me off guard, and I had flashbacks of my children and concerti, sonatas, "Jesu Joy," on and on—things I had not thought of for years, but I guess are buried somewhere in my subconscious. You probably know I am more than satisfied and very grateful to be able to contribute still with my teaching and at church, and no way would I want to be back in the stress of those years, beautiful though they were, and well-received as my children's music was. It was certainly an example of the power of music."

February 2012 Mark and Margie have been planning trip to Peru for several weeks, but had been unable to firm up plans until Margie's visa was in hand. Have set February 14 as arrival date in Peru, but want to keep date a secret from Margie's family. Plan to arrive at front door, ring doorbell, and place baby Matthew in other grandmother's arms. … Family arrives later than anticipated in Pisco; no one is at home. Goes downtown, sees Margie's sister Erica walking towards them on sidewalk. Erica catches sight of Matthew, puzzled by sight of baby who looks very much like her little nephew, and is then blocked by young woman standing in her path. Suddenly realizes that it is her sister—great excitement, and much hugging! … Family migrates to grandmother's workplace, comes up behind grandmother, who is alerted by co-workers that her daughter is behind her. Again, much excitement and joy as grandmother scoops up first grandchild and hugs daughter and son-in-law.

MATTHEW

Anonymity to Spectacle, two versions (same person): **December 10, 1996** (sixteen years ago—from 1996's Digest) Mother *[Louise]* looks for excuse to go for a walk, decides to deliver flyer information to customer several blocks away. Dons padded winter coat and woollen gloves, happily strides down Saanich Road to crosswalk at Quadra. Eyes two lanes of traffic approaching on other side of road; stands back on sidewalk to await their passing. To her surprise, both lanes come to a halt. Mother looks left to closest two lanes and is startled to see that they, too, have stopped. Cars stretch down both sides of road as far as can be seen. Mother hurriedly steps into crosswalk, feeling very conspicuous. Halfway across, drops letter onto damp pavement, desperately tries to retrieve it, hampered by thick gloves and long, bulky coat; is very conscious of four lanes of traffic waiting patiently. Spends next three blocks musing on how a few moments can transform one from a comfortable anonymity to a most uncomfortable spectacle. **May 2012** version, as related by grandmother: I experienced a similar, and more spectacular, transformation, as I checked out some of the science fair exhibits at UVic. Grandson Eric was participating, and his grandfather and I decided to give him a little support; we knew his project was well done. Things went fine at first. Eric surfaced from within the crowd and proceeded to take us to his exhibit. He also pointed out an exhibit that had taken his fancy: a hydrofoil experiment operated by a vacuum cleaner. The earnest young exhibitor showed us how it worked and Eric suggested I get on it. I replied that someone smaller should try it, and was assured by the exhibitor's partner that not only had they already had "tall" people try it, but the contraption would hold up to 300 lbs. Having spent nearly 52 years trying to affirm (i.e., teach) children and teenagers, I thought I would give it a shot. So I stood on the platform (approximately

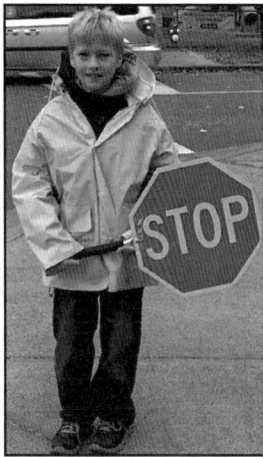

ERIC

two feet in diameter), feet on the indicated spots, and took the piece of twine that supposedly would give some semblance of balance. I assumed the platform would lift sedately up a couple of inches and then, equally sedately, return to its place of origin. Not so. Almost immediately the platform starting tilting, and I, who almost always have a hand near a handrail, wall or counter to ensure I don't fall, found myself catapulted to the floor. There were immediate cries of "Are you OK?" and "Are you hurt?" I assured them I wasn't hurt—only my dignity had suffered. My dear husband is torn between amusement at the sight and the contemplation of the potential seriousness of such a fall; daughter Margaret cautiously e-mailed: "Let us know when enough time has passed that we can look back on the visual with a smile."

June 14, 2012 Louise is at large circle garden in back yard, shovelling out gallons of beautifully friable compost into large pots. Becomes aware of raucous cawing above her head. Two crows, agitated, swoop back and forth. She inserts rake into soft earth; hopes tines will act as scarecrow. Failed manoeuvre, as birds fly even lower. Takes hose, sprays upwards. Law of gravity takes over, bringing deluge of water down on top of her. Takes hose back to holder, leaning over to avoid frantic birds; passes raspberry patch, has peculiar sensation of being watched. Suddenly catches sight of two glowing black eyes among the raspberry leaves: a baby crow!

SEEN AND HEARD ...

... grandparents exploring the Arizona desert with brother Eric Forsberg and wife Wynne, gaining more appreciation for Louise's and Eric's parents love of the unobtrusive beauties of that desolate land ... Louise touching teddy bear cholla cactus with its—from-a-distance—soft needles; discovers that tiny barbs at needle ends are removed only with exquisite pain ... Louise eating a very fresh grapefruit every day for a week—picked right off the tree in front of brother's home in Arizona ... Bruce and Louise marvelling at (from a distance at first) the Grand Canyon, and thoroughly enjoying the variety of songs and instrumentation at the Grand Ole Opry in Phoenix ... screensaver which suddenly appeared on our computer—little Matthew in sailor suit worn by his Uncle Mike 42 years ago, and by his father 33 years ago ... hundreds of snowdrops faithfully making their annual appearance in February, a legacy of an unknown gardener from 60 or 70 years ago ... Tori commenting on the trip up to Victoria about some birds flying overhead, "You know why they're flying in the shape of a V, Mom and Dad? Because they're going on 'Veecation!'" ... the

TORI

Bucher van enduring three one-hour waits in Olympic National Park as snow is ploughed on Highway 101, at one point sliding within inches of a seven-foot drop, pulled out by a passing tow truck a few minutes after car had left road (grandmother learned during the middle of the night that 101 had been closed, envisioned family trapped in that huge park) … Geordon and Marilyn hiding in bedroom (in Argentina), only room in house not occupied by family or guests, talking with Marilyn's parents via laptop: "We're not sure right now just who is in this house—four children, two interns, Josh's friends, couple of Canadians who found us on the internet—planning to bike from here to Alaska," and, laughing, "We know you have always had lots of people in your house, but you *produced* most of them!" … Geordon and Marilyn repeating their wedding vows 25 years later at a simple but lovely service on August 10, with family and friends in attendance … Bruce patiently listening to longish story from wife; recognizing that she has something else to share, reaches up, smiling mischievously, to remove hearing aids … mallard and hen feasting on duckweed in front pond, feathers glowing in the spring sunshine (duckweed apparently is not only valuable as food source—with potential as human food—but serves as a water purifier and mosquito inhibitor) … Stark family leaving Victoria's two-degree weather and rain in March for three weeks of Johannesburg's sunshine, jumping into their friends Michael and Dawnmaree's swimming pool a day later … note from son-in-law: "We woke up at 4:30 a.m. to get Anna up and off on her seven day band trip today. I took her to Reynolds for 5:15 a.m. and while waiting there with her she surprisingly remembered she needed to take her flute." … (November update: Anna received straight As on her report card.) … pink Easter lilies at UVic housing complex—bring back memories of Louise's first encounter with pink lilies at the age of three at the air force base in Coal Harbour … Granddaughter Joy: "It's just at the tip of my … nose" … Grandson Michael identifying flower as "fox mittens," quickly correcting to "foxgloves" … Michael playing on Gold

JOY AND JOLYN

JOSHUA   JORDAN

soccer team … note from son Michael: "I crossed a milestone on my most recent flight (to Glasgow), that of accumulating 10,000 hours of flight time. For those familiar with author Malcolm Gladwell's book *Outliers*, 10,000 hours is about where one starts to get good at something, which should be a relief to my passengers. By my own calculation it represents about 417 days of spending every hour of every day aloft." … Mark's "cherub schedule," listing days and times when aunts and cousins have the privilege of babysitting little Matthew when both father and mother are at work and school … Margie's final course marks: A+ and A+ … Jordan graduating from high school in Buenos Aires on June 9; Joshua at grade eight promotion ceremony June 13; family leaving South America for meetings in Denver on June 14, the day Marilyn's cohort is graduating from Royal Roads University; Marilyn in mortarboard and gown at Royal Road's October convocation, happily accepting her Masters of Art in Leadership diploma … large deer with impressive antlers outside kitchen window, checking out plant smorgasbord on other side of fence (Louise not too happy); month later: same buck on inside of fence, mowing down grape hyacinth leaves (Louise even less pleased, as her plants are destined for youth project) … little Matthew bent double as he peers

MARILYN, WITH A MASTER IN LEADERSHIP

ANNA

at Grandma's feet, fascinated with toenails which Grandma has painted red (for perhaps the third time in her life) in preparation for her trip to the desert … Melissa following through on her 2011 Christmas gifts to her Stark niece and nephews, an "adventure" of their choice: Anna, a visit to Adrena LINE (zipline adventure) and overnight at the lake; Eric, a trip to Vancouver, overnighting in a hotel; and Michael, an excursion to WildPlay Nanaimo, a high ropes course, followed by Monopoly and chess time at the lake (rumour has it that while Michael balanced happily on the ropes and platforms, his companion had a much greater affinity for anything she could get her hands on or arms around) … 11 little scrolls around the Christmas tree, guaranteeing Melissa at least 11 more adventures with her nieces and nephews in 2013 … little Matthew standing by a downstairs heat register, laughing as the blasts of heat send his wispy hair flying (grandmother's relationship to heat vent not as cheerful, as it lives only a foot away from two outside doors which are all too often left open) … fantastic thunder and lightning storm which greeted parents on first morning of their stay in Dubai, resulting in huge torrent of water down the apartment

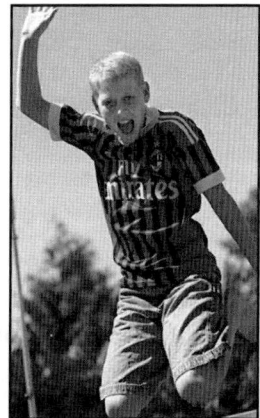

MICHAEL

block's exterior, deep puddles of water on streets which do not have drains, and intermittent flashes of lightning throughout the day … Melissa celebrating Canada Day with sunrise on the east coast and fireworks on the west coast … grandmother watching video replay of Rendle and Stark grandchildren (seven cousins) and their parents providing a Christmas programme (singing, piano, violin) at Central Care Home and Mt. Edwards Court, reminded of years past when seven siblings and their violins gave similar concerts at these residences, and others … little Matthew's fa-

MICHAEL AND GEORDON

vourite toy: a $200+ Tonka toy fished out of the upstairs toilet by the plumber (the *toy* did not cost $200) … anecdote from Geordon: "The little girls are working with their mommy sorting clothes, passing on some to other friends and cousins, packing for the winter, the summer and the container. In the midst of all of that, they came downstairs last night dressed in some truly beautiful summer gowns. Bless Jordie's heart; his response, that just melted their hearts with joy, was, 'Would you girls come with me to my Prom?'"… a description of

first-class treatment on an Emirates Boeing 777-200LR (a revelation to those who had until now flown only economy class): "14 hours is quite a long flight, but certainly being in first class ameliorated both the length and any discomfort. We were offered fresh juice, and a hot towel (several times), then dates and Arabic coffee, and then an unlimited menu, which could be ordered from at any time. The little room had a basket of cookies, chocolate bars, and Pringles chips, a bar filled with six or seven juice and pop containers, a tray of creams and scented packages, a deluxe writing set,

another silky bag of toiletries, and a pajamas/ slippers/nightshade set. At bedtime, an attendant made the seat into a bed with mattress and duvet, and, after an excellent meal, we each raised the walls of our 'rooms' and slept quite well. There are eight first class seats on a B777, with four attendants, and two washrooms close by." [*It's instructive that the person who wrote this description forgot to mention the hundreds of movies or varieties of music available; even at 35,000 feet, reading is still her preference.*] … a view of the Himalayas over Pakistan: a huge expanse of snow-topped mountains under a layered sky—pastel pink at the top; intense turquoise in the middle, shading to a soft turquoise near the peaks …

JONATHAN IN UNCLE MIKE'S UNIFORM

Chapter 59: A Christmas Digest, 2013

EDITORIAL *by Louise*

December 29 Poised between the celebration of our Saviour's birth three days ago and the entering of a new year three days from now, my mind returns to the words of an old hymn: "Guide Me, O Thou Great Jehovah, pilgrim through this barren land. I am weak, but Thou art mighty, Hold me with Thy powerful hand." ... I do not live in a "barren" land, but I do feel relatively powerless in the face of an unknown future. I pray for guidance in this new year for myself, my family, and my friends and acquaintances. May 2014 bring us a measure of health and happiness, and opportunities to relieve the sufferings of those around us.

We are fortunate to have Mark and Margie and little Matthew (as distinct from "big" Matthew, his uncle) sharing our home. Our little grandson is a delight, but not free from some of the characteristics of a typical two year old. His parents recently shared, with some disbelief and embarrassment, that this beautiful child flew into a "full-out" (his father's word) tantrum at the grocery store when his time at pushing the shopping cart was through. His mother hurriedly picked him off the floor while his father paid their bill, and both exited the store on the run, with Junior Holland howling. Grandma, as caretaker of family memories, was prompted to share a couple: the first, her second child lying face-down on the floor in the middle of our tiny house, banging his little fists on the wooden floor and crying in frustration over the world's (i.e., his parents') injustice, the display prompting his older, less easily-unsettled, sister to give this novel activity a try a few hours later, without much success; the second, an anecdote recorded by Granny Anna, relating how her eldest at the age of three, had transplanted her grandmother's carrots into another area of the garden. Upon being reprimanded a year later for picking a bouquet of flowers from the neighbour's garden and being told she would have to return them to the neighbour, stamped her foot and said angrily to her mother, "Mommy, you are a *stinker!*" (Vocabulary acquired at air force base in Coal Harbour.) *[Update to 2013: the little boy of 42 years ago now responds to the terms "Captain" or "Commander"; the little girl of nearly 70 years ago spends considerable time outside among the flowers, propagating hundreds of plants for her benefit project.]*

This year's highlight had to be our foray into Europe. Melissa said three years

ago, as she started her Master's programme through the University of Edinburgh,
that she would take us to her graduation.
True to her word, she not only did that,
but took us on side excursions to Sweden
(home to my paternal grandparents),
Denmark (origin of my maternal grandparents), and England (to visit Bruce's
relatives)—all crammed into eleven days,
and involving much walking and the riding of many conveyances: airplane, train,
bus, rented car. Melissa had synchronized
these modes of travel with bookings in
hotels in Malmo (Sweden), Copenhagen
and Bov (Denmark), and Edinburgh, and

TRAVELLING TO MELISSA'S GRADUATION IN SCOTLAND

activities involving sightseeing, shopping, and culture (Edinburgh symphony on one
evening; a very interesting lecture on early instruments in St. Cecilia's Hall Museum
of Instruments on another)—a huge undertaking, with not much margin for delayed
flights or rides. We enjoyed the train ride from Scotland to the Midlands (Uttoxeter)
in England for two days with Bruce's Hollingsworth cousins at the end of our trip.
After a night in a London hotel, and a walk through part of the incredible Hyde Park,
we continued on the train to Heathrow—and home.

My mother had saved a box of my great-aunt's diaries and artwork for over 50
years, and at her passing in 2002, I became caretaker of these documents. Great Aunt
Anna (1870–1951) was a writer, first in Old German, with smatterings of Danish—the
family lived in the Schleswig-Holstein area which was claimed in turn by Germany
and Denmark—and, after her move to Canada in 1912, in increasingly fluent English,
punctuated with the occasional frustrated "O Canada!" She was also very artistic,
leaving beautiful samples of needlework and several coloured drawings of both the
area around Flensburg (now German; Flensborg when it was Danish) and her farm in
Saskatchewan. It has been very interesting to correlate Aunt Anna's writings and
artwork and my mother's autobiography and relate them to some of the places we
saw in our travels. We were able to find several of the European buildings in
Auntie's pictures from more than a century ago, and have been able to get more information from the Internet. We learned from the archives in Bov that my great-
grandfather, a coppersmith who specialized in the rolling of copper into thin sheets,
died in 1878 at 37 after five days of illness probably related to copper poisoning, leaving children 8 (Aunt Anna), 6, 4 and 2 (my grandfather) behind. Twenty-eight years
later my grandfather and my beautiful young Danish grandmother emigrated to
Manitoba in 1906, along with two toddlers, both of whom died in the next few

months, just before my mother's birth in 1907. The little girl had been named Anna, so that became my mother's name as well. When we were in Sweden, I also gave some thought to my young Swedish grandparents leaving the cold and hardships of Sweden for the probably equally challenging climates of North Dakota and, eventually, Saskatchewan. My 14 Swedish aunts, uncles and father were born over a period of 27 years; my grandmother, Lovisa, had her first baby at 16 in Sweden and her last at 43 in Canada.

Our boarders Jasmine Montgomery-Reid and Brandon Fyall left us in June, and we welcomed sister and brother Rosalea and Dalton Pagani, grandchildren of our church friends, John and Rona Slomke. Rosalea and Dalton are both attending Camosun College. We enjoy their company very much, and they in turn seem happy here, especially on the days when our youngest grandchild turns up at the table downstairs. Our boarder of many years, Steven De Vries, left us on December 23 to marry Andrea Cave, also a musician and at one time my student. We will miss Steve; it has been a privilege to share our home with him.

PERSONAL GLIMPSES

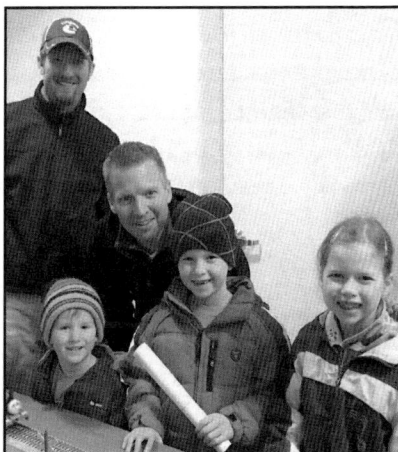

MATT WITH MIKE AND BUCHER CHILDREN

Matthew continues to develop and modify Level Ground's order management system, a positive challenge as the company expands. We are thankful for his help with computer challenges, only a block (or a click of the mouse) away, and for his steadying influence on family dynamics. He recently found himself at a production of *The Nutcracker* in Salem with brother Mike, watching niece Tori dance as both mouse and angel. Matt maintains his interest in roller hockey and volleyball.

Mark and **Margie** and little **Matthew** continue to share our roof, hopefully to their advantage, and definitely to our pleasure. Mark deals (in a friendly manner, we have heard) at the border with visitors to our country. Margie has completed several courses towards possible training in nursing. Matthew makes a daily run through the bottom of the house, a car in each hand, to check that Grandpa and Grandma are there, and then scampers off for a busy

MATTHEW WITH HIS PERUVIAN GRANDMOTHER

STARK FAMILY

day upstairs.

Richard and Melody lend their talents and energies to Level Ground Trading and La-Z-Boy Furniture Galleries, and coordinate the activities of three very active young people: Anna [16], Michael [14] and Eric [11]. Anna enjoyed her five weeks as Counselor in Training at Camp Qwanoes this summer, and is involved with several leadership and musical activities at school and church. Michael and Eric take piano lessons with Grandma, counterbalancing that activity with soccer. Michael is in Reynolds School's Centre for Soccer Excellence, Eric is in gymnastics, and both are in French immersion. They and father Richard biked up and down Hurricane Ridge (Port Angeles) in support of Opportunities International, a micro-loan NGO that enables those in poverty to start small businesses. Melody joined Melissa and the Rendles on *El Camino* (Spain) in August, spent three days in Paris with Melissa, and flew to Seattle from Germany via Dubai on Emirates flights, somehow managing to acquire first-class accommodation.

Melissa works part-time as paediatric nurse and part-time in education through contracts with UVic, instructing

MELISSA ON GRADUATION DAY

students who come through the Paediatric Unit. This summer she completed her Master of Science in Clinical Education from the University of Edinburgh, just in time to lead/accompany some of her family on *El Camino* for much of August. She walked 350 km on the *Camino Primitovo* route, up early each morning to start in the dark and beat the heat, enjoying the welcome of the Spanish people and the many nationalities she met on her journey. In November she guided her parents through Sweden, Denmark, Scotland, and England (Uttoxeter).

Margaret and Chris celebrated Christmas in Salem for the first time, establishing their own family traditions. They, along with Tori [8],

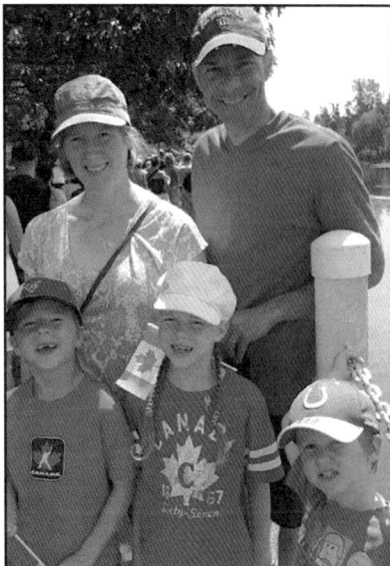
BUCHER FAMILY

Jonathan [6 1/2] and **Justin** [3 1/2] joined Chris's family for American Thanksgiving. They would have stayed with Chris's parents, but the parents' home in Washington, Illinois, was lifted from its foundation on November 17 by a tornado—total destruction. Both parents had rushed to the basement for protection and were safe, if stunned. Chris's father gave thanks to God on local TV that he and Chris's mother were still alive (video clip picked up by chance in Dubai). Cars were shifted to other lots; appliances have not been found. Much was irretrievable, although some items (including his mother's wedding ring) were found in the area surrounding the cul-de-sac, and one photo surfaced 100 miles away in Joliet. Back home in Salem, Tori and Jonathan are thriving in an inner-city Spanish immersion school, and Justin keeps Mommy company during school hours. Chris and Margaret are active in a large Alliance church; Chris continues to oversee road construction and maintenance across an extensive area of Oregon.

MICHAEL AND HIS NAMESAKE

We have had **Michael** here for the month of December, a rare treat. He is just completing his seventh year in Dubai, and we are hoping he decides in the near future to find lodging a little closer to this side of the planet. His work takes him all over the world, often on long flights. We sometimes think of the comment he once shared regarding flying: "99% pure boredom and 1% sheer terror!" I tried not to think of that statement as we flew in and out of several airports on our trip.

Geordon and **Marilyn** are settling into a new home in Denver, Colorado, with **Joshua** [15], **Jolyn** [10] and **Joy** [9]. Joshua attends an inner-city high school with a good academic reputation, and Jolyn and Joy attend a Spanish-immersion school in the neighbourhood. **Jordan** [19] is in his second year at Trinity Western University (Langley) in the theatre programme, but managed to get to Colorado for Christmas. Geordon's position as President of Youth for Christ International starts in January. With their transition over the past several months, the family is becoming prepared for this new stage in their lives. Visas should be available in January, after which their belongings

RENDLE FAMILY

can be moved from Victoria.

And the parents... We continue to enjoy sharing This Old House with both family and friends: the three Ms in half of the upstairs, three (now two) boarders and ourselves in the other half, with access for all to the downstairs level. And Melissa, Melody and her family, and Matthew are very near; Marilyn, Michael and Margaret are available on Skype. **Bruce** keeps the household running; shops for and prepares most meals. **Louise** happily shares her piano skills three days a week with a wonderful group of young people and maintains both her plant and recycled card projects—the first a fund-raiser for youth, the second for an orphanage and hospital in Haiti, and both excuses for indulging in pastimes she enjoys.

LIFE'S LIKE THIS

Plus ça change, plus c'est la même chose—The more things change, the more they stay the same. ... **September 1958** The Forsberg family has just moved to Victoria from a more rural area, with their children aged 17, 16, 15, 13, and 10. The eldest wants to attend the youth group at Central Baptist, which is approximately 10 blocks from her home near Victoria High School. For several weeks she walks to the meeting because she is afraid the bus will not let her off at the right place. ... **September 2013** The eldest has decided to acquire some skill in the Spanish language, and has registered at UVic. The bus terminus is at the university, so, in spite of some self-consciousness at being the only over-30 passenger (and at that considerably over 30), her ride was uneventful. It wasn't until the return trip that she suddenly realized there were no cords to pull. Trying to remain calm, she finally got up enough courage to ask a lovely young student nearby if the yellow buttons on the poles were for signalling the wish to get off. She kindly said they were, and conversed pleasantly with the mature but obviously somewhat sheltered student for the rest of her ride.

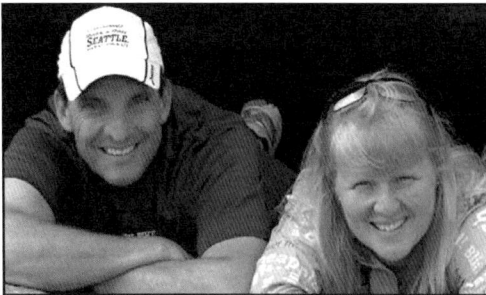

GEORDON AND MARILYN

September 11, 2013 (unprecedented flooding in the Denver area due to heavy rains) ... Meanwhile, inside the Rendle home: Marilyn arrives back at 6:40 a.m., after dropping Geordon off at airport. Opens door to sound of *rushing* water. River from upstairs bathroom is pouring through living room ceiling. Joshua meets mother on stairs, says shower tap broke off inside the wall; cannot be turned off. Water continues down through basement ceiling lights. Mother calls town home emergency hotline; children run around putting plastic garbage cans and laundry baskets under the running water and laying towels on the floor. Maintenance man calls, gives directions for turning off tap. ... Aside from huge mop-up operation, complicated by the family's flight 48 hours later to join Geordon in Colombia, the only permanent damage is one very damp library book.

SEEN AND HEARD ...

... Tori, Jonathan and Justin, hairnets in place, helping move coffee bags at Level Ground, under Auntie Melissa's (and LG worker's) surveillance ... Joy's response to No Trespassing sign: "So if four of us go over that fence it would be fine, right? It just says No TRES ['three' in Spanish] passing." ... Matthew's first haircut January 14, the relinquishing of babyhood with a few scissor snips ... Brandon's lemon meringue pie, with double meringue, tall and delicious ... Tori's recipe for water: take it from the tap; drink and enjoy! ... Tori's recipe for blossom drink: "1) 5 cups blossoms. 2) 5 cups of water (put in cup that you drink in). 3) put in one cup of blossoms in each cup. Makes 5." ... Michael and Eric playing piano pieces on the gorgeous Casavant organ after an organ concert in the Alix Goolden Hall ... Melissa swimming in the North Sea in November, racing to the sauna to warm up ... Edinburgh Castle brooding over the city from its position on Castle Rock ... Castle from below: a forbidding gray presence, lightened

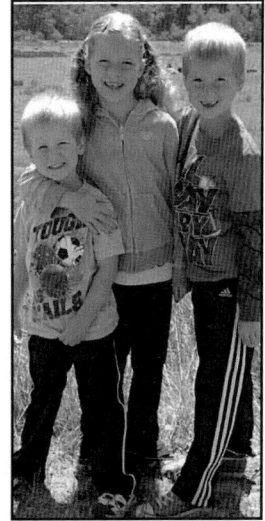

JUSTIN, TORI, JONATHAN

by the occasional golden larch tree, still holding its leaves in November, and a flock of white pigeons rising up its side ... Melissa arriving at first *Camino* hostel after 27 km of hot walking to find Geordon, Jordan and Joshua already booked in, although they had arrived a day later in Oviedo—thanks to a taxi ride ... Melissa soaking her aching feet in every pilgrim fountain and cold pool, stream and river along the *Camino* ... Joshua and a couple of friends pulling a powerhouse 50 km on the last day, arriving in Santiago at 1:00 a.m. ... Jolyn [then 9] and Joy [8], upon receiving the news that father Geordon had been appointed International President for Youth for Christ, commenting that if Jolyn were elected President, Joy could be her assistant, both breaking into gales of laughter at the prospect (their mother's comment: "We just don't get any respect around here!") ... video of children from Luswisi school, Tanzania, calling out "ANNA, ANNA, THANK YOU, ANNA" for her gift of money for school supplies

JOY AND JOLYN

(raised largely by baking and selling cookies), delivered by father Richard and Level Ground's Hugo Ciro as they visited coffee suppliers in Africa ... Bruce's hospital menus from bypass operation nine years ago, dated November 30 and December 2, surfacing unexpectedly from a pile of miscellaneous papers, a reminder of the gift of prolonged life given at that time, and the large Christmas meal prepared in instalments by the patient three weeks later ... lecturer at St. Cecilia's Hall, Edinburgh University (built in the late 1600s), performing on keyboards 300 to 500 years old, one of which was played by Mozart ... more than a dozen e-mails within the family trying to figure out a

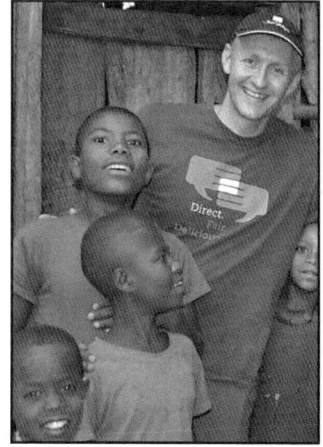

RICHARD VISITING AFRICA

date for Uncle Matt's April 22 birthday meal (21st? Maybe 14th? 19th? 28th? etc., etc.); Matt's "possible solution": "I'm fine without any birthday hoopla." ... Chris holding ten-pound salmon on fishing trip with Richard and friend ... substantial garden shed and play area designed and built by Chris in backyard: three swings, fort, slide, monkey bars ... Grandma working with six of her grandchildren at the piano ... Joshua completing the requirements for Grade VIII Piano and Advanced Rudiments

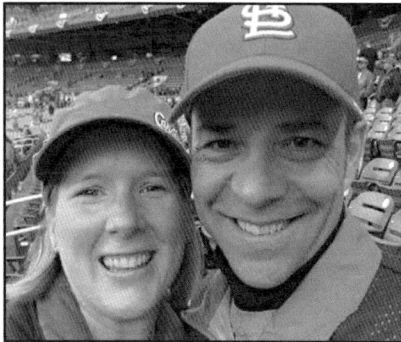

MARGARET AND CHRIS

before his departure to Denver ... Jordie "off the grid" (no texting, no Facebook) near Prince George, experiencing the highs and lows of tree planting for several weeks ... Anna, flute in hand, interviewed by *Times Colonist* reporter after playing in Reynolds band for the May parade ... Horne Lake: torrents of rain on metal roof, fragrance of cedar and firs after heavy rainfall, continuous changing of colours and textures on the lake, sound of deep forest resisting the wind, isolation ... Richard and Matthew pulling apart the old dock and building a new one, sawing the old cedar logs (some almost a metre in diameter) into rounds ... Michael and Eric chopping chunks of cedar into kindling to

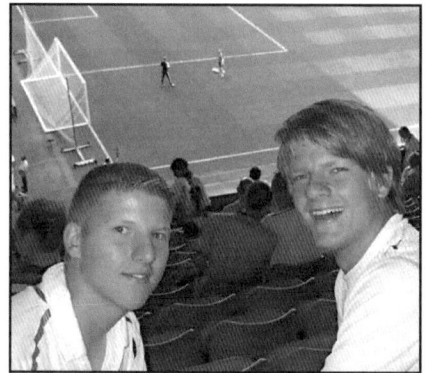

JOSHUA AND JORDAN

sell ... Melissa meeting her supervisors and classmates from around the world for the first time off-screen, at their graduation in Edinburgh November 26 ... parents startled to hear Melissa's programme director in Edinburgh inviting her to apply for work with them in their programme … Anna's monthly "date" with Grandpa, as they both help out with the Breakfast Club for street people … Joy's comment at the end of two back-to-back 25-km days on the *Camino* which brought her to Santiago de Compostela ahead of

ANNA   MICHAEL   ERIC

schedule, when asked what she would like to do with the extra time: "I don't want to do anything with my feet!" … Matt fixing Melissa's faucet, which had been dripping for a month, in an hour and without the flood that Melissa is sure would have resulted if she had enough strength to get the faucet off … Matt remotely accessing the Buchers' internet system in Salem, temporarily restoring the old system so he and Mike can get the new system sorted out for Chris and Margaret … *Thank you* from four sisters to three special brothers—all of us appreciate the multi-tier tech support we receive. From setting up networks or doing photos for Marilyn's newsletter from Dubai (Mike), to arranging the photos for the Christmas letter (Mark), to formatting Melissa's dissertation (Matt)—basically being available for all computer crises. …

Chapter 60: A Christmas Digest, 2014

EDITORIAL *by Louise*

December 5 Melody is 40 today, and her father and I have just had the privilege of taking her out to her favourite Thai restaurant for a birthday lunch. Such an occasion has her mother's thoughts flipping back across four decades to her first encounter with her youngest daughter, and, as many of you will not be surprised to learn, Mother has immediate access to her perspective at that time; her *"Hey, there's no violin in this case!"* sits on our computer desktop for quick reference. According to this mini-encyclopedia, our newest cherub was "7 1/8 pounds of cuddly brunette with soft, fuzzy hair, velvety cheeks, a quivery chin, flickering eyelids, and a tiny mouth that puckers even when Mommy isn't kissing her." Her parents went on to describe her as "enchanting." They would probably describe her a little differently now: determined, highly efficient, hospitable, a loving wife and mother (and daughter), excellent student, inspirational. And she, of course, will be a little unsettled at being put under this spotlight.

Melody's is the first of three December birthdays in our family (Melissa, 23rd; Marilyn, 30th), but the birthday that takes even more of our attention during this month is "the Birthday of a King," the Birthday of *the* King, our Saviour. We praise God for His salvation, and for His peace in troubled times. May 2015 bring you much contentment and joy.

PERSONAL GLIMPSES

Our "away" family lives in Colorado (Marilyn and Geordon, Joshua, Jolyn and Joy; Jordie is in Langley at school), Dubai (Mike), and Oregon (Margaret and Chris, Tori, Jonathan, and Justin). Our "here" family lives right around us: Melissa and Matthew in side-by-side condo buildings a block away, Melody and Richard and family eight blocks away, and Mark and Margie and little Matthew upstairs.

We all feel the loss of our dear Auntie Hildegard, widow of Bruce's Uncle Gordon, who passed away in May six weeks ahead of her 97th birthday. Having escaped from East Germany, Hildegard contributed much to her new country in the area of physiotherapy, at one time heading up the physio department at the Royal

Jubilee Hospital. She was a loving, generous support to our family and many others.

We enjoy sharing our home with Dalton and Rosalea Pagani, Camosun students. Quiet, studious, and helpful, they are great company. As top history student, Dalton has just received a $500 scholarship. Rosalea's room is filled with ribbons and trophies from horse-riding competitions; she occasionally returns home to Powell River to have some time with her horse, Lenny.

RENDLE FAMILY

Marilyn and **Geordon** are settling into their new home in Denver (Aurora), Colorado. **Jordan** is in his third year at Trinity Western, across the border here in Canada. **Joshua** is taking the IB programme at George Washington High School, an urban, multi-ethnic high school, and **Jolyn** and **Joy** attend Denver Language School, a Spanish immersion, public charter K-8 school. Geordon's responsibilities as President of Youth for Christ International take him all over the planet. Marilyn tends the home fires, and assists in the YFC work in the Americas. In September the family spent 10 days in Thailand, as Geordon was commissioned by YFCI leaders in the company of more than 500 delegates representing over 70 different nations.

Mike is completing his eighth year in Dubai, flying as an Emirates Airline captain to many exotic destinations (and some not so), maintaining an unpredictable schedule as he departs from airports at random times of the day. Probably his least favourites are the after-midnight flights which necessitate wake-up times 3 1/2 hours ahead of take-off time.

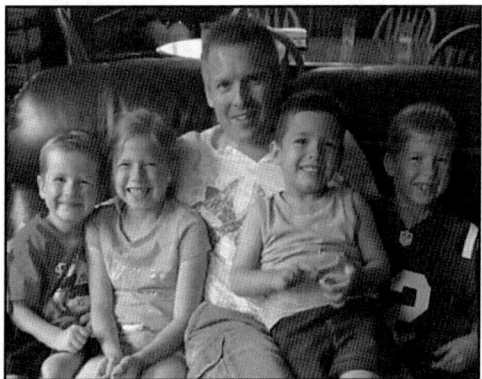
UNCLE MIKE WITH JUSTIN, TORI, MATTHEW AND JONATHAN

Home for Christmas, he shared some professional knowledge with his young niece and nephews: "Push forward, houses get bigger. Pull back, houses get smaller. Keep pulling back, houses get bigger again. And that's it!"

Margaret and **Chris** and three little ones—**Tori** [9], **Jonathan** [7 1/2], **Justin** [4 1/2]—are thriving in Salem, Oregon. Chris utilizes his engineering skills in highway management; Margaret provides a warm, welcoming refuge for her family, and gives considerable assistance to projects at the children's school. Tori and Jonathan, in Spanish immersion, play league soccer. Tori enjoys swimming as well, and Jonathan is involved in the Upward basketball league, with his dad as team coach. Jonathan, newly bespectacled, works on his multi-page "series" of "fiction" and "non-fiction" essays and drawings dealing with the solar system, birds, and sharks—all researched from books and encyclopedias not included in his Grade 2 school curriculum. Both enjoy time at the piano, practising their assignments as well as improvising their own melo-

BUCHER FAMILY

dies. Justin has one more year before he heads down the school path. He also enjoys music and is, according to his mother, their "hands-on child," testing every knob, door, switch, latch, etc., constantly questioning how things work. He also enjoys raking and digging with Daddy. The Buchers are building a strong home in their com-

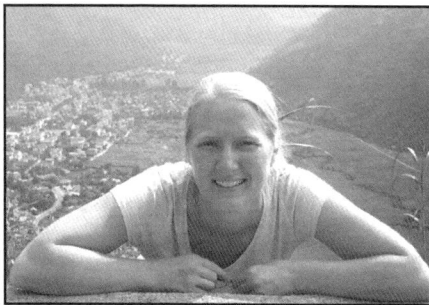

MELISSA

munity and appreciate the resources their church offers. They frequently welcome members of their Canadian family for visits.

Melissa continues to fulfill multiple roles with her nursing: 12-hour shifts as a paediatric nurse, clinical instructor for nursing students who come through Paediatrics, camp nurse at Camp Qwanoes, and supervisor for a Masters student through the University of Edinburgh. She enjoys it most when her roles overlap; not only is this timesaving, but it is also satisfying to see experience gained in one area useful in another. A highlight of her year was a trip to Thailand for the YFCI General Assembly, which also included a side trip on her own to Vietnam.

Richard and **Melody** celebrated their 20th anniversary this year. Richard and the children—**Anna** [17], **Michael** [15], **Eric** [12]—have recently supported Melody through an intensive three-month, full-time course at UVic. The equivalent of one year of university study, the course has given her a Certificate in Business Administration. A couple weeks after completing the course,

STARK FAMILY

she began working in the Victoria School Board office, and is really enjoying her new job (on call with SD61). Anna, set to graduate next June, sings in the school choir, and received a Youth Now award in the "green" category for her efforts at school with chickens and garden. She also won the $500 Generations to Come award, sponsored by the Principals and Vice-Principals Association. Michael, in Grade 10, towers over his mother. Although he is doing very well at the piano, his heart is on the soccer field; a broken arm this fall put a damper on both activities. Eric, in Grade 7 at Cedar Hill, plays saxophone in the band and, like Michael, takes piano lessons with his grandmother. He and Anna burn off energy at gymnastics once a week. All three enjoy serving with Grandpa at our church's Breakfast Club for street people.

Mark and **Margie** and little **Matthew** are our closest neighbours, as they continue to live in half of the upper floor of our home. Mark welcomes visitors at the border, firearm on hip (a commentary on the changes 9/11 brought to Canadian security), and Margie is enjoying the freedom a driver's license brings. Matthew, now 3 1/2, carries sunshine and mischief from floor to floor of his home. A trip to Peru is scheduled for February and March.

MARGIE, MATTHEW, MARK

Matt quietly supports his family, especially in the area of computer technology. He oversees the IT component of Level Ground Trading, which continues to grow, maintaining its mandate for direct fair trade with integrity. Matt has organized every aspect of the company into an order management system, and continues to make changes to it as the need arises. He and Mark make a great team on the roller hockey rink, the result of over 25 years of playing together. (Mother goes back to the beginning: two little boys, 8 and 5 1/2, dressed in oversized and mismatched "uniforms," including bike helmets, hitting around a puck for hours on the backyard concrete pad, aiming for the net set up at one end.)

MATT

Bruce and **Louise** just celebrated their 53rd anniversary (December 21), 85 years to the day that his parents were married, and 74 years to the day of her parents' marriage. They are blessed with good health and many interests and responsibilities. Bruce does almost all of the shopping and most of the cooking, and serves in various venues at our church (Central Baptist). Louise works at the piano with a wonderful group of young people, contributes some leadership and keyboard skills to the Hymns and Heart services at church, and alternates between her two fundraising projects: perennials—in support of young people—and making recycled cards—in support of the Canadian Foundation for the Children of Haiti <cfchcanada.ca>.

LOUISE AND BRUCE

LIFE'S LIKE THIS

January 8, morning Louise is getting her hair done when a second customer comes in for her appointment and chats with the hairdresser, whom she obviously knows well. Louise joins in the conversation and the hairdresser mentions that she teaches piano. The new customer asks if Louise knows a piano teacher named _____ and Louise responds enthusiastically, "Yes, I do; I just love her! She's so conscientious and competent and cheerful." To Louise's surprise, the lady says, "She's my daughter." (To be added to the list of *Ways to Make People Happy Without Even Trying!*)

January 14, afternoon Husband brings a cup of coffee at just the right time to music room (the usual coffee-preparer, outside gathering twigs, suddenly realized it was ten minutes to teaching, and had to make a choice between coffee and a change of clothes). Student comments, "He sure is nice." Teacher replies, "Yes, he is very kind to me."

March evening Grandma is putting small grandson to bed; tells him who loves him: "God, Daddy, Mommy, Grandpa, Grandma, Auntie Marilyn" and on through extended family. Grandma gets to Bucher family, randomly names Tori, Jonathan, and Justin, Auntie Margaret—at which point her mind skips to the other daughter who most resembles Margaret (Melody), lists her, Uncle Rick, Anna, etc., continuing through other aunts, uncles and cousins. There is a short pause, and then a little voice murmurs, "And Uncle Chris." Grandmother realizes her inadvertent omission, which has not gone unnoticed by sleepy child, and places her beloved American son-in-law back into the family lineup.

April 25 Boarders departed two weeks ago for summer break; Margie and little Matthew left for 3 1/2 weeks in Peru on April 21; Mark and Matt leave today for Dubai for visit with Mike, as Melissa flies to Denver to visit Marilyn and family: there is no one else in this house except the two aging owners! But there are at least six other "houses" on this property that are not so empty: a bushtit's bag nest hanging, unseen for weeks, above the front sidewalk; a birdhouse near the kitchen now housing a chickadee family; a nest inside the carport holding several Bewick wren chicks; a mallard's nest in the jungle of vines and shrubs near the carport; a towhee's home in the ivy-covered oak tree on the lowest level, threatened by crows and squirrels; and a sparrow household attached to the fir tree behind the swing. No wonder there is birdsong from 5:00 a.m. until nightfall!

April 26–May 6 Jordie accompanies senior staff member of YFC USA World Outreach, Bill Housley, on a supervisory trip to Chile, Argentina and Uruguay to interpret language and cultural aspects involved in expat missionaries' work. Bill and Jordie are sharing a simple motel room one night when a cell phone starts ringing in the wee hours. Awakened by the sound and groggy, each one mentally starts berating the other: Why is he not turning that noise off?! A knock at the door—the cleaning person apologetically says she thinks she left her cell phone in the room. After a search of both beds, it is finally found between the sheets and blankets of Bill's bed and is returned to its rightful owner. A few chuckles are shared, and the men relax into a more peaceful sleep.

October 4 Connecting across the cultures—Melissa is sharing a train compartment with an older Vietnamese woman on a 30-hour trip from Hanoi to Ho Chi Minh City. The woman brings out a picture of herself in full traditional dress at a special ceremony, likely from where she has just been. In turn, Melissa pulls out her iPad and flips through a couple of photos, trying to communicate in simple English. There is no flicker of recognition or interest until Melissa shows a photo of her parents, at which point the woman points excitedly at Melissa and taps enthusiastically on the photo; as Melissa comments, "Evidently there are some familial characteristics handed down."

October evening Grandma has come down from music room for supper break, is eating with husband, boarders, daughter-in-law, and grandson. Three-year-old grandson spills a little of his dessert; for reasons unknown and hopefully never to be repeated, Grandma's dish of applesauce flips into her lap. Grandson's comment: "Just like me, Grandma!"

MATTHEW AND JUSTIN

SCENE IN PASSING ...

... Mark and Matt starting off New Year and new roller hockey season with their team's victory 12 to 5 (Mark five goals, one assist; Matt one goal, six assists) ... nuthatches answering each other a semitone apart (four Bs, answered by four Cs) ... four large loads of sheets waving in the July breeze on newly-installed clothes lines strung between the backyard oaks: fourteen sheets and multitude of towels used by 22 family members on overnight stay at Horne lake (only absentees were Mike in Dubai and Mark guarding the Canadian border in Victoria) … Melissa hanging out her own laundry, taking advantage of continuous summer sun … Mike running on the rubberized track at Safa Park, Dubai, at 9:30 p.m.—39°C and very humid: "Just me and the Indians and Arabs and the local women walking in their abayas with their sneakers and iPods" … Jordie struggling with knee brace and then ACL surgery related to sports injury … nine fluffy ducklings and mother duck swimming in the front pond; babies, with their yellow and black markings, look like large bumblebees … glimpses of life at Horne Lake: Geordon swimming to island in middle of lake; Jolyn and Tori

taking turns in kayak; Justin catching fish off end of dock; three little girls playing endless card games and reading books; *no TV*; Melissa with little Matthew out in kayak and in boat; Grandpa enjoying the antics of Michael and Eric on the tube … little Matthew and Grandpa cleaning car of Horne Lake Road dust … Jordan, laughing at his Auntie Melissa's comment: "Hmm… this looks a little sketchy." Both are wandering on mopeds at

ELEVEN GRANDCHILDREN VISITING HORNE LAKE

midnight on the backroads of Ao Nang Beach, Thailand. *[Yet another example of how it is better that parents/grandparents learn some things after the fact.]* … bushtits on half of little tree accidentally sprayed by hose, daintily drinking water from the fir needles … beautiful auburn-coloured laying hens sunning themselves along the step at the Starks' house; keep family well supplied with eggs … Anna working all summer at Qwanoes, following in the footsteps of the two generations ahead of her; Michael spending three weeks at Qwanoes in the Step Out Program … little Matthew figuring out how to get Daddy's cookie, after he and mother have eaten theirs, and he has been told last cookie is for his father: "Mommy, can I be Mark?" "Yes, that's fine." "OK then, can I have that cookie?" (Response: "No.") … Tori setting up her own science experiments and exploring her new microscope's possibilities … definition of "exquisite": three tiny golden-crowned kinglets sipping water on concrete pad in back yard, meticulously picking up morsels of tree debris with minuscule beaks, hopping around gardener's feet … gorgeous song of equally diminutive winter wren filling gloomy February morning with cheer … Matthew's "That's OK, Glamma" to

Grandma's "Sorry, Matthew," after asking student Matthew to play his solos at recital, and noticing little grandson's consternation … Mike, violin refurbishing in mind, exploring the inner workings of a violin repair shop in Houston, Texas, as the owner (Phil Gold) meticulously manufactures a new bridge for a young violinist … Tori creating theatrical productions for friends and family, and participating in Worship Dance workshops … blackhooded juncos picking up scraps dropped from feeder, occasionally making an awkward foray up to nibble on suet … snowdrops flooding bank beside waiting room door for 48th year; also found in clumps in other areas of property … hummingbird keeping Grandma company in greenhouse, whirring from geranium to geranium; later shares same area with Grandpa … Grandma driving out to Brentwood for Spanish lessons with UVic *profesora*, an enjoyable challenge with an outstanding teacher (Sra. Maria-Elena Cuervo-Lorens), and a nostalgic trip along the road of her childhood (West Saanich) … special Christmas gift from Grandpa to Grandma: a Spanish Bible (Santa Biblia); *El Señor es mi pastor; nada me falta. (Salmo 23:1)* … May hailstorm in Denver causing $4,500 in damage to front and top of Rendle car in spite of position, along with several others, under overpass—terrifying, with prospect of windshield shattering in on family … Father Mark "chasing" Matthew with Matthew's battery-operated car, as Matthew tries to keep ahead on his tricycle (newly-acquired skill) … Matthew interrupting piano lesson to give Grandma a kiss; bestows one on delighted student as well … Marilyn playing violin at four consecutive church services on Christmas Eve, after pastors learn of her musical background, an eight-hour commitment … three different woodpeckers at feeder: downy (small), pileated (large) and northern flicker (large); last two, as well as the handsome and raucous Steller's Jay, do not receive a warm welcome, beautiful though they are … grandparents visiting Denver, Colorado, with eldest daughter and family, exploring the mile-high city, checking out family's church and children's schools, visiting a most interesting Jewish museum, and taking in a Canucks game (Grandma's earplugs made the experience a happy one, although the final score, in the Avalanche's favour, was a little disappointing.) … hummingbird flashing emerald green and hot pink in the sun, attracted to the spray from the hose … Mark and Matt ending year with their team's victory and trophy; score is 8 to 8, with Mark scoring 9th goal in overtime (Mark three goals, one assist; Matt one goal, five assists) …

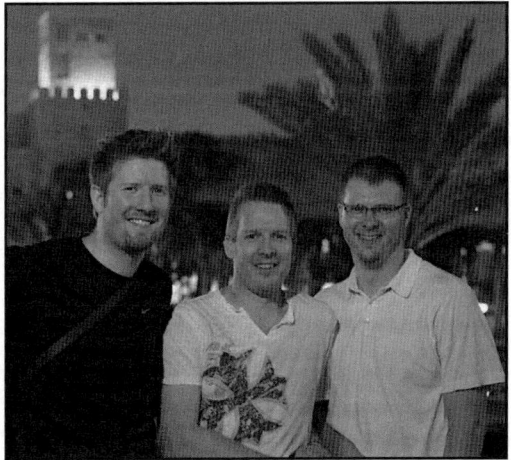

MATT AND MARK VISITING MIKE IN DUBAI

Chapter 61: A Christmas Digest, 2015

EDITORIAL *by Louise*

December 21, 6:30 a.m. The rain runs in silvery streaks down the windows. It is chilly and dark outside, but cozy here in front of the screen, with the furnace on and an afghan over my knees. It is also our wedding anniversary, and the dreary weather is reminiscent of that special day 54 years ago when the evening gloom was also punctured and dispersed by the light of candle and bulb. I have given myself the task of sharing, for the 50th time, news from this place on the rocks. As I do this, I pray that your 2016 will be filled with many blessings, that our world will be given a measure of peace, and that we all may be given the resources to lend support to those less fortunate than ourselves.

Our household consists of Bruce, myself, and university students Jessica and Jeffrey Curtis, from Comox. Our previous boarders, Rosalea and Dalton Pagani, left us last April, one to study in Nanaimo, the other to live on his own closer to the university. We are enjoying our times with Jessica and Jeffrey, and hope they are comfortable in this rather quiet setting, a contrast both to their own home of four children and to this home twenty and thirty years ago. Mark and Margie and not-

LOUISE AND BRUCE

so-little Matthew live in the upstairs suite. Bruce shops and cooks and involves himself in several service projects, and I continue to teach piano four afternoons and evenings each week, provide some music at church, organize a couple of projects to help young people in different settings, and study Spanish, all activities supported by a patient and loving husband.

But life does not always run smoothly. We were shattered early on the morning of October 2 to learn that our beloved sister-in-law, Wynne Forsberg, had passed away suddenly of a pulmonary embolism the evening before, on the eve of her 50th wedding anniversary. This has been devastating for my brother Eric and his family, and we ourselves have difficulty accepting the situation. One of our sons commented that this is the "new reality" he will be dealing with over the next few years: the loss of those who have been an important and beloved part of his life. Ecclesiastes reminds us that "there is a time to be born and there is a time to die," and we trust in the One who controls these times. There is still dismay and grief when such hard things come our way.

A year ago four of our children lived very near us, and three were away. This year the numbers are reversed, as Melissa (our "Honeybee") has again flown away—this time for a year in Saudi Arabia, leaving an empty condo in the neighbourhood, and a void in the lives of her Victoria family. So we now have children in Colorado, Dubai, Oregon and Saudi Arabia. We have visited the first three areas, and Melissa assures us that we, as her parents, would be welcome to visit her. Melody and her family live a few blocks away, and Matt just a block away. It is our hope that a year from now, we will be able to share the news, God willing, that a little girl arrived in March to become the twelfth grandchild. She will also live at this address!

We made two trips south this year, one in April to visit the Buchers in Salem, the other in November to spend some time with the Rendles in Colorado. On the second trip, we drove 14 hours with five of our favourite people—only Jordie was not included—to Mesa, Arizona, with an overnight stay in Albuquerque, New Mexico, and had a pleasant visit with my brother Eric before we flew home from Phoenix.

We are delighted that my sister Harriet has returned to Victoria, after fifty years of living elsewhere in BC and in the United States (Alaska, Montana, Minnesota, Hawaii, Oregon). Our sister Jeannie and her husband Barry have renovated a large house near the top of Triangle Mountain. Harriet and daughter Tricia, along with Barry and Jeannie, now live in what has been transformed into a very beautiful home with an outlook over the Esquimalt Harbour.

PERSONAL GLIMPSES

Marilyn and **Geordon**, **Joshua** [almost 18], **Jolyn** [12] and **Joy** [11] enjoy their home and work in Aurora (Denver), Colorado. Eldest son **Jordan** has nearly completed his degree at Trinity Western University and will be marrying **Rachel Bell** on August 13. Joshua graduates from high school with an IB diploma in June and is looking for a university

GEORDON AND MARILYN

that offers both a sports management degree and the opportunity to play soccer—and, ideally, scholarships. Jolyn and Joy attend a Spanish-immersion school. Geordon oversees the work of Youth for Christ International in over 100 nations, both by conference call and e-mail, and by travelling to

JORDAN AND RACHEL

areas as needed; Marilyn lends assistance to YFC work in the Americas, makes use of her piano and violin skills, and sometimes travels with Geordon.

Michael will be flying for China Airlines out of Taipei, starting in April. With scheduled flights confined to two-thirds of the month, he should be free to travel home more frequently, and we are looking forward to that. He fulfilled his goal of bringing his parents and each of his siblings to Dubai, when Margaret joined him on his side of the planet in October.

Margaret and **Chris**, **Tori** (Victoria) [10], **Jonathan** [8] and **Justin** [5] continue to thrive in Salem, Oregon, although a much-anticipated pre-Christmas trip to Victoria was sabotaged by illness, and a box of Christmas gifts languishes in our guest room. All three children now attend Grant Community School in

BUCHER FAMILY

Spanish immersion classes, and Tori and Jonathan work with Margaret on piano and violin. Tori enjoys ballet and swimming. Jonathan has just finished fall soccer and is starting basketball season with Dad as coach. Justin, now in Kindergarten, is often found drawing and painting, and designing his own Lego creations. Chris continues to travel through a large area of Oregon, checking out road and bridge conditions, and Margaret has spent a few hectic months serving as co-chairman of the school's parent auxiliary.

Melissa counts among the highlights of her year a "bucket list" trip to Cape Scott, right up at the north-western tip of Vancouver Island. To her parent's relief, Richard, Melody, Michael and Eric joined her at the last minute. Judging by the complaints about aches and pains from most involved, the hike must have been challenging. She found it satisfying to have her Master's research published after working through a couple of initial rejections; as she says, perhaps "third time's the charm."

MELISSA HIKING WITH STARK FAMILY

This summer Melissa was graciously granted a year's leave of absence from nursing and supervision of nursing students here in Victoria and, after a seemingly interminable wait for a visa, left for Saudi Arabia at the end of October to do similar work in a hospital in Riyadh. She lives in a compound of ex-pats representing a variety of countries, and is pleasantly surprised at the variety of foods and other merchandise available in Riyadh (most imported and at three times Canadian prices). Although she is required to wear an abaya much of the time she is in public, she is able to dress in western clothes in and around the hospital, as well as in other compounds around the city. Despite the numerous cultural differences, her transition has been smooth and she feels well-supported in her new role.

MELISSA IN SAUDI ARABIA

Melody and **Richard** are experiencing the first phase of their "empty nest" syndrome, as **Anna** [18] is away at the eight-month Kaléo leadership programme at Camp Qwanoes, up-Island at Crofton. Although Anna's programme, sponsored by Briercrest Bible College and Seminary in Caronport, Saskatchewan, is heavy—she describes one course as "drinking out of a fire hose"—she has been able to come home for the occasional overnight visit. In addition to academic studies, she has

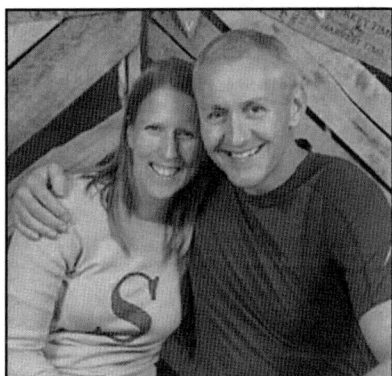

MELODY AND RICHARD

enjoyed a trip on the sailing ship *Pacific Grace*, a wilderness hike on Mount Albert Edward, and surfing at Tofino. **Michael** [16] stands a head above his mother and siblings, and has been very busy with a business course at Camosun College, in addition to his Grade 11 studies. He invests an hour each week in piano and theory studies with his grandmother, and spends even more time on the soccer field. **Eric** [13] also spends time at the piano with Grandma. He has won several awards in bike racing, and since returning to soccer has enjoyed having his brother and dad as the coaches of his team. Richard continues to manage

ERIC, MICHAEL, ANNA

sales at Level Ground Trading, which has had its best year yet, and Melody is very happy in her new job as Accounts Clerk at Central Middle School.

Mark and **Margie** and **Matthew** [4] live on their own upstairs, but frequently find themselves in our section of the house—welcome, and often helpful, company. Mark continues to screen visitors to our country at the border, and Margie works to keep their home comfortable and welcoming. Young Matthew is growing into a lov-

MATTHEW, MARK, MARGIE

ing, considerate little boy, a joy to family both on and off this property. He is looking forward with great anticipation to the arrival of a little sister in the spring. Mark received kudos from his co-workers for his help in making the new office computer system more user-friendly.

Matt is our computer magician, working with his complex order management system and at-times temperamental computers at Level Ground on a regular basis, and on family computers whenever the need arises. We computer-challenged relatives are often amazed to see problems that have plagued us for hours disappear with a few quick movements of the mouse. Matt still forms a formidable duo with brother Mark on the roller hockey rink.

MATT

SEEN AND HEARD ...

... January's gift: bright green leaves and lacy white blossoms of the native Indian plum shrub ... news of the spelling bee contest in Denver, where both Jolyn and Joy made the top 10: "Congratulations to Joy Rendle

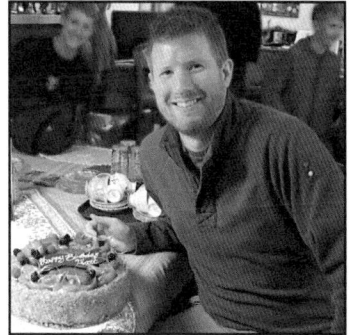

MATTHEW ON FIRST DAY OF PRE-SCHOOL

... the Champion for the entire inter-school competition!" ... Little Matthew kissing his mommy's tummy, as she leaves for ultrasound ... Mark, Margie and Matthew dressed as bunnies for church's family group fall party ... Joshua's photograph in newspaper with favourite soccer team, Tottenham Hotspur, from London, who were visiting Denver ... Louise under hawthorn tree, working at plant table, inundated with hawthorn berries chewed and spit out by squirrel above her head ... joy personified: little Matthew on a trail-a-bike, in helmet, gloves, and kneepads, gliding down driveway behind father, grinning from ear to ear ... evidence that other creatures also use this property to raise their young: nest in basket full of gardening gloves (Bewick wren), constructed of moss, fir and oak twigs, dryer lint, and a feather; bag nest on patio (bushtit), made of lichen, rose campion leaf, moss, and feathers, carefully held together by spiderwebs; nest in rubber boot inside of greenhouse (bird unknown), with small white egg

... query from youngest grandson: "Daddy doesn't need to know this, does he?" ... Anna receiving both the "Dogwood District Award" and the "Saanich-Gulf Islands Green Party of Canada Scholarship for Civic Engagement" for her many hours of volunteering ... Matthew to Auntie Melissa (July 22): "I woke up this morning and I was so surprised I was 4!" ... "Flat Jonathan" (a life-size paper doll coloured to represent grandson Jonathan, and sent on a trip around the world as a Grade 2 writing project in Salem) travelling from Salem to Victoria, Denver, Chicago, Central Illinois, Baltimore, Dubai and then back to Oregon, where the real Jonathan wrote up his travels ... Uncle Mike's contribution to nephew's "Flat Jonathan" project: photographs of the paper doll on the flight deck during an actual flight—Mike's comment: "First Officer Jonathan! hahah"—serving drinks and "receiving" first aid, oxygen and CPR; in front of the Burj Khalifa in Dubai; in Washing-

UNCLE MIKE WITH "FLAT JONATHAN" IN DUBAI

ton, DC; and at the Hatta Dam, near the border of Oman, with camels (one of which tried to eat him) and sand dunes. This project involved some sacrifice of dignity for Captain Mike: "I felt a bit dumb, a middle-aged man taping a paper person to a park bench in front of the Washington Monument but hey, what can you do?" ... Jonathan completing a September to November soccer season without one practice or game in the rain—and this in the Pacific Northwest! ... well-antlered buck stripping kale, grape hyacinth and pole bean plants (leaves but not beans) in back yard, thankfully ignoring most of Louise's hundreds of sale plants; handsome but unwelcome ... Louise and Mark assisting moped rider at front of house, stunned by force of deer striking vehicle ... Mark drags moped to hiding spot behind trees; rider is taken to hospital, found to have broken ribs. ... grandson Michael receiving a first-class mark on his Level VII piano exam, in spite of soccer schedule that demands up to four sessions a day on the field ... Jolyn and Joy joining cousin in exam success, at Levels VI and V ... Tori joining Stark and Rendle cousins in Grandma's year-end recital in June—a fortuitous coinciding of family schedules ... Geordon speaking at YFC 50th anniversary celebration in Sri Lanka

JOLYN, JOSHUA, JOY

and 20th anniversary in Rwanda, with stopover in Ghana, a 28,000-mile round trip … Joshua, captain and centre-back of his soccer team, receiving an All-City award as one of the top 11 high school soccer players in Denver … December visitors at bird feeders: dainty bushtits and chickadees, sparrows, nuthatches, and tiny ruby-headed

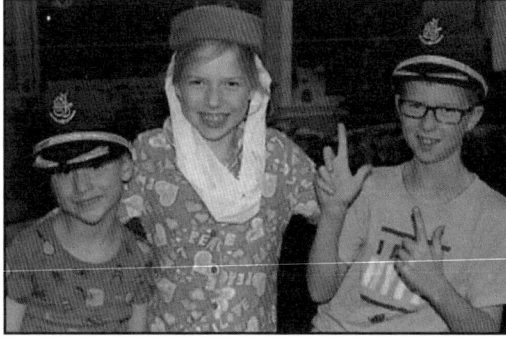

JUSTIN, TORI, JONATHAN

kinglet zoom in and out of area, occasionally scattered by appearance of larger Northern flicker or Steller's jay; fox sparrows, towhees and juncos scrabble on ground below for morsels of suet and fallen seeds … Tori digging in school garden as Portland TV station cameras roll … Mark's carpentry projects: refinishing garden bench, re-boarding laundry stand, replacing rotted boards and steps of playhouse originally built by Grandpa Norman Holland over 40 years ago, new set of display shelves for Louise's plants … Tori's and Jonathan's baptisms in June, a solemn yet joyous occasion … Anna, beautiful in long graduation gown custom-tailored by dear friend Pat Robbie, surrounded by family and friends at the backyard tea in her honour … **Christmas morning** Louise sorting through place cards to decorate for table of 16, setting aside names of those who will not be here in the evening, thinking with a pang of those whose place cards will never be at this table again … Bruce's 50-foot "corridor" kitchen, spreading from dining-room (slow cooker, frying pan), down hallway to laundry-room (hot plate, coffee-maker, sink for dishes, refrigerator), to office (microwave)—source of meals for nine long weeks as kitchen was completely remade, a project necessitated by water damage around sink … from Mike, regarding a special guest in the cockpit: "The whole thing was a bit surreal though—the Indian ground staff nervously checking their watches, as some guy from Canada, an Arab guy 20 years his junior [the First Officer], the Duchess of York, and her Spanish travel escort all have a nice little visit in the flight deck of an

ANNA WEARING HER GRADUATION REGALIA

Emirates B777 in Bangalore. I wasn't about to be rushed, and they couldn't exactly hurry up the VIP guests." …

LIFE'S LIKE THIS

Saturday, May 9 (night before Mother's Day) Joshua has delivered his mother

to the airport for a 7:00 p.m. flight to South Africa. It is snowing heavily, and the road is slippery. ... Marilyn boards plane, sits as the hours pass. Has a chat by Skype with Mike in Moscow. After six hours, announcement is made that flight is cancelled and passengers are told to de-plane. Taxi loaded with fellow passengers returns her to home in wee hours, in time to play in snow with children on Mother's Day. ... Josh again takes mother to airport later in the day.

September 17, 6:00 a.m. Louise is out delivering plant notices house-to-house along Lodge Avenue. Memories from 20 and 30 years ago flood her consciousness as she travels on sidewalks and paths and up and down stairs made familiar by years on the paper-route with her children: ... *fragrance of freshly-baked bread wafting down Lodge Avenue from bakery at Lake Hill* ... **5:50 a.m. summer morning, 1985** *Police car slides up beside Mike and his assistants-in-training, Margaret and Melissa; driver asks to see date on newspaper to be sure trio are not up to mischief* ... **December 1984** *Thigh-high snow obliterates stairways, under fluffy pink clouds reflecting city lights. Family walks from home to routes spread across district, dragging and carrying newspaper bundles; all routes are finally delivered by noon.* ... **November 1991** *Mother, out delivering family flyers at 4:30 a.m. at the corner of Lodge and Saul to get a head start on morning deliveries, is suddenly blinded by powerful flashlight, and surrounded by several squad cars. Officer asks what she is doing, tells her that homeowner has reported "17-year-old youth in navy-blue windbreaker" prowling neighbourhood. With an additional 30 years in her history, Mother regards navy-blue sweater and marvels at its powers of rejuvenation.* ... **January 1996** *Terror grabs Mother as she starts driving down steep hill on Saul Street towards Lodge: stream of water that normally crosses street has frozen, and car lurches wildly from side to side of short street, miraculously missing several parked cars, coming to a standstill on lawn across Lodge* ...

October 18, 3:00 p.m. Eldest daughter picks up parents at Denver airport, a 25-minute drive from home in Aurora. Casually mentions that supper is being prepared for 25 people, including 16 members and wives of YFC's international board. Fragrance of dozens of potatoes baking greets parents at door. Son-in-law has stripped five large Costco chickens onto platters, saving bones for father-in-law to make into broth. Daughter transforms heads of romaine into caesar salads, puts out loaves of artisanal bread and a variety of juices. Dessert is provided by enormous (and delicious) Costco pumpkin and pecan pies, with whipped cream. Coffee and tea, and *voilà!*—*¡ya está!*—a meal for 25! Guests from Jamaica, Germany, New York, Bangladesh, Maryland, Denver, Ghana, Australia, and Colombia spread throughout dining and family rooms, enjoying meal in the comfort of an American-Canadian home.

Chapter 62: A Christmas Digest, 2016

EDITORIAL *by Louise*

December 12, 6:15 a.m. I am again sitting in front of the computer, cozy in several layers of dressing-gowns and afghans, my only company the sizzling of sleet against the window. (I recently learned that "sleet" is *"aguanieve"* in Spanish: "water" + "snow"; should be able to remember that.)

We recently received an invitation from The Siblings to a celebration code-named "80-75-55." This (on the 22nd, d.v.) will no doubt be a happy occasion, but the numbers are a little startling. The first two represent birthdays, and the third, an anniversary. A fourth could also have been added: "50," to mark how long we have lived in This Old House. And "51," the number representing this letter. The opening sentence from 1983's Christmas Digest, with a couple of changes, could have served as the beginning to this letter: ... "It is no doubt part of the '**Elderly**-And-How-Did-We-Get-Here-So Fast' Syndrome, but it seems a very short time ago that we were as-sembling **2015**'s annual letter."

8:45 a.m. Mark has just returned with Matthew from an abandoned trip to school, as the roads between here and Doncaster Elementary proved very treacherous. The *aguanieve* has become *nieve*, and the view from every window is stunning.

FAMILY AT 55TH WEDDING ANNIVERSARY CELEBRATION (MELISSA IN SAUDI ARABIA)

December 23 Last evening was indeed a happy occasion—a party at Geordon and Marilyn's home, with all of our grandchildren except Jordie and Rachel, and all of our children in attendance—even Melissa, by Skype. Three of my four siblings and all of Bruce's shared in the fun. A large "55" made up of dozens of photos had been assembled in Salem and carefully transported to Murray Drive to decorate the living room wall, and a continuous stream of photos and short videos from over five decades was projected on the computer, thanks to Mark's expertise. Clips of seven violins playing in different settings brought a wave of nostalgia to the group's accompanist.

We hope you have had a wonderful Christmas, and will experience a New Year filled with many blessings from the hand of God.

PERSONAL GLIMPSES

JORDAN AND RACHEL

Marilyn and **Geordon** are back in Victoria for what we hope will be an extended period of time. It is so good to have them and the girls, **Jolyn** [13] and **Joy** [12], within hugging distance again. In the spring, **Jordan** [22] graduated from Trinity Western University in theatre and married **Rachel Bell**, also a theatre grad, on August 13, and they are happily juggling several jobs on the mainland. **Joshua** [18] is in first year studies (sports management) at TWU, playing centre defensive mid-field on the Spartans soccer team. Jolyn and Joy have adapted well to their new school (Shoreline Community Middle School), and are involved in choir, enrichment, and violin (Joy), as well as youth group at church. They are also completing requirements for the Royal Conservatory of Music Levels VII and VIII.

JOLYN

JOY

JOSHUA

Geordon and Marilyn are finishing up a few months of sabbatical after going through considerable adjustment when, due to lack of alignment between him and the board of directors, Geordon was asked to resign from his position as President/CEO of Youth for Christ International at the beginning of September. Youth for Christ Canada, as Geordon and Marilyn's sending agency, has been very supportive as they process future opportunities with Geordon and encourage Marilyn in her role, spanning 26 years, which includes coaching and administration.

GEORDON AND MARILYN

Positive messages from many co-workers around the globe have been very affirming, and Geordon and Marilyn know God has a plan for them (Jeremiah 29:11).

MIKE AND MELODY

Michael, after nine years of flying for Emirates Airline in Dubai, has moved to China Airlines in Taipei, again as captain of the Boeing 777. Although he lacks the ability to converse in Mandarin and at times feels isolated, he is impressed by the kindness of his colleagues and those he meets in other settings. The move allows him more consecutive days of leave, and we enjoyed his time here this Christmas.

Margaret and **Chris** and our three very dear American grandchildren, **Tori** [11], **Jonathan** [9 1/2] and **Justin** [6 1/2] were able to join us for a few days ahead of Christmas, this year with no travelling problems. A year ago, colds and the flu kept them State-side (resulting in the freezing of the abundance of baked goodies Margaret had prepared

BUCHER FAMILY

for her Canadian family); the previous year, they slid to the edge of a snowy road in Olympic National Park on their way here, and were assisted by a ranger who "just happened" to be patrolling their section of that beautiful but twisty road.

Chris continues to check out road and bridge conditions over a large area of Oregon, and this year spent over eight weeks in various US locations for additional training and consulting. Bringing her years of teaching experience to bear, Margaret invested huge amounts of time and energy into school projects until June as co-president of the parents' association, and now serves in an advisory role. Tori and her brothers have weekly Skype visits in front of the piano keyboard. All are progressing well at school, studying in the United States' second prominent language, Spanish.

Melissa is preparing to come home to Victoria in late March, after almost a year and a half in Saudi Arabia. She managed to make her way to Jordie and Rachel's wedding in Langley, but other than that, we have not been able to visit with her in person since her departure in October of 2015. She has been working, as she says, "more hours than ever before in a nursing position," serving alongside a "diverse, multicultural, and ever-changing staff." She has travelled much within the country, in green areas as well as in the rocky wilderness and on the sandy desert, on occasion sharing coffee and dates and even complete meals in Saudi homes. Along with her teaching/nursing responsibilities, she has taken advantage of further training, provided free at the hospital. In August, she was joined by brother Matt and niece Anna on a trip to Denmark and Sweden to explore family roots. She looked for a place to stay in the small Swedish town (Tyngsjö) where her great-grandfather's family had grown up, and found online a comfortable cottage which the owner had just started to rent to travellers. When she told him that she was

MELISSA IN SAUDI ARABIA

coming to learn more about her family's origins, he said he would do his best to help her. Much to their mutual astonishment, it was discovered that his grandmother was Melissa's great-grandfather's sister. In an age without today's technology, his family, who had moved only five miles from their birthplace, lost track of the brother who had moved to North America (North Dakota, and then Saskatchewan) in 1902, as well as the other ten siblings. Melissa and her travelling companions enjoyed the

STARK FAMILY

incredible beauty of the area, visiting the original homestead, and uncovering family history right back to the 1500s.

Richard rides his bike out to Level Ground Trading in Saanichton, where he and his associates are bringing the company to yet another level of success: "success" being growth in business, and, even more important, helping the disadvantaged by paying fair prices to the farming families, and in many cases providing access to education and health care. Richard is planning to join his children around the study table as he starts MBA studies at Royal Roads in January. **Melody** rides her bike most days in the other direction, downtown to Central Middle School, where she enjoys her position as Accounts Clerk. **Anna** [19] has just completed a successful semester at UVic after a year at Kaléo, a Bible and Leadership programme held at Camp Qwanoes in partnership with Briercrest Bible College. **Michael** [17] is scheduled to graduate from Reynolds Secondary in June, and has completed a first-year course in preparation for business studies at UVic. He sings in the school choir and plays on the U-18 Lakehill soccer team. **Eric** [14] also attends Reynolds, where he plays saxophone in the band. He enjoyed travelling to an isolated community up-Island with a group from our church (Central Baptist) to do maintenance work at the camp at Esperanza. A highlight of the family's year was hiking the West Coast Trail together—eight challenging days of making family memories and meeting all sorts of interesting people along the way.

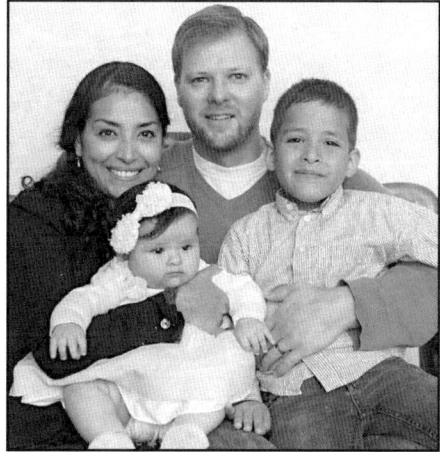

HOLLAND FAMILY

Mark and **Margie** presented the family with a very special gift in March: baby **Mia** ("mine" in Spanish, the name chosen by brother Matthew) **Michaela** (in honour of Mark's other brother) **Luciana** (after both of her great-grandmothers)—a happy, healthy baby who insists on growing too quickly right in front of our eyes. Mark has two more months of paternity leave, returning in March to his place at the border. Little **Matthew** [5 1/2] is in Kindergarten French immersion at Doncaster School and is Grandma's youngest piano student. He also enjoys swimming and soccer.

Matthew continues to work with Level Ground's OMS (order management system). Hockey and volleyball provide a change of pace, as did his trip to Scandinavia with sister and niece. Sister Melissa was very grateful for his adaptability regarding the "whims" of his companions, and for his expertise with Excel sheets and GPS. Grandparents and parents were thankful to have him accompany Anna both to and from Canada, as Melissa had different routings. He kindly sent a requested care package (mostly warm clothes), organized by her father, to Melissa when she spent a few days in Halifax in February, and included some items on a hard drive which were password protected. (She shouldn't have had to ask him for the password, which was "Honeybee"—the meaning of the name Melissa.)

MATT

Bruce and **Louise** fill their days with shopping and cooking activities (Bruce), teaching responsibilities (Louise) and family interactions (both). They share their part of the upstairs with a lovely, conscientious UVic student, Patricia Engler, from St. Albert, Alberta.

Bruce has participated in several service opportunities over the past year, including the church's monthly breakfast at Our Place, and helping with the Sunday evening Hymns and Heart service. He had the novel experience of serving as executor on a will for someone he hardly knew who had, without his knowledge, put his name on her will 18 years ago at the age of 84. Although it was a small estate and relatively straightforward, there were beneficiaries he had to track down, eventually through a tracking agency. The project, while satisfying, involved considerable paper-work and time. Louise, during her non-teaching hours, wanders from the back yard, where she propagates perennials in support of young people, to the music-room where she recycles used greeting cards and other normally-discarded paper into new cards, in support of the Canadian Foundation for the Children of Haiti—a pleasant activity no doubt associated with her frugal upbringing. Her special privilege is working at the piano with eight grandchildren—three in Salem, Oregon (by Skype), and the other five in Victoria.

SEEN AND HEARD ...

... Melissa, with her blonde hair an anomaly in Saudi Arabia, amused by the surreptitious taking of photos on cell phones as she walks, in a flowing abaya, through the crowds ... Melissa in abaya and niqab, eyes barely visible, visiting in the most conservative area of Saudi Arabia ... Mark and Matt scoring six of the seven goals in the semifinal game of roller hockey tournament ... under the dripping maples and cedars at Horne Lake: profound silence save for the peeping of a tiny green tree frog; sword, maidenhair and lady ferns, horsetails and apple-green vanilla plants decorate side of gravelled road ... Michael's version of "Which One is Different?": his flight roster, a listing of 18 names, all Chinese except for one Canadian ... Tori, Jonathan and Justin receiving their Canadian citizenship in August, on the other side of the border ... Margie also receiving Canadian citizenship; now has two red-and-white flags that are especially meaningful to her, as the Peruvian flag shares Canada's colours ... 4-year-old grandson: "Grandma, you are a *good woman!*" ... former student driving past our house, sideswiped by car making wide turn from Lakeview Avenue; incident in which thankfully, only cars received damage, witnessed by daughter Melody, who happened to be following student's car ... student's cousin receiving special award for high mark (90) on Grade (Level) VIII piano examination, much to student's and teacher's delighted surprise ... scarlet runner vines and flowers serving as deer's breakfast, resulting in harvest of eight pods of beans ... recipe for happy plants: barrels of grass from Michael and Eric's lawn mowing + kitchen scraps from the two households on this property + Garry oak leaves = soil usable (after six to nine months) for plant project ... Melissa playing Christmas carols on her violin in the back of a taxi after the Embassy Christmas service, as requested by her two (female) companions, for the benefit of her favourite taxi driver, a Muslim, who kept saying, "One more!" … Michael and Eric on piano (duet), Anna on flute, Melody on violin, Great-Auntie Marilyn reading a couple of her own Christmas poems, and Grandma on piano for singing at recent care-home programme … from Mike, re. time zones: "I leave Taipei at around 11:30 p.m. on Monday night and land 12 hours later in Vancouver around 7 p.m. … Monday night." … re. darkening sky: "Oh well, I've seen thunderstorms in Winnipeg, tornadoes in Texas, monsoons in India, why not typhoons in Taiwan? 180 mph winds should be something. (That's 290km/h. Giddyup.)" … from Los Angeles: "Just on the bus from LAX airport to the crew hotel. Me and 17 Taiwanese crew, I totally blend in." … little Matthew, making a special trip to the downstairs kitchen to talk to his grandfather: "Grandpa, please pray for me. I'm getting my shots." … Mark receiving a "Peace Officer Exemplary Service Award" (the "Above and Beyond Award") for his efforts in making the new Canada Border Service database system more user-friendly for his colleagues, at a 2:45 p.m. ceremony at the Vancouver airport … son Matthew having adenoids removed at 8:00 a.m. that morning, able to see father as he comes out of anesthetic, just before Daddy leaves for float plane downtown … Tori, apparently a recipient of her grandfather's culinary excellence genes, winning a "Fun Foods Award" for her pineapple ham muffins, using her own recipe … Tori and father exploring gluten-free/vegan options in response to dietary restrictions; most recent success is a delicious g.f. vegan chocolate cupcake. … mournful occasion: Mark "recycling" beloved old Jeep; father not unhappy to have parking space back … Melissa, playing Lego game with a five year old on his iPad who, jabbering away in Arabic, keeps grabbing her hand to show her where to put it (Melissa noted, ironically, that the mother, in a country which does not allow women to drive, had him change the driver of the car to a female.) … Geordon canoeing to school and back with his daughters … Tori and Jonathan singing Spanish Christmas song with members of the Rendle and Stark families, along with one older member of the Holland family, at a recent night of music at our church …

TORI, A BUDDING CHEF

LIFE'S LIKE THIS

May 18, 5:00 p.m., Juan de Fuca Rec Centre Eric [13] is entered in the School Bike League BMX competition. He has won several competitions in the past, and is looking forward to today's challenge. However, as he makes the first turn of the first race, the rider just ahead of him slows. Eric's bike catches his wheel, and his bike topples, scraping elbow, knees, and bike: end of that race for Eric. He takes second place in second race, third place in third race; not eligible for semi-finals. … Rider slated for semifinals leaves early; Eric is asked to take his place. ... Results: Eric receives first place for both semifinals and finals. Abrasions forgotten as he stands on podium with his award.

Acquiring Humility ... **December 18, morning church service** Louise enjoys playing a piano prelude of Christmas music. Walks across platform and down stairs back to seat. Friend, sitting in row behind her, stops her and gently removes green velcro hair roller from fuzzy sweater, hands it to her. Owner realizes that roller has travelled under coat to church and across platform, and is thankful that its perch was on left side, facing back of stage.

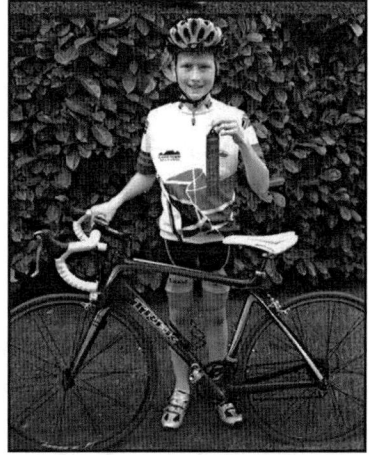

ERIC WITH RIBBON

Chapter 63: A Christmas Digest, 2017

EDITORIAL *by Louise*

PARENTS AND CHILDREN

February 6 A couple of months ago, I started 2016's Christmas Digest, bundled in afghans and dressing gowns, in a house silent except for the spitting of sleet against the windows. During the intervening two months, Victoria uncharacteristically has seen at least four snowfalls come and go, and today is hopefully the last one for the season. *La nieve* is very beautiful, and also very disruptive.

Outside the dining room window the winter birds of my childhood—juncos, with their coal black (male) and charcoal (female) heads—hang clumsily from the feeders, along with the more-coordinated chickadees, bushtits, downy woodpeckers, towhees, nuthatches and one plump Bewick wren. Juncos are much happier on the ground, picking up scraps that fall from the feeders, and leaving tiny tracks in the snow. These dainty markings are identical to those in the woods of West Saanich Road, where as a child I used to sit quietly on a log, enjoying the silence of the snow and watching the juncos nibble fallen cedar seeds and make trails on the pristine surface.

February 7 There are huge marshmallows topping the flower pots, quantities of meringue on the fir branches, and layers of icing covering the oaks and other deciduous trees, transforming this property into a white wonderland. A four-inch layer of snow has brought beauty and muffled sounds to those of us sticking close to home, and anxiety to those who have to get out and drive in it.

November 13 Since the above was written, there has recently been another small but very cold and windy snowfall which sent us scurrying to get the tender perennials into the greenhouse, with icy fingers and the wish we had been smart enough to finish the job before the end of October.

Several creatures large and small share our property, along with a multitude of birds, to both good and bad effect: handsome but voracious deer, visiting through the night, devour bean, strawberry and raspberry leaves (but not the beans, strawberries or raspberries), kale, grape hyacinth and bluebell leaves, and anything else green and tender; little brown (native) and green (introduced) lizards bask on the rocks in the summer sunshine; raccoons churn up/aerate the compost piles (a good thing) and chew holes in the flooring of the garden shed (not a good thing; necessitated a new floor above a layer of teeth-jarring metal mesh); and squirrels dig holes all over the yard, upset and empty pots of plants, climb the bird feeders, and provide entertainment as they chase each other through the trees.

Bruce and I are grateful that we are still able to live in the family home and continue sharing it with others. Patricia Engler, completing fourth-year Bachelor of Science courses at UVic, moved in a year ago, and this September Sandra Lee, a UVic student now at Camosun College in the nursing programme, joined her, across the hallway. Both are lovely young women, and wonderful company. Mark and his family share the other half of the upstairs, and everyone seems to get along well.

The proliferation of new calendars with 2018 imprinted on them is yet another reminder of the passage of time. Alternate weeks I drive to Brentwood for Spanish lessons, past the home of my childhood—a pleasant and nostalgic trip. It is difficult to believe that I left our home (now Heavenor Farm) on West Saanich Road near Durrance Road nearly 60 years ago. Even more sobering is the site of the old Prospect Lake School, a couple of miles south of our home, where my father worked as custodian for several years, sometimes accompanied by two or three of his grumbling children during the holiday breaks for a thorough clean-up of the school. This included cleaning windows, desks, and washrooms, and spreading and sweeping up Dust-bane on the oiled floors. Today not only is there no vestige of the old school, but the site is now an inaccessible forest of shrubs and trees, mostly alder, and blackberry vines, with a stream running through it.

Such retrospective thinking brings an acknowledgement of God's faithfulness to me and my family, and gratitude for the many years of provision, protection and blessing He has given us, by His grace.

COUSINS ON CHRISTMAS HILL

May this grace and these blessings be extended to you and your families in the New Year!

SEEN AND HEARD ...

... Bruce and Louise eating five large grapefruit off brother Eric's tree over three days in Mesa, Arizona, during a January respite from Victoria's dampness and dark ... an educational and enjoyable visit to the Musical Instrument Museum in Phoenix, which houses an interactive display of over 6,500 instruments from around the world ... **January 27** exuberant trilling of winter wren heard for first time this year ... Louise's halting introduction of husband to lovely Peruvian guest (Margie's mother, Margarita): *"Permítame presentarle a mi esposo, Bruce."* Spanish-speaking members of family patiently stand by ... Melissa, weary, in Riyadh airport near departure gate for Egypt but not sure where loading gate is, answering phone: "I can see you, you need to come over to the gate!" Call is from anxious flight service manager, flanked by six male attendants waiting to take her boarding pass; Melissa wonders where manager obtained her phone number but glad he had it ... Boarder Patricia and granddaughter Anna waiting for bus with hundreds of other UVic students in the snow, deciding to walk the five kilometres home, stopping at Tim Horton's for hot chocolate and doughnuts—an unusual adventure in the city of January snowdrops and February daffodils ... recently discovered note from late 1970s that indicates Marilyn was already headed for leadership: "Michael, Since you told daddy there were books outside I am going to tell TARA, TANYA, and GABY. <u>TOGETHER</u> we will beat up on you. MARILYN (PS IF YOU TELL THAT I WROTE THIS NOTE YOU are in <u>MORE</u> TROUBLE.)" ... Marilyn's comment regarding discovery: "I have repressed this memory... but Mike might still be seeking therapy." ... And Mike's: "It does answer a few questions." ... six precious words: "Grandma, can I tell you something?" ... white lilac fills music room window in May, especially radiant at twilight; fragrance wafting through surrounding area ... Justin [7] using large needles to make a fuchsia-coloured scarf for Margaret's Mother's Day gift, supervised by big sister Tori ... Mother leafing through her seven children's primary school journals which are filled with much humour, usually unintended, and nostalgia, sharing with her family interesting items as they surface ... Launch of six Level VIII students after their RCM piano exams in June resulting in welcome reduction of teaching schedule to three days, in spite of influx of several sweet be-

JUSTIN

TORI

ginners ... six grandchildren and two of their cousins plus three parents and the aunt who organized the troops (Melissa), raking the annual fall of leaves—a gift from the 30+ Garry Oaks to the compost piles; the workers were enticed to the job on a very cold afternoon with the promise of hot chocolate at Starbucks afterwards ... grandparents grateful for the help ... Louise harvesting hundreds of gallons of fertile soil from the compost piles for her plant project ... birds trying to find their way to the feeders past deer fencing, flying up and over, or down and under, or, in the case of the tiny bushtits, right through the one-inch grid ... the *clip clop, clip clop* of Mia's tiny boots as she approaches the downstairs kitchen on a laminated floor, catapulting Grandma's mind back several decades to the story of "Three Billy Goats Gruff," which she read to her first class of 42 Grade Two children. In the story, each of the goats crossed a bridge *trip trap, trip trap*, under which lived the fearsome Troll, who threatened to eat them. One of the novice teacher's more unruly pupils had just been reprimanded and, as Louise passed his desk, she heard him mutter, in reference to herself, "the ugly old troll," which brought a certain degree of merriment to her family at home when they learned of the description. She was 19. She still has two "ugly troll" dolls given to her at that time by the young man who would very soon also be giving her a diamond ring. ... Melissa requesting exit ticket home to take her east first, rather than west, returning from Saudi Arabia via Beijing, Shanghai, Hong Kong and Taipei, which enabled her to drop in on brother Mike ... bittersweet parting with cabin at Horne Lake, a place of much beauty and many memories ... note to Grandma from Joy: "I opened this pea pod and how many peas were there? Seven, and that made me think about my mom and her six siblings, which made me think of you. Love you, Joy" ... Grandma's response: "Yes, there were seven peas in the pod, but each one was uniquely different—and very special." ... Matthew and Grandma and a new song: Grandma says she wants to sing a song for him that she will teach him next week, called "Praise Him, Praise Him, All Ye Little Children." Matthew rolls his eyes, smiles knowledgeably and says, "I bet this is about God," and as she finishes it ("God is love"), he exclaims triumphantly, "I *knew* it!" ... seven siblings on their violins, sharing a couple of hymn arrangements from years ago, at family's

ERIC

Thanksgiving meal ... Eric enjoying this year's fall cyclocross racing season; keeps up with a group of elite bicyclists on 70-kilometre ride ... Jolyn spending two life-changing weeks in Slovakia, working (painting, digging, renovating) with YFC's Project Compassion; father Geordon accompanied her to Vienna, and left her after a couple of days to meet with YFC colleagues in other parts of Europe ... recent addition to Mia's vocabulary: "No, no, no, no... NO!" ... Eric's parents threatened with poverty as he collects on his straight A report cards … Melissa, on one of her rowing excursions, settling her boat near the Inner Harbour and the *M.V. Coho*'s route, ensuring that her little passenger, nephew Matthew, can wave goodbye to his Bucher relatives as they return home from a visit to Victoria … Mike, giving some older, top-ranked badminton players in Brentwood—home for over 65 years to some of BC's badminton champions—some stiff competition; learns that his friendly and very skilful opponents attended high school with his mother …

LIFE'S LIKE THIS

January 10, 4:00 p.m. Grandpa brings cup of coffee to Grandma while she is working with youngest grandson at the piano. Grandma: "Thank you, Darling." Turning to grandson: "Do you know what 'darling' means?" "It's what *I* am." (Grandma and grandson have discussed this subject previously.)

January 1983 Mark's Grade One journal includes multiple entries relating to the progress of the second addition onto our house, from the initial announcement of an "adishin," through descriptions of work on the attic, roof, windows, walls, insulation, stucco, painting, to "specers" for the "stereow." The entries, punctuated hopefully every so often by "It is nearly finisht," extend into June. … **April 2011** Mark and Margie move into this suite, where they have since been joined by little Matthew and Mia, living amicably beside the appreciative grandparents now for 6 1/2 years. Little did Mark know 34 years ago that his "helping" the workmen by tidying up and sweeping was in fact contributing to his future home …

Fall morning Mother is sitting at computer at end of family room. Explosion at gate near window at other end of room sends her running to the window. Eight-foot bamboo pole and deer netting are in shambles across fence. Mother rushes through porch to check out fate of deer who either thought he could sail over nearly-invisible wall of netting, or did not see it. Is sure deer must have somersaulted over fence and will be in bad shape. Discovers very large, antlered buck 50 metres away on neighbouring lawn, blinking at her across fence. Wonders at creature's resiliency, is thankful it was not hurt. … Father replaces pole, decorates netting with shiny pinwheels.

PERSONAL GLIMPSES

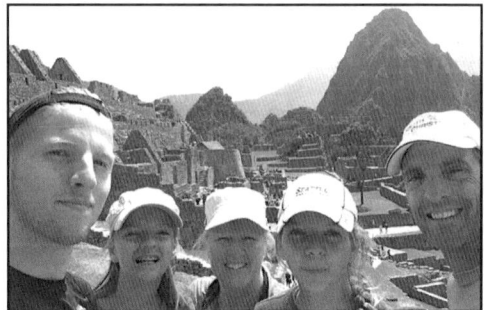

RENDLE FAMILY

Marilyn and **Geordon** (Rendle) continue their work with Youth for Christ, Geordon as Global Youth Advocate, and Marilyn as Global Connector, both under the umbrella of YFC Canada. Geordon, Marilyn, **Jolyn** [14], and **Joy** [13] travelled to Peru for three weeks in the summer, where Geordon spoke in a variety of settings, and Marilyn and the girls provided music. In October, Geordon spent ten days speaking to youth leaders in the mountains of Nepal, glad that he was on his own, given the travelling challenges. A trip to Israel in November was a first-time experience for Geordon and father Don, and was followed by Geordon's trips to Montreal and India. In his absences, Marilyn managed the household of five teenagers (three of her own and two charming homestay students from Italy and Spain). On the mainland, **Jordie** [23] and **Rachel** keep busy with their jobs at BC Ferries and Pacific Bottleworks Company. In September, **Josh** [19] made the decision to transfer from Trinity Western University to Camosun College in Victoria, where he has found the second year in the Bachelor in Sports Management programme an excellent fit. He now plays for both Division 1 and 2 Gorge men's teams. Jolyn is at Esquimalt Secondary, the only Grade 9 student on the senior basketball team. Joy is still at Shoreline Middle School, in Grade 8. Jolyn completed requirements for Level VIII piano in June, and is taking a break from lessons; Joy is now working at that same level.

JORDAN AND RACHEL

Michael continues to fly with China Airlines, out of Taipei. His contract allows more family visiting time; we have enjoyed several visits with him this year. Among his varied gifts to his parents is the replacement of dim lights with bright LED fixtures throughout the house. The new lighting in the music room has been a wonderful gift to the piano teacher. In addition to the routine responsibility of navigating hundreds of passengers across thousands of miles, Mike is forced at times to put his experience and expertise to the test as his B-777 encounters difficult weather conditions. Hurricane-force winds in Frankfurt forced two aborted landings, and an eventual landing in Amsterdam. Even worse than the buffeting from the hurricane was Typhoon Nesat in Taipei which threw the plane around like a cat with a mouse; using every resource available to him, Mike managed to divert to Hong Kong. Learning of these incidents after the fact is probably best for parental peace-of-mind.

MIKE WITH HIS SISTERS

Margaret and **Chris** (Bucher), **Tori** [12], **Jonathan** [10 1/2], and **Justin** [7 1/2] have recently moved to another area of Salem, from their beautiful custom-built home to a spacious fixer-upper closer to school, church and community. As is often the case with older homes, some problems don't surface until the family actually starts living in the "new" home, so the family's engineer is finding his training put to use in several areas. A tear-out of the kitchen at the end of the year will initiate the renovation season. Tori is in middle school at Howard Street Charter School, a school

BUCHER FAMILY

of the arts, and the boys are still in Spanish immersion at Grant Elementary School. Grandma has the pleasure of their company each week on Skype, as they share their progress at the piano with her. Tori plays violin in the school orchestra; Justin picks out tunes on his ukulele. Aesthetics are balanced with swimming (Tori is on a swim team), cross-country, basketball, and baseball.

MELISSA

We are very happy to have Auntie **Melissa** back in the neighbourhood, after a year and a half in Saudi Arabia. She is maintaining some contact with the Middle East as she studies Arabic through Continuing Studies at UVic. Although she misses many aspects of the unique Middle Eastern culture and the friends she made, she enjoys her return to Canadian freedoms such as being allowed to drive, and to drive when and where she wants, to understand what is spoken around her, and to not being viewed as an oddity to be recorded on ever-present cell phones as she goes about her day-to-day activities. Her new position at Victoria General Hospital involves both the educating of paediatric nurses and keeping her hand in clinical practice.

Melody and **Richard** (Stark) are adjusting to a household of three university students: Richard has been working towards his MBA at Royal Roads University, and **Anna** [20] and **Michael** [18] are both at UVic, Anna in second year Education, and Michael, following his graduation in June from Reynolds Secondary, in the Peter B. Gustavson School of Business. **Eric**

STARK FAMILY

[15] continues at Reynolds in Grade 10, supplementing his studies with a pre-engineering programme at Camosun College. Most weeks Michael and Eric touch bases with Grandma on the piano bench, sometimes discussing family history alongside their piano studies. Melody keeps the accounts in order at Central Middle School, assisting the school in adopting the district's newest financial software. Richard continues to oversee the sales growth of Level Ground Trading; a move to a new 20,000-square-foot warehouse near their current facility is scheduled for December 15th, opening up opportunity for even further growth. Anna spent the summer working with Extreme Outreach in addition to separate short-term mission trips to Mexico and Japan, and continues volunteering each week at Our Place and with Street Ministries on Pandora Avenue, reaching out to our city's most vulnerable and at-risk citizens. Michael and Eric spent much of the summer at Camp Qwanoes in leadership and in the practical ministries of the dish pit and maintenance.

Matthew and Mark

Mark continues to welcome visitors to Canada at the border, trying to winnow out those who have a negative motivation for making the trip to the Island, and assisting those who are legitimately in need of guidance. **Margie** enjoys working in the home with their two little ones, and continues to share recipes and menus with her father-in-law. She was delighted to have both mother Margarita and sister Erica visit earlier this year. **Matthew** [6 1/2] is in French-immersion Grade One at Doncaster Elementary, and little **Mia**, at 20 months, brings an extra sparkle into the household.

Margeliza and Mia

Matthew plays league roller hockey with brother Mark. His order management system at Level Ground continues to deal with all aspects of the business; he spends work time tweaking the programmes in response to management's requests, and dealing with the company's computer needs. The family appreciates the quick fixes he gives to home computer problems, and his ability to listen patiently to the more voluble members of his family (adjective contributed by the talkative sister who lives nearest him). He hosts an occasional movie night for various family members when schedules permit, and accompanied Melissa on her back-home burger quest last summer, patronizing a variety of restaurants in search of the quintessential hamburger.

Mia, Uncle Matt, Matthew

Chapter 64: A Christmas Digest, 2018

EDITORIAL *by Louise*

We extend to you our sincere good wishes for a 2019 filled with God's best blessings. Our love and appreciation for your friendship and kindness to us and our family come along with this letter.

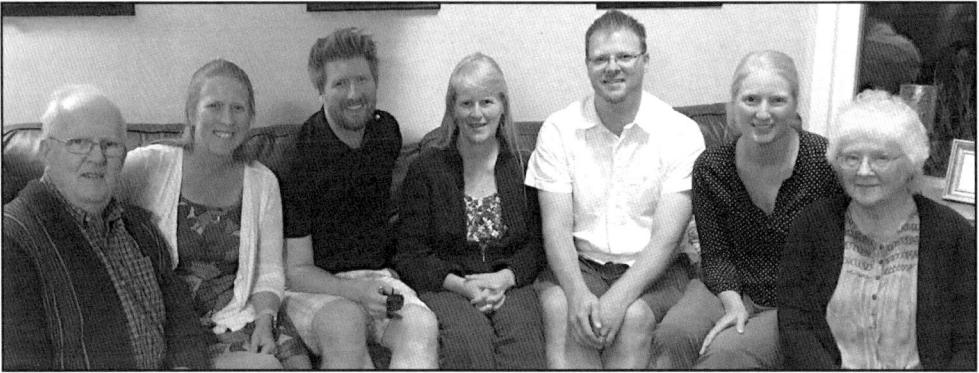

PARTIAL FAMILY GATHERING AT STARKS'

This is the most recent in a long series of long letters to leave This Old House at the end of each year. The property again hosts millions (billions?) of oak leaves, most raked and carried to a large pile at the back for composting. The rocks are green with moss and licorice ferns, and other little plants and fungi. Although there has been light frost on the rooftops, the water has still not been turned off *[December 15]*—a task that usually takes place in late October. Pink bergenia and multi-coloured poly-anthus think it is spring, and the holly tree will soon add colour to our Christmas table. The large (60- to 70-year-old) cotoneaster shrubs are also laden with red ber-ries, soon to be decimated by the annual influx of robins.

And this letter, God willing, will be added along with the most recent nine let-ters to *"Hey, there's no violin in this case!"*—published in 2009, and hopefully, to be re-published in 2019. I intend to bribe my grandchildren into ploughing through this compilation of family history which extends from a young mother-to-be's insomniac musings of 51 years ago, through her tumultuous middle years (children, children, and more children: her own, and students—all gifts; music, music, and more music—also a gift) into a more sedate old age. *[Children's response to "sedate": Really?]*

PERSONAL GLIMPSES

Marilyn and **Geordon** (Rendle) are four months into a four-year Youth for Christ commitment in the United Arab Emirates. Earlier this year Marilyn received a request to become director of Youth for Christ/ Youth Unlimited for the United Arab Emirates, working with some of the 600,000 young people in the country.

RENDLE FAMILY AT JORDIE'S GRADUATION

After much heart-searching, prayer and family support, the family yet again emptied their home and made it available to renters. Son **Josh**, studying Sports Management at Camosun College, lives in the basement. Son **Jordan** and wife **Rachel** live on the Mainland, working at several jobs. **Jolyn** [15] and **Joy** [14] are finding their new country "different," but apparently are adapting well to the IB (International Baccalaureate) programme. Jolyn, an outstanding basketball player at Esquimalt Secondary last winter, has managed to attract a team around her, with her sister as team-mate and father as coach.

JOSHUA AND JORDAN

Michael is now flying the Dreamliner (Boeing 787; Wikipedia says it costs up to $325 million each) for Norwegian Air out of London (Gatwick). Much as he appreciated the kindness shown to him by his Taiwanese friends and colleagues at China Airlines, he felt somewhat isolated by the language barrier. He now is happily dealing with the eccentricities of Britain as he communicates with ease in his native tongue, and takes advantage of the centuries of culture and beauty.

MIKE IN STAFFORDSHIRE, HOME OF HOLLAND RELATIVES

Margaret and **Chris** (Bucher), **Tori** [13], **Jonathan** [11], and **Justin** [8] continue to renovate their 1950s home in Salem, Oregon with satisfying results. They are looking forward to a completed kitchen by Christmas, after ten months of dealing with an

BUCHER FAMILY

over-extended contractor, and are thankful for a new craftsman who has done an excellent job finishing up another's work. Margaret is relieved finally to be able to start putting her kitchen in order, after living off counters, tables and unfinished cupboards for many months. Chris continues to travel the south-west corner of the state, supervising Federal Highway projects in that region. Grandma has the pleasure of listening to her grandchildren's piano pieces from across the border most Wednesdays; Tori and Jonathan also continue the family tradition of violin studies through their fine arts-focused Charter Middle School (supervised by their mom) and both enjoyed being part of the school's cross country team this fall. Justin, transferring to their neighbourhood school this year, has been quick to make new friends and enjoys being part of an enrichment Japanese class and choir after school.

Melissa divides her time between nursing, where orientation and support of new staff is a primary part of her role, behind-the-scenes activities at our church, lending her violin expertise to instrumental ensembles, and exploring distant lands: Australia and New Zealand in April; the Emirates, Jordan, Palestine, and Israel in November/December. In October she hosted her lovely namesake from Switzerland, born on her birthday 16 years ago this December and named Melissa. The Swiss Melissa's father accompanied her to Victoria to celebrate the birthday, and Vancouver Island cooperated by sparkling in sunshine and warmth.

MARILYN, JOLYN, JOY, AND MELISSA IN ABU DHABI

Melody and **Richard** (Stark) live just a few blocks from here, for which we are thankful. **Anna** [just turned 21], **Michael** [19], and **Eric** [16]—all significant birthdays in our cul-

STARK FAMILY

ture—are studying conscientiously at UVic and Reynolds Secondary. Anna is in the third year of a BEd programme, Michael in the second year of a BComm programme, and Eric attends Reynolds for band only, taking a variety of high school and university courses online. Richard, too, has passed a significant birthday, and is completing his MBA at Royal Roads. Richard continues to work in management at Level Ground and Melody keeps everything financial organized at Central Middle School. Both ride bikes to work most days—one travelling to the north (Saanichton), the other to the south (Victoria).

HOLLAND FAMILY

Mark and **Margie**, little **Matthew** [7] and **Mia** [2 1/2] continue to provide us with good company and entertainment, as they complete their eighth year of house-sharing. We cannot believe how quickly the time has passed, and how amicable the relationships have been. Mark continues as an officer with the Canadian Border Services Agency in downtown Victoria. Little Matthew, in French immersion, is acquiring an accent that his grandmother, even with six years of high school and university studies in that language, will never match.

MATTHEW   MIA

Matthew is facing his mother's book project in the new year. He continues to fine-tune Level Ground's order management system during his working hours, and plays several sports during his downtime. His namesake and tiny niece think Uncle Matt is pretty special, and that sentiment seems to be shared by all other members of the family. We are also grateful that he and Melissa, in their respective condos, live only two half-blocks away.

And *les parents/los padres*? **Bruce** continues to keep this household running, and helps out with several projects for those in need. He is the main shopper, cook, car tank filler, bookkeeper and chequebook balancer. His help-mate would be independently wealthy if she had $1 for every lunch she has made over the past 45 years. Her other activi-

MATT

ties are related to music (teaching, supplying some music at our imperfect—according to our pastor—and wonderful church), recycling cards in support of the Canadian Foundation for the Children of Haiti <cfchcanada.ca>, and propagating plants to sell in support of young people. Both thank God for the multiple blessings they have been given.

LIFE'S LIKE THIS

February 2018 Marilyn is playing hymns and classical pieces on her violin in Lebanon's refugee tents, receives warm reception. Hosts and hostesses ask to have photo taken with violin. (Mother thinks of the many years of violin lessons for eldest daughter and her siblings, and weeps inwardly for those who will never have that privilege, whose distress in life is not precipitated by incessant practising and lessons but by the threat of bomb-ings and starvation.)

March 6, 5:30 a.m. local time Michael has just returned to Taipei from Los Angeles. Trudges wearily through the Taoyuan air-port to catch his bus home. 14-hour flight has been exhausting, but he is satis-fied it went safely and effi-

MIKE WITH FLIGHT CREW IN TAIWAN

ciently. Only thoughts are of the bed waiting. ... Passenger approaches pilot and asks if he was the captain on the China Airlines flight from LAX. Receiving a slightly guarded affirmative, comments on the excellent landing; as experienced travellers, he and his wife have rarely experienced such a smooth landing. As in so many times in the past, pilot is appreciative of the kindness of strangers; weight of fatigue lifts a bit.

July 15, first round of roller hockey play-offs Matt lands 6 of team's 12 goals, without the setups of his longtime linemate, Mark, on duty at the border, who is cha-grined to think he might now be rendered useless. *[Parent's comment: Not likely.]*

August 10, 9:15 p.m. Mother is watering plants in backyard, hears scratching on bark of oak tree beside playhouse. Is not surprised to see quintet of rac-coons—mother and four babies—climbing down on their way to their nocturnal ad-ventures, which often involve the overturning and emptying of pots. Mother rac-coon is on the ground. Her human counterpart approaches the little creature, who rises on hind legs and growls. Larger mother comes closer. Smaller mother runs up trunk, jumps to playhouse roof, a very few feet from larger mother's head. Little rac-coons make way up into higher branches, eventually followed by their mother. Gar-dener's last sight is that of five masked bandits peering down at her around trunk of tree.

August 21 Geordon and Marilyn, Jolyn and Joy alight from plane in Abu Dhabi.

Thermometer registers 41 degrees. Marilyn, somewhat intimidated by reputation of country to which she has been called, mutters to husband, "Remember—*low profile!*" Geordon nods amiably in assent. ... Family stays in Anglican vicarage for two weeks while apartment-hunting; vicar introduces Geordon to key people in government. Within days, Geordon is invited to participate in a Ministry of Tolerance three-day workshop, working with and lecturing to bright young people in their 20s; apparently his "excellent leadership style and standard of English" (thanks in part to Royal Roads University) have influenced this startling development. He appears on video and is quoted at length in the newspaper. So much for "low profile." *[See also December 15.]*

September 11, 10:00 a.m. Piano teacher is completing tidy-up of music room for first day of teaching. Eldest daughter, sorting boxes as she left for Middle East, has given mother box of old cards which could be used for mother's card project. Mother comes across 1991 card sent to eldest daughter on her 24th birthday from sister four years younger: "<u>For You</u>, Sister, Another Birthday ... another year closer to looking *like Mom,*" surrounded by happy faces. *[Margaret had drawn these in.]* Mother smiles as she realizes that daughters would not anticipate this card in their mother's hand 27 years later, and imagines younger sister's delight when she spied the card.

Fall night, 1:30 a.m. Mark returns from work, turns into driveway, and notes sensor light on in carport through which he will be making his way to the house. But not right away. Through the carport a huge, well-antlered buck is striding toward him, no doubt with a satisfying taste of the property's vegetation still in his mouth. Mark waits in car until deer has sauntered back to Saanich Road.

December 15 Geordon takes out subscription to Gulf News in Abu Dhabi, intending to take advantage of its coverage of world news. **December 16** Receives phone call informing him that he has won 2018 Audi A4 in draw for subscribers. Initial disbelief explodes into exhilaration as he discovers call is legitimate. Tells Gulf staff that family has been praying for a new car since their arrival in the Emirates in August. Newspaper and video interviews follow this happy event.

SCENE IN PASSING ...

... Melissa asking Mike, in response to photos of his Christmas Day flight across Russia to Frankfurt, which included spectacular pictures of the Northern Lights: "The lights are amazing! But my question is: Did you see Santa Claus? You were practically at the North Pole; maybe you saw him heading home for the day/year?" ... Anna spending six weeks in Quebec in summer French Immersion programme,

ANNA IN OTTAWA

enjoying the train ride home … Melissa floating in hot air balloon over 3,000 feet above Mansfield, Australia (*Man from Snowy River* country) … Grandmother, daughter and granddaughters celebrating the family's fourth and final Level VIII Piano exam with lunch at Government House's Rudi's Place and excursion through surrounding gardens, surveying the flights of eagles and crows through the woods below … observation of four-year-old piano student, who was learning about musical rests at previous lesson: "Do you know what is in that rest *[a whole rest, which is a tiny black rectangle attached below the fourth line on the staff]*?" "Lots of tiny notes." *[There are no notes in the measure, so wouldn't one assume they had to have gone somewhere? Fifty-plus years of teaching piano, and instructor had never before been confronted with this concept.]* … another four year old referring to piece played by more advanced student: "I liked the *quickly* piece she played best." … Grandson Michael, exhausted on his day off from a full summer

MICHAEL

at Qwanoes, fast asleep on the beach while brother and cousins play in the surf … Richard and Melody touring Beijing with an Educators' tour, accompanied by Eric … Tori receiving most valuable runner award at the end of season … Anecdote found on 1985 calendar: Mother is teaching Junior Church class of six to eight year olds about life in Bible times: no TV, no cars, no airplanes. Asks class what kind of jobs people had in those days. Family member responds enthusiastically, "Washing cars!" At

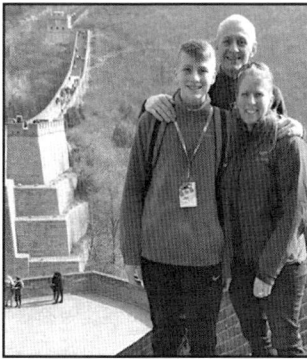

ERIC, RICHARD AND MELODY ON GREAT WALL OF CHINA

this moment, Mother would not be able to foresee that a couple of decades later, he will graduate from university in the top 10% of that year's class. … Grandson Eric, at 15 the youngest in men's 92-kilometre cycling event in Penticton (the *Gran Fondo*), finishing 10th of 700 participants, allowing him to enter 160-kilometre race in August … friend's observation: "How can our children be middle-aged, when *we're* still middle-aged?" … Jonathan teaching himself ukulele and playing "Somewhere Over the Rainbow" with classmate for fifth grade promotion ceremony … Melissa and Melody cycling in July through the Pacific Northwest from Victoria through Anacortes around to Port Angeles, enjoying lots

CHRIS AND TORI AFTER RACE

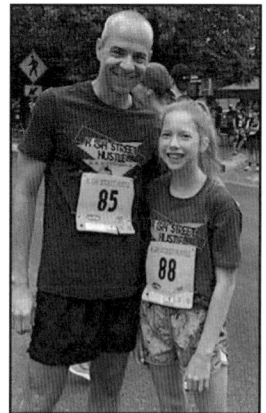

JONATHAN

of sunshine and beautiful scenery … *la estudiante anciana* searching for *actitudes y comportamientos cristianos* (Christian Attitudes and Behaviours) from Spanish Bible … the hands of several Middle Eastern leaders rising when asked if they knew the hymn "Jesus Loves Me"—they had been influenced by their Filipina nannies … Michael's 49th birthday celebration in segments: morning spent touring *HMCS Vancouver* with new commander of ship, his friend of over 20 years (the drummer in a worship band where Mike played bass guitar and violin; one has risen through naval ranks, the other has gradually mastered nine increasingly-sophisticated aircraft); lunch with brothers and a sister; cake with a couple dozen closest relatives at sister's home in evening; and, finally, family supper at parents' home next evening *[So what can we do for the 50th?]* … Justin planting seeds from his lunch apple, marking the spot with pencil flag marked "**ASS**"; responding to mother's raised eyebrow, "Mom, it's to show where I planted my **Apple SeedS!**" … boarder Patricia Engler, now graduated and travelling through university campuses in the southern hemisphere, interviewing students and those who work with students <patriciaengler.com> … privilege and pleasure of sharing our home with other boarder, nursing student Sandra Lee … large compost areas "roto-tilled" by family of raccoons during the night, resulting in acceleration of breakdown of oak leaves, kitchen scraps, grass, and plant

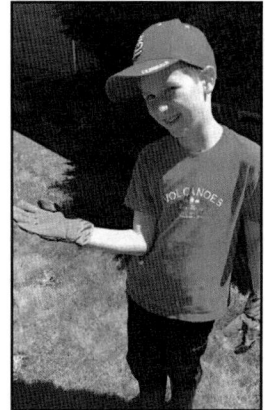

JUSTIN

debris into hundred of gallons of beautiful soil … watering hundreds of potted plants, day after day, week after week, during summer heat … Tori making a *Día de Muertos* altar in remembrance of her Aunt Leslie for Spanish class … wide grin as Spanish-speaking seven-year-old grandson gets the humour on Christmas card: sheep in Santa hat on outside, "¡Fleece Navidad!" inside … eldest son renting and building three-storey scaffolding so he can scrape down and repaint metal flagpole and replace disreputable flag at its peak; middle brother helping him dismantle boards and tubing; brilliant red and white flag flying from sparkling white pole, with boisterous piano rendition of "O Canada" spilling out of open window, eliciting a grin from father … Eric's adorable little hedgehog, Seven, cuddling into his soft blanket during the day, running the treadmill through the night … Melissa dealing with flood damage throughout her condo early this year, allowing her to spend time with Jolyn and Joy and two international students at the Rendle home while the parents were travelling and workmen were mopping up and restoring … "Flat Justin," a paper representation of grandson Justin travelling around North America, Taiwan and the Czech Republic; PDFs assembled by Uncle Mike and friend Katerina provide imaginative photo essays of Flat Justin's travels …

Afterword: Third Edition

August 31, 2019

53 years on this property; 53 years of family activities and memories—what a privilege for me to have been able to share my perspective and experiences with family and friends!

As I write this ending to my book of letters, I am in a peaceful place, still blessed to have my four siblings, my dear, loving husband, my seven children and twelve grandchildren within my call, either in person, or by phone, e-mail, or Skype. I do not take this idyllic situation for granted, as circumstances can change in an instant, and I know that the next few years will bring significant shifts in the family structure. But I trust that the God who is grace and love is in control; as has been said, "I do not know what the future holds, but I know Who holds the future."

My love and best wishes come to you, the reader, along with this book.

Louise

Printed in Canada